BUTTERWORTHS
Legal Research Guide

Guy Holborn MA LLB ALA
Librarian, Lincoln's Inn Library

Butterworths
London, Boston, Brussels, Dublin, Edinburgh, Hato Rey,
Kuala Lumpur, Singapore, Sydney, Toronto, Wellington
1993

United Kingdom	Butterworth & Co (Publishers) Ltd, 88 Kingsway, LONDON WC2B 6AB and 4 Hill Street, EDINBURGH EH2 3JZ
Australia	Butterworths, SYDNEY, MELBOURNE, BRISBANE, ADELAIDE, PERTH, CANBERRA and HOBART
Belgium	Butterworth & Co (Publishers) Ltd, BRUSSELS
Canada	Butterworths Canada Ltd, TORONTO and VANCOUVER
Ireland	Butterworth (Ireland) Ltd, DUBLIN
Malaysia	Malayan Law Journal Sdn Bhd, KUALA LUMPUR
New Zealand	Butterworths of New Zealand Ltd, WELLINGTON and AUCKLAND
Puerto Rico	Equity de Puerto Rico, Inc, HATO REY
Singapore	Butterworths Asia, SINGAPORE
USA	Butterworth Legal Publishers, AUSTIN, Texas; BOSTON, Massachusetts; CLEARWATER, Florida (D & S Publishers); ORFORD, New Hampshire (Equity Publishing); ST PAUL, Minnesota; and SEATTLE, Washington

A CIP Catalogue record for this book is available from the British Library.

ISBN 0 406 00596 6

Printed by Mackays of Chatham PLC, Chatham, Kent

Preface

This book has been written partly with those undertaking legal research courses in mind. For undergraduate law students the basics for finding their way round the law library are fully covered and there is a particular slant towards the needs of would-be solicitors on the Legal Practice Course and would-be barristers on the Bar Vocational Course. The new emphasis being placed on legal research skills in legal education is a welcome development, but it is still only a relatively small part of the curriculum, so this book is also intended to be a practical work of reference to be used when the classes at law school are a rather dim memory and the trainee solicitor, pupil barrister, or new post-graduate student is having to grapple with a research problem for real. I would also be pleased if more experienced lawyers found it useful as a reminder of the ever expanding range of research tools available and as a source of information on areas not encountered every day, for example local legislation. I hope it might be of some help to librarians and information professionals too, whether in their day to day enquiry work or in legal research training.

This rather all-purpose approach has its drawbacks; first year undergraduates do not need to know where to find an unpublished local statutory instrument and an experienced lawyer might resent being told when to use square brackets in a citation. To mitigate this, and also to try to import some practicality into the work, it is presented in two halves. The first half is a narrative text, which, with worked examples and illustrations, is particularly aimed at those on taught courses, but which also gives more detailed guidance to others if needed. The second half is a Quick Reference Guide which gives in summary form solutions to common problems, evaluations of alternative sources, and practical advice to anyone doing legal research without the need to wade through pages of text.

The first half, after an initial chapter of general research techniques, covers the three main areas of secondary sources, legislation and case law. The chapter on legislation is quite substantial since it covers not only statutes and statutory instruments but also EC legislation, local legislation, other subsidiary legislation and quasi-legislation. It then goes on to look at legislative history and proposals for legislation. The need to have a grasp of these latter sources has received a particular impetus from the recent House of Lords decision to relax the prohibition on citing *Hansard* in court. At the end of the chapter is an extended worked example involving, in a single problem, statutes, Statutory Instruments, government circulars, Bills, debates and government reports.

The chapter on case law includes EC case law; in general the policy throughout the book is to treat EC materials alongside English materials, rather than to consign them to a chapter on their own. This is on the grounds that for any research problem an English lawyer ought these days to consider whether there is a European angle and that there is an increasing overlap between the research tools that cover English law and those that cover EC law. The chapter on case law also covers unreported cases and, as a coda, the increasingly important area of European Convention on Human Rights case law.

Chapter 5 covers treaties, again both from the point of view of the practitioner and the academic researching public international law; and chapter 6 rounds up those official publications not covered in the preceding chapters. The detailed descriptions in the first six chapters are mostly concerned with the law of England and Wales. However, both the practitioner and the academic for a variety of reasons may be faced with the law outside England and Wales and might welcome some guidance. The treatment of this in chapter 7 is necessarily limited and for the larger jurisdictions other research guides already exist. But some pointers are given, with the emphasis being on the jurisdictions most likely to be encountered by an English lawyer, namely the other parts of the British Isles and the common law countries. The last chapter deals with directories and subjects adjacent to law. The latter is again somewhat cursory, but it is hoped it might give some idea of the possible sources of use to the lawyer outside the law library.

The Quick Reference Guide largely follows the same order of treatment. If each section is to be reasonably self-contained and provide an immediate answer without endless cross-referencing, a certain degree of duplication in the description of various tools that solve more than one kind of problem is inevitable; so for that I do not apologise. Under each heading references to the paragraph numbers in the main text are given should more detailed explanation be required.

Throughout the book account is taken of electronic sources, whether on-line, such as Lexis, or on CD-ROM. In the first chapter the new student is exhorted always to check at what date a publication states the law. As it is probably in respect of CD-ROMs that this book will get out of date most rapidly, I perhaps ought to say, in analogous fashion, that it covers products known to me at 1 December 1992.

Guy Holborn

January 1993

Acknowledgments

It is necessary to acknowledge the considerable assistance I have received from various quarters in preparing this book. First, to the following publishers for their kind permission to reproduce material in the illustrations:

Butterworths
Her Majesty's Stationery Office
Incorporated Council of Law Reporting for England and Wales
Legal Information Resources Ltd
Mansell
Martindale-Hubbell
Office of Official Publications for the European Communities
Sweet & Maxwell.

Sally Phillips, Supreme Court Librarian, was at the same time as this was being written preparing a leaflet on transcripts and she kindly allowed to me to use in the Quick Reference Guide her format and some of her information. Jules Winterton, Librarian of the Institute of Advanced Legal Studies, kindly came to my assistance when I was faced with various last-minute authorial panics. Loyita Worley, Librarian of solicitors Richards Butler was very helpful with some of the materials mentioned in chapter 8. Steve Harwood, Librarian of the British Institute of International and Comparative Law lifted my veil of ignorance of Council of Europe human rights documentation.

None of the above is of course responsible for any errors that may appear. The assistance and forbearance of all my colleagues at Lincoln's Inn are also gratefully acknowledged. Finally, the very least I can do by way of reparation to my wife, Sophie, and my children, Jack and Lucy, is let them see their names in print.

Contents

4. Case law   123

B. QUICK REFERENCE GUIDE   231

Contents   232

A. Legal research explained and illustrated

1. Introduction: aims and techniques of legal research

How to find a telephone number

1.1   I want to telephone an acquaintance who works at London University, but who is not at work. I remember he was staying at a hall of residence. How do I find its telephone number? Look in the phone book. Is the University in the business pages or is the hall of residence in the residential pages? Is it under London University or University of London? I find the number, and when I ring I am told he moved out a few months ago. So I ring Directory Enquiries, but then realise I do not know his new address and his name is John Smith. Pause for thought. Do I know someone else who would know his number? His girlfriend would. She works in a firm of estate agents, but I cannot remember their name. Ah, I think they were on the corner of High Holborn and Chancery Lane. Is there a directory that lists businesses by street — there is Kelly's Post Office directory isn't there? I look in the local public library. The Kelly's on the shelf looks rather out of date. I ask the librarian who says it is not longer published but gives me the *London Business Finder* instead. I find the name of the firm. I ring them, but forget that it is an 071 number (British Telecom have not charged you for this call). Try again, success, I speak to her. He has gone to visit relatives in New York, and she gives me the number of an uncle there who will know where he is. Start to dial the New York number, then realise my phone bill has recently been getting out of hand and I cannot afford a transatlantic call. Decide it is not that urgent, and send him a letter at his University department instead.

This story is contrived to illustrate some recurring themes in legal research. Indeed it could be said that if you can find a telephone number you can find the law — it merely requires the application of common sense and a little experience. However, the aims of this book are to make explicit the intuitive steps that may count as 'common sense' and to shorten the learning curve that may count as 'a little experience', and thereby place legal research among the essential skills to be gained early on by any lawyer or would-be lawyer.

Recurring themes in legal research

No single source is comprehensive

1.2   Like the London phone books, research tools cover different categories of materials or are designed to solve different sorts of problems. Even those tools that are multi-purpose and that aim at some degree of comprehensiveness — such as *Current Law*, which used to boast 'all the law from every source', or Lexis with its gigabytes of full text data — cannot be the last word. One reason for this is that there are bound to be time lags — the information may have changed or been added to in the last few weeks, or days, or hours. But also, the quantity of information that might be of use to a lawyer is just not finite.

1.3 Two consequences flow from this. The first is the importance of being aware of the scope of particular sources, and not being misled by their titles. It is helpful when the sources themselves set out clearly their editorial policies. For example, the *Legal Journals Index* does this, explaining its coverage of all legal journals *published* in the UK. If you aware of that, you will realise that despite the mine of information to be found in it, there might be other articles in English on English law not indexed in it. Another example is *The Law Reports Index*. On its front cover it lists the series of law reports it indexes. These are neither just the 'official' law reports nor all the law reports there are, but only a selection of the major series. This makes it a very handy tool, but is not necessarily appropriate for in-depth research.

1.4 The other consequence is the converse: the importance of being aware of the overlap between different sources. Just as the phone book is not the only place to find a telephone number, there is more than one way of finding the law, and indeed the heading of this section could well have been another recurring theme of legal research: there is no single 'right' way to tackle a research problem. Although this flexibility is sometimes convenient, it can also mean that if you want to be thorough and squeeze the last pips out of a problem the research can be tedious and repetitive as you hunt through alternative sources hoping to find something the others have missed. But then there are plenty of other activities in the law that are tedious and repetitive.

Choosing a starting point

1.5 Given this variety of sources, an effective research strategy depends on choosing the best starting point. The most important step, dealt with below (paras 1.27-1.28), is identifying the legal issues involved. Having got that, you still need to know, for example, whether the area is primarily statute-based or governed by common law cases. Date is very important too. For example, if you are wanting to find cases on a particular subject it is sensible to try to find first the most recent case because it is likely that it will cite all the earlier cases of importance on the subject. On the other hand the sources offering the greatest currency are not necessarily those offering the greatest coverage. For example, the *Daily Law Reports Index*, though offering excellent currency, would not necessarily be the best place to start unless you happen to know that there was a major case in the area in the last few weeks. It might be better to start with *The Digest* or *Current Law*, then do a quick update.

1.6 Another factor in choosing a starting point is how comprehensive you need to be and how much time you have. If you are involved in a case in the House of Lords, then you are likely to want to pull out all the stops to track down an obscure Commonwealth case given among 10 other authorities in footnote 14 on p 1268 of *Rayden on Divorce*. On the other hand, if you are appearing before Highbury Magistrates Court in five minutes, a scan of the 150 volumes of the *Canadian Abridgement* is not going to get your client off driving without due care and attention.

Choosing your words carefully

1.7 The success of a search depends on thinking through at the outset the relevant terminology. Whether the phone book chooses to use 'London University' or 'University of London' is an elementary illustration. Often there is no difficulty because much of the law is framed in specific technical language, but frequently there are synonyms or alternative expressions for the same legal concept or topic, eg 'land law' or 'real property', 'labour law' or 'employment law', 'revenue law' or 'tax law', 'conflict of laws' or 'private international law', 'retention of title' or 'reservation of title' or 'Romalpa clauses', 'commercial lease' or 'business tenancy'. There may be alternative English and Latin expressions, eg 'stare decisis' and 'precedent'. Awareness of synonyms is all the more important when using non-technical terms, especially in free text retrieval systems such as Lexis, eg 'buyer and seller' as opposed to 'purchaser and vendor'. The last example also illustrates the need to think of antonyms as well as synonyms; other examples are debtor and creditor, legitimate and illegitmate.

1.8 Broader and narrower terms need to be thought of too. If you are looking for a specific term in an index it may entered directly or as a subdivision of a broader heading. Similarly, if you are looking for a book or article on a particular subject it may be dealt with in a book or article on a larger topic. Construct mentally a hierarchy of possible terms on the lines of the following two examples:

>   Remedies
>   Equitable remedies
>   Injunctions
>   Mareva injunctions

>   Tort
>   Negligence
>   Professional negligence
>   Medical negligence
>   Wrongful birth

1.9 As well as thinking through synonyms and a hierarchy of broader and narrower terms, one must bear in mind related terms and also disentangle different meanings that the same terms may have in different contexts. Examples of closely related, but not synonymous or identical, terms or subject areas, are 'immigration' and 'nationality', 'competition law' and 'monopolies', 'consumer protection', 'product liability' and 'sale of goods', 'mergers' and 'take-overs'. Some examples of the same terms being used in different contexts are: 'taxation' which will usually mean revenue law, but may well refer to the taxation of costs; 'privilege' which may arise in the context of defamation or of discovery; 'caution' in the sense of a police caution or a caution on the land register; 'forfeiture' in the sense of criminal confiscation orders or in the context of forfeiture of leases (or forfeiture of an inheritance under the Forfeiture Act 1982); 'ultra vires' in administrative law or in company law.

1.10 The same terms, while not representing different concepts, may be applied in different areas of law, the most obvious examples being torts which may also be crimes, such as conspiracy, assault, and nuisance. The same term may be used in a loose general sense or in a specific technical sense. For example a 'settlement' may refer generally to a disposition of property, or specifically to a settlement under the Settled Land Act 1925 as opposed to a trust for sale. A 'warranty' may be used loosely for any guarantee or assurance, or specifically as a contract term whose breach only gives rise to a right to damages not to rescission.

1.11   If your research takes you into materials or writings from other jurisdictions, it is also necessary to be alive to the possibility that terms may differ from their English usage. For example in the United States (and other jurisdictions) 'judicial review' will usually refer to the courts reviewing whether legislation is constitutional rather than the review of administrative action. Scottish law is replete with its own technical terms which should not be confused with their appearance in ordinary English usage, such as 'diligence' or 'irritancy'.

1.12   Change of terminology over time should be appreciated, especially if your research takes you into older materials. This may be the result of changes in fashion — for example in contract law 'exclusion clauses' were often and may still occasionally be called 'exception clauses'. The umbrella term 'intellectual property' for copyright, designs, and patents has only relatively recently become the preferred term — 10 or 20 years ago it would have been 'industrial property'. It may be the result of changes in the boundaries and classication of subjects. It was only in 1966 that the first English textbook on the law of 'restitution' was written. Before then it would have been considered under the head 'quasi-contract' in contract books or dispersed in equity texts. The law, and so its terminology, may have mirrored changes in social conditions — the law of 'master and servant' and 'husband and wife' are now employment law and family law. Changes may also result from the intervention of legislation. Entire legal concepts may disappear as the result of legislation — since 1967 the student has not had to worry about the distinction between 'felonies' and 'misdemeanours', yet an appreciation may still be necessary for reading old cases. Or there may be a substitution of terminology — theft for larceny (Theft Act 1968), criminal damage for malicious damage (Criminal Damage Act 1971), personal insolvency for bankruptcy (Insolvency Act 1985), inheritance tax for capital transfer tax (Finance Act 1986). (The last example incidentally was unusual in having retrospective effect, so that the Capital Transfer Act 1984, as it was called on its enactment, is to be cited as the Inheritance Tax Act 1984.) The extent to which these changes are merely substitutions of terminology or introduce entirely new statutory regimes varies, but even with major changes an awareness of the previous legislation and its own terminology is often necessary. Income support was preceded by supplementary benefit, driving dangerously by reckless driving, and we have had the merry progression from the rates, via the community charge, to the council tax.

1.13   These changes often present problems in using indexes, particularly to major works such as *Halsbury's* produced over a period of time and serial works such as *Current Law*. Cross-references may be provided, but it is as well to prepare mentally one's own in advance. *Current Law* also exemplifies another problem which can occur with any serial publication — namely changes not in the terminology of the subject matter as such but in indexing policy. From 1987 there were major changes in the headings used both in the body of the main work and in the index. For example, in the main work the heading 'Criminal law' was split into three separate headings 'Criminal law,' 'Criminal procedure and evidence' and 'Criminal sentencing'; 'Divorce and matrimonial causes' became 'Family law'. In the index there was much greater use of direct headings, so that, for instance, 'Mareva injunctions' and 'Anton Piller orders' now have their own headings rather than appearing as sub-headings of

'Practice'. The *Legal Journals Index* and *Daily Law Reports Index* follow an elaborate structured thesaurus for their subject indexing. A much expanded and revised edition of the thesaurus was prepared in 1990, and is revised continuously with the introduction of new terms as required; this again must be borne in mind when searching the older volumes.

1.14 Although the emphasis on thinking through terminology has here been in the context of subject searching because that is where it is most pertinent, the same general advice applies to searching for names, whether as authors in catalogues, or as parties in cases or indeed as subject terms. Names of corporate bodies are the most likely to cause trouble. The London University problem of inversion is a common one: Commissioner of Police for the Metropolis or Metropolitan Police Commissioner, Secretary of State for the Environment or Environment Secretary, Law Reform Commission of Australia or Australian Law Reform Commission, Court of Justice of the European Communities or European Court of Justice. Changes of name, mergers and demergers are another common problem: Liberty was the National Council for Civil Liberties; The International Stock Exchange was the Stock Exchange; the Department of Trade and the Department of Industry merged to become the Department of Trade and Industry; the Department of Health and Social Security split into the Department of Health and the Department of Social Security. Acronyms and initialisms as opposed to the full name often occur. Occasionally a body may have a popular name and an official name, for example the Ombudsman is formally known as the Parliamentary Commissioner for Adminstration. Policy in indexes and tables varies on the treatment of corporate bodies in the form of personal names, eg Arthur Andersen or William Hill — they may be entered directly under the first element or inverted like a personal name.

1.15 Personal names do not present great problems — basic phone book skills are all that are needed. The unhyphenated double-barrelled surname versus the second (or third) forename is the standard problem: S.A. De Smith, Sir William Clarke Hall, E.R. Hardy Ivamy, T.A. Blanco White. For some reason the surname of the author of the well-known work on personal insolvency (previously bankruptcy) is often assumed to be Muir Hunter, rather than just Hunter. Peerage titles that differ from the original family surname can occasional confuse, though usually this arises in the case of old rather than modern writers: Charles Abbott or Lord Tenterden, Edward Sugden or Lord St Leonards, Quintin Hogg or Lord Hailsham of St Marylebone.

Currency

1.16 Well over 3000 new reported cases are digested by *Current Law* each year; over 2500 statutory instruments (SIs) are made; 7000 articles appear in British legal periodicals. Taking these sources alone 50 new items of legal information appear every working day. This rapid level of change makes it essential that your legal research is as up to date as possible.

Ensuring that the results of your research are as up to date as possible entails three elements: awareness of how particular sources are updated, awareness of which sources offer the greatest currency, and awareness at each stage of the precise date to which your research has taken you. In the course of this work many particular works will be examined and their updating mechanisms explained, but the basic principle when using any unfamiliar work is to ask onseself if and how it is updated — read any prefatory or explanatory matter. The tools offering the greatest currency for any particular problem will also be highlighted, but if in doubt ask someone, such as the law librarian or information officer, whether there is anything else more up to date. Most legal sources will say up to what date the law is stated — in textbooks look at the preface, in looseleaf works look at the latest filing instructions.

1.17 In the quest for currency it should not be overlooked that old law can sometimes help. A particular section of a statute hot off the Queen's printing press may in fact merely re-enact a previous provision. Old legal concepts may be resuscitated to meet novel problems — for example Peter Sparkes in an article, [1986] *Conveyancer* 107, canvassed the application of the remedy of distress damage feasant, classically employed in the case of straying cattle, to the problem of private car clamping.

Needles in haystacks

1.18 The John Smith problem is one quite often encountered in legal research. It is not restricted to common names when searching for authors in catalogues or parties in tables of cases. In the *Current Law Case Citator* for 1977-1988 there are over 500 reports under the heading 'Practice direction'; in 1989 there were 43 SIs with the title 'Air Navigation (Restriction of Flying)' regulations. Sometimes there is no alternative but to plough through masses of material until you find what you want, but often the search can be approached from a different angle that yields a more specific result or can be narrowed in some way. One of the techniques of legal research is striking a balance between over-retrieval and under-retrieval. In the first example, if you were looking for a particular practice direction but did not know its precise title, then rather than wading through the lists in *Current Law* under title, you might try a subject approach, or better still find the relevant part of the *White Book* where it is more than likely to be cited. In the second example, if you only had manual sources at your disposal, you would probably be stuck, but if you had access to Lexis or SIs on CD-ROM it would a simple matter to add the place name to the search request to find the restriction of flying regulation for a particular locality. The second example also illustrates the fact that with a manual index how broad or narrow your search can be is dictated to you by the particular indexing policy and method, whereas with on-line searching it is largely in your hands. Because of that flexibility, the best general advice for on-line searching is start with a broad search and gradually make it more specific — it is a safer to retrieve some material that you do not need than to miss some material that may be relevant.

Shortcuts: people sometimes better than books

1.19 'Ask the girlfriend' in the phone number illustration is by no means a flippant precept for legal research. In a law firm, barristers chambers, or law school, there may well be someone else with expertise in the particular field you are researching who is able to say off the top of their head what the leading case is or what the best article is. Empirical research in the scientific research community has repeatedly shown that this form of informal 'networking' comes ahead of libraries or databases as a source of information, and experience shows that this is the case in the law too. Even if there is no one of your immediate acquaintance who can help, it can often save a lot of time if you can go straight to the horse's mouth. If you are struggling with the EC regulation of seed varieties, ring Legal Division A2 in the Ministry of Agriculture;

if you are unsure whether the United Kingdom has ratified a treaty, ring the Treaty Department at the Foreign and Commonwealth Office; if you want to know whether a decision of the Court of Appeal has gone to the House of Lords, ring the Judicial Office of the House of Lords; if you think the regulations governing authorised unit trust schemes have been amended, ring the Unit Trust Association and so on. In chapter 8 use of various directories to find such sources of information is discussed; the only bit of advice given here is that when contacting government departments it is best if you can find the number of the particular section or individual rather than try the general switchboard and in general if you can find the name of a particular person to contact, so much the better.

The half-remembered

1.20 As with finding the name of the girlfriend's firm, much legal research does not start completely cold. In fact what goes under the name of legal research is often no more than trying to find that case you saw in *The Times* a couple of weeks ago. The danger is that usually it turns out that it was not *The Times* but *The Independent*, it was not a couple of weeks ago but a couple of months ago, and that though 100% certain that the name of one of the parties was Ede it was in fact Ravenscroft. Despite these pitfalls, if you do have some point of reference at the back of your mind to start from it can save considerable time in tackling a research problem. For this reason browsing journals and using current awareness services, be they published or in-house productions such as many large law firms and other organisations circulate, is a healthy exercise even if every item within your field of interest is not noted there and then. Not only lawyers but also the information professionals and librarians to whom this book is also addressed should make a point of scanning the legal press.

Lateral thinking

1.21 As with any research, speed and proficiency in legal research depend on a certain degree of luck and intuition as well as experience and knowledge. The ability to think round a problem and come up with alternative approaches when first attempts fail is probably not something that can readily be taught. Edward de Bono's book *Teaching Thinking* (Penguin) perhaps shows that, on the contrary, it can be taught, and certainly his most well-known book *Lateral Thinking* (Penguin) is relevant to research skills, and well worth reading. But having a crossword mentality does help. This book can elucidate the equivalent of the conventions that signal the presence of an anagram in a crossword clue, but it cannot tell you in every case how to rearrange the letters to get the solution.

Knowing your sources and how they work

1.22 If lateral thinking cannot be taught, knowledge of the range of available sources is something concrete that can and should be assimilated, and indeed accounts for much of the content of this book. It should be emphasised though that familiarity with the materials is best gained from using them as much as from reading about them. Until that familiarity is gained, the best assumption to work on is that for most research problems there is a tool designed to solve it: if while tackling a problem you are thinking 'There must be an easier way of doing this', there usually is. The benefit of making the small effort to acquire the necessary knowledge is not just that you can go straight to the right place, but you will know when there definitely is no research tool designed for your problem before tackling it the hard way.

1.23 However, outside the mainstream tools dealt with in this book, there is a vast range of sources, some specialised or obscure and not necessarily widely available. The range of tools is not static either. Even if you have access to a large and well-equipped law library, there is always a danger of forgetting that there might be better sources elsewhere. It should also be remembered that law librarians and information officers are not only paid to answer questions but actually quite enjoy being asked. Furthermore, apart from being trained, they have usually clocked up more 'flying hours' doing legal research than many lawyers for whom research is necessarily only a small part of their work. So although this book aims to make the lawyer reasonably self-sufficient, asking for help is not a sign of failure but often a sensible and time-saving move.

Costs, benefits and time

1.24 The decision whether to ring the States or send a letter requires only a fairly basic application of cost/benefit principles. Applying the same principles to legal research does not require much greater sophistication, but is a necessary discipline. The classic illustration is the decision whether to use an on-line service, such as Lexis, which will cost money or do a manual (or CD-ROM) search, which is free (ignoring of course the original purchase price of the materials). The variables are the quality of information required, the value of that information to you, the speed with which it is required and the cost (or value) of your time. It may be that the on-line source is in fact the only source — for example, Lexis for the transcript of an unreported case. Or the quality or quantity of information from the on-line source is better — for example as with Lexis by retrieving many more references than the manual citators to statutes judicially considered. In those eventualities a judgment has to be made as to how badly you need the information. Depending on the context, the cost may seem cheap at the price, may be grudgingly met, or may be deemed too much because you can make do without the information. In many circumstances, the same information may be retrieved from manual sources but it takes much longer. If the matter is very urgent there may be no choice; if you are a solicitor using up billable hours it may well be cheaper to spend the money on an on-line search; even if your time does not directly cost money, there be better things you could be doing with it.

1.25 Another typical illustration of cost, benefits and use of time is delegation of research, be it to a trainee solicitor, to a pupil barrister, to a research assistant, or to a law librarian or information officer. Similar variables apply. As it is more likely that those categories of person — rather than the senior partner, silk, or professor — will be reading this, the important point here, if the research is to be more cheaply done by you, is getting the research request absolutely clear. The assumption is often made by those delegating the task that what they really need is readily transmitted by telepathy. Sometimes a certain firmness of purpose is required to elicit what exactly is wanted. Find out why it is wanted, how much is wanted, and when it is wanted (usually yesterday).

Back to square one: approaching the problem from a different angle

1.26   As has emerged above, throughout the research process choices have to made — of starting points, of terminology, of sources, and so on. Frequently the wrong choice may be made and a dead end reached. Even where the problem has been tackled in the most efficient and elegant way, there is always the chance that a fresh approach will yield something more. If time allows double-checking is always a wise precaution — even the most reputable sources sometimes have errors or omissions. Illustrations of this will be given in the subsequent chapters, and the point is but one specific example of the general application of lateral thinking in legal research. At this stage it is just worth emphasising, however, that research tools that have one purpose can often be used in roundabout way for another purpose. *Halsbury's Statutes* can be used to find cases, both cases and legislation can be traced through the *Legal Journals Index*, information on government publications can be found in *Current Law Statutes Annotated*, and so on.

Getting off the runway: from fact to law

1.27   In practice the most difficult aspect of legal research, especially for the new practitioner, is not the grasping of such points as those listed above. Rather, the difficulty is conceptual. Legal problems as they arrive on the solicitor's or barrister's desk (or indeed in the student's examination paper), are not dressed as such, but usually come in the form of more or less complex fact situations. The first step in researching the problem has to be translating the fact situation into legal issues. The skills needed for spotting the relevant legal issues can only be acquired through experience and knowledge of the substantive law, and this book must assume such competence. If some practice is needed there are some useful self-assessment practical exercises, where factual situations requiring identification of the legal issues are given, in Victor Tunkel's *Legal Research* (Blackstone Press, 1992). Or approaching it the other way, inventing facts to fit a legal issue, the following exercise, a sort of legal trivial pursuits, can be tried.

1.28   A brick comes through your window. Those are the facts of the case, what are the legal issues? On the basis of these facts alone, criminal damage may be the first thing that springs to mind. Inventing the fewest additional facts, use your legal imagination to raise other legal issues. Score highest for the most far-fetched legal topic arrived at with the addition of the fewest facts. For example trespass or negligence would be fairly low scoring. An ecclesiastical law point might be higher. And indeed, a quick look at the ecclesiastical law title in *Halsbury's Laws* indicates that, if we suppose the window is a church window and you are a vicar conducting a service inside, the following possiblities might arise: riotous or indecent behaviour contrary to s 2 of the Ecclesiastical Courts Jurisdiction Act 1860; obstructing or assaulting a clergyman in the discharge of his duties contrary to s 36 of the Offences Against the Person Act 1861; and a common law offence of disturbing a priest in the perfomance of divine worship (*R v Parry*, (1686) Trem PC 239). For a higher score try, say, copyright, *donatio mortis causa*, EC law.

The research cycle summarised

1.29 Distilling what has been said so far, the following is the strategy to aim for:
(1) identify the point of law;
(2) choose your terminology: think of key words, broader terms, narrower terms, related terms, synonyms, antonyms;
(3) choose a starting point: eg textbooks, *Halsbury's*, case-finding aids, legislation-finding aids;
(4) choose a starting date and work backwards;
(5) bring yourself up to date: supplements, etc;
(6) double-check using alternative sources;
(7) start again from a different angle.

Physical format of legal materials and their finding aids

1.30 Although most of them will be familiar to anyone who has set foot in a law library, it is worth at the beginning running briefly through the variety of physical formats that are encountered in legal research, and highlighting any particular hazards.

Printed sources

1.31 The main point to be aware of in using ordinary printed sources is the method, if any, of updating. Many standard hardbound and softbound books are simply reissued in new editions from time to time, without any intermediate supplementation. Some are reissued regularly on an annual basis — *Blackstone's Criminal Practice*, the recent rival to *Archbold*, has chosen that method to avoid the cumbersomeness of supplements; it is also the standard way of issuing many tax handbooks after each budget. But many practitioners' works have supplements between editions. Usually these are cumulative, but occasionally there may be more than one supplement to consult. In the past English legal publishers have occasionally followed the American practice of having 'pocket part' supplements that are physically inserted in a pocket inside the back cover, but usually they are kept (or lost) separately.

1.32 Looseleaf works have long been a solution to the updating of legal books. If properly maintained and organised, they are a great boon, but it is always essential to check when the last release of new material was inserted, because otherwise they can give a false sense of security as to their currency: the publishers may be tardy in issuing new releases, there may be a backlog of looseleaf filing in the library or office, the subscription may have lapsed or been cancelled. The pagination of looseleaf works is necessarily more complicated. Apart from making it sometimes difficult to find the relevant page, it can conceal the fact that some pages are missing or misfiled (which can all too easily happen after a trip to the photocopier). Apart from allowing updating proper, they also allow the publication of a work before it is complete. This does allow the publication of what is available more quickly, but can be a test of the scrupulosity of publishers in their marketing. It is also necessary to be aware that the looseleaf format is not proof against the need for supplements as well. The looseleaf

Statutes in Force resorts to cumulative supplements as well as replacing pages in the main work, and some of the large looseleaf encyclopedias do not consolidate their tables and indexes with every release but issue supplementary ones.

1.33 Large multi-volume works such as *Halsbury's* or *Atkin's Court Forms* may use a combination of the above methods of updating. Individual bound volumes are reissued from time to time, a cumulative supplement is published annually, and a looseleaf service contains new materials pending the reissue of a bound volume and provides a noter-up to catch developments between annual supplements.

1.34 Serial publications such as law reports and journals do not have any great problems. It is worth remembering, though, that while some only have indexes for each volume, others might have separate cumulative indexes, or, as can be easily overlooked, cumulative indexes covering several volumes bound in with one particular volume. An often unavoidable frustration is that the loose parts of serials have to go away to be bound up, though many series do have bound volume services whereby the publishers provide a bound volume as well as the loose parts. For finding aids and indexes issued in serial loose part format the pattern of cumulation should be noted. For example *Legal Journals Index* cumulates quarterly and annually, so there is no need to consult the superseded monthly parts if they have been inadvertently left on the shelf. The entries in the body of the monthly parts of *Current Law* are only cumulated annually (into the *Current Law Yearbook*) but many of the tables and indexes cumulate each month.

Microforms

1.35 The use of microforms, whether in the form of roll film or fiche, may be dwindling in the face of electronic media, but they will continue to be encountered for some time in law libraries. Apart from being a space-saving format for very bulky material (official publications such as Parliamentary papers and European Community documentation are often held in microform), they are used as a cheap way of republishing out of print material, and as a preservation medium for old materials that in their original paper format are distintegrating. Computer output microfiche (COM) was until recently one of the preferred methods of printing out large quantities of computer data, such as library catalogues and bibliographical tools like *British Books in Print*, that had to be updated and reissued frequently. Although being gradually ousted by on-line systems and CD-ROM, there continue to be many COM fiche products. Ordinary microforms may use positive or negative images, but many reader-printers allow the printing out of negative microform in positive format like the photocopy of an ordinary page. COM fiche require a higher magnification lens than ordinary microforms. If you have not used microfiche before and are struggling to insert them in the reader the right way round, follow the mortuary adage: face up, feet first.

Computerised sources

1.36 There are a number of computer databases either accessible from a terminal via a telephone line (on-line) or in the form of CD-ROMs (Compact Disk — Read Only Memory). They fall into two broad categories according to the nature of the data they hold. The first are full text systems, which include the legal database best known in this country, Lexis. The entire text of the law reports and legislation is loaded and any word, bar a very few words such as 'the' or 'and', wherever it occurs can be found. It is not thus an index — the user is the indexer. The only intervention by the suppliers of the database is to code segments of each item — for example, the name of the court, the head note, the names of counsel, in a law report — so that they can be searched individually without searching all the text in every item. The second category is the purely bibliographical database, which indexes the material but merely give the references to where the printed source may be found. The Lexis style system thus provides for one-stop shopping if required (though many users will read the retrieved material in its printed form, rather than on screen or from printout), but a purely bibiographical system is only a substitute for a conventional index. Although they are more common with scientific databases, a hybrid of these two categories may be encountered, namely databases that provide full indexing facilities but also give summaries or abstracts of the material indexed rather than full text.

1.37   In all the systems, not only can any single term in the database be searched for, but combinations of terms can be specified. This is done using what is grandly called Boolean logic. The actual commands that need to be keyed in vary but the three main ways of combining terms are by using the logical connectors AND, OR, or AND NOT. 'Blood' AND 'Guts' retrieves only items containing both the terms 'Blood' and 'Guts'. 'Blood' OR 'Guts' retrieves any item containing either the term 'Blood' or the term 'Guts'. 'Blood' AND NOT 'Guts' retrieves only those items that contain 'Blood' which do not also contain 'Guts'. AND is thus a way of making a search more specific. If you are only interested in damages in libel cases, then 'Damages' AND 'Libel'. AND NOT is a useful way of excluding references to a term used in a different context. 'Arrest' AND NOT 'Ship' would prevent the criminal lawyer from running to a whole series of references in *Lloyd's Law Reports*. OR is a way of broadening a search — 'Copyright' OR 'Passing off' — or in full text systems a way of allowing for synonyms or alternative spellings — 'Vehicle' OR 'Car', 'Judgement' OR 'Judgment'.

1.38   As well as these basic techniques, most systems offer additional facilities. A refinement of AND searching particularly useful in large full text systems is proximity or adjacency searching. This confines the search to those items where the two terms are not merely anywhere in the same item but are within a certain distance of each other, for example in the same paragraph or within so many words. If you are searching for material on negligent valuations, to search for the complete phrase 'Negligent valuation' would not retrieve material where the matter was phrased as 'a valuation was alleged to have been carried out negligently'; on the other hand to search for just 'Negligent' AND 'Valuation' might retrieve a mass of irrelevent material where these two quite common words are separately mentioned in entirely different contexts in the same item. To able to specify only those items where the two terms are near each other is likely to be much more successful. On Lexis the search would be phrased Negligent w/10 Valuation, which would retrieve items where the word Negligent appeared within 10 words of the word Valuation.

1.39   The last example also illustrates the utility of being able to truncate search terms, which is a refinement of OR searching. In a free text system without truncation one would have to enter 'Negligent' OR 'Negligence' OR 'Negligently'. Most systems allow for the search on a truncated stem, 'Negligen', thereby retrieving all the possible variations automatically. On Lexis this is done using a !, thus 'Negligen!'; other systems may use different symbols. Lexis automatically searches for both the singular and plural form without truncation being specified, but in other systems the apppropiate symbol may need to be used. A similar feature but used within a word rather than at the end is the wildcard character, for example wom*n would retrieve both woman and women, and indeed any other word, if there were any, that contained any letter of the alphabet in the position of the asterisk. A table setting out the symbols and commands used in a selection of on-line and CD-ROM systems is given in the Quick Reference Guide (QR1.1).

On-line

1.40 Most on-line databases are provided by commercial vendors, in other words they cost money. It is important to be aware of the charging structure of a particular database to avoid running up unpleasant bills and to make the most cost-effective use of them. There are usually four cost elements: a subscription to the service which has to be paid whether the system is used or not; a connect time charge, so much per minute that you are connected to the computer while searching; a search charge — this is not universal, but is a particular feature of the Lexis charging structure and is incurred each time a new search is entered; and lastly telecommunications costs, ie the phone bill — many systems, even where the main computer is overseas, allow access via a local 'node', so that long distance rates are not incurred, but it is worth bearing in mind, even though this is usually the smallest element in the costs, the difference between peak and off-peak phone charges.

1.41 If you are using a PC as a terminal it may be possible to download the results of your search (though beware of copyright problems if this is not sanctioned by the vendor) for perusal later at your leisure. This is particularly useful with systems with a high connect time rate, or where the search has resulted in a large number of 'hits'. On the other hand the Lexis charging structure, with its relatively low connect time charge, is designed to encourage on-screen browsing, but it places a premium on formulating the initial search correctly — although the search may be modified to make it more specific without extra charge, if the search is started afresh another, quite hefty, search charge is incurred.

1.42 Like looseleaf works in the printed field, one of the advantages of on-line systems is of course that they can be constantly updated. But as with looseleafs it is important not to be misled as to their actual currency. Some systems, such as those providing financial information or news services, are indeed updated daily or more frequently, but with others there may be a time lag. Usually a front screen will give the date of the latest information added. Lexis, for example, will be up to date to within the last three or four weeks; on the other hand, the data on Celex, the EC official database, can be months behind.

CD-ROM

1.43 The format of a CD-ROM will be familiar to anyone with a modern hi-fi system at home, but the CD player is plugged into a PC rather than an amplifier. Their high storage capacity allows each CD to act as a mini database in its own right, and search software loaded onto the PC allows it to be searched like any on-line system. The publications loaded in this format may be the full text of, for example, law reports or SIs, or may be a convenient format for indexes and other finding tools, such as *Current Law* or the *Index to Legal Periodicals*. The great advantage of the format is that you can carry out on-line type searches without the associated costs. Having paid for the CD, there are no other charges to be met. The two disadvantages are frequency of updating and size limitations. Although the cost is falling, at the time of writing only those CDs with a large circulation, such as the American-based *Index to Legal Periodicals*, can afford to issue new, cumulated, disks every month; quarterly updates are the norm. Some CD vendors, notably Justis, are also on-line hosts and so can mitigate the problem. The advantage claimed for a combined CD and on-line search is that the best search strategy can be evolved at your leisure at no cost on the CD and the bulk of the material retrieved there; the on-line service is then used only briefly to check on any more recent material added since the last issue of the CD. Although seemingly vast quantities of data can be stored on a single disk — the equivalent of the entire *Encyclopaedia Britannica* or *Oxford English Dictionary* — their capacity is still no match for the big on-line systems, such as Lexis. At the moment the CD publishers are naturally confining their attentions to current material with only limited retrospective conversion, so that most legal products only occupy a single disk; but with the passage of time, searching of multiple disks will be required.

Viewdata

1.44 This is an on-line source in the sense that there is a remote computer which is accessed via a telephone line, but the way in which the searcher interacts with the system is different from the conventional on-line databases described above. Ceefax on the BBC is a species of viewdata — the screen is merely a substitute for the printed page, and indeed viewdata systems are usually arranged in numbered pages. Rather than entering search terms and using Boolean logic, the on-screen equivalent of printed indexes are used to find the information. The main legal database in viewdata is Lawtel, which operates via BT's Prestel service. It indexes and provides summaries of a range of current legal sources such as cases, legislation and bills. The vendors also provide a research bureau service and the system is used as a form of electronic mail for subscribers to send their research requests to the bureau and receive the answers back; these answers remain on the system as a source of information for other users. Lawtel operates via subscription; on top of that there is Prestel's (low) connect time charge, and the phone costs. Much of the information on Prestel itself, which includes a very wide range of useful sources from train timetables to cricket scores, is charged for on a per page viewed basis. Lawtel is updated daily.

In-house databases

1.45 Many law firms and some libraries may have their own in-house computer databases. As well as conventional catalogues they may contain such material as counsel's opinions and drafting precedents. They may also provide indexes to articles, newspaper law reports and other published materials in a form more suitable to local needs and with greater currency than the commercially available services, whether printed or computerised. A hybrid of the in-house service and the conventional commercial service is the electronic version of the *Daily Law Reports Index* and the *Legal Journals Index*. Rather than offering a remote on-line service, the publishers provide fortnightly the entire database on magnetic tape which subscribers then load onto their own computer system, and search using their own preferred search software. C-Text, which contains the various financial services regulatory materials and is used by some of the large City practices, works in a similar way.

2. Starting from square two: textbooks and other secondary sources

Introduction

2.1 Later chapters of this book are devoted to finding the primary sources of the law — legislation, cases, treaties, and various other official publications. Certainly it is necessary for lawyers to be able to find these materials for themselves from scratch in some circumstances, but in real life the first port of call in solving a legal problem is not usually the indexes to the law reports and statutes, but textbooks and other secondary sources. Someone has already done the research for you — why do it the hard way? It may then be wise to check for yourself the primary sources cited, and also to check for recent developments since the textbook was updated, but attacking the raw data of the primary sources completely cold is seldom necessary.

The range of secondary sources

2.2 The pre-eminent secondary source is *Halsbury's Laws of England*. You cannot go far wrong by starting virtually any legal research here. Arranged by topic in 45 brown volumes, it provides an authoritative statement of the law by experts. Some large topics may be covered in a more condensed fashion than in the equivalent practitioners' textbook, but there is always more than ample citation of authority. On the other hand, because it is completely comprehensive, it treats some topics not covered at all by the textbooks. For example, the law relating to barristers warrants a 165 page section, yet is not the subject of any current textbook. Volumes 52 and 53 covering the European Communities deserve special mention. Because there was no equivalent practitioners' work on an equivalent scale, and because of the problems of integrating the updating with the main work, these have been developed into a spin-off publication, David Vaughan's *European Community Law*. As well as being comprehensive and authoritative, *Halsbury's Laws* is also very current. A section below (paras 2.6-2.10) is devoted to how to use it and get the most out of it.

2.3 Textbooks come in a variety of shapes and sizes. There are the large (and expensive) practitioners' works such as *Chitty on Contracts* or *Phipson on Evidence*. There are concise guides aimed at the practitioner in a hurry, such as the *Longman Practitioner Series*. Of books aimed at undergraduates, the nutshell type of guide is going to be of limited value for legal research, but some of the substantial academic texts, eg *Megarry and Wade on Real Property*, *Treitel on Contract*, *Smith and Hogan on Criminal Law*, are highly regarded and so are used by practitioners too and have been cited in court. Not only for academic or comparative research, but also for the practitioner faced with a novel or doubtful point, textbooks from the other major common law jurisdictions should not be overlooked. The Americans, in particular, have a tradition of producing exhaustive treatments on a grand scale — the current editions of *Corbin on Contracts* and *Wigmore on Evidence* each run to many volumes, and the *Restatements* prepared by the American Law Institute, which if we had the equivalent would be analogous to *Halsbury's Laws* rewritten by the Law Commission, are occasionally cited in the English courts.

2.4   Although many practitioners' textbooks that would previously have been published in ordinary bound form are now appearing in looseleaf format, the traditional application of the looseleaf format is to subject encyclopedias, often multi-volume, which reprint in amended form all the primary materials, such as statutes and SIs for a particular area (the term 'encyclopedia' in this context refers to their compendious nature rather than implying an A to Z arrangement). They also often contain introductory matter, substantive commentary and annotations to the primary materials. However, the ratio of such added-value material to material merely reprinted varies. For example, the *Encyclopedia of Insurance Law*, while usefully bringing together the statutory material, has little by way of text, whereas the *Encyclopaedia of Banking Law* has two volumes of text which are as highly regarded as any of the bound textbooks on the subject. As emphasised in the first chapter, it is important to be aware of the date the law is stated to be at, whether the book is bound or looseleaf.

2.5   Articles in periodicals are the other main secondary source. There are over 200 legal periodicals published in the UK alone. Again there is a wide range of form and substance. There are the long-established generalist heavyweights such as the *Law Quarterly Review*; there are the weeklies such as the *New Law Journal*, *Law Society's Gazette*, *Solicitors Journal*; and there is the ever-increasing number of specialist titles, which may offer substantial articles such as the *Construction Law Journal* or may be more in the form of a newsletter such as *Corporate Briefing*. All are valuable for current awareness and for catching recent developments since the last update to a textbook; they may be the only source of information for topics barely covered in the textbooks; and they may provide a depth of analysis for which there is not space in the textbooks. They may contain reports of cases in full or short form, as well as commentary on cases. As well as UK journals, there are English language journals from other parts of the world to bear in mind, especially for academic and comparative research, or research involving an international element. The tradition of every law school in the United States producing its own law review (the larger schools often producing ones in specialist areas, such as international law, as well the main one) accounts for the very large number of American titles.

Also covered in this chapter are legal dictionaries and sources for forms and precedents. The latter provide pro-forma examples as aids to drafting pleadings, particular types of contract, wills, trusts and all sorts of other legal documents.

Using *Halsbury's Laws*

2.6   *Halsbury's Laws* is arranged alphabetically by broad topic. Large topics may occupy a whole volume, or even two volumes, while several smaller topics may be

fitted into a single volume. Note that there is a separate index to each topic at the back of each volume; if there is more than one topic, there is more than one index. The numbered paragraphs, rather than the pagination, provide the principal reference system within volumes, and the numbering runs throughout each volume whether or not it contains more than one topic. All the references in the various tables and indexes are to paragraph, not page, numbers.

2.7   It is kept up to date in three ways. First, when the quantity and importance of new material warrants it, individual volumes are reissued in revised form. This does not usually create any difficulty — the spine will be marked 'reissue' and the date will be given on the title page. However, the current edition of *Halsbury's* started life 20 years ago and major changes in the law occasionally call for some restructuring of the arrangement and allocation of the broad topics. During a transitional period, it may be that a volume on the shelf contains the latest version of one topic, but that other topics in it have since been reassigned to another volume that has been reissued. A temporary label on the spine may cover the topics in it that are redundant.

2.8   The second updating mechanism is the cumulative supplement, issued annually in two bound volumes. It mirrors the volume and paragraph numbering of the main work. Then, thirdly, there is a noter-up, arranged in the same format as the supplement, in one of the two looseleaf 'Current Service' volumes. Issued monthly, it provides updates between annual supplements. See figure 2.1, which illustrates a page from volume 9 under the title Coroners. The cumulative supplement (figure 2.2) shows that the information in para 1105 has been superseded by new Coroners' Rules. The looseleaf noter-up (figure 2.3) shows that there has also been a recent relevant decision from the House of Lords.

2.9   The second of the two looseleaf 'Current Service' volumes contains *Halsbury's Laws Monthly Reviews*. These reviews, though flying the *Halsbury's* flag and having the same subject headings, are really a separate feature. They provide summaries of the latest cases and statutes, rather than relating directly to the text of the main work, and are not dissimilar to the monthly digests of *Current Law*, issued by rival publishers, Sweet & Maxwell. They can be used in the same way to check for very recent material or to browse as a current awareness tool (they are in pamphlet form to facilitate circulation round the office or chambers before being filed in the binder). Their coverage is perhaps not as comprehensive as *Current Law*, but they are strong on some areas such as summaries of unreported cases on quantum of damages for personal injuries. There is a looseleaf index which cumulates with every issue during the year. The references in the index are to the paragraph numbers which run consecutively in one sequence through the year. A confusing, not to say eccentric, feature of this numbering system, however, is that the sequence starts in November not January. Thus paras 92/276–92/374 are in the December 1991 review. The monthly reviews are then cumulated into the *Annual Abridgement*, which again are analogous to the *Current Law* yearbooks.

2.10   There are several ways of accessing the main work of *Halsbury's Laws*. Often all that is necessary is to browse along the shelf to find the appropriate volume and then to browse through the contents page for the particular topic. Otherwise you can approach it by using the subject indexes, or, if you know the name of a relevant case or statute by using the tables of cases or statutes. Each volume has its own indexes (as mentioned, one for each topic in the volume) and tables, but at the end of the work volumes 53 to 55 comprise a consolidated table of legislation, a consolidated table

Figure 2.1   Halsbury's Laws: *main work*

(1821) 4 B & Ald 218, and *R v Judge, ex parte Isle of Ely JJ* [1931] 2 KB 442, DC, both refer obiter to the power of inferior courts to commit absent witnesses and jurors though without any particular reference to the powers of a coroner. In a Canadian case, *R v Little, R v Miller* [1926] 2 WWR 762 (Man.), it was held that a coroner has power to commit for contempt a witness who refuses to testify. It seems that the status of a coroner's court as a court of record (see para. 1002, ante) implies power to commit for contempt; see *Beecher's Case* (1608) 8 Co Rep 58a at 61a; and see COURTS. The duration of the committal by the coroner for contempt is uncertain.

As to the right of appeal in cases of contempt of court, see the Administration of Justice Act 1960, s. 13, and CONTEMPT, paras. 107 et seq., ante.

4 See para. 1101, ante.

1104. Prohibition of photographs and sketches. It is a statutory offence to take or attempt to take in court any photograph or, with a view to publication make or attempt to make in court any portrait or sketch, of the coroner, of a juror, or of a witness, or to publish any photograph, portrait, or sketch so taken or made[1].

1 Criminal Justice Act 1925, s. 41 (1), (2) (a), (b). The prohibition extends to the precincts of the court building: s. 41 (2) (c).

1105. Application of laws of evidence. A coroner's inquest is not bound by the strict laws of evidence[1]. In practice, however, the laws of evidence are usually observed by coroners especially in cases where the coroner's inquisition may charge a person with murder, manslaughter or infanticide. Documentary evidence as to how the deceased came by his death is not admissible at an inquest unless the coroner is satisfied that there is good and sufficient reason why the maker of the document should not attend the inquest[2]. If such documentary evidence is admitted at an inquest, the inquest must be adjourned to enable the maker of the document to give oral evidence if the coroner or any properly interested person so desires[3].

All exhibits produced in evidence must be marked with consecutive numbers, each number being preceded by the letter "C"[4].

1 Per Wills J in his charge to the Grand Jury, Times, 18th March 1890; *R v Divine, ex parte Walton* [1930] 2 KB 29 at 36. As to the laws of evidence, see EVIDENCE.
2 Coroners Rules 1953, S.I. 1953 No. 205, r. 28 (1).
3 Ibid., r. 28 (2). The Report of the Committee on Death Certification and Coroners 1971 (Cmnd. 4810), para. 16.63, recommends that, subject to the same right of objection for properly interested persons as exists under the present law, coroners should in future have a general discretion to accept documentary evidence from any witness at an inquest.
4 Coroners Rules 1953, r. 29.

1106. Incriminating evidence. A witness is not bound to answer any question which may incriminate him[1]. Where it appears to the coroner that a witness has been asked such a question he must inform the witness of his right to refuse to answer[2]. This, however, does not entitle a witness to refuse to enter the witness box on the ground that he may be asked such questions. The objection can only be considered in relation to a particular question.

1 Coroners Rules 1953, S.I. 1953 No. 205, r. 18 (1).
2 Ibid., r. 18 (2).

1107. Competency of witnesses. The statutory provisions and common law rules as to the competency of witnesses[1] are in practice followed by coroners although it is doubtful whether strictly the statutory provisions apply to inquests[2].

Figure 2.2   Halsbury's Laws: *cumulative supplement*

right to direct a post-mortem examination and may only refuse a request by an interested party on good grounds: *R v Greater London Coroner, ex parte Ridley* [1986] 1 All ER 37.

TEXT and NOTE 9—Maximum fine now £400: 1988 Act supra, s 10(1). This amount may be further altered by order to take account of changes in the value of money: Magistrates' Courts Act 1980, s 143(1), (2)(f), Sch 6A; Criminal Justice Act 1982, s 48(1), (2), Sch 5; 1988 Act supra, Sch 3.

1099   Request for post-mortem examination by jury
NOTE 1—1887 Act consolidated in Coroners Act 1988, see table in para 1200A post.

1101   Fining of recalcitrant witnesses
TEXT and NOTES—A fine imposed by a coroner is enforceable by the magistrates' court for the area in which the coroner's court was held, as is a recognisance forfeited at an inquest: Criminal Justice Act 1988, s 67. 1887 Act consolidated in Coroners Act 1988, see table in para 1200A post.
TEXT and NOTE 1—Maximum fine now £400: 1988 Act supra, s 10(1). This amount may be further altered by order to take account of changes in the value of money: Magistrates' Courts Act 1980, s 143(1), (2)(f), Sch 6A; Criminal Justice Act 1982, s 48(1), (2), Sch 5; 1988 Act supra, Sch 3.

1102   Arrest of witnesses
NOTE 1—1887 Act consolidated in Coroners Act 1988, see table in para 1200A post.
NOTE 2—1952 Act consolidated in Magistrates' Courts Act 1980; see ss 125, 126.

1103   Committal for contempt
NOTE 2—See also *R v West Yorkshire Coroner, ex parte Smith (No 2)* [1985] QB 1096, [1985] 1 All ER 100, DC.

➧ 1105   Application of laws of evidence
TEXT and NOTES 2, 3—Replaced. At an inquest a coroner may admit documentary evidence relevant to the inquest from any living person, which in his opinion is unlikely to be disputed. Such documentary evidence may be objected to and may still be admitted if the coroner believes that the maker of the document is unable to give oral evidence within a reasonable period of time. Before admitting such evidence the coroner must, at the beginning of an inquest, announce publicly that such documentary evidence may be admitted, giving the name of the maker of the document and allowing any person to object to the admission of such evidence. Such a person may see a copy of the documentary evidence if he so wishes. Any documentary evidence so admitted must be read aloud at the inquest. Further a coroner may admit as evidence any document made by a deceased person if it is relevant to the purposes of the inquest: Coroners Rules 1984, SI 1984/552, r 37.
NOTE 4—See now ibid, r 38.

1106   Incriminating evidence
NOTES 1, 2—Replaced: SI 1984/552, r 22.

1107   Competency of witnesses
NOTE 2—Now 1898 Act, s 6(1); SL(R)A 1981.

1108   Examination of witnesses
NOTE 1—1887 Act consolidated in Coroners Act 1988, see table in para 1200A post. For form of oath see now 1984 Rules, SI 1984/552, Sch 4, Form 9.
NOTE 3—See now ibid, r 21.

1109   Depositions of witnesses
TEXT and NOTES 1–3—Repealed: Criminal Law Act 1977, Schs 12, 13.
NOTE 4—Replaced: SI 1984/552, r 39.

1110   Scope of inquest
TEXT and NOTES—1953 Rules consolidated: SI 1984/552.
TEXT and NOTES 1–3—See now ibid, r 36(1). The duty of a coroner's jury to name the person they find guilty of causing a death as abolished by the Criminal Law Act 1977, s 56(1), Sch 13, is now omitted from the 1984 Rules.
TEXT and NOTE 4—Replaced by ibid, r 36(2) which states that neither the coroner nor the jury may express any opinion on any matters outside the scope of the inquest. The jury is not entitled to make recommendations, even if they do not form part of the verdict: *R v Shrewsbury Coroners Court, ex parte British Parachute Association* (1987) 152 JP 123, DC.

1111   Speeches and summing up
TEXT and NOTES—Replaced: Coroners Rules 1984, SI 1984/552.
NOTE 1—See now ibid, r 40.
TEXT and NOTES 2, 4—See now ibid, r 41 and also rr 42, 43 and para 1120 post. For directions to be given where there are allegations of lack of care by police, see *R v West London Coroner, ex parte Gray* [1988] QB 467, [1987] 2 All ER 129, DC; *R v Wolverhampton Coroner, ex p McCurbin* [1990] 2 All ER 759, CA.

Figure 2.3   Halsbury's Laws: *looseleaf noter-up*

Noter-up   **Volume 9**

---

101   Committal
TEXT and NOTES—see *Duo v Duo* [1992] 3 All ER 121, CA and *Smith (CM) v Smith (S)* [1992] 2 FCR
33, CA.

CONTRACT

297   Duress
NOTE 3—See also the Australian case of *Scolio Pty Ltd v Cote* (24 April 1992, unreported) (Supreme
Court of Western Australia) (threat of criminal prosecution did not vitiate contract).

366A.5 (Supplement)   Further prevention of avoidance
NOTE 3—See *Stewart Gill Ltd v Horatio Myer & Co Ltd* [1992] 2 All ER 257, CA.

418   Business organisation and registration of business names
TEXT and NOTE 5—See now Business Names Act 1985.

507   Account current
NOTE 3—See also *Barlow Clowes International Ltd (in liquidation) v Vaughan* [1992] 4 All ER 22, CA.

622   General
TEXT and NOTE 9—The bar in *King v Hoare*, cited, to further actions once judgment has been obtained
against one or more, but not all, persons jointly liable in contract for the same damage has been removed:
Civil Liability (Contribution) Act 1978, s 3.

624   Judgment against one joint debtor
TEXT and NOTES—The bar to further actions once judgment has been obtained against one or more,
but not all, persons jointly liable in contract for the same damage has been removed: Civil Liability
(Contribution) Act 1978, s 3.

625   When judgment against one joint debtor no bar
TEXT and NOTES—The general rule that judgment against one joint debtor bars an action against the
others has been abrogated: Civil Liability (Contribution) Act 1978, s 3.

628   Accord and satisfaction
TEXT and NOTES 3, 4—The bar in *King v Hoare*, cited, to further actions once judgment has been
obtained against one or more, but not all, persons jointly liable in contract for the same damage has been
removed: Civil Liability (Contribution) Act 1978, s 3.
See *Deanplan Ltd v Mahmoud* [1992] 3 All ER 945.

681   Stakeholder
TEXT and NOTE 1—See *Rockeagle Ltd v Alsop Wilkinson (a firm)* [1991] 4 All ER 659.

COPYHOLDS

No further updating since publication of the 1992 *Cumulative Supplement.*

COPYRIGHT

888–905A (Supplement)   The Copyright Tribunal
NOTE 4—SI 1989/1129 amended: SI 1992/467.

927   Educational uses
TEXT and NOTES 16, 17—SI 1990/879 amended: SI 1992/211.

967   Extension to areas within jurisdiction
TEXT and NOTES 26–29—See SI 1992/1306, 1313.

CORONERS

1036   Inquests and post-mortem examinations
NOTE 4—See *R v Poplar Coroner, ex p Thomas* [1992] 3 WLR 485, DC.

1105   Application of laws of evidence
TEXT and NOTES 2, 3—See *Devine v Attorney General for Northern Ireland; Breslin v Attorney General for
Northern Ireland* [1992] 1 All ER 609, HL.

CORPORATIONS

1211   Name essential
NOTE 6—Charities Act 1960, s 31 omitted: Charities Act 1992, s 47, Sch 3.

Halsbury's Laws Current Service   November 92/Binder 2/Noter-up/19

of cases, and a consolidated index. Bear in mind that, though these are reissued from time to time, they may pre-date a very recent reissue of a volume of the main work, in which case the precise paragraph references given may no longer be accurate. This will be apparent when you reach the volume of the main work — it is then simply a matter of readjusting the references using the volume's own index or tables. Having found the relevant section of the main work, always then check the cumulative supplement and looseleaf noter-up for any subsequent changes. The three step process — main work/cumulative supplement/noter-up — should be an automatic routine whenever you use *Halsbury's Laws*.

Finding textbooks

2.11   The first step is naturally to be familiar with the way your law library organises its shelves and its catalogues, but you may well need to find out what might be available beyond your own library. Unfortunately there is no one comprehensive bibliography of all legal textbooks. The nearest to a one-stop tool is Donald Raistrick's excellent *Lawyers' Law Books: a Practical Index to Legal Literature*. The only caveat, which as time passes becomes an increasingly pronounced one, is that the last edition was back in 1985. It lists by subject all law books of current value, with an author index. It spreads its wings beyond UK textbooks, by including selected texts that might be of value to the English lawyer from other common law jurisdictions and on European and international law. Its selection of English textbooks usefully includes ancilliary material such as Law Commission reports, and at the head of each listing of books the relevant volumes of *Halsbury's Laws* and *Statutes*, *Encyclopaedia of Forms and Precedents*, *Atkin's Court Forms*, are given along with the titles of any periodicals devoted to the subject.

2.12   Although not designed as a bibliography as such, remarkably useful is the catalogue produced by Hammicks, the legal booksellers. It lists most English legal books in print by broad subject, with an author index. It is prepared annually. A minor hazard is that, in the interests of currency, it does contain some titles not yet published but which are supposedly coming out within the lifetime of the catalogue, but they are usually marked 'NYP'. It is also of course of no assistance for titles that are out of print.

2.13   Guides to books in print will cover the bulk of material of practical value, on the reasoning that if it is in print it is likely to be recent and if not recent of importance. There are two competing US publications specifically devoted to legal books in print, *Legal Books in Print*, published by Glanville (a division of Oceana publications) and *Law Books and Serials in Print*, published by Bowker. The Glanville publication, though US based and US biased, covers English language material from all over the world; the Bowker publication is mostly confined to US materials but a sister publication, *International Legal Books in Print* described below, is designed to cater for non-American material. The Glanville publication is now produced every three years in about six volumes. In between editions it is supplemented by the twice-yearly *Law Books Published*. The Bowker publication began as a way of updating another of its publications *Law Books 1876-1981*. It is published annually with quarterly cumulative supplements. Both publications allow access by author or subject and give full bibliographical details. The subject headings used by the Glanville work are probably the easier of the two to use, unless one is a devotee of

Library of Congress subject headings which are used by Bowker. Not a guide to material in print as such, but mainly of use for current materials because it is not cumulated, is the annual *Bibliographic Guide to Law* published by G.K. Hall, which lists all the law material, both domestic and foreign, catalogued by the Library of Congress.

2.14   *International Legal Books in Print* mentioned above was first published by the UK branch of Bowker in 1990 with the aim of making English language material from outside the United States more accessible than could the two US publications discussed above. It does contain a wealth of data, but it has to be said that it suffers from the somewhat indiscriminate use of computer data without sufficient editorial control, leading to some inaccuracies, inconsistencies and lack of currency. It is unlikely to be of use for checking English publications, but if you need to find material from other jurisdictions apart from the US then it may be better than nothing.

2.15   Returning to domestic products, another source that may help is *Current Law*. Inside the back cover of each digest there is a list by author of legal books published that month; this list is not particularly useful as a finding aid as such but it is interesting to browse through it as a current awareness exercise if you have time. These books, though, are listed under the appropriate subject headings within the monthly parts; the cumulative subject index in the latest monthly part can save looking through each part — the entries in the index are marked 'book' to distinguish them from case references. In the yearbooks, rather than being included in the body of the work as with the monthly digests, the books for that year are listed by subject at the back.

2.16   There are also general bibliographical tools to bear in mind, especially for areas on the fringe of law which might not appear in specifically legal sources. Most large libraries will have the *British National Bibliography* in one form or another. It is published in hard copy, fiche and on CD-ROM, as well as being available via the British Library's on-line service, Blaise. It should theoretically cover all books published in the UK, and the file goes back to 1950. *British Books in Print*, which is available in annual bound-volume form, on monthly cumulated fiche, or on the CD-ROM product, *Book Bank*, can help too, though it does not have a subject arrangement — one can only check under likely sounding titles.

2.17   Apart from academic research in legal history, it is sometimes necessary to find older law books. There are a few treatises such as *Coke's Institutes*, *Hale's Pleas of the Crown*, or *Blackstone's Commentaries* that rank as authorities in their own right and continue to be cited in court from time to time — for example Hale, written in the 1670s, featured in the series of cases on marital rape that culminated in the House of Lords ruling in 1991 in *R v R* [1992] 1 AC 599. These do not represent great difficulties — if the library does not have original editions they may have facsimile reprints. But you may need to follow up what the law used to be on some point, to make sense of an old reported case for example, and this may require greater research. The standard bibliography is the *Legal Bibliography of the British Commonwealth* compiled by W. Harold Maxwell and others, but generally known as 'Sweet & Maxwell' after its publishers. Volumes 1 and 2 cover English law. The first volume, published in a second edition in 1955, goes up to 1800 and is arranged by subject with an author and title index. The second volume covers 1801 to 1954 and is arranged by author with a subject index. More recently the *Bibliography of Eighteenth Century Legal Literature* by J.N. Adams was published, and a companion work *Bibliography* *of Nineteenth Century Legal Literature* has started publication (note that its coverage, at this stage at any rate, is only up to 1870, not the whole century). Neither are the easiest publications to use, though the latter incorporates some improvements. The first is a classified subject arrangement with an author index on fiche, the second is by author with a subject index on fiche. Both products are promised on CD-ROM, which will make a big difference to their accessibility. As well as being purely bibliographical tools, they also give locations for items in the major law libraries with historical collections. For the eighteenth century as well as the above tools there is the *Eighteenth Century Short-title Catalogue* (ESTC). This vast database, based on the holdings of many libraries both here and in the USA, is not confined to law but lists all books printed in Great Britain, or printed in English from 1701 to 1800, and gives locations for them. It is available on-line on Blaise, but is also available on CD-ROM. The CD-ROM version demonstrates the enormous benefits of this medium for bibliographical materials.

2.18   Apart from bibliographies as such, library catalogues are a valuable source of information. Traditionally many law libraries produced printed catalogues to enable wider circulation. Until a few years ago, this tradition was continued by the reproduction and publication, either in hard copy or microform, of the card catalogues of major collections, such as that at the Institute of Advanced Legal Studies. But with computerisation remote access to on-line catalogues is now possible. In this country the main source will be university libraries with large law collections, which can be accessed via JANET (the Joint Academic Network). Some academic libraries will also have access to the big American automated co-operative catalogues which cover hundreds of libraries, such as OCLC.

Finding articles

Legal Journals Index

2.19   This process has been revolutionised by the *Legal Journal Index*, which began publication in 1986. Before then the main alternatives were either to use *Current Law*, which covers selected articles in the main English legal periodicals, but not very effectively — it is subordinate to its main function of covering case law and statutory materials; or to use the American-based *Index to Legal Periodicals*, whose coverage and currency for English periodicals is less than adequate.

2.20   *Legal Journals Index* (LJI) covers all legal journals, or journals regularly carrying legal items, published in the UK. Newletters merely digesting primary materials are not covered. Every article, law report, case note, book review and editorial are indexed. Only news, or other ephemeral, items of less than a page are not indexed. It is published in monthly parts which cumulate quarterly and annually. Since January 1993 articles on EC law (other than those dealing specifically with UK implementation) have no longer been indexed in it but appear instead in the new parallel service *European Legal Journals Index* (ELJI), which also includes coverage of journals on European law in English not previously indexed because they were published outside the UK.

2.21   The whole database (including both LJI and ELJI) is now also available in electronic form. Although a CD-ROM version may appear in due course, this is currently supplied in the form of magnetic tape every fortnight, which subscribers then load onto their own computer system — many of the large firms of solicitors use it in this way. The advantages of the electronic version are that one does not have to look through a whole series of volumes and parts, it is possible to search on elements such as title terms that are not conventionally indexed, and that it incorporates any editorial corrections made retrospectively to the database after it is original creation. However, the description here concentrates on the hard copy form (and applies to both LJI and ELJI), as that is the most widely available and the search software used on the electronic version varies from subscriber to subscriber. If, though, the hard copy version proves inadequate for the kind of search you wish to do and you do not have access to the electronic version, the publishers will, for a charge, carry out a search on the database for you: see the front of any part for details.

2.22 It comprises five separate indexes: subjects, authors, cases, legislation and book reviews, together with, at the front, lists of abbreviations of the journals indexed. It is important to grasp the way the subject approach is tackled, as it is rather different from some traditional legal indexes. A page is illustrated (see figure 2.4). It works by means of headings using rotated keywords. Specific keywords are assigned to the entry from a strictly controlled list (a thesaurus). Where more than one term is assigned to a particular article, entries are made under each in rotation. For example an article on EEC competition law relating to insurance would be found under any of the following three headings:

COMPETITION LAW. EEC law. Insurance
EEC LAW. Insurance. Competition law
INSURANCE. Competition law. EEC law

Only the most specific term provided in the thesaurus is assigned, and in some areas these can be very specific. In the printed version, cross-references are not given between broader and narrower terms, so it is a matter of thinking of the most specific term for yourself and then thinking of possible broader headings and synonyms. In most cases the right keywords will be found without difficulty, but if help is needed some libraries may have the full printed version of the thesaurus which lists the terms used and the terms that are broader, narrower or related to any particular term; the thesaurus can also be viewed on the electronic version. The extract from the thesaurus below shows how a hierarchy of terms is created; it also illustrates how, in those subject areas with a large quantity of journal literature, the terms at the bottom of the hierarchy are quite narrow:

FINANCE
   FINANCIAL INSTITUTIONS
      BANKING
         LOANS
            EQUITY LENDING
            EUROLOANS
            FACILITY LETTERS
            LOAN AGREEMENTS
            LOAN NOTES
            LOAN STOCK
            MEDIUM TERM NOTES
            MULTI CURRENCY LOANS

NEGATIVE PLEDGES
PERSONAL LOANS
SPECIAL DRAWING RIGHTS
SUBORDINATION
SWAP AGREEMENTS
SYNDICATED LOANS

2.23 The author index is self-explanatory. Entries are given for both authors if there are two, but only under the first named if there are more than two. The book review index is by both the author and the title of the book reviewed (but not by name of reviewer).

2.24 The case index covers material of two different kinds. On the one hand there are reports of cases, such as those that appear in the *New Law Journal, Estates Gazette, Criminal Law Review* and so on. On the other hand there are articles or notes commenting on particular cases. Entries for the first category will simply comprise the citation under its name. For the second, there will be a title (if necessary supplied or expanded) of the article or note (and author if named) followed by the reference to the journal article itself. Thus

IDC GROUP LTD v CLARK [1992] E.G.C.S. 93 (CA)

— a case reported in the *Estates Gazette Case Summaries*

R v CANTERBURY CITY COUNCIL EX P. HALFORD [1992] 2 P.L.R. 137. Conservation areas. (Judicial review of planning authority's decision to designate conservation area). *E.G. 1992, 9228, 117*

— an article in the *Estates Gazette* commenting on a case reported in the *Planning Law Reports*.

The case reference given in the second kind of entry will be to the citation (or citations) used in the article itself. Remember that there may be other reports of the case, and indeed in the case index to *Legal Journals Index* different articles on the same case may appear with different citations in the heading. Helpfully, the case index provides cross-references from the names of defendants to the main entry under plaintiff.

2.25 The legislation index is broad in scope and covers articles commenting not only on particular UK statutes (or sections of statutes) but also on SIs and other regulations, EC legislation, Bills and other draft legislation, international treaties and conventions, and foreign legislation. Until 1990 this index was arranged in one alphabetical sequence by title. From 1991 (though this new arrangement is under review) it is divided into five sequences: England and Wales, other UK (ie Scotland, Northern Ireland, Channel Islands and the Isle of Man), EEC and Europe, individual countries A-Z by country, and international — the last division comprises multilateral treaties other than European ones; bilateral treaties will be found in the relevant country section. Use of the EEC legislation division needs care: the first filing element in the title may be 'Commission' or 'Council' depending on where the Directive or Regulation emanated from; to complicate matters where there have been a number of Directives on a subject the first filing element may be 'First', 'Second'

Figure 2.4 Legal Journals Index

SUBJECT INDEX

LUMP SUM PAYMENTS. Commutation. Occupational pensions
Exchanging pension for cash. (Inland Revenue commutation rules and formulae used in ten company schemes).
IDS P.S.B. 1992, 60, 3-6

LUMP SUM PAYMENTS. Investments. Money purchase schemes. Personal pensions
More surprises? (Possible liberalisation of rules governing post retirement investment of capital which must currently be invested only in annuities). David Evans.
Pen. World 1992, 21(11), 57-58

LUXEMBOURG. Dentists. EEC law. Freedom of establishment
Right of establishment: "single-surgery" rule contrary to equal treatment principles. (Rule discriminating between national and foreign dentists' opportunities to work not justified on medical grounds). Commission of the European Communities v Luxembourg Case C-351/90.
E.B.L.R. 1992, 3(11), 320

LUXEMBOURG. EEC law. Mergers. Subsidiary companies. Taxation
Luxembourg implements the EC directives. (Parent/subsidiary and merger tax directives). Jean-Francois Hein.
I.T.R. 1992, 4(1), 34-35

LUXEMBOURG. Listing. Stock exchange
Listing on the Luxembourg stock exchange. (Basic procedure for applicants for listing - includes table of fees). Alex Schmitt.
B.J.I.B. & F.L. 1992, 7(11), 514-517

MAGISTRATES. Breath tests. Drink driving offences
Reasonable excuse - personal knowledge of justices. (Whether magistrates may rely on own knowledge of medical conditions raised as excuse for failing to give breath specimen). D.P.P. v Curtis Times, September 7, 1992 (QBD).
W.R.T.L.B. 1992, 9(9), 69-70

MAGISTRATES. Criminal procedure. Prisoners rights
R. v Cambridge Justices Ex p. Peacock (1992) 156 J.P.N. 732 (QBD).

MAGISTRATES. Family proceedings. Judgments and orders
Hertfordshire C.C. v W (1992) 89(39) L.S.G. 33 (Fam Div).

MAGISTRATES. Freedom of information. Locus standi. Media
R. v Clerkenwell Stipendiary Magistrate Ex p. Daily Telegraph (1992) 142 N.L.J. Rep. 1541 (QBD).

MAGISTRATES CLERKS. Bias
The reasonable onlooker and the clerk. (Principles and tests applied in cases involving role of court clerk). Adrian Turner.
J.P. 1992, 156(46), 723-725

MAGISTRATES COURTS. Compensation orders. Statutory nuisance
Statutory nuisance: civil or criminal? (Powers of magistrates' court to make compensation order). Herbert v Lambeth L.B.C. (1992) 156 J.P. 389 (QBD).
J. Crim. L. 1992, 56(4), 333-334

MAGISTRATES COURTS. Criminal law. Fees. Legal aid
Many set to drop out of criminal work - survey. (Solicitors' attitude to fixed fee legal aid proposals).
L.S.G. 1992, 89(41), 5

MAGISTRATES COURTS. Criminal law. Fees. Legal aid
PCC - a ray of hope? (Law Society's "price per case" proposals). Jane Ahrends.
Lawyer 1992, 6(45), 7

MAGISTRATES COURTS. Criminal law. Fees. Legal aid
Soft approach gets a grilling. (National Legal Aid Practitioners Group meeting in Birmingham on proposed standard fees in magistrates courts).
Lawyer 1992, 6(46), 7

MAGISTRATES COURTS. Criminal law. Fees. Legal aid
The fixed fees battle. (Introduction of standard fees for magistrates' court criminal legal aid). Lee Bridges.
Legal Action 1992, Nov, 7,24

MAGISTRATES COURTS. Custodial sentences
The restrictions on custodial sentences in the Criminal Justice Act 1991 - sentencing guidelines from the Criminal Justice Act 1982: Part 1. M.D. Dodds.
J.P. 1992, 156(44), 691-694

MAIL ORDER. Enforcement. Exports. Registration. VAT
Distance selling - is it enforceable? (New VAT registration system as part of single market initiative and prospects of international agency cooperation). Value Added Tax Act 1983 Sch.1A. Bob Davies.
Pract. VAT 1992, 6(10), 80-82

MAINTENANCE. Cars. Champerty. Credit. Hiring
Run off the road. (Whether credit hire companies' provision of cars at no charge to plaintiffs after road traffic accidents falls foul of common law rules of maintenance and champerty). Stuart Catchpole and Iain Tenquist.
L.S.G. 1992, 89(39), 28

MAINTENANCE. Child support
Child maintenance: Child Support Act 1991. (Outline of provisions).
P.C.L.B. 1992, 5(9), 99-101

MAINTENANCE AGREEMENTS. Competition law. Computers. United States
Anti-trust enforcement in the United States: Eastman Kodak revives tie-in claims. (Legality of policy of supplying replacement parts only along with maintenance service under US competition law). Eastman Kodak Co v Image Technical Services Inc (1992) 112 S.Ct. 2072. Richard H. Stern.
E.I.P.R. 1992, 14(10), 369-371

MALICE. Mens rea. Murder
Intention in a joint or common enterprise. (Mens rea required to commit murder as party to common enterprise). R. v Roberts Independent, October 22, 1992 (CA).
J.P. 1992, 156(47), 737-738

MALICE. Mens rea. Murder. Remoteness
R. v Roberts (1992) 142 N.L.J. Rep. 1503 (CA).

MALICE AFORETHOUGHT
See Malice

MALICIOUS FALSEHOOD. Abuse of process. Defamation
Joyce v Sengupta: what difference will it make? (Whether writ for malicious falsehood abuse of process). Defamation Act 1952 s.3. Alan Williams.
I.M.L. 1992, 10(10), 76-77

MALICIOUS FALSEHOOD. Defamation. Legal aid
Joyce v Sengupta (1992) 89(39) L.S.G. 35 (CA).

MALPRACTICE
See Professional negligence

MANAGEMENT. Codes of practice. Health and safety at work
Blueprint for future health and safety management. (Code of Practice published). Management of Health and Safety at Work Regulations 1992.
H. & S.M. 1992, 15(12), 1-5

MANAGEMENT. Environment. Information retrieval
Getting IT started. (Using computers to manage environmental information). Malcolm Wicks.
Env. Risk 1992, Oct, 23-25

MANAGEMENT. Intellectual property
Crucial issues in IP commercialisation. (Advice to companies on good management of IP). Clive Elliott.
M.I.P. 1992, 24, 13-16

MANAGEMENT. Law firms
Action for survival: Part 2. (Guidance on practice management for small firms). Adrian Pike.
L.S.G. 1992, 89(39), 26-27

MANAGEMENT. Law firms
Managing beyond the corporate model. (Advice on implementation of inventive management strategies in law firms). David Jabbari.
Legal Bus. 1992, Nov, 47-50

MANAGEMENT. Law firms
Re-engineering the structures. (Current management trends in large and small law firms).
Lawyer 1992, 6(45), 14

MANAGEMENT. Law firms. Networks
Partners, please: Part 1. (Profile of Nexus Law Group Ltd). Martin Read.
S.J. 1992, 136(43), 1121

MANAGEMENT AGREEMENTS
See Management contracts

MANAGEMENT COMPANIES. Local authorities. Privatisation. Real property
Host potential. (Case study of transfer of Oxford C.C.'s property workload to private firm). David Young.
L.G.C. 1992, 6536, 22

MANDAMUS. Acquittals. Certiorari. Informations. Prosecutions
R. v Hendon Justices Ex p. D.P.P. (1992) 156 J.P.N. 746 (CA).

MANSLAUGHTER. Accomplices. Mens rea. Murder
Joint enterprise - mens rea of secondary party to murder. Hui Chi-Ming v R. [1991] 3 All E.R. 897 (PC). R.J. Cooper.
J. Crim. L. 1992, 56(4), 396-398

MANSLAUGHTER. Accomplices. Mens rea. Murder
Joint unlawful enterprises and murder. Hui Chi-Ming v R. [1991] 3 W.L.R. 495 (PC). Andrew L.-T. Choo.
M.L.R. 1992, 55(6), 870-875

MANSLAUGHTER. Drink driving offences. Jury directions. Scotland
Brodie v H.M. Advocate 1992 S.L.T. 925.

MANSLAUGHTER. Jury directions. Mistake. Self defence
Mistaken belief in self-defence. (Need for jury directions on mistaken belief when self defence in issue). R. v Oatridge (1992) 94 Cr. App. R. 367 (CA). R.J. Cooper.
J. Crim. L. 1992, 56(4), 377-379

MANUFACTURING AGREEMENTS. Contractual liability. EEC law. Jurisdiction. Sale of goods

etc. Enacted legislation will be identified by its number and so files before draft legislation identified by its title alone. Intermingled with the legislation will also be conventions and treaties. An abbreviated illustration of the filing order with the filing elements indicated in bold is as follows:

COMMISSION DIRECTIVE 89/48 ON MUTUAL RECOGNITION OF DIPLOMAS

COMMISSION DIRECTIVE 91/242 ON HIGH DEFINITION TELEVISION

COMMISSION DIRECTIVE ON LIFE INSURANCE (DRAFT)

COMMISSION DIRECTIVE ON THE AWARD OF PUBLIC SERVICE CONTRACTS (DRAFT)

COMMISSION DIRECTIVE ON THE LANDFILL OF WASTE (DRAFT)

COMMISSION REGULATION 2349/84 ON PATENTS

COMMISSION REGULATION 556/89 ON KNOW-HOW LICENSING AGREEMENTS

COMMISSION REGULATION CONCERNING ADMINISTRATIVE CO-OPERATION IN THE FIELD OF INDIRECT TAXATION (DRAFT)

COMMISSION REGULATION ON ENVIRONMENTAL AUDITING (DRAFT)

COMMISSION REGULATION ON RESTORATION OF PATENT TERMS FOR PHARMACEUTICALS (DRAFT)

CONVENTION ON INSIDER TRADING 1989 (COUNCIL OF EUROPE)

CONVENTION ON JURISDICTION AND ENFORCEMENT OF JUDGMENTS IN CIVIL AND COMMERCIAL MATTERS 1968

COUNCIL DIRECTIVE 76/207 ON EQUAL TREATMENT FOR MEN AND WOMEN AS REGARDS ACCESS TO EMPLOYMENT

COUNCIL DIRECTIVE 76/768 ON COSMETIC PRODUCTS

COUNCIL DIRECTIVE ON COMPARATIVE ADVERTISING (DRAFT)

COUNCIL DIRECTIVE ON MUNICIPAL WASTE WATER TREATMENT (DRAFT)

COUNCIL DIRECTIVE ON THE LIABILITY OF SUPPLIERS OF SERVICES (DRAFT)

COUNCIL REGULATION 4064/89 ON THE CONTROL OF CONCENTRATIONS BETWEEN UNDERTAKINGS

COUNCIL REGULATION 2726/90 ON COMMUNITY TRANSIT

COUNCIL REGULATION FOR SUPPLEMENTARY PROTECTION CERTIFICATES FOR MEDICAL PRODUCTS (DRAFT)

COUNCIL REGULATION ON THE STATUTE FOR A EUROPEAN COMPANY (DRAFT)

COUNCIL REGULATION ON TRADE IN DANGEROUS CHEMICALS (DRAFT)

EUROPEAN CONVENTION ON HUMAN RIGHTS 1950

EUROPEAN PATENTS CONVENTION 1973

FIRST COUNCIL DIRECTIVE 77/780 ON THE COORDINATION OF LAWS RELATING TO THE BUSINESS OF CREDIT INSTITUTIONS

FIRST COUNCIL DIRECTIVE 79/267 ON THE COORDINATION OF LAWS RELATING TO DIRECT LIFE INSURANCE

PROTOCOL ON SOCIAL POLICY (MAASTRICHT) 1991

SECOND COUNCIL DIRECTIVE 90/619 ON THE COORDINATION OF LAWS RELATING TO DIRECT LIFE INSURANCE

SECOND COUNCIL DIRECTIVE 92/30 ON SUPERVISION ON A CONSOLIDATED BASIS OF A CREDIT INSTITUTION

SEVENTH COUNCIL DIRECTIVE 83/439 ON HARMONISATION OF GROUP ACCOUNTING PRACTICES

SIXTH COUNCIL DIRECTIVE 77/388 ON A COMMON SYSTEM FOR VAT

THIRTEENTH COUNCIL DIRECTIVE ON COMPANY LAW CONCERNING TAKEOVER AND OTHER GENERAL BIDS (DRAFT)

TREATY OF ROME 1957

These complications do not arise of course if one is using the electronic version.

2.26 Apart from producing the index itself, the publishers also provide a document delivery service, which can be particularly useful as few law libraries, if any, take all 200 journal titles indexed. For a charge, photocopies of any article (except those from a very few titles which do not have copyright clearance) can be supplied by post, fax or document exchange. Details appear in the front of each issue.

Other sources

2.27 As already mentioned the main source prior to 1986 when the *Legal Journals Index* started publication was the American based and long-standing *Index to Legal Periodicals* published by H.W. Wilson. It continues to be of value for articles on English law published outside the UK, particularly in an academic or comparative context, and for articles on the law of other jurisdictions, particularly of course the United States. The *Index to Legal Periodicals* has been going since 1908, but since 1980 it has had a competitor in the form of *Current Law Index* (not to be confused with the UK publication, *Current Law*), published by Information Access in California. This aimed to overcome certain perceived shortcomings of the Wilson product in terms of coverage, currency and arrangement. It is true that in face of this competition *Index to Legal Periodicals* has made a number of improvements, but the *Current Law Index* probably remains the superior, albeit more expensive, product. Because of its cost, it is not, however, as widely available in UK law libraries. *Index to Legal Periodicals* is published in monthly parts cumulated quarterly and annually. There used to be triennial cumulations but they ceased in 1979. Partly in order to solve the problem of cumulation and also to provide better access there is a CD-ROM version, *Wilsondisc*, which cumulates the whole database back to 1981 every month. This provides excellent search facilities, and may be available in some UK law libraries (there is also an on-line version). Information Access, as well as providing its printed index to periodicals, has produced a larger database covering newsletters and newspapers, *Legal Resources Index* which is available on-line and in microform. A CD-ROM version of this, *Legaltrac*, is also published, but its current availability in UK law libraries is limited.

2.28 Two other American products should be mentioned. The *Legal Bibliography Index* published annually since 1978 picks up bibliographies in books and journals and may save you the effort of compiling your own bibliography. The *Index to*

Periodical Articles Related to Law now has a 30-year cumulation covering 1958 to 1988 and is updated regularly. It is useful for material, for example of a criminological or sociological nature, that is not picked up by the main legal journal indexing services.

2.29 The above products are confined to English language materials. Foreign language material is covered by the *Index to Foreign Legal Periodicals*. This is only going to be needed rarely by the English practitioner, but its existence should be noted, especially as comparative materials, particularly on Europe, assume increasing importance.

2.30 Lexis now includes a small number of journals in addition to its main coverage of cases and legislation. Coverage is currently limited to: *Estates Gazette* (from 1991), *Law Society's Gazette* (from 1986), *New Law Journal* (from 1986) and the *Journal of the Law Society of Scotland* (from 1990). As with all Lexis materials these are in full text and so would come into their own for searching in a way not catered for by the conventional indexes. Examples might be searching for individuals or companies mentioned in news items, or searching for cases or legislation mentioned in articles, but not sufficiently prominently to be picked up by *Legal Journals Index*. Apart from these English and Scottish periodicals, Lexis also includes a large number of American law reviews. Lawtel also includes selected articles from the main law journals.

2.31 *Current Law* is the only indigenous source for articles before *Legal Journals Index* started in 1986, and remains a fallback if it is all that is to hand in the office or chambers. In the monthly digests articles are listed at the end of each main subject heading. They are also included (marked 'article') in the cumulative index for the year in the latest monthly part, where they may be more specifically indexed. In the yearbooks, however, they are only listed separately after the list of books in the 'Books and articles' section at the back of the volume. Here only the main digest headings are used and they are not included in the main index to the volume, so any more specific indexing they may have received in the monthly parts is lost. There is no access other than by subject and they are not included in the CD-ROM version.

2.32 So far it is is general legal bibliographies and bibliographical tools that have been discussed. Articles (and books) may also be listed is specialist subject bibliographies. These may be serial publications, such as *Public International Law*, which is an index to the the periodical literature in that field, or one-off lists that may or may not be supplemented, for example *Bibliography of British and Irish Labour Law* by B.A. Hepple and others. Specialist journals may carry regular bibliographies of recent writings in their field, as does the *Industrial Law Journal*.

2.33 For EC matters, access to a large body of literature is provided by SCAD, the documentation service of the Commission, which since it became available on CD-ROM (marketed in two versions by Justis as SCAD and by ILI as EC Infodisk) is of considerably more value than it used to be. As well as indexing various classes of official documents (including one-off reports and the like) it covers a wide range (not just legal) of articles and documents received by the Commission library. To get the best out of it, however, does require some practice. The printed version, *SCAD Bulletin*, is issued weekly and so functions largely as a current awareness tool. From time to time *SCAD Bibliographies* on particular subjects are issued, as are *SCAD Bibliographical Files* which provide synopses as well as bibliographical references.

As well as the *SCAD Bulletin*, there are a number of other current awareness services, of which *European Access* published by Chadwyck-Healey in conjunction with the UK offices of the European Commission, probably provides the fullest coverage of recent secondary literature. For articles that discuss particular ECJ cases a supplementary source of information is the *Guide to EC Court Decisions* prepared by the T.M.C. Asser Institute. The cases are arranged by ECJ number and at the end of each entry which gives various details an 'Annotations' section lists journal articles, though many of them will be in continental legal journals.

2.34   Apart from articles in journals and textbooks proper, collections of essays and papers should be briefly mentioned at the end of this section on secondary sources. Typically issued in honour of someone distinguished (*Festschriften*) or resulting from a conference, such collections are frequently fairly miscellaneous in scope and the contents may not be apparent from the standard catalogue entry for the book as a whole, which may only have the broadest of themes. An *Index to Legal Essays*, designed to solve this problem, was published in 1983 and covered the period 1975 to 1979, but unfortunately has not been updated since. Unless they are cited in other secondary sources, one's only tool is thus serendipity.

Obtaining books and articles

2.35   As already mentioned photocopies of articles from those journals indexed by the *Legal Journals Index* are obtainable from the publishers of the index. Most academic libraries also operate an inter-library loan service which enables photocopies and loans to be obtained via the British Library's Document Supply Service. They have in stock at Boston Spa a wide range of English and foreign legal periodicals; if they do not have the title in stock they will pass it to back-up library. The Institute of Advanced Legal Studies in the University of London published a *Union List of Legal Periodicals*, which lists the holdings of all UK law libraries, but unfortunately the last edition was in 1978 and it is unlikely to updated in the near future. The Institute of Advanced Legal Studies also offer a document delivery service on a commercial basis to non-academic users, but to gain access to this an annual subscription must be taken out, though they permit access to personal callers on payment of a daily fee.

Theses

2.36   Doctoral and other theses are going to be needed primarily in connection with academic research (though the practitioner should not dismiss this possibility in an area devoid of other secondary literature). Because they are in their nature unpublished they are usually only obtainable via inter-library loan from the British Library (who hold many in microform) or have to be consulted at the university concerned. As well as for their content, information on theses will be needed by prospective research students in order to see whether their projected topic has been covered already. The Institute of Advanced Legal Studies (who incidentally receive copies of all legal theses througout the University of London) used to prepare two publications on legal theses. *Legal Research in the United Kingdom*, consolidated from time to time, listed completed research since 1905; the last edition goes up to 1984. The annual survey *List of Current Legal Research Topics* listed dissertations in progress (which was no guarantee of eventual completion), but its publication has been suspended, the last edition being in 1988. Wider than law, but including law, are Aslib's *Index to Theses* (also available on CD-ROM), which covers British and Irish theses accepted, and the social sciences volume of *Current Research in Britain*, which covers research projects (not just dissertations) in progress and is published by the British Library. If you wish to research theses beyond British ones, the main tool, which covers all subjects not just law, is the vast *Dissertation Abstracts International: Series A: Humanities and the Social Sciences*. There are cumulative indexes to this in the form of *Comprehensive Dissertations Index*. The labour involved in searching these has been greatly alleviated since their availability on CD-ROM.

Forms and precedents

2.37   There are two main general collections of forms and precedents, which set out standard or common forms of documents as aids to drafting. *Atkin's Court Forms* contains those that may be required in civil proceedings. It is arranged in 41 volumes; individual volumes are reissued from time to time; there is an annual cumulative supplement, and an interim Service Booklet between supplements. It is arranged by subject matter with each group of forms preceded by a substantial commentary. The quantity and quality of the commentary can sometimes be overlooked: the work forms a substantive and comprehensive guide to civil litigation, and is not merely a collection of forms. In the indexes — there is a consolidated index to the whole work reissued each year and indexes in the individual volumes — the references are to volume and page numbers; those in square brackets refer to forms, those without to commentary. A useful feature, whose presence is not always appreciated, is the table at the front of the cumulative supplement which correlates the Rules of the Supreme Court to the appropriate volume of the main work; there is a similar table for the County Court Rules.

2.38   The other major work is the *Encyclopaedia of Forms and Precedents*, which contains the full range of documents and forms that may be needed by practitioners for all aspects of their work other than litigation. Most of the planned 42 volumes of the fifth (grey) edition have now been published, but until it is complete some volumes of the fourth (green) edition may need to be consulted. A table to be found in service binder E of the fifth edition shows the destination of corresponding material from the fourth edition, and indicates which volumes of the fourth edition have been entirely superseded. The volumes of the fifth edition are not being issued in strict numerical order, so until it is complete do not (necessarily) be alarmed by apparent gaps on the shelf. The updating of the fifth edition is entirely looseleaf (though it is envisaged that volumes of the main work will be reissued when necessary). The five looseleaf service binders mirror the volume numbering and arrangement of the main work and contain material which updates, replaces or supplements the corresponding section of the main work; service issues are quarterly. Like *Atkin's Court Forms*, there is a substantial amount of commentary as well as the text of the forms and precedents themselves. The numbering and reference system, however, is slighly different from *Atkin's* and requires some elaboration.

2.39   Like *Atkin's,* in each *title* (there is usually more than one title per volume) the paragraphs of commentary are conventionally numbered in bold at their start and the forms that follow have their own sequence of numbers at their head. However, running through the entire volume — and through commentary and forms alike — is a separate single sequence of paragraph numbers given on the right of the page in square brackets. It is these that are referred to in the indexes; the source of possible confusion, though, is that here the square brackets are omitted if the reference is to commentary rather than to a form. In the first illustration (see figure 2.5), the index, under 'Party walls — inner London — disputes' refers to **16** 353, ie paragraph [353] in volume 16. Because the index omits the square brackets you know that it is referring you to commentary. In the second illustration (figure 2.6), under 'Fence — agreement to erect and maintain boundary fence', the reference is **16** [361]. Because the square brackets are included you know that it is referring you to a form.

2.40 Cross-references within a title, on the other hand, will be to the commentary paragraph number or form number for that title, though the square bracket paragraph reference may be added too, eg 'See Paragraph 20 ante [145]' or 'See Form 16 post [276]'. Cross-references to other titles will give the volume number and title as well, eg 'See vol 36 SALE OF LAND Paragraph 161 [1201]'. To reiterate, in the last example the reference is to paragraph 161 of the commentary to the title 'Sale of Land' which is paragraph [1201] of volume 36; in the indexes this reference would appear just as: **36** 1201. The indexes consist of a softbound consolidated index to the whole work which is replaced every year, an index to each volume, and an index to the service binders which is filed in binder E.

2.41 Apart from the *Encyclopaedia*, there is one other general collection of precedents which should be mentioned, *Kelly's Draftsman*. This contains, in a handy one-volume format, the commonest forms and precedents needed by solicitors in general practice. There are, however, quite a number of specialist works with which to supplement the general collections above. On the contentious side, *Bullen and Leake* is devoted to pleadings, and there are particular works covering the precedents needed in the Queen's Bench Division, the Chancery Division, and the county court. Textbooks on the practice and procedure in the various courts will often include relevant forms and precedents as appendices. On the non-contentious side, there are a number of subject collections — conveyancing naturally enough receiving particular attention. The publishers Longman have produced a useful series of looseleaf collections covering commercial documents, matrimonial precedents, wills, trusts and other topics. Standard textbooks, again, often include forms and precedents as appendices, as do many looseleaf encyclopedias.

2.42 Some publishers offer a version of their precedents on floppy disk as well as, or instead of, a printed version. These can then be loaded direct onto the solicitors' word processor without being retyped. Sweet & Maxwell, in their *Magna Legal Precedent* series, have developed this approach most fully. Many firms of solicitors also maintain their own in-house collections of precedents, nowadays usually in the form of word-processed documents.

Legal dictionaries

2.43 The materials under consideration in this section are adjuncts to the finding aids for statute and case law discussed in the following chapters, as well as to the textbooks and other secondary sources discussed in this chapter. There are tools that perform one or more of the following functions: explaining the meaning of technical

Figure 2.5   Encyclopaedia of Forms and Precedents:
index volume and main work (commentary)

[354–360]   VOL 16: FENCES, BOUNDARIES AND PARTY WALLS   152

1 See the London Building Acts (Amendment) Act 1939 s 56 (1) (a), (b), (c), (d) (26 Halsbury's Statutes (4th Edn) LONDON).
2 See ibid s 56 (6). Only the building owner who incurs expenses may recover (*Re Stone and Hastie* [1903] 2 KB 463, CA (not a subsequent tenant)) but where an adjoining owner makes a later use of the works, a successor to the building owner may recover: *Mason v Fulham Corpn* [1910] 1 KB 631.
3 See the London Building Acts (Amendment) Act 1939 s 58 (1); *Spiers & Son Ltd v Troup* (1915) 84 LJKB 1986.
4 See the London Building Acts (Amendment) Act 1939 ss 50 (2) (d), 56 (1) (e).
5 See ibid s 56 (3).
6 See ibid s 57 (1) and Form 17 [411] post.
7 See ibid s 57 (2).
8 See ibid s 57 (2), (3).   **[350]**

28 Execution of work and rights of entry. Rights conferred on the building owner are to be exercised in the prescribed manner[1], and there are rights of entry for this purpose[2]. The building owner, in the exercise of any rights conferred under the Act, is not authorised to interfere with any easements of light or other easements in or relating to a party wall[3]. The building owner may remain liable to carry out work after conveying his title[4].   **[351]**

1 See the London Building Acts (Amendment) Act 1939 s 51 (1), (2) (26 Halsbury's Statutes (4th Edn) LONDON).
2 See ibid s 53 (1), (2), (3).
3 See ibid s 54; *Burlington Property Co Ltd v Odeon Theatres Ltd* [1939] 1 KB 633, [1938] 3 All ER 469, CA. There must be some doubt about the judgment of McCardie J in *Selby v Whitbread & Co* [1917] 1 KB 736 that the statutory code in London overrides common law rights: it is submitted that there are no clear provisions to allow the withdrawal of a right of support; this is supported by *Upjohn v Seymour Estates Ltd* [1938] 1 All ER 614 where the Law of Property Act 1925 s 38 was held to preserve a right of user and support to a party wall despite work carried out following a party wall award under what is now the London Building Acts (Amendment) Act 1939.
4 See ibid s 57; *Selby v Whitbread & Co* [1917] 1 KB 736.   **[352]**

29 Determination of disputes. Detailed provision is made for the determination of differences and disputes between building owners and adjoining owners[1]. Unless the parties agree to the appointment of a single surveyor, each must appoint a surveyor and the two surveyors must then appoint a third surveyor[2]. The agreed surveyor, or the three surveyors, or any two of them, must settle by award any matter in dispute before the work is begun, or during the carrying out of the work[3]. If no two surveyors can agree, the selected third surveyor must make an award within 14 days of being requested[4]. The award must deal with the work required, the manner of executing it, costs and supervision of the work[5]. The award is conclusive subject to appeal within 14 days of delivery of the award[6]. Where the title to any property is registered, notice of a party wall award may be entered on the register[7].   ➡ **[353]**

1 See the London Building Acts (Amendment) Act 1939 s 55 (26 Halsbury's Statutes (4th Edn) LONDON).
2 See ibid s 55 (a) (ii) and Form 18 [412] post.
3 See ibid s 55 (i).
4 See ibid s 55 (j).
5 See ibid s 55 (k), (l).
6 See ibid s 55 (m), (n). For the date of delivery of an award see *Riley Gowler Ltd v National Heart Hospital Board of Governors* [1969] 3 All ER 1401, CA; *Leadbetter v Marylebone Corpn* [1904] 2 KB 893 (award invalid if it relates to work which is not the subject of the building owner's notice); *Marchant v Capital & Counties plc* (1983) 267 Estates Gazette 843 (award may impose a continuing obligation on the building owner to keep the party wall weatherproofed, although it is preferable for permanent work that will ensure weatherproofing to be specified).
7 See the Land Registration Act 1925 s 49 (1) (f) (37 Halsbury's Statutes (4th Edn) REAL PROPERTY). Registration is as a notice or caution: see ibid s 54.   **[354–360]**

Figure 2.6   Encyclopaedia of Forms and Precedents:
main work (forms) and index volume

Precedents

1

AGREEMENT for the erection and maintenance of a boundary fence (with
variations for replacement and a maintenance contribution)[1]

THIS AGREEMENT is made the ...... day of .... BETWEEN (1) (*name of first
owner*) of (*address*) ('the First Owner') and (2) (*name of second owner*) of (*address*) ('the
Second Owner')   ➡ **[361]**

WHEREAS

(1) The First Property
The First Owner is [[entitled to be] registered with absolute freehold title No ... to *or*
the owner of the fee simple of] the property known as (*address or description*) ('the First
Property')

(2) The Second Property
The Second Owner is [[entitled to be] registered with absolute freehold title No ... to
or the owner of the fee simple of] the property adjoining the First Property on the
[north] side and known as (*address or description*) ('the Second Property')

(3) The Boundary of the First Property
The boundary between the First Property and the Second Property [between points A
and B as marked on the attached plan] consists of [[(*brief description of fence*) *or* wire
strands supported by wood posts] standing on and belonging to the First Property ('the
Original Fence') *or* no marked physical feature] and the parties to this agreement have
agreed that a fence shall be erected on the First Property along the said boundary on
the terms set out below

NOW IT IS AGREED as follows:

1 Erection of new fence
The First Owner shall within ... months or within such longer period of time as may
from time to time be agreed in writing between the parties [remove the original fence
and in its place] erect [along the whole boundary between the First Property and the
Second Property *or* between points A and B as marked on the attached plan] a fence
in accordance with the specification contained in the schedule below

2 Maintenance of fence[2]
The First Owner and his successors in title shall forever thereafter [at his or their own
expense] maintain the said fence in good repair and condition

terms, assembling the definitions given by the courts to words or phrases that have required construction be they in a statute or other document, assembling the definitions given in the statutes themselves, and translating foreign legal terms.

2.44 The leading 'explanatory' dictionary is *Jowitt's Dictionary of English Law*. Reference will be given to any statutory or judicial definitions, but this is the place to look if you wish to know what an advowson is or what the York-Antwerp rules are; in effect it is a mini-encyclopedia of the law. It also performs a translating function for a wide range of Latin tags. It is published in two volumes with a cumulative supplement. There are are also a number of smaller works of a similar nature that may be convenient alternatives, such as *Mozley and Whiteley's Law Dictionary* or *Osborn's Concise Law Dictionary*. The long-standing American publication, *Black's Law Dictionary*, is a valuable supplement to the English products.

2.45 A rather different kind of work in the 'explanatory' category is the *Oxford Companion to the Law* by David M. Walker. It is aimed at readers in other disciplines as well as at lawyers, but is nonetheless remarkably useful. It can be best described by quoting from the dust jacket: '[It] is neither a legal dictionary, nor an encylopaedia of legal rules, still less a legal guide for laymen. It is a compendium of information about branches of legal science, legal systems, institutions such as courts and juries, notable judges and jurists, legal concepts and ideas, major legal principles and important documents and cases'. It is particularly useful for historical material and for the explanation of terms and concepts from civil (including Scots) law which may not be covered in English sources. For a work of reference, the author's personal views are sometimes expressed with a surprising forthrightness (see, bearing in mind the work was published in 1980, the entry on trade unions).

2.46 There are also a few dictionaries confined to particular branches of law, such as insurance and banking. The *Oxford Encyclopaedia of European Community Law* by A.G. Toth, as its preface explains, elucidates a host of legal terms and concepts which either have no equivalent in national law or have acquired an entirely new and independent meaning in the context of a supranational Community law. It acts as a dictionary in that each entry provides a short and concise definition, but these are followed by longer and more detailed explanations, which, together with its A to Z arrangement, make it encyclopedic in the conventional sense: it is not a looseleaf compilation of primary materials like many legal works called 'encyclopedias'. Three separate parts, covering institutional law, substantive law, and common policies, are plannned.

2.47 *Stroud's Judicial Dictionary*, published by Sweet & Maxwell, is the main work devoted, as it name implies, to the decisions of the courts that have interpreted the meaning of particular words and phrases. With one or two exceptions statutory definitions are not included unless they themselves have been subject to judicial interpretation. The current (fifth edition) is in five volumes with a cumulative supplement. In preparing the fifth edition there was substantial pruning of older cases and of Scottish, Irish and Commonwealth material; so on an obscure point it may be worth consulting the fourth edition too.

2.48 A competitor to *Stroud*, but wider in scope, is *Words and Phrases Legally Defined*, published by Butterworths. As well as judicial definitions, it includes definitions from statutory material; it also has extensive references to Common-wealth materials, to which in the latest (third) edition have been added selected references to US material. It is published in four volumes with a cumulative supplement. There are helpful cross-references to *Halsbury's Laws*.

2.49 Words and phrases that have been judicially considered are also covered by *Halsbury's Laws Monthly Reviews* and by *Current Law*. Because of their frequency of updating, these will be more current than the supplements to *Stroud* and *Words and Phrases*. The index to words and phrases in the monthly reviews is filed in the looseleaf noter-up service volume to *Halsbury's Laws*, not in the binder containing the monthly reviews themselves. There is a table of words of phrases at the front of the *Annual Abridgement*, which cumulates the monthly reviews. There is a cumulative table of words and phrases for the current year in the latest monthly digest of *Current Law*, and this is incorporated into the yearbook in due course. *The Law Reports Index*, which covers mainstream cases, has an entry 'words and phrases' in its subject matter index.

2.50 Lexis is particularly well suited to this kind of research. To find the mere occurrence of a particular word or phrase is of course straightforward; to limit the search to those cases where the term is actually analysed, a suggested strategy is to use a proximity search, so that the word or phrase appears near the words 'meaning', 'interpretation', or 'construction' and their equivalents in other grammatical forms. Thus to find any cases on the meaning of 'best endeavours', the search statement would be: best endeavours W/15 meaning OR interpret! OR constru!

2.51 There are quite a number of dictionaries that translate legal terms to and from English. Ordinary English legal dictionaries will cover many Latin words, but there is also *Latin Words and Phrases for Lawyers* by R.S. Vasan (Lewis Books, 1980). If you are tempted to follow up references to very old cases or treatises, remember that they may well turn out to be in Law French, which was the language of the courts before 1600 and continued to be used during the seventeenth century. If still undeterred, J.H. Baker's *Manual of Law French* (2nd ed, Scolar Press, 1990) may assist. In the modern context, linguistic problems are most likely to be encountered in connection with European Community materials. The Council Secretariat have a Terminology Office which has produced glossaries translating terms between the Community languages. For other language dictionaries, and indeed for all kinds of legal dictionaries (only a small selection of the most useful have been mentioned by name in this chapter), consult the list provided in Raistrick's *Lawyers' Law Books* (under 'Dictionaries') and in the Hammicks catalogue (in the 'Reference' section).

3. Legislation

Forms of legislation

3.1 In the United Kingdom, as in most jurisdictions, there are two main classes of legislation. Primary legislation consists of the Acts — or statutes, the terms are interchangeable — passed by Parliament itself. The other class, usually published in the form of statutory instruments (SIs), is variously termed secondary, subsidiary, subordinate or delegated legislation. The last term most accurately reflects its nature as this is legislation made under powers delegated by Parliament, typically to government ministers. It may (or may not) receive limited Parliamentary scrutiny, but Parliament itself does not have time, even if it were desirable in principle, to enact all the rules, regulations and matters of detail required in the adminstration of the modern state. However, the power to make secondary legislation must derive from primary legislation — a section in an Act will set out by whom and how the secondary legislation may be made, for example:

> The Secretary of State shall by regulations make a scheme providing for payments to be made to a person to whom this section applies by their former registered employers ... The power to make regulations under this section shall be exercisable by statutory instrument subject to annulment in pursuance of a resolution of either House of Parliament.

Apart from the difference in how they are made, there is another important distinction between primary and secondary legislation. Unlike in many jurisdictions which have written constitutions and constitutional courts, the legality of primary legislation in the United Kingdom cannot be challenged in the courts. Only secondary legislation can be subject to judicial review, if it is made in excess of its enabling powers (ultra vires).

3.2 There is one obvious proviso to the last proposition, which qualifies the traditional two-fold classification of legislation set out, namely the European dimension. European Community legislation, although in a sense delegated legislation, does not fit neatly into either category and needs to be treated separately. Another category of material that will be discussed in this chapter is not strictly speaking legislation, in that it is not directly legally enforceable, but it nonetheless may have legal consequences. It is highly miscellaneous, but is compendiously described as quasi-legislation, codes of practice being perhaps the most commonly cited example. At the end of the chapter Bills, proposals for legislation and the various materials that precede or are involved in its making are described.

Public General Acts

3.3 Primary legislation comes in two main forms, Public General Acts and Local and Personal Acts. The latter are encountered much less frequently and are dealt with separately later (paras 3.121-3.134). (For the sake of completeness, it should also be mentioned that in ecclesiastical matters the Church of England Synod — formerly the Church Assembly — pass Measures, which have a similar status to Public General Acts and are printed and issued with them.) Public General Acts form the main body of statute law and as their name implies they are usually of general not merely local application and affect the community at large not just particular persons. They can be amended or repealed, either expressly or impliedly, only by another Act of Parliament (though occasionally an Act will run the risk of constitutional impropriety and incorporate a power to amend by delegated legislation — a so-called Henry VIII clause). Otherwise an Act will remain in force indefinitely. The *Chronological Table of Statutes* published by HMSO starts in 1235, and shows that many ancient provisions are still on the 'Statute Book', though various programmes of statute law revision have steadily removed obsolete material. It should also be borne in mind that not all new Acts enact new law. They may simply bring together for the sake of convenience and clarity a number of Acts on a particular area that have been passed over a period and which have progressively amended each other. These are called consolidation Acts.

3.4 About 60 or 70 Public General Acts are passed each year. Apart from identifying which statutes apply to a particular area, the two main tasks the legal researcher has to perform are establishing whether an Act or part of an Act is still in force on the one hand, or yet in force on the other. The latter exercise is necessary because, though some Acts come into force immediately on passing through the requisite stages in Parliament and receiving Royal Assent, many do not. The Act itself may specify a later commencement date, or it may contain a power for a minister subsequently to appoint a date. Usually this is only a matter of concern if one is dealing with recent legislation, but occasionally there can be long delays in bringing an Act into force. For example, the Easter Act 1925, which provides that Easter should fall on a fixed date, is neither repealed nor in force.

Anatomy and citation

3.5 A typical modern Act in its official form is illustrated (figure 3.1). (1) is the short title, the official name of the Act. It only became the established practice to include a short title at the end of the nineteenth century. To facilitate the citation of earlier statutes with only long titles, the Short Titles Act 1896 retrospectively assigned short titles to over 2000 Acts then in force, and the Statute Law Revision Act 1948 added a further list. Note that no comma appears between the title and the year — this has been the official practice since 1963, and should be followed even when citing earlier Acts. (2) A 'chapter' number, abbreviated as c. (or sometimes ch.), was originally assigned to each Act passed in a particular Parliamentary session. Since 1963 they have been assigned to each Act passed in a particular calendar year. The

Figure 3.1

---

① # Protection of Badgers Act 1992

② ### 1992 CHAPTER 51

③ An Act to consolidate the Badgers Act 1973, the Badgers Act 1991 and the Badgers (Further Protection) Act 1991.   [16th July 1992] ④

⑤ **B**E IT ENACTED by the Queen's most Excellent Majesty, by and with the advice and consent of the Lords Spiritual and Temporal, and Commons, in this present Parliament assembled, and by the authority of the same, as follows:—

Offences

⑦

⑥   1.—(1) A person is guilty of an offence if, except as permitted by or under this Act, he wilfully kills, injures or takes, or attempts to kill, injure or take, a badger.

Taking, injuring or killing badgers.

(2) If, in any proceedings for an offence under subsection (1) above consisting of attempting to kill, injure or take a badger, there is evidence from which it could reasonably be concluded that at the material time the accused was attempting to kill, injure or take a badger, he shall be presumed to have been attempting to kill, injure or take a badger unless the contrary is shown.

(3) A person is guilty of an offence if, except as permitted by or under this Act, he has in his possession or under his control any dead badger or any part of, or anything derived from, a dead badger.

(4) A person is not guilty of an offence under subsection (3) above if he shows that—

    (a) the badger had not been killed, or had been killed otherwise than in contravention of the provisions of this Act or of the Badgers Act 1973; or

1973 c. 57.

    (b) the badger or other thing in his possession or control had been sold (whether to him or any other person) and, at the time of the purchase, the purchaser had had no reason to believe that the badger had been killed in contravention of any of those provisions.

Interpretation.

1968 c. 27.

14. In this Act—

"ammunition" has the same meaning as in the Firearms Act 1968;

"badger" means any animal of the species *Meles meles*;

"badger sett" means any structure or place which displays signs indicating current use by a badger;

"firearm" has the same meaning as in the Firearms Act 1968;

"sale" includes hire, barter and exchange and cognate expressions shall be construed accordingly.

Short title, repeals, commencement and extent.

15.—(1) This Act may be cited as the Protection of Badgers Act 1992.

(2) The enactments mentioned in the Schedule to this Act are repealed to the extent specified in the third column of that Schedule.

(3) This Act shall come into force at the end of the period of three months beginning with the day on which it is passed.

(4) This Act does not extend to Northern Ireland.

⑩ SCHEDULE

REPEALS

Chapter	Short title	Extent of repeal
1973 c. 57.	The Badgers Act 1973.	The whole Act.
1981 c. 69.	The Wildlife and Countryside Act 1981.	Section 73(4). In Schedule 7, paragraphs 8 to 12.
1985 c. 31.	The Wildlife and Countryside (Amendment) Act 1985.	Section 1.
1986 c. 14.	The Animals (Scientific Procedures) Act 1986.	In Schedule 3, paragraph 9.
1990 c. 43.	The Environmental Protection Act 1990.	In Schedule 9, paragraph 6.
1991 c. 28.	The Natural Heritage (Scotland) Act 1991.	In Schedule 2, paragraph 5.
1991 c. 35.	The Badgers (Further Protection) Act 1991.	The whole Act.
1991 c. 36.	The Badgers Act 1991.	The whole Act.
1991 c. 53.	The Criminal Justice Act 1991.	Section 26(3).

number is given in arabic numerals (before 1803 they were printed in capital roman numerals). (3) is the long title, which sets out in greater detail the purpose of the Act; in this case it is a consolidation Act, re-enacting three earlier Acts as one. (4) The date given beneath it in square brackets is the date of Royal Assent, which as already mentioned may or may not be the date of commencement into force. (5) is just a standard enacting formula. (6) Long Acts or ones covering separate areas may be divided for convenience into Parts, but the sections and subsections will be numbered consecutively throughout the Act. Later Acts sometimes amend earlier Acts by means of inserting new sections into the old Act. Such sections are identifed by the addition of a letter, so that, for example the new section 14A will appear between the old sections 14 and section 15. The same procedure can apply to subsections. (7) The marginal notes are not technically part of the Act, but are a general convenience and may in some circumstances be used as aids for statutory interpretation. (8) An interpretation section, setting out definitions of particular terms used, is usually found near the end of the Act before the schedules. (9) The last section of the Act usually provides for commencement and geographic extent. For commencement one of three formulas may be used: a specific day may given, a period after the passing of the Act may be specified, eg three months (as here), whenever that should fall depending on the actual date of Royal Assent, or it is simply left to come into force on a day to be appointed by, for example, the Secretary of State. If the Act contains no commencement provision it comes into force at the beginning of the day on which it receives Royal Assent — Interpretation Act 1978 s 4(b). If the Act is not to apply to the whole of the United Kingdom, this will be stated; here the Act applies to England, Wales and Scotland but not to Northern Ireland. (10) Appended to the Act may be one or more schedules which are referred to in the body of the Act. They have equal force but are a convenient means of setting out matters of detail such as procedural rules, tables of fees, and lists of various kinds. Repeals of earlier legislation are often given in schedules, as here. The numbered parts within schedules are referred to as paragraphs rather than as sections.

3.6 Modern Acts are usually cited simply by their short title (which includes the year), eg Road Traffic Act 1991. For brevity they may also be cited by just year and chapter number, eg 1991 c 40. For completeness, though it is not strictly necessary in order uniquely to identify the Act, both forms may be used, eg Road Traffic Act 1991 (c 40). Older Acts, however, were cited by chapter number and the regnal year of the session of Parliament in which they were passed. Parliamentary sessions, which usually run from November to July, will frequently straddle more than one regnal year, the regnal year being calculated from the date of accession of the reigning monarch. Thus 30 & 31 Vict c 27 refers to the 27th Act passed during the session of Parliament that was held during the 30th and 31st years of the reign of Queen Victoria. If citing a particular section, the abbreviation s. is used (or ss. for sections in the plural).

3.7 Some older Acts were known by popular names taken from the name of the promoter of the Act or its subject matter. For example the Marriage Act 1753 was known as Lord Hardwicke's Act and the Sunday Observance Acts were often called the Lords' Day Acts. A selective list of these giving their official references is in an appendix to *Craies on Statute Law* (7th ed, 1971) and the *Oxford Companion to Law* has entries for some. A new list is planned for the new edition of *Craies*, which when it comes will provide the fullest information. In the meantime probably the fullest list, though it may not be readily available, is the Table of Short and Popular Titles in volume 16 of *Chitty's Statutes of Practical Utility* (6th ed, Sweet & Maxwell, 1916).

Sources for the text of Acts

3.8 In most large law libraries you will be spoilt for choice if all you need is the unamended text of a recent Act. But, depending on the nature of your enquiry, you need to be aware of the pros and cons of the different forms of published Acts.

Halsbury's Statutes

3.9 This commercially published set is usually the best source: it prints the text of the Act as amended (or enables you readily to check whether the text has been amended), it is updated frequently, and it has annotations giving cross-references to other parts of the Act, to other Acts, to relevant SIs and to relevant case law. It is arranged in 40 or so bound volumes by broad topic. There is a softbound tables and index volume to the whole work which is replaced annually. It is kept up to date in four ways. First, individual volumes of the main work are reissued from time to time when the quantity and importance of new material warrants it. Secondly, recent statutes are issued in looseleaf 'Current Statutes Service' volumes pending incorporation in a bound volume. For the sake of currency these may initially be issued in unannotated form and are then reissued when the necessary editorial work has been carried out. Thirdly, a cumulative supplement, arranged according to the same volume numbers of the main work, is issued annually in bound volume form. Fourthly, a looseleaf noter-up, arranged in the same way as the supplement, captures developments between annual supplements. The fourth edition (in grey covers) of the main work is now complete, but earlier editions remain useful for legislation no longer in force, which sometimes needs to be referred to.

3.10 One limitation to bear in mind is that, as its full title — *Halsbury's Statutes of England* — indicates, it does not cover statutes which apply to Scotland only. However, it does include Church Measures and, very selectively, some Local and Personal Acts, principally those relating to London. An occasional drawback is that because of its subject arrangment, the text of a particular statute may be split between different volumes if it covers separate topics. For example, the text of the Police and Criminal Evidence Act 1984 is split between volume 12 on Criminal Law and volume 17 which includes the title Evidence. To the newcomer *Halsbury's Statutes* may seem a little daunting, but a small effort early on to discover how it works will be amply repaid. How to use it for different types of research will be explained in detail at the appropriate points below. Although widely used throughout the legal profession, it is not of course an official text — for court purposes the official text is that produced by HMSO.

Queen's Printer Copy

3.11 The official text of individual Acts published by HMSO is known as the Queen's Printer Copy. They are printed and issued usually within a few days of Royal Assent (though occasionally longer delays can occur). They are subsequently reissued as annual bound volumes (the modern ones in red covers), which include tables and indexes. The loose prints are the only source for the text of very recent statutes that have not yet appeared in the commercially published series. If you have a citation that includes the year it is straightforward to find them on the shelf. The obvious limitation to using the statutes in this form is that the text is only as it was on the date it was passed. However, for many purposes, if you know that it has not been amended, this is all that is needed. They are also a source if you need the text of statutes that are no longer in force.

3.12 Some libraries may take the *Law Reports Statutes* which are exactly the same as the official text but reprinted by authority for the Incorporated Council of Law Reporting and issued in a uniform binding to the *Law Reports*.

Statutes in Force

3.13 This is the official text, published by HMSO, of all Public General Acts in force, including those covering Scotland, as amended. It includes a dozen or so Local Acts of general interest — fewer than *Halsbury's*. It does not include Northern Ireland leglislation, other than UK Acts made at Westminster that extend to Northern Ireland — there is a separate looseleaf edition, *Statutes Revised: Northern Ireland*. *Statutes in Force* is arranged by topic and occupies over 100 dark brown looseleaf volumes. The topics, termed groups, are arranged alphabetically, but are also assigned a number. A group is subdivided into sub-groups and may occupy more than one volume; conversely some volumes may contain more than one group. It began publication in 1972 and replaced the third edition of *Statutes Revised*, which was a consolidation in bound volume form of all statutes in force as at 1948. Although efforts have been made to improve its currency and arrangement, it has to be said that few lawyers use it as a first port of call. It is looseleaf but individual Acts are printed as stapled pamphlets and are only reissued if subject to significant amendment. Otherwise amendments appear in cumulative supplements filed in separate binders at the start of the work. It is important to note the date of the last revision of a particular Act and its supplement. Annotations are not given beyond indicating authorities for amendments, repeals and commencement provisions. It is sometimes preferable to *Halsbury's* if you do not need annotations and want a more compact text, for example for photocopying purposes. Occasionally, heavily amended text might have been more recently reissued than the equivalent text in *Halsbury's*. As mentioned, it will help, where *Halsbury's* cannot, if you need a Scottish Act. For court purposes, unlike *Halsbury's*, it is an officially recognised text.

Individual Acts from *Statutes in Force* may be purchased from HMSO.

Current Law Statutes Annotated

3.14 Whereas *Halsbury's* is the commercially published value-added alternative to *Statutes in Force*, *Current Law Statutes* offer a similar alternative to the Queen's Printer Copy; that is, they are arranged chronologically and the text remains as it was when originally passed, but they have the addition of explanatory annotations. The extent of the annotations varies according to the importance of the Act. The general notes at the start of a statute are often excellent, and can provide fuller information than *Halsbury's* on the legislative background to the statute — full references are given to any preceding green papers, white papers, Royal Commission or Law Commission reports and to the relevant Parliamentary debates. For important statutes, the annotations often extend much more than *Halsbury's* to substantive commentary rather than just cross-references, but of course this information remains static. For this reason their value declines with age. They go back to 1947 and form part of the *Current Law* service published by Sweet & Maxwell (though they are available separately and may or may not be shelved in the library with other parts of *Current Law*). Individual statutes are issued soon after Royal Assent and are filed in a looseleaf service volume. For the sake of currency an unannotated version, printed on blue paper, may be issued in advance. The looseleaf issues are replaced by three or four blue bound volumes each year. The looseleaf service volume also contains a subject index which is updated three times a year. At the end of the year this is incorporated at the back of the last bound volume. Since 1990 an index has also been supplied for each individual Act, which is a useful feature for long Acts. Until 1991 the standard version of this service excluded exclusively Scottish Acts, but there was a separate version, *Scottish Current Law Statutes Annotated* (which also included all the English material in the standard version). Now there is only the one version which includes all Acts.

Butterworths Annotated Legislation Service

3.15 This service by rival publishers is similar to *Current Law Statutes* in that it publishes statutes as they come out in annotated form. Its arrangement is slightly different however. It does not have a looseleaf service; major Acts are published as separate bound volumes, with shorter Acts grouped in a miscellaneous manner. Its index is only published every two years but is cumulative back to 1939. It is widely available, but it is probably fair to say that it is less popular than *Current Law Statutes*.

Lexis

3.16 Lexis contains the full text of all statutes in force as amended. The date at which the database stands is displayed on the file display screen; check this as in the past there have been delays in getting statutory material on. They are found in the STAT file in the ENGGEN library. If preferred, they can be searched together with SIs in the combined STATIS file. One feature to appreciate, especially if one is more used to searching the cases file, is that each section of an Act rather than the Act as a whole is treated as a separate item. It is also necessary to be aware of the conventions used for indicating amended text. Square brackets are placed round new words that have been added. Three dots show the omission of words repealed, and underlining is used to show words that are prospectively repealed or repealed with savings. Note that underlining may not appear on printouts. The text of each section of an Act is headed with the date it came into force, and at the foot is the annotations segment which gives full details of derivations, commencement provisions and amending legislation.

3.17 In the discussion of various types of research problem in this chapter emphasis will be laid on when Lexis may be preferable to manual sources and conversely when manual sources are as good and the cost of a Lexis search would not normally be justified. But these comparisons are of course based on the assumption that both sources are equally available. Not all students (nor for that matter, yet, all practitioners) have access to Lexis. On the other hand, if you do have access to Lexis, especially as it is now available through a PC without a dedicated terminal, you can still have at your finger tips the full text of the statutes without being anywhere near a library.

Looseleaf encylopedias

3.18 Convenient sources for the text of legislation are subject-based looseleaf encyclopedias. Often accompanied by expert commentary or annotations, they are as good a source as any. For some major subjects there may be more than one to choose from, produced by different publishers. Always check the date of the latest release.

The main function of looseleaf encyclopedias is to reproduce primary materials in convenient form, but of course standard bound textbooks may also reprint selected statutory materials as appendices.

Handbooks and subject collections

3.19 Statutes on a particular subject are often published in single volumes, usually softbound, as handbooks as in the series published by Butterworths or in collections of cases and materials designed for students. Convenience and portability (unlike the big looseleafs) are their virtues, though their date of publication should always be noted. Their availabilty, though, is confined to the major subject areas, eg. property law, company law, family law.

Older Acts

3.20 Sessional volumes of Acts have been officially printed since 1483, but very few sets exist before the eighteenth century. However, there have been numerous unofficial compilations at various dates. Probably the most widely used is *Statutes at Large*, which was originally compiled by Owen Ruffhead and hence is sometimes referred to simply as 'Ruffhead'. In the edition by Runnington it covers statutes from Magna Carta to 1785 (25 Geo III). However, for statutes before 1714 the most authoritative edition (and recognised as such by the Interpretation Act 1978) is *Statutes of the Realm* prepared by the Record Commissioners and published in 10 volumes 1810-22. The drawback to using them is that they are extremely hefty folio volumes. Unless one is in weight-training, *Statutes at Large* are sufficient for most everyday purposes. Ruffhead's *Statutes at Large* are, however, only one edition of several with the same title published in the eighteenth and nineteenth centuries. The bibliography and interrelationship between the various editions is complex. If further guidance is needed, reference should be made to Sweet & Maxwell's *Guide to Law Reports and Statutes* (4th ed, 1962), pp 11-16. All these editions omit statutes passed during the Commonwealth. These are only going to be of historical interest, but they have since been published by the Statute Law Committee under the editorship of C.H. Firth in 1911, *Acts and Ordinances of the Interregnum 1642-1660*.

The range of finding aids

3.21 Most of the sources described above have their own tables and indexes. Lexis, of course, is its own finding aid. But there are one or two separately published finding aids. HMSO publishes two works, *Index to the Statutes* and the *Chronological Table of Statutes*. Issued annually, each in two black volumes, they are authoritative guides, but for most enquiries they are not the first place to look, their main limitation being that they are usually at least two years behind.

3.22 Included in the *Current Law Statutes Service* is a *Statute Citator*. This is also issued as a stand-alone publication, now called the *Legislation Citator*. Two bound volumes list chronologically all statutes up to 1988 that have been passed since 1947 and all earlier statutes amended or repealed since that date. (It also includes SIs made under those Acts and references to case law.) The bound volumes are supplemented by a softbound volume covering from 1989 to the pre-current year. The current year is covered by the cumulative statute citator in the monthly parts of *Current Law* — note, though, that this is updated only every two months, not in every issue.

Summaries of legislation are provided by topic in the monthly parts and yearbooks of *Current Law*.

3.23   *Is it in Force?* published by Butterworths is issued to subscribers to *Halsbury's Statutes*, but is also available separately. It is mainly a guide to commencement provisions for Acts passed since 1966, but is does also indicate amendments and repeals, though not the authorities for them. It is arranged chronologically, but with the statutes listed alphabetically (not by chapter number) within each year. It is published annually. Between editions the equivalent information is given in the *Is it in Force?* section in the service volume to *Halsbury's Statutes*.

3.24   Lawtel, the viewdata system that operates through British Telecom's Prestel service, includes summaries, but not the full text of statutes passed since 1980. As the service also summarises Bills, it is able to incorporate Acts very quickly after they are passed. It is updated daily.

3.25   Titles and catalogue information for statutes, SIs and Bills since 1980 are on the UKOP (United Kingdom Official Publications) CD-ROM issued by HMSO in conjunction with Chadwyck-Healey. Statutes and Bills (but not SIs) are also included in the HMSO monthly and annual catalogues.

3.26   The *House of Commons Weekly Information Bulletin* is a useful source for recent legislation as it includes all Public Bills before Parliament in the current session, and will include date of Royal Assent and chapter number as soon as they are passed.

3.27   Most of the main journals, such as the *New Law Journal*, the *Solicitors Journal*, and the *Law Society's Gazette* summarise recent legislative developments either in current awareness sections or as the subject of separate articles in the case of important statutes. For this reason, although it is not its main function, the *Legal Journals Index* can sometimes be a back door route to finding statutes. As well as its main subject index by key words, there is a separate legislation index, by title, which picks up articles on specific legislation (and Bills).

Finding Acts by title

3.28   For statutes in force there are alphabetical lists in the tables and index volume of *Halsbury's Statutes* and in the first volume of *Statutes in Force*. Note that in *Halsbury's Statutes* the letter (S) following a volume number indicates the looseleaf 'Current Statutes Service' volumes, which mirror the arrangement of the main work. It can occasionally occur that a volume of the main work is reissued after the Tables and Index Volume was last issued. This might cause two small hiccups. First, the page number for the statute given in the Table and Index volume will no longer be accurate. However, the volume number will remain the same and when you get to it, it will be apparent that you have got a very recent reissue; it is then straightforward to relocate the item from the volume's own table. Secondly, if the statute is listed as being in a 'Current Statutes Service' (S) volume, it may in fact have since been incorporated in the reissued bound volume, so if the statute is no longer in the looseleaf binder do not necessarily assume it has been stolen; check the equivalent volume of the main work.

3.29 Volume 53 of *Halsbury's Laws* also contains an alphabetical list of statutes mentioned in that work, which is likely to be very comprehensive though it may not coincide totally with the contents of *Halsbury's Statutes*. There is an alphabetical table of statutes in the *Current Law Legislation Citator 1972-1988*, its softbound supplement and from 1992 in the looseleaf service volume of *Current Law Statutes Annotated*, but not in the first volume of the citator, 1947-1971, nor in the monthly digests. The table in the 1972-1988 citator will include all statutes affected during that period as well as those actually passed so its coverage is wider than its dates might suggest.

3.30 If the year of the Act is known it is a simple matter to go the annual volumes of Public General Acts or *Current Law Statutes* which contain alphabetical tables for each year. To find the chapter number of very recent statutes not yet in *Halsbury's* or *Statutes in Force*, the table of Public Bills in the *House of Commons Weekly Information Bulletin* or Lawtel will give the answer, though it would not take much longer simply to browse along the shelf of Queen's Printer copies.

3.31 For old Acts not found in the above sources, there is no single alphabetical listing, so a search by subject matter will be needed (see para 3.37).

3.32 Unless you wish to look at the text itself (for example, if it has been heavily amended and has not yet been consolidated in *Halsbury's Statutes* or *Statutes in Force*), Lexis would be an expensive way of simply identifying a statute from its title. But if you do need to search Lexis by title, search on the title segment, eg TITLE(MARINE INSURANCE). But you may retrieve a large number of items if you have not specified a section number or if there are several statutes with the same title. To confine the search to a particular year and section number type TITLE(MARINE INSURANCE W/5 1906) AND SECTION(9).

Finding Acts by subject

3.33 Subject-based looseleaf encyclopedias, if there is one for the area in question, are often the most convenient source. Otherwise *Halsbury's Statutes* is the best place. There is a consolidated index to the whole work in the Tables and Index volume. Note that this index is in *two* sequences. The first and longest covers the bound volumes of the main work. The second sequence covers statutes in the looseleaf 'Current Statutes Service' volumes. The same problems as described in para 3.28 can occur if the relevant volume in the main work has been reissued since the index volume was last issued: the page references in the main sequence may not be accurate and the material referred to in the service sequence may have been incorporated into the main work. However, individual volumes of the main work also have their own indexes, so as long as you can get to the right volume there should be no problem. Having found the relevant matter in the main volumes and/or the 'Current Statutes Service' volume, always double-check the annual cumulative supplement and looseleaf noter-up for any more recent developments.

3.34 The *Index to the Statutes* published by HMSO is another possibility, but is less current and less convenient than *Halsbury's Statutes*. However, it does cover Scottish Acts, and one of its useful features is that geographical extent within the United Kingdom is indicated by the abbreviations E, W, E & W, S, or L (for London). It was first published in 1870, but now also serves as an index to *Statutes in Force*. It is arranged by broad heading, eg Road Traffic, and at the start of the entry all the relevant statutes are listed by title and chapter number and with group and sub-group references for *Statutes in Force*. Most topics are then broken down by sub-heading and by geographic extent with detailed index entries to particular sections of Acts. In this part of the index the references are by chapter number only — the short title is not given. Within the detailed sub-headings, cross-references are given to other headings.

3.35   Lexis is well suited to subject searching, and in some ways searching statutes on it is more straightforward than searching for cases in that statutory language tends to be more consistent and formalised than the language used in judgments. However, as most standard research problems involving statutes can usually be answered satisfactorily and reasonably quickly by manual means, in practice resort to Lexis tends to be confined to unconventional searches. It is particularly useful for tracing concrete entitites that may treated in legislation covering entirely different topics. For example, a search on 'caravans' will not only retrieve the Caravan Sites Act and various statutes you might expect relating to housing, planning and rating, but also sections from the Timeshare Act, Norfolk and Suffolk Broads Act and the Public Order Act among others.

3.36   Lawtel and *Current Law* in its monthly digests and yearbooks both summarise statutes by subject. In this context they are more appropriate for current awareness than in-depth research. They could also be used as a convenient way of checking the exact title of a statute that you only vaguely recollect was passed recently.

3.37   Usually one only needs to find statutes that are no longer in force by subject when tracing the history of a particular provision, in which case one can just look at the current statute and see what it repeals, and then see what that statute repealed and so on. But otherwise one could use superseded editions of *Halsbury's Statutes*, the first edition of which was published 1929-1931. For statutes before 1786 *Statutes at Large* has an index volume, as does, for statutes before 1715, *Statutes of the Realm*. Old editions of standard textbooks would also be a practical way to approach this.

Worked example: using the subject indexes to Halsbury's Statutes

3.38   Under which statute are orders to destroy dangerous dogs made?

1. VOLUME INDEX

The main alphabetical subject index in the 'Table of Statutes and General Index' volume is in two sequences. The first sequence, the 'Volume Index', covers the main bound volumes. The following entry will be found:

dog
        dangerous, order for destruction **2**, 191

At page 191 in volume 2 will be found the Dogs Act 1871, s 2 of which provides for the destruction of dangerous dogs. See figure 3.2.

2. SERVICE INDEX

In the same 'Tables of Statutes and General Index' volume as above is a second, much shorter, sequence, the 'Service index', which covers the looseleaf 'Current Statutes Service' volumes. The following entry will be found:

dogs
     dangerous, additional powers of court on complaint about, **2**, *Animals*, 53-54

Look in the binder of the looseleaf current statutes service that covers volume 2 material (Binder A: vols 1-11). Within the section for volume 2 material (there are divider cards) each main topic covered is separately paginated (unlike the main bound volume which is continuously paginated across topics). At pages 53 and 54 of the *Animals* section will be found the Dangerous Dogs Act 1989 which supplements the 1871 Act. See figure 3.3.

3. ANNUAL CUMULATIVE SUPPLEMENT

There is nothing further here in the part covering volume 2 at the relevant pages.

4. NOTER-UP

However, if you look in the looseleaf noter-up volume at the section covering volume 2, there is an annotation to pages 191 to 192, which shows that the 1871 Act has been further supplemented by the Dangerous Dogs Act 1991 and a reference is given to Vol 2(S) (ie the current statutes service volume covering volume 2 material) title *Animals*. This Act was issued after the annual tables and index was prepared, and so was not found under step 2 above. Although no page reference is given, it is found easily enough at the end of the *Animals* section in the volume 2 division. See figure 3.4.

Finding amendments and repeals

3.39   *Halsbury's Statutes* or *Current Law Legislation Citators* are usually the best places to check whether a particular statute has been amended or repealed. My own preference is to use *Halsbury's* first, then to check the statute citator in the *Current Law* monthly digests for any amendments since the last noter-up to *Halsbury's* was issued.

3.40   Find the statute in *Halsbury's* by looking either in the alphabetical list or the chronological list of statutes which are both in the Table and Index volume. Having found the statute in the main work you will have the text as amended at the date that particular volume was issued. Check for later amendments first in the annual cumulative supplement under the same volume number and page as the main work, and then in the looseleaf noter-up service (printed on blue paper), which is arranged in the same way.

3.41   The *Current Law* statute citators are arranged chronologically by chapter number. In the monthly digests the statute citator section is cumulative for that year so it is only necessary to refer to the latest monthly part, though, as already noted, it is updated only in every other issue — the date to which it is current is given at its

Figure 3.2 Halsbury's Statutes: *Table of statutes and general index volume and main work*

---

documents—*continued*
administration of estates, in—*continued*
examination of persons as to, **17**, 383
place for deposit of, **17**, 384–5
subpoena to bring in, **17**, 384
ancient, presumption as to, **17**, 129
concealment, fraudulent, **37**, 309
conveyancing, production and safe custody, **37**, 164
copy—
acceptance of, **17**, 162
meaning, **17**, 168
Director of Public Prosecutions, delivering to, **12**, 939
false certification of, **17**, 88
false, issue of, **38**, 486, 1030
falsification of seal etc, **17**, 82
foreign, proof and effect, **17**, 126, 151
forgery etc, penalty, **17**, 100
judge's signature, judicial notice of, **17**, 81
land registration—
acknowledgment of, **37**, 634
inspection, **37**, 611–12
production to registrar, **37**, 633
legal estates, relating to, **37**, 93
meaning, **17**, 129, 168
microfilm copies, **17**, 210
official—
communicating, **12**, 177–9
possessing, **12**, 192
retaining for prejudicial purpose, **12**, 192
tampering with, **12**, 192
powers of attorney, for, proof of, **17**, 130
production—
acknowledgment, **37**, 140, 164
friendly societies—
Chief Registrar's powers, **19**, 139

documents—*continued*
title, of—*continued*
loss or destruction—*continued*
proof, **37**, 143
responsibiltiies, **37**, 165
possession—
owner's consent, deemed to be with, **1**, 47
when deemed to be in, **1**, 45
production—
expenses of, **37**, 164–5
obligation, **37**, 164
order of court for, **37**, 165
regulations respecting, **37**, 213
transferring, mode of, **1**, 51
vendor—
indemnity to, **37**, 143
retention by, **37**, 140
Welsh language, in, **41**, 754–5

dog
breeding establishment—
diseases, prevention of spread, **2**, 367
inspection, **2**, 367
keeper, death of, **2**, 366
licence—
breach of conditions, **2**, 366
cancellation, **2**, 367
conditions for granting, **2**, 365
disqualification for, **2**, 367
duration of, **2**, 365–6
grant of, **2**, 365
refusal of, appeal from, **2**, 365
requirement for, **2**, 365
meaning, **2**, 368
offences and penalties, **2**, 367
cruelty to, disqualification for keeping for, **2**, 236
dangerous, order for destruction, **2**, 191 ◀

DOGS ACT 1871 s 2 191 ◀

---

4 Provisions of 11 & 12 Vict c 43, extended to this Act

The powers and provisions of the Summary Jurisdiction Act 1848 shall extend and apply to this Act, and to all proceedings, matters, and things to be taken, had and done, and to all persons to be proceeded against or taking proceedings under this Act.

NOTE

Summary Jurisdiction Act 1848. This Act was repealed by the Magistrates' Courts Act 1952, s 132, Sch 6 and the Courts Act 1971, s 56, Sch 11, Pt IV. Summary jurisdiction and procedure are now mainly governed by the Magistrates' Courts Act 1980, Vol 27, title Magistrates, and by rules made under s 144 of that Act.

5, 6 (*S 5 repealed by the SL(R) Act 1976; s 6 repealed by the Courts Act 1971, s 56(4), Sch 11, Pt IV.*)

DOGS ACT 1871

(34 & 35 Vict c 56)

An Act to provide further Protection against Dogs [24 July 1871]

Northern Ireland. This Act applies. Ss 3, 5 and the Schedule were repealed by the Diseases of Animals (Northern Ireland) Order 1975, SI 1975/418.

1 (*Repealed by the Dogs Act 1906, s 10, Schedule.*)

2 Dangerous dogs may be destroyed

Any court of summary jurisdiction may take cognizance of a complaint that a dog is dangerous, and not kept under proper control, and if it appears to the court having cognizance of such complaint that such dog is dangerous, the court may make an order in a summary way directing the dog to be kept by the owner under proper control or destroyed, and any person failing to comply with such order shall be liable to a penalty not exceeding [£1] for every day during which he fails to comply with such order.

Figure 3.3 Halsbury's Statutes: *Service index and current statutes service volume*

---

disclosure of information. *See* **information**

disconnection
service pipe, of, **49** Water 158–60

discovery
High Court's power to order, repeal of, **2** Arbitration 16

discrimination
barrister, by or in relation to, **4** Barristers 3–5
racial. *See* **racial discrimination**
sex. *See* **sex discrimination**

discs
capital allowances, **42** Taxation 419–21

disease
compensation payment in respect of, **40** Soc Sec 338–41, 359–71

dismissal
unofficial industrial action, those taking part in, **16** Employment 15–16

disposal licence
meaning, **49** Water 238

document—*continued*
conveyancing services, relating to, power to require production of, **11** Courts 68–70
identity, false statement in connection with, **4** Aviation 20, **34** Ports & Harbours 31–2
interpretation of reference to service of, **49** Water 324–5
registered patent agent, preparation by, **41** Solicitors 7
registered trade mark agent, preparation by, **41** Solicitors 7
service of—
Aviation and Maritime Security Act 1990, under, **34** Ports & Harbours 37–8
interpretation of reference to, **49** Water 324–5
taxation. *See* **taxation**

dogs
collars, enforcement of orders about, **2** Animals 61
control of—
collars, enforcement of orders about, **2** Animals 61
stray dogs. *See* stray *below*
tags, enforcement of orders about, **2** Animals 61
dangerous, additional powers of court on complaint about, **2** Animals 53–54 ◄

DANGEROUS DOGS ACT 1989

(1989 c 30)

An Act to extend the powers available to a court on a complaint under section 2 of the Dogs Act 1871 together with additional rights of appeal and enhanced penalties
[27 July 1989]

Northern Ireland. This Act does not apply; see s 2(5) post.

1 Additional powers of court on complaint about dangerous dog

(1) Where a magistrates' court makes an order under section 2 of the Dogs Act 1871 directing a dog to be destroyed it may also—

(*a*) appoint a person to undertake its destruction and require any person having custody of the dog to deliver it up for that purpose; and

(*b*) if it thinks fit, make an order disqualifying the owner for having custody of a dog for such period as is specified in the order.

Figure 3.4 Halsbury's Statutes: *looseleaf noter-up volume and current statutes service volume*

ANIMALS

VOLUME 2

Game Act 1831 (c 32)

165   Section 18
         Licensed to deal in game. A person licensed to deal in game under this Act is a "licensed game dealer" for the purposes of the Deer Act 1991, s 10, Vol 2(S), title Animals.

Game Licences Act 1860 (c 90)

186–   Section 14
187   *Persons licensed . . . to deal in game.* A person licensed to deal in game under this Act is a "licensed game dealer" for the purposes of the Deer Act 1991, s 10, Vol 2(S), title Animals.

Dogs Act 1871 (c 56)

191–   Section 2
192n   *General Note.* An order may be made under this section regardless of whether the dog is shown to have injured any person, and may specify the measures to be taken for keeping the dog under proper control; see the Dangerous Dogs Act 1991, ➡ s 3(5), Vol 2(S), title Animals.

➡ ## DANGEROUS DOGS ACT 1991

(1991 c 65)

Preliminary Note

This Act, which received the Royal Assent on 25 July 1991 and, apart from s 8 (which came into force on that date), came into force on 12 August 1991 (the day appointed by the Secretary of State under s 10(4)), imposes restrictions on certain types of fighting dogs, and provides for restrictions to be imposed on other types of dangerous dogs. It creates the offence of having a dog dangerously out of control in a public place, and provides that magistrates may specify the type of control measures to be applied to dangerous dogs.

S 1 provides that it is an offence to breed, transfer or advertise the American pit bull terrier, the Japanese tosa, and any other type of fighting dog prescribed by the Secretary of State, or to have such a dog in a public place without it being muzzled, or to abandon such a dog or allow it to stray. After 30 November 1991 (the day appointed by the Secretary of State under sub-s (3) of this section) it will be an offence under this section to possess such a dog.

S 2 gives the Secretary of State reserve powers to designate a particular breed which is a serious danger to the public, and to impose muzzling or leashing restrictions upon that breed. This power may only be exercised with the approval of both Houses of Parliament.

S 3 creates the offence of allowing any dog to be dangerously out of control in a public place, which is an aggravated offence if the dog causes injury to any person; it also creates an offence of allowing a dog to enter a place which is not public but where it is not permitted to be and there are grounds for apprehension that it will cause injury, which is an aggravated offence if the dog causes injury. Sub-s (5) of that section clarifies that under the Dogs Act 1871, s 2, Vol 2, p 191, a magistrates' court may place restrictions on a dog about which a complaint has been made, whether or not the dog is shown to have injured any person.

head. All statutes, of whatever date, that have been amended or repealed in the current calendar year will be listed and the chapter number and section (but not the short title) of the amending or repealing statute given. See figure 3.5. If you wish to use the earlier statute citators in preference to *Halsbury's Statutes*, you will need to look in the two bound volumes covering statutes affected 1947-1971 and 1972-1988, the softbound supplement covering 1989 to the pre-current year, and also, depending on the time of year and whether the softbound supplement has come out yet, the statute citator section in the December issue of the monthly digest for the previous year. The statute citator for the current year is also issued in looseleaf form as part of the service volume to *Current Law Statutes Annotated*, but is not issued as frequently as it is in the monthly digests and for some reason even on issue it is not as up to date. The *Current Law* statute citators, unlike *Halsbury's Statutes*, all cover Scottish Acts.

3.42 *Statutes in Force* would of course be another way of checking for amendments and repeals, but it is an approach that does not have anything special to recommend it, unless the relevant volumes of *Halsbury's* are missing from the shelf. Having checked the text in the main work, look in the cumulative supplements which are in the binders shelved at the start of the work.

3.43 Lexis is certainly another way of approaching this problem. It is particularly valuable for heavily amended text, which can be found in a single step whereas to establish how the text stands from *Halsbury's Statutes* you may need to look in four places. *Current Law* statute citators are even less useful in these circumstances: you will get all the necessary references but you will still have to work out for yourself from these how the text now stands. But check the date of the statute database on Lexis.

3.44 The *Chronological Table of the Statutes* published by HMSO can be used as an alternative to the above sources, as long as it is remembered that it is likely to be two years or so out of date. But it is the only way of checking when and how older statutes that are no longer in force (which may be outside the scope of *Halsbury's* or *Current Law*) were repealed. It lists by chapter number all statutes since 1285 and shows whether any section has been amended or repealed and if so by what. The titles of Acts still in force in whole or in part are printed in bold and the titles of Acts that have been wholly repealed are printed in italic. See for example the Royal Marriages Act 1772 (12 Geo 3 c 11) in figure 3.6. For the purposes of the Abdication Declaration Act 1936 (chapter 3 of the Parliamentary session that spanned the first — and last — year of the reign of Edward VIII and first year of the reign of George VI), it was excluded. Section 2 was partly repealed by the Statute Law Revision Act 1888 and section 3 was repealed by the Criminal Law Act 1967. Otherwise it is still in force.

Worked example: finding amendments and repeals in Halsbury's Statutes and Current Law Statute Citators

Has s 42 of the Gaming Act 1968 (restrictions on advertisements relating to gaming) been amended or repealed?

1. *HALSBURY'S STATUTES:* MAIN WORK

3.45 Find the statute in the main work. The alphabetical list of statutes in the 'Tables of Statutes and General Index' volume is the quickest way. The reference **5**, 98 is given. Go to volume 5, which contains the title 'Betting, Gaming and Lotteries',

Figure 3.5   Current Law: *monthly digest statute citator*

STATUTE CITATOR
(Up-to-date to August 21, 1992)

Acts of the Parliaments of England, Great Britain and the United Kingdom

CAP.

29 Car. 2 (1677)

3. Statute of Frauds 1677.
s. 4, see *Elpis Maritime Co.* v. *Marti Chartering Co. Maria D., The* [1991] 3 W.L.R. 330, H.L.

1 Will. & Mar., Sess. 2 (1688)

2. Bill of Rights 1688.
Art. 4, see *Woolwich Building Society (Formerly Woolwich Equitable Building Society)* v. *I.R.C.* [1991] S.T.C. 364, C.A.

25 Geo. 2 (1751)

36. Disorderly Houses Act 1751.
s. 8, see *D.P.P.* v. *Curley and Farrelly* [1991] C.O.D. 186, D.C.

6 Geo. 4 (1825)

120. Court of Session Act 1825.
s. 40, see *Laing* v. *Scottish Grain Distillers, The Times,* March 25, 1992.

2 & 3 Will. 4 (1832)

71. Prescription Act 1832.
see *Jones* v. *Price, The Independent,* January 16, 1992, C.A.; *Marine & General Mutual Life Assurance Society* v. *St. James' Real Estate Co.* [1991] 38 EG 230, H.H. Judge Ross-Martyn.

5 & 6 Will. (1835)

50. Highways Act 1835.
s. 72, see *Baron* v. *Chief Constable of Devon and Cornwall* [1991] Crim.L.R. 631, D.C.

7 Will. 4 & 1 Vict. (1837)

28. Wills Act 1837.
s. 9, see *Wood* v. *Smith, The Times,* March 4, 1992, C.A.

3 & 4 Vict. (1840)

110. Loan Societies Act 1840.
s. 27, repealed in pt.: 1992, c. 40, schs. 21, 22.

CAP.

5 & 6 Vict. (1842)

55. Railway Regulation Act 1842.
s. 17, repealed in pt.: 1992, c. 42, s. 40, sch. 4.

8 & 9 Vict. (1845)

19. Lands Clauses Consolidation (Scotland) Act 1845.
s. 19, see *Royal Bank of Scotland, The* v. *Clydebank District Council,* 1992 S.L.T. 356.
20. Railways Clauses Consolidation Act 1845.
s. 75, amended: 1992, c. 42, s. 49.
33. Railways Clauses Consolidation (Scotland) Act 1845.
s. 6, see *Royal Bank of Scotland, The* v. *Clydebank District Council,* 1992 S.L.T. 356; *Loch Ryan Oyster Fisher* v. *British Railways Board* (O.H), 1986 S.C. 84.
s. 68, amended: 1992, c. 42, s. 49.
109. Gaming Act 1845.
see *City Index* v. *Leslie* [1991] 3 W.L.R. 207, C.A.

10 & 11 Vict. (1847)

27. Harbours, Docks and Piers Clauses Act 1847.
ss. 33, 83, see *Peterhead Towage Services* v. *Peterhead Bay Authority* (O.H.), 1992 S.L.T. 593.

12 & 13 Vict. (1849)

51. Judicial Factors Act 1849.
s. 34A, Act of Sederunt 92/272.

18 & 19 Vict. (1855)

111. Bills of Lading Act 1855.
repealed: 1992, c. 50, s. 6.

19 & 20 Vict. (1856)

29. National Gallery Act 1856.
repealed: 1992, c. 44, sch. 9.

20 & 21 Vict. (1857)

43. Summary Jurisdiction Act 1857.
s. 6, see *Griffith* v. *Jenkins* [1992] 2 W.L.R. 28, H.L.

Figure 3.6   Chronological Table of the Statutes

136   CHRONOLOGICAL TABLE OF THE STATUTES

c. 87   ..   *Staffordshire roads.*—r., 53 G. 3. c. cxxxv; Annual Turnpike Acts Cont. 1887 (c. 64).
c. 88   ..   *Leicester roads.*—r., 11 G. 4. & 1. W. 4. c. iii.
c. 89   ..   **Bradford to Idle canal.***
c. 90   ..   *Ayre and Lanark roads.*—r., 54 G. 3. c. ccii.
c. 91   ..   *Lancaster roads.*—r., 1-2 G. 4. c. xv.
c. 92   ..   *Worcester and Warwick roads.*—r., 59 G. 3. c. xlix.
c. 93   ..   *Liverpool and Preston road.*—r., 26 G. 3. c. 126.
c. 94   ..   *Sussex roads.*—r., 2-3 W. 4. c. lvii.
c. 95   ..   *Salop and Denbigh roads.*—r., 19-20 V. c. ciii.
c. 96   ..   *Pembroke roads.*—r., 48 G. 3. c. cxxxix.
c. 97   ..   *Berks. and Wilts. roads.*—r., 21-2 V. c. xlii.
c. 98   ..   *Sussex roads.*—r., 53 G. 3. c. ccviii; 3-4 W. 4. c. xliv.
c. 99   ..   *Sussex roads.*—r., 11 G. 4 & 1 W. 4. c. civ.

1772 (12 Geo. 3).
cc. 1, 2   *Exportations and importation.*—r., S.L.R., 1871.
c. 3   ..   *Land tax.*—r., S.L.R., 1871.
c. 4   ..   *Mutiny.*—r., S.L.R., 1871.
c. 5   ..   *Marine mutiny.*—r., S.L.R., 1871.
c. 6   ..   *Malt duties.*—r., S.L.R., 1871.
c. 7   ..   *East India Company.*—r., S.L.R., 1871.
c. 8   ..   *Plymouth: improvement.*—r., 5 G. 4. c. xxii.
c. 9   ..   **Bedford level.***
c. 10   ..   *Papists.*—r., S.L.R., 1871.
➡ c. 11   ..   **Royal Marriages.**
             excl.—His Majesty's Declaration of Abdication, 1936 (1 E. 8 & 1. G. 6. c. 3), s. 1 (3).
             s. 2 r. in pt.—S.L.R., 1888.
             3 r.—Crim Law, 1967 (c. 58), s. 13, sch. 4 pt. I.
c. 12   ..   *Mutiny in America.*—r., S.L.R., 1871.
c. 13   ..   *Militia pay.*—r., S.L.R., 1871.
c. 14   ..   *Great Yarmouth: improvement.*—r., 5-6 W. 4. c. xlix.
c. 15   ..   *Edinburgh: improvement.*—r., 11-2 V. c. cxiii.
c. 16   ..   *Port Glasgow Harbour.*—r., 27-8 V. c. cxl.
c. 17   ..   *London: streets.*—r., 5 G. 4. c. cxxv.
c. 18   ..   *Chatham: streets.*—r., Local Govt. Supplemental, 1860 (No. 2) (c. 118).
c. 19   ..   *Crown lands in Fenchurch Street, London.*—r., S.L.(Reps.), 1978 (c. 45), s. 1 (1), sch. 1 pt. XIV.
c. 20   ..   *Felony and Piracy.*—r., S.L.R., 1948.
c. 21   ..   *Municipal corporations (mandamus).*—r., S.L.R., 1887.
c. 22   ..   **Ayr Harbour.***
c. 23   ..   *Relief of insolvent debtors, etc.*—r., S.L.R., 1871.
c. 24   ..   *Dockyards, etc., Protection.*—r., Crim. Damage, 1971 (c. 48), ss. 11 (2) (8) 12 (6), sch. pt. III.
c. 25   ..   *Naval prize.*—r., Naval Prize Acts Repeal, 1864 (c. 23), s. 1.
c. 26   ..   **Drainage: Cambridge, Isle of Ely.***
             r. in pt., am.—Land Drainage (Benwick Internal Drainage District) Provisional O. Conf., 1941 (c. viii), sch. s. 3, schs. 1, 2.
c. 27   ..   **Drainage: Isle of Ely.***
c. 28   ..   **Watford Churchyard and Workhouse.***
c. 29   ..   *Spurn Point lighthouse.*—r., S.L.R., 1861.
c. 30   ..   *Salaries of Justices of Chester, etc.* r., S.L.R., 1861.
c. 31   ..   *Indemnity.*—r., S.L.R., 1871.
cc. 32, 33   *Importation.*—r., S.L.R., 1871.
c. 34   ..   *Workhouse, Westminster.*—r., S.R. & O. 1901/278.
c. 35   ..   *Crown lands at Richmond, Surrey.*—r., S.L.(Reps.), 1978 (c. 45), s. 1(1), sch. 1 pt. XIV.
c. 36   ..   *Richmond chapel, Lancs.*—r., 4 E. 7. c. c. s. 25, sch. 2.
c. 37   ..   **Market Weighton.*** am.—S.I. 1983/52
c. 38   ..   **Christchurch, Middlesex.***
c. 39   ..   *Unfunded debt.*—r., S.L.R., 1871.
c. 40   ..   *St. Marylebone Church.*—r., 51 G1 3. c. cli.
c. 41   ..   *Maidenhead Bridge.*—r., 4 E. 7. c. xcv.
c. 42   ..   **Duchy of Lancaster (precinct of Savoy).***

and at page 98 the Act starts (see figure 3.7). It is worth noting at this stage, for use later with *Current Law*, that the chapter number for the Act is c 65. Also note from the spine or title page that the volume is a 1989 reissue — the page after the title page indicates that the law is stated as at 1 July 1988. Turn to s 42, and at the end the notes to the section state that the text is as amended by the Lotteries and Amusements Act 1976, the Magistrates Courts Act 1980 and the Cable and Broadcasting Act 1984 (see figure 3.8).

2. *HALSBURY'S STATUTES*: CUMULATIVE SUPPLEMENT

3.46 Go to the annual cumulative supplement (the bound volume), which is arranged by the volume and page numbers of the main work. It will be found that s 42(8) has been further amended by the Broadcasting Act 1990 (see figure 3.9). To find the amending text itself go to the Act in Vol 45.

3. *HALSBURY'S STATUTES*: NOTER-UP

3.47 Go to the looseleaf noter-up, which is arranged exactly like the cumulative supplement. At the front it will state the date to which it is current. No further amendments to the s 42 are given: in figure 3.9 it will be seen there is nothing added between s 22 and s 48.

4. *CURRENT LAW*: STATUTE CITATORS IN MONTHLY DIGESTS

3.48 Find the statute citator in the latest monthly digest from the contents page. The statutes are arranged chronologically by chapter number. To save time, we have already noted from *Halsbury's Statutes* that the Act is chapter 65 of 1968. The following entry will be found (see figure 3.10):

   65. Gaming Act 1968
      s. 42, amended: 1992, c. 10, s. 1

As this, at the time, would be a very recent Act, it would probably be only available in the form of an HMSO Queen's Printer copy. Looking through the loose Acts, chapter 10 will be found to be the Bingo Act 1992, and s 1 amends s 42 of the 1968 Act with regard to bingo advertising. Depending on the date of the last issue of the *Halsbury's Statutes* noter-up and the time of year, it may also be necessary to look at the statute citator in the December *Current Law* monthly digest for the previous calendar year.

STATUTES IN FORCE: A COMPARISON

3.49 By the way of a footnote to the above example, it is worth comparing the result of the same search using only *Statutes in Force*. To find the Act use the alphabetical list of Acts in the 'Guide to the Edition' binder, usually shelved at the beginning of the set. Reference is given to Group 12 Subgroup I. In the binder for Group 12, after the divider card for Subgroup I, the Act will be found. The cover states that it is revised to 1 October 1977, and indeed turning to s 42 it will found that it only incorporates the first amendment we found — the Lotteries and Amusements Act 1976. If the equivalent group is found in the cumulative supplement binders, amendments to 1 July 1989 are given, and so the amendment by the Cable and

Figure 3.7 Halsbury's Statutes: *Table of statutes and general index volume and main work*

33	ALPHABETICAL LIST OF STATUTES	gre

Free and Voluntary Present to His Majesty (1661) **10**, 40
Friendly and Industrial and Provident Societies Act 1968 . . . . . **21**, 1;50
Friendly Societies Act 1896 . . . . **19**, 3
Friendly Societies Act 1955 . . . . **19**, 64
Friendly Societies Act 1971 . . . . **19**, 77
Friendly Societies Act 1974 . . . . **19**, 77
Friendly Societies Act 1981 . . . . **19**, 176
Friendly Societies Act 1984 . . . . **19**, 176
Fugitive Offenders Act 1967 . . . . **17**, 517
Further Education Act 1985 . . . . **15**, 320

G

Game Act 1831 . . . . **2**, 146
Game Act 1970 . . . . **2**, 303
Game Laws (Amendment) Act 1960 . . . . **2**, 250
Game Licences Act 1860 . . . . **2**, 171
Gaming Act 1710 . . . . **5**, 7
Gaming Act 1738 . . . . **5**, 9
Gaming Act 1835 . . . . **5**, 11
Gaming Act 1845 . . . . **5**, 12
Gaming Act 1892 . . . . **5**, 16
Gaming Act 1968 . . . . **5**, 98

---

98   VOL 5 BETTING, GAMING AND LOTTERIES

(8) (*See Vol 24, title* Licensing and Liquor Duties.)

NOTES

The words in square brackets in sub-s (3)(*a*) were substituted by the Customs and Excise Management Act 1979, s 177(1), Sch 4, para 12, Table, Pt I.
Sub-s (3)(*b*) was repealed by the Finance Act 1972, ss 54(8), 134, Sch 28, Pt II.
Sub-s (3)(*d*), (*e*) were repealed by the Income and Corporation Taxes Act 1970, s 538(1), Sch 16.
Sub-s (3)(*h*) was repealed by the Capital Gains Tax Act 1979, ss 157(1), 158(1), Sch 6, para 10, Sch 8.
Part I (except sections 8 to 12 and Schedules 7 and 8). Ie ss 5 and 7.
Construed as one. Ie the enactments in question are to be construed as if they were contained in one Act, unless there is some manifest discrepancy; see eg *Phillips v Parnaby* [1934] 2 KB 299 at 302. Accordingly definitions in the earlier Act may be relevant to the construction of provisions of this Act (see *Solomons v R Gertzenstein Ltd* [1954] 2 QB 243, [1954] 2 All ER 625, CA; *Crowe (Valuation Officer) v Llcyds British Testing Co Ltd* [1960] 1 QB 592, [1960] 1 All ER 411, CA), though this principle should not be pressed too far in construing revenue Acts (see the opinion of Lord Simonds in *Fendoch Investment Trust Co v IRC* [1945] 2 All ER 140, HL).
A later Act may not be referred to for the purpose of interpreting clear terms of an earlier Act which the later Act does not amend, even though both Acts are by the express provision of the later Act to be construed as one; but if the earlier Act is ambiguous the later Act may be used to throw light on its interpretation; see *Kirkness (Inspector of Taxes) v John Hudson & Co Ltd* [1955] AC 696, [1955] 2 All ER 345, HL.
Customs and Excise Management Act 1979. See Vol 13, title Customs and Excise.

(*Schs 1, 3, 4 repealed by the Finance Act 1968, s 61(10), Sch 20, Pt I; Sch 2 repealed by the Finance Act 1969, s 61(6), Sch 21, Pt I; Sch 5 repealed by the Hydrocarbon Oil (Customs & Excise) Act 1971, s 24(2), Sch 7 and the Alcoholic Liquor Duties Act 1979, s 92(2), Sch 4, Pt I; Sch 6 repealed by the Finance Act 1976, s 132(5), Sch 15, Pt I, the Customs and Excise Management Act 1979, s 177(3), Sch 6, Pt I, and the Alcoholic Liquor Duties Act 1979, s 92(2), Sch 4, Pt I; for Sch 7, see Vol 24, title Licensing and Liquor Duties; Sch 8 (which applied to Scotland only) repealed by the Licensing (Scotland) Act 1976, s 136(2), Sch 8; Sch 9 repealed by the Customs and Excise Management Act 1979, s 177(3), Sch 6, Pt I and the Alcoholic Liquor Duties Act 1979, s 92(2), Sch 4, Pt I; Schs 10, 11 repealed by the Income and Corporation Taxes Act 1970, ss 538(1), Sch 16; Sch 12 repealed by the Finance Act 1972, ss 122(5), 134(7), Sch 28, Pt IX; Sch 13 repealed by the Capital Gains Tax Act 1979, s 158(1), Sch 8; Schs 14, 15 repealed by the Finance Act 1971, ss 55(1), 69(7), Sch 14, Pt III; for Sch 16, Pts I, II, see Vol 24, title Licensing and Liquor Duties; for Sch 16, Pts III, IV, VI–VIII, X, see Vol 41, title Stamp Duties; Sch 16, Pt V repealed by the SL(R) Act 1971; Sch 16, Pt IX repealed by the Provisional Collection of Taxes Act 1968, s 6(2), Schedule.*)

GAMING ACT 1968

(1968 c 65)

Figure 3.8   Halsbury's Statutes: *main work*

➤ **42 Restrictions on advertisements relating to gaming**

(1) Except as provided by this section, no person shall issue, or cause to be issued, any advertisement—

(a) informing the public that any premises in Great Britain are premises on which gaming takes place or is to take place, or

(b) inviting the public to take part as players in any gaming which takes place, or is to take place, on any such premises, or to apply for information about facilities for taking part as players in any gaming which takes place, or is to take place, in Great Britain, or

(c) inviting the public to subscribe any money or money's worth to be used in gaming whether in Great Britain or elsewhere, or to apply for information about facilities for subscribing any money or money's worth to be so used.

(2) The preceding subsection does not apply to any advertisement in so far as it relates to gaming which is, or is to be,—

(a) gaming as an incident of an entertainment to which section 33 of this Act applies, or

(b) gaming to which section 41 of this Act applies, or

(c) gaming on any premises to which paragraph 4 of Schedule 9 to this Act applies and in respect of which a permit under section 34 of this Act is for the time being in force, or

(d) gaming on any premises to which paragraph [3 of Schedule 3 to the Lotteries and Amusements Act 1976 applies and in respect of which a permit under section 16] of that Act is for the time being in force, or

(e) gaming at any travelling showmen's pleasure fair.

(3) Subsection (1) of this section does not apply to—

(a) the display, on any premises in respect of which a licence under this Act is for the time being in force, of a sign or notice indicating that gaming takes place, or is to take place, on those premises, whether the sign or notice is displayed inside or outside the premises, or

(b) the publication or display of a notice, where the notice is required to be published or displayed by any provision of Schedules 2 to 4 to this Act and the publication or display is so made as to comply with the requirements of that provision, or

(c) the publication in any newspaper of a notice stating that a licence under this Act has been granted, if the notice is published not later than fourteen days from the date on which the licence was granted or from such later date as may be appointed by the licensing authority by whom the licence was granted, and the notice is in a form approved by the licensing authority;

and, in the case of any premises in respect of which a club is for the time being registered under Part II or Part III of this Act, subsection (1) of this section shall not apply to any advertisement by reason only that it contains the name of the club.

(4) Subsection (1) of this section does not apply to the publication of an advertisement in a newspaper which circulates wholly or mainly outside Great Britain.

(5) Where a person is charged with an offence under this section, it shall be a defence to prove that he is a person whose business it is to publish or arrange for the publication of advertisements and that he received the advertisement in question for publication in the ordinary course of business and did not know and had no reason to suspect that its publication would amount to an offence under this section.

(6) For the purposes of this section an advertisement issued by displaying or exhibiting it shall be treated as issued on every day on which it is displayed or exhibited.

(7) Subject to subsection (5) of this section, any person who contravenes subsection (1) of this section shall be guilty of an offence and liable—

(a) on summary conviction, to a fine not exceeding [the prescribed sum];

(b) on conviction on indictment, to a fine or to imprisonment for a term not exceeding two years or to both.

(8) In this section "advertisement" includes every form of advertising, whether in a publication or by the display of notices or by means of circulars or other documents or by an exhibition of photographs or a cinematograph film, or by way of sound broadcasting or television [or by inclusion in a cable programme service], and references to the issue of an advertisement shall be construed accordingly; and "the public" means the public in Great Britain, and includes any section of the public in Great Britain, however selected.

NOTES

The words in square brackets in sub-s (2)(d) were substituted by the Lotteries and Amusements Act 1976, s 25(2), Sch 4, para 4.

➤ The reference to the prescribed sum in sub-s (7)(a) is substituted by virtue of the Magistrates' Courts Act 1980, s 32(2), title Magistrates.

The words in square brackets in sub-s (8) were inserted by the Cable and Broadcasting Act 1984, s 57(1), Sch 5, para 22.

Figure 3.9   Halsbury's Statutes: *annual cumulative supplement and looseleaf noter-up*

Vol 5 (1989 Reissue)   BETTING, GAMING AND LOTTERIES

PAGE
　　　　　Gaming Act 1968 (c 65)—*continued*
139–　　　Section 42
140　　　　Sub-s (8) is amended by the Broadcasting Act 1990, s 203(1), Sch 20, para 14,
　　　　　　Vol 45, title Telecommunications and Broadcasting.

Vol 5 (1989 Reissue)   BETTING, GAMING AND LOTTERIES

PAGE
　　　　Betting, Gaming and Lotteries Act 1963 (c 2)—*continued*
　　　　　　　""'qualified accountant" means a person who is eligible for appointment
　　　　　　　　as a company auditor under section 25 of the Companies Act 1989;".
　　　　　　For transitional provisions as to termination and resignation of appointments,
　　　　see reg 4 of those regulations.

　　　　　Schedule 1, para 20
67n　　　　The Betting, Gaming and Lotteries Act 1963 (Variation of Fees) Order 1987,
　　　　　　SI 1987/95, is revoked and replaced by SI 1991/2176.

68n　　　　*Orders under this paragraph.* The Betting, Gaming and Lotteries Act 1963,
　　　　　　(Variation of Fees) Order 1987, SI 1987/95, is revoked and replaced by SI
　　　　　　1991/2176.

75　　　　Schedule, 2, paras 10, 11
　　　　　　In para 11, for the sum of "£350", there is substituted the sum of "£464", by the
　　　　　　Betting, Gaming and Lotteries Act 1963 (Variation of Fees) Order 1991, SI
　　　　　　1991/2175, reg 2 (revoking SI 1982/572).

85–　　　Schedule 3, para 12
86　　　　　In para 12(1), (3), for the sum "£35", there is substituted the sum "£46", and in
　　　　　　para 12(2), for the sum "£350", there is substituted the sum "£464", by the
　　　　　　Betting, Gaming and Lotteries Act 1963 (Variation of Fees) Order 1991, SI
　　　　　　1991/2175, regs 3–5 (revoking SI 1982/572).

　　　　　Gaming Act 1968 (c 65)
　　　　　　Section 14
112n　　　*Regulations under this section.* The Gaming Clubs (Hours and Charges)
　　　　　　Regulations 1984, SI 1984/248, reg 5, is further amended by SI 1991/871 (sub-
　　　　　　stituting for the sum "£5", the sum "£5.70", in both places where it occurs, and
　　　　　　revoking SI 1989/535).

116–　　　In sub-s (3), for "£4,000", there is substituted "£4,500", by the Gaming Act
117　　　　(Variation of Monetary Limits) Order 1991, SI 1991/870, art 2.
　　　　　　In sub-s (8), for "£1,750", there is substituted "£2,000", by the Gaming Act
　　　　　　(Variation of Monetary Limits) Order 1991, SI 1991/870, art 3.

117n　　　*Regulations under this section.* The Gaming Act (Variation of Monetary
　　　　　　Limits) Order 1989, SI 1989/536, is revoked and replaced by SI 1991/870.

　　　　　Section 22
120n　　　*Regulations under this section.* The Gaming (Record of Cheques) Regula-
　　　　　　tions 1988, SI 1988/1251, are amended by SI 1991/1892.

145n　　　Section 48
146　　　　Sub-ss (3)(*a*), (*b*), (*f*), (*g*), (4)(*a*), (*b*) are amended, by the Gaming Act (Variation
　　　　　　of Fees) Order 1991, SI 1991/60 (amending SI 1990/386), as follows—

Halsbury's Statutes 3rd Edn Service: Issue 153/ 4th Edn Service: Issue 44

Figure 3.10 Current Law: *monthly digest statute citator and* Queen's Printer copy

Bingo Act 1992

↑ **1992 CHAPTER 10**

An Act to amend the Gaming Act 1968 with respect to bingo; and for connected purposes. [6th March 1992]

BE IT ENACTED by the Queen's most Excellent Majesty, by and with the advice and consent of the Lords Spiritual and Temporal, and Commons, in this present Parliament assembled, and by the authority of the same, as follows:—

1.—(1) Section 42 of the Gaming Act 1968 (restrictions on advertisements relating to gaming) shall be amended as follows.

(2) In subsection (1), at the end of paragraph (c) there shall be inserted "or

(d) containing an inducement to the public to take part as players in a game of bingo, or to become members of a club to which section 20 of this Act applies, or

(e) containing any such matter relating to any relevant premises, to any activities carried on at any relevant premises or to any club operating from any relevant premises as may be specified or described in regulations made by the Secretary of State."

(3) After that subsection there shall be inserted—

"(1A) For the purposes of this section any advertisement displayed on a sign or notice which—

(a) is within 400 metres of any relevant premises;

(b) contains sufficient information about the premises" to indicate their location; and

---

STATUTE CITATOR

AP.

1968—cont.

64. Civil Evidence Act 1968.
s. 3, see *Sphere Drake Insurance v. M. E. Denby, Posgate v. Alexander & Alexander Services, The Times, December 20, 1991,* Kershaw J.

65. Gaming Act 1968.
s. 14, regs. 92/431, 750(S.).
s. 16, see *Crockfords Club v. Mehta* [1992] 1 W.L.R. 355, C.A.
s. 20, orders 92/426, 751(S.).
s. 20, amended: order 92/751(S.).
s. 21, order 92/429.
s. 42, amended: 1992, c. 10, s. 1.
s. 48, orders 91/2499(S.); 92/93, 410(S.).
s. 48, amended: orders 91/2499(S.); 92/93.
s. 51, orders 91/2499(S.); 92/93, 410(S.). 426, 429, 751(S.); regs. 92/431, 750(S.).

67. Medicines Act 1968.
modified: regs. 92/605.
s. 1, regs. 91/2605.
s. 4, order 92/606.
s. 7, amended and repealed in pt.: regs. 92/604.
s. 8, amended: *ibid.*
ss. 18, 24, regs. 92/755.
s. 40, regs. 92/32.

Current Law August Digest 1992

Broadcasting Act 1984 is picked up. But the 1990 and 1992 amendments will not be found.

Is it in force yet?

3.50   As explained above (para 3.4), many Acts are only brought into operation in whole or in part on a date subsequent to their passing by means of commencement orders which are published (with a single exception in recent times: see para 3.58) as SIs. *Is it in Force?* issued annually goes back to 1966 and is the best place to start for a statute passed before the current year. It is arranged by year and alphabetically within each year. In the example in figure 3.11, it will be seen that the Social Security Act 1990 received Royal Assent on 13 July 1990. Commencement provisions are contained in subsections 23(2) and (3) of the Act, and three commencement orders have been made to date. The date of entry into force of each section is given with the authority — either the section number of the Act or the SI number of the commencement order. Some sections, eg s 17, are not yet fully in force.

3.51   The looseleaf noter-up volume of *Halsbury's Statutes* contains a supplement to *Is it in Force?*. It is in two parts. The first part adds commencement dates to the statutes listed in the main *Is it in Force?* volume that have been announced since it was last issued. The second part contains commencement dates for statutes passed in the current year.

3.52   However, updated more frequently is the table of Commencement of Statutes that appears in the monthly parts of *Current Law*. It is cumulative through the year so it is only necessary to look in the latest monthly part, but remember that it only lists commencement dates announced during the current calendar year. Until about June each year, when the *Current Law* yearbook for the previous year is issued and the monthly parts are replaced, the table of commencement dates in the December issue of the previous year's monthly parts can be referred to. The table is illustrated in figure 3.12. The layout is slightly different from *Is it in Force?*, but the same information is given. It will be noticed that further subsections of s 17 (not yet in force at the date of the last edition of *Is it in Force?*) have now been brought in. The references to 'C.L.' in the authority column after the SI numbers are to the month and paragraph of *Current Law* where the SIs were originally digested.

3.53   If you wish to check commencement dates before the current year using *Current Law* rather than *Is it in Force?*, you will need to use the *Statute Citators*. These will not give actual commencement dates, but the SI numbers for all commencement orders are given — the orders themselves have to be then consulted to establish the actual dates. It is the current practice for all the commencement orders to be given at the head of the entry for the Act, but for earlier Acts they are only listed under the relevant enabling section of the Act — you will thus need to know which section of the Act contains the commencement provisions. If you approach the problem this way and find there are several commencement orders, look at the most recent one first — the provisions of previous orders are usually summarised in a note at the end. As well as in the statute citator section, the *Current Law* legislation citators include an alphabetical list of all SIs; as the title of those that are commencement orders is invariably the same as the name of the Act (eg Companies Act 1989 (Commencement) No 3 Order 1991) they can be easily spotted there as well. An alternative to the table in current monthly parts of *Current Law* for recent commence-

Figure 3.11   Is it in Force?

586	1990

Social Security Act 1990 (c 27)

RA: 13 Jul 1990

Commencement provisions: s 23(2), (3); Social Security Act 1990 (Commencement No 1) Order 1990, SI 1990/1446; Social Security Act 1990 (Commencement No 2) Order 1990, SI 1990/1942; Social Security Act 1990 (Commencement No 3) Order 1991, SI 1991/558

s 1	1 Oct 1990 (SI 1990/1446)
2	1 Oct 1990 (for the purpose of authorising the making of regulations) (SI 1990/1942)
	3 Dec 1990 (otherwise) (SI 1990/1942)
3(1)–(5)	1 Oct 1990 (SI 1990/1446)
(6)	13 Jul 1990 (s 23(2), (3))
(7), (8)	1 Oct 1990 (SI 1990/1446)
4	6 April 1991 (SI 1991/558)
5, 6	13 Jul 1990 (s 23(2), (3))
7	See Sch 1 below
8	15 Oct 1990 (SI 1990/1446)
9	*Not in force*
10	13 Jul 1990 (s 23(2), (3))
11(1)	17 Aug 1990 (for purpose only of giving effect to s 11(3)) (SI 1990/1446)
	Not in force (otherwise)
(2)	See Sch 2 below
(3)–(6)	17 Aug 1990 (SI 1990/1446)
12(1)	See Sch 3 below
(2)	1 Oct 1990 (SI 1990/1446)
13	18 Jul 1990 (SI 1990/1446)
14	See Sch 4 below
15(1)–(10)	13 Jul 1990 (s 23(2), (3))
(11)	*Not in force*
16(1)	13 Jul 1990 (s 23(2), (3))
(2), (3)	18 Jul 1990 (SI 1990/1446)
(4)–(8)	13 Jul 1990 (s 23(2), (3))
(9)	18 Jul 1990 (SI 1990/1446)
(10)	13 Jul 1990 (s 23(2), (3))
➡ 17(1)–(6)	*Not in force*
(7)	See Sch 5 below
(8)–(10)	*Not in force*
18–20	13 Jul 1990 (s 23(2), (3))
21(1)	See Sch 6 below
(2)	See Sch 7 below
(3)	13 Jul 1990 (s 23(2), (3))
22, 23	13 Jul 1990 (s 23(2), (3))
Sch 1	13 Jul 1990 (s 23(2), (3))
2	*Not in force*
3	18 Jul 1990 (for the purpose of authorising the making of regulations under the Social Security Pensions Act 1975, s 59C(5), as inserted by Sch 3, which are expressed to come into force on or after 1 Oct 1990) (SI 1990/1446)
	1 Oct 1990 (otherwise) (SI 1990/1446)
4, para 1	22 Oct 1990 (for the purpose only of authorising the making of regulations) (SI 1990/1942)
	12 Nov 1990 (otherwise) (SI 1990/1942)

Figure 3.12 **Current Law:** *monthly digest —table of commencement of statutes*

DATES OF COMMENCEMENT—STATUTES		
Statute	*Commencement*	*Authority*
Sexual Offences (Amendment) Act 1992 (c.34)		
s.8	March 16, 1992	s.8(3)
Remaining provisions	August 1, 1992	S.I. 1992/1336
Social Security Act 1990 (c.27)		
s.17(1)–(6), 10	April 6, 1992	S.I. 1992/632 [1992] 6 C.L. 383
s.14 (part), Sched. 4, para. 2	June 29, 1992	S.I. 1942/1532
Social Security (Mortgage Interest Payments) Act 1992 (c.33)		
All provisions	March 16, 1992	Royal Assent
Stamp Duty (Temporary Provisions) Act 1992 (c.2)		
s.1	January 16, 1992	s.1(4)
s.2	February 13, 1992	Royal Assent
Still-Birth (Definitions) Act 1992 (c.29)		
s.3	March 16, 1992	Royal Assent
ss.1, 2, 4	October 1, 1992	s.4(2)
Statute Law (Repeals) Act 1989 (c.43)		
s.1 (part)	June 1, 1992	S.I. 1992/1275 [1992] 7 C.L. 565
Taxation of Chargeable Gains Act 1992 (c.12)		
All provisions (in part)	April 6, 1992	s.289
Timeshare Act 1992 (c.35)		
All provisions	October 12, 1992	S.I. 1992/1941
Tourism (Overseas Promotion) (Wales) Act 1992 (c.26)	May 16, 1992	s.3
Traffic Calming Act 1992 (c.30)		
All provisions	May 16, 1992	s.3
Transport and Works Act 1992 (c.42)		
s.70	March 16, 1992	Royal Assent
ss.45, 46, 49, 57–60, 63, 65(1)(a), (e), (2), 66, 67, 68(1) (in part), 69, Sched. 3, Sched. 4, Pt. I (in part), Pt. II	July 15, 1992	S.I. 1992/1347
Trade Union and Labour Relations (Consolidation) Act 1992 (c.52)		
All provisions	October 16, 1992	s.302
ss.45, 46, 49, 57–60, 63, 65(1)(a), (e), (2), 66, 67, 68 (in part), 69, Sched. 3, Sched. 4, Pt. I (part), Pt. II	July 15, 1992	S.I. 1992/1347
Tribunals and Inquiries Act 1992 (c.53)		
All provisions	October 1, 1992	s.19(2)
Weights and Measures Act 1985 (c.72)		
s.43	April 1, 1994	S.I. 1992/770

ment dates is the Commencement of Statutes section in the looseleaf noter-up volume of *Halsbury's Laws* (as distinct from the *Statutes*). This is updated monthly, and unlike *Is it in Force?*, is arranged alphabetically regardless of year.

3.54 Although commencement orders are usually issued reasonably ahead of the date on which the statute is to be activated and so a check in the latest monthly part of *Current Law* is safe enough, you might well want to check whether any commencement orders have been issued more recently. Lawtel and the on-line database that supplements the Justis CD-ROM of SIs will both do this. If you do not have access to those, the safest method, if somewhat tedious, is to check every *Daily List* issued by HMSO back to the last update of *Current Law*. All SIs issued on a particular day are listed at the end. The process is not quite as time-consuming as it sounds because any commencement orders are given first in the SI section of each list — you do not have to read through the whole lot (see figure 3.13).

3.55 If you do not have access to the *Daily Lists*, or are not prepared to wade through them, the weekly journals (*New Law Journal, Law Society's Gazette*, the *Solicitors Journal*) list recent commencement orders.

3.56 Lexis provides full details of commencement provisions — the date is given at the head of each section and the authority for it in the annotations at the foot, but is probably an expensive way to proceed unless you are looking at the section on Lexis anyway.

3.57 If you cannot find a commencement order but wish to know whether there are plans to issue one in the near future, the government department concerned may be able to help. Rather than ringing the main switchboard, try to identify the correct section in the department from the *Civil Service Yearbook* — this publication is now also available on CD-ROM and that format would be ideal for this kind of enquiry especially if it is not clear which department is the one concerned. The press office or library of the relevant department may also be able to put you on to the right official to speak to. Also ministers sometimes announce their intention to bring out a commencement order by way of an answer to a Parliamentary question.

3.58 It is worth mentioning in conclusion, because conceivably it could happen again, that there was one recent instance of a commencement order not being published as an SI. Due to a drafting error in its commencement section, the Competition and Service (Utilities) Act 1992 could not be brought into force by SI — the Department of Trade and Industry had to issue its own commencement orders. These were published by HMSO and attention was drawn to them in the *Daily Lists*; most libraries would have filed them with the SIs at the end of the numerical sequence for the year.

Worked example

Which provisions of the Road Traffic Act 1991 are in force?

1. *IS IT IN FORCE?*

3.59 *Is it in Force?* appears annually around June each year, covering statutes passed up to the end of the previous year. The 1992 edition will cover this Act and any commencement orders made up to the end of 1991. The Acts for each year are

Figure 3.13   HMSO Daily List

List no. 3, Wednesday 6th January 1993

United Nations

Teaching about human rights. – [6], 34p.: ill.: 28 cm. – UN publication sales no.E.91.I.38. – 92 1 100459 4 *£6.25*

Treaty series: treaties and international agreements registered or filed and recorded with the Secretariat of the United Nations.ISSN 03798267. – Irregular

   Vol. 1263. 1982. I. Nos. 20754-20766 II. No. 901. – xiv, 497p.: 24 cm. – In several languages. – 0 11 910320 6 *£15.25*

   Vol. 1314. 1983. I. Nos. 21887-21898. – xvi, 381p.: 24 cm. – In several languages. – 0 11 910319 2 *£15.25*

   Vol. 1330. 1983. I. Nos. 22312-22325. – x, 349p.: 24 cm. – In several languages. – 0 11 910321 4 *£15.25*

United Nations. Economic Commission for Europe

Annual review of the chemical industry 1990. – x, 238p.: chiefly tables: 30 cm. – ISSN 2554291. – UN publication sales no. E.92.II.E.21: ECE/CHEM/84. – 92 1 116546 6 *£27.00*

United Nations Environment Programme. Industry and Environment Programme Activity Centre

Technical report.

   11 From regulations to industry compliance: building institutional capabilities. – 62p.: 30 cm. – UN publication sales no. E92.III.D.11. – 0 11 910318 4 *£9.25*

United Nations Industrial Development Organization

Industry and development.ISSN 02507935. – irregular

   No. 30. – iv, 125p.: tables: UN publication sales no. E.92.III.E.1: ID/SER.M/30. – 92 1 106272 1 *£18.25*

STATUTORY INSTRUMENTS

Issued on 5th January 1993

Commencement orders (bringing into operation an act or part of an act). 1992

3241   **The Local Government Act 1992 (Commencement No. 2) Order 1992.** – 2p.: 30 cm. – *Enabling power:*Local Government Act 1992, s. 30 (3). Bringing into operation various provisions of this Act on 04.01.93. - for art. 2; 14.02.93. - for art. 3; 14.03.93 - for art. 4. – *Issued:*05.01.93. – *Made:*14.12.92. – *Effect:*None. – *Territorial extent & classification:*E/W/S. General. – 0 11 025138 5 *£0.65*

3253   **The Environmental Protection Act 1990 (C. 101)(Commencement No. 12) Order 1992.** – 4p.: 30 cm. – *Enabling power:*Environmental Protection Act 1990, s. 164 (3). Bringing into operation various provisions of this Act on 01.02.93. - for art. 2, & 01.02.93. for art. 3. – *Issued:*05.01.93. – *Made:*18.12.92. – *Laid:*01.01.93. – *Effect:*None. – *Territorial extent & classification:*E/W/S. General. – 0 11 025142 3 *£1.05*

Other statutory instruments. 1992

3023   **The Council Tax (Prescribed Class of Dwellings) (Wales) Regulations 1992.** – 4p.: 30 cm. – *Enabling power:*Local Government Finance Act 1992, ss. 12, 113 (2), 116 (1). – *Issued:*05.01.93. – *Made:*02.12.92. – *Laid:*03.12.92. – *Coming into force:*07.12.92. – *Effect:*None. – *Territorial extent & classification:*E/W. General. – 0 11 025133 4 *£1.05*

3199   **The Child Abduction and Custody (Parties to Conventions) (Amendment) (No. 5) Order 1992.** – 4p.: 30 cm. – *Enabling power:*Child Abduction and Custody Act 1985, s. 2. – *Issued:*05.01.93. – *Made:*17.12.93. – *Coming into force:*01.02.93. – *Effect:*S.I. 1986/1159 amended & S.I. 1992/2662 revoked. – *Territorial extent & classification:*GB. General. – 0 11 025141 5 *£1.05*

3209   **The Social Security (Austria) Order 1992.** – 8p.: 30 cm. – *Enabling power:*Social Security Administration Act 1992, s. 179. – *Issued:*05.01.93. – *Made:*17.12.92. – *Coming into force:*31.12.92. – *Effect:*1992 c. 4, 5; S.I. 1981/605 amended. – *Territorial extent & classification:*E/W/S. General. – 0 11 025134 2 *£1.90*

3210   **The Social Security (Finland) Order 1992.** – 4p.: 30 cm. – *Enabling power:*Social Security Administration Act 1992, s. 179. – *Issued:*05.01.93. – *Made:*17.12.92. – *Coming into force:*31.12.92. – *Effect:*1992 c. 4, 5; S.I. 1984/125 amended. – *Territorial extent & classification:*E/W/S. General. – 0 11 025128 8 *£1.05*

3211   **The Social Security (Iceland) Order 1992.** – 4p.: 30 cm. – *Enabling power:*Social Security Administration Act 1992, s. 179. – *Issued:*05.01.93. – *Made:*17.12.92. – *Coming into force:*31.12.92. – *Effect:*1992 c. 4, 5; S.I. 1985/1202 amended. – *Territorial extent & classification:*E/W/S. General. – 0 11 025129 6 *£1.05*

3212   **The Social Security (Norway) Order 1992.** – 4p.: 30 cm. – *Enabling power:*Social Security Administration Act 1992, s. 179. – *Issued:*05.01.93. – *Made:*17.12.92. – *Coming into force:*31.12.92. – *Effect:*1992 c. 4, 5; S.I. 1991/767 amended. – *Territorial extent & classification:*E/W/S. General. – 0 11 025131 8 *£1.05*

arranged alphabetically by title. The entry shows that the Act received Royal Assent on 25 July 1991, and the commencement provisions are in s 84(1). One commencement order under that section, SI 1991/2054, has been made to date. The effects of that order are then listed section by section.

A further check in the *Is it in Force?* section of the looseleaf noter-up volume to *Halsbury's Statutes* will give any further developments since the annual volume, but as it is not updated as frequently as *Current Law*, it may be as quick to skip it and go straight to *Current Law*.

2. *CURRENT LAW:* DATES OF COMMENCEMENT TABLE IN MONTHLY DIGESTS

3.60   The table of commencement cumulates in every monthly issue throughout the calendar year. The title page of the latest monthly issue will give a page number for the table. In June 1992 the latest monthly part was the May issue. Two further commencement orders, SIs 1992/199 and 1992/421, are given together with their effects. For one of them a reference — [1992] 4 C.L. 319 — is also given. This is merely the entry in the main monthly digest — paragraph 319 in the April issue — where the SI was noted, but it does not add any further information.

3. *HMSO DAILY LISTS*

3.61   In June 1992 that would give the full picture of which provisions were in force. It would have been noted, however, that the main substantive provisions of the Act, which make major changes in the law relating to road traffic offences, were not yet in force. The supplement to *Wilkinson's Road Traffic Offences* notes that these provisions were expected to have been brought into force in December 1991. Comment elsewhere might also alert you to the possiblity that an announcement was imminent. To check whether any commencement orders have been made since the May issue of *Current Law*, the most systematic method is to look through every *Daily List* since then. SIs are listed at the end of each list, and if there are any commencement orders issued on that day they appear before other SIs. A flick through will reveal that a fourth commencement order was issued on 9 June. The *Daily List* merely tells you that the order, SI 1992/1286, brings into operation 'various provisions of this act on 01.07.92'. Inspection of the SI itself shows that it does indeed cover most of the main sections of the Act (see figure 3.14). An explanatory note on the back of the SI also helpfully summarises the effect of the previous three orders (see figure 3.15).

ALTERNATIVE ROUTES

3.62   The above three-stage search is certainly to be recommended as being safe, accurate and reasonably quick if you have only manual sources to hand. If, however, you have access to it, Lawtel is excellent for this type of search, because all the above three stages will be covered in one fell swoop. Find the entry for the Act in the statutes section; they are arranged alphabetically by title.

3.63   Lexis would be one way, but there would still be a currency gap for the very latest orders. In this instance where we are looking at the whole of a large Act, it would make sense to search for the commencement orders in the SI file rather than looking for the Act, where we would have to read the annotations of every section. Choose ENGGEN library, SI file:

TITLE(ROAD TRAFFIC ACT 1991 w/5 COMMENCEMENT)

Figure 3.14

STATUTORY INSTRUMENTS

1992 No. 1286 (C.42)

ROAD TRAFFIC

The Road Traffic Act 1991 (Commencement No 4 and Transitional Provisions) Order 1992

Made - - - -   *3rd June 1992*

The Secretary of State for Transport, in exercise of the powers conferred by section 84 of the Road Traffic Act 1991(**a**) and of all other enabling powers, hereby makes the following order:

PART 1

GENERAL

Citation and Interpretation

1.—(1) This Order may be cited as the Road Traffic Act 1991 (Commencement No. 4 and Transitional Provisions) Order 1992.

(2) In this Order–
"the 1981 Act" means the Public Passenger Vehicles Act 1981(**b**);
"the RTA 1988" means the Road Traffic Act 1988(**c**); and
"the RTOA 1988" means the Road Traffic Offenders Act 1988(**d**);
"the 1991 Act" means the Road Traffic Act 1991.

Commencement of Provisions

2. The provisions of the 1991 Act specified in the first column of the Schedule to this Order which relate to the matters specified in the second column of that Schedule shall come into force on 1st July 1992 subject to the limitations (if any) specified in the third column of that Schedule.

SCHEDULE   Article 2

PROVISIONS BROUGHT INTO FORCE ON 1ST JULY 1992

1 *Provisions of the Act*	2 *Subject matter of the provision*	3 *Limitation of the provision*
Section 1	Offences of dangerous driving.	
Section 2	Careless and inconsiderate driving.	
Section 3	Causing death by careless driving when under the influence of drink or drugs.	
Section 4	Driving under the influence of drink or drugs.	
Section 5	Disapplication of sections 1 to 3 of the Road Traffic Act 1988 for authorised motoring offences.	
Section 6	Causing danger to road users.	

Figure 3.15

EXPLANATORY NOTE

(This note is not part of the Order)

The Order brings into force on 1st July 1992 certain provisions of the Road Traffic Act 1991 including those relating to:–

(1) the replacement of reckless driving offences with the new dangerous driving offences;

(2) the extension of the scope of careless and inconsiderate driving to any mechanically propelled vehicle and to public places other than roads;

(3) the creation of a new offence of causing death by careless driving when under the influence of drink or drugs;

(4) the disapplication of sections 1 to 3 of the Road Traffic Act 1988 for authorised motoring events.

(5) the creation of a new offence of causing danger to road users in England and Wales;

NOTE AS TO EARLIER COMMENCEMENT ORDERS

(This note is not part of the Order)

Provision	Date of commencement	S.I. No
s.35	1st October 1991	1991/2054
	2nd March 1992	1992/199
s.43 (except in respect of Scotland)	1st October 1991	1991/2054
s.44	1st October 1991	1991/2054
s.47	1st April 1992	1992/421
s.48 (partially)	1st October 1991	1991/2054
	1st April 1992	1992/199
	1st April 1992	1992/421
ss.50 to 63	1st October 1991	1991/2054
ss. 64(2)	1st October 1991	1991/2054
ss. 73 to 78	1st October 1991	1991/2054
ss. 80	1st October 1991	1991/2054
ss. 81 (partially)	1st October 1991	1991/2054
ss. 82	1st October 1991	1991/2054
ss. 83 (partially)	1st October 1991	1991/2054
	1st April 1992	1992/421
Schedule 3 (except in respect of Scotland)	1st October 1991	1991/2054
Schedule 4 (partially)	1st October 1991	1991/2054
Schedule 5	1st October 1991	1991/2054
Schedule 7 (partially)	1st October 1991	1991/2054
Schedule 8 (partially)	1st October 1991	1991/2054
	1st April 1992	1992/421

3.64   Of printed sources, the Commencement of Statutes section in the second looseleaf current service volume (the noter-up volume) to *Halsbury's Laws*, would in this instance have been a good alternative choice, and in fact picks up in one search all three commencement orders we found in the first two stages above. The table is simply arranged in one alphabetical sequence. In June 1992 it was updated to May 1992 and covered all statutes not in force, or not wholly in force at 1 November 1991. However, if the Act we were looking at had in fact been brought fully into force before 1 November 1991, it would not have given us the answer and we would still have had to look at *Is it in Force?*. Likewise if the latest looseleaf service issue had not been as up to date as the latest monthly part of *Current Law* (which, depending on the efficiency of your library, can happen through delay in filing rather than delay in issue), then we still would have had to look at the latter as well.

Statutory instruments

3.65   Statutory instruments (SIs) form the main category of subsidiary legislation. (For the few categories of subsidiary legislation not issued as SIs see paras 3.135-3.142.) The nomenclature of the different kinds of SI varies: rules, regulations and orders are the most common. The generic term, statutory instruments, and the rules for their promulgation and publication, derive from the Statutory Instruments Act 1946. Before that they were called Statutory Rules and Orders (SR & O), but they are a relatively modern phenomenon. Separately published annual volumes began only in 1890. There were some Statutory Rules earlier in the nineteenth century but their publication was entirely ad hoc. The original Rules of the Supreme Court were published as a schedule to the Judicature Act 1875.

3.66   Over 2000 SIs are made each year. They may be purely local in application, for example authorising a bypass or trunk road. They may be very short, for example substituting one sum for another in a social security regulation. They may be in force for only a brief period; for example 14 successive orders concerning fishing of shellfish were made and revoked during 1991. On the other hand, they may enact substantial bodies of law; the Insolvency Rules 1986, for example, run to 784 pages. Because of their number, they can be harder to track down than statutes. Apart from finding them by title or subject, there is the problem, as with statutes, of checking whether they have been amended or revoked (note the terminology, SIs are revoked, statutes are repealed). But with a rare exception (see para 3.99) there is not the problem of finding commencement dates: they almost always bear this on their face. A particular problem with SIs not encountered with the statutes is that not all of them are necessarily printed (see para 3.68).

Anatomy and citation

3.67   See figure 3.16. The year and the number of the SI in that year are given at the head. This is the main means of identification and citation: in this case SI 1992/1751. There may also be another number in brackets after it preceded by an abbreviation, eg (C 42) — see figure 3.14. These are subseries of particular classes of SIs. However (with the exception of the NI — Northern Ireland — series) they are not necessary for identification or citation purposes and are mainly a convenience for those who do not wish to subscribe to all SIs from HMSO. The main subseries are: C (Commencement Orders), L (Legal: fees or procedure in the courts), and S (Scotland). The NI series is rather different. These are SIs made under the Northern Ireland Act 1974 at Westmimster, but equate in substance to primary legislation and would have been passed by the legislature in Northern Ireland if there still was one; though UK SIs, they are Northern Ireland statutes, and are generally cited not by the SI number but by the NI number, which is thus in effect a chapter number. *Subsidiary* legislation for Northern Ireland, the equivalent of SIs in England, Wales and Scotland, is issued entirely separately by HMSO in Belfast as Northern Ireland Statutory Rules and Orders. Beneath the number will be found the date it was made, the date on which it was laid before Parliament (if it was required to be laid — see para 3.167), and the commencement date. The numbered parts of the SI are not called sections. If the SI is an 'Order' they are called paragraphs, but if the SI is in the nature of 'Regulations' or 'Rules', then they are referred to simply as regulation 1, 2 etc or rule 1, 2 etc, the usual abbreviations being reg. and r. respectively. As with the statutes, schedules giving various detailed provisions, often in tabular form, may be included after the main body of the text. At the end an explanatory note is usually printed (see figure 3.17). It is not part of the instrument, but helpfully summarises the purpose of the SI, earlier SIs amended or revoked and any EC legislation that it implements.

Sources for the text of SIs

3.68   The choice is not as wide as for statutes, but there are a number of alternatives. The official text is published by HMSO, who treat them in three categories: SIs of general application (which are all printed), SIs of only local application but of sufficient importance to be printed, and SIs of local application that are not printed. The first two categories are issued individually on a daily basis, and equate to the Queen's Printer copies of Acts. The SIs in the last category, which may for example merely provide for a one-way street in Nether Wallop, will in practice usually only be needed in connection with some local authority matter and the authority concerned should have access to the text. Otherwise the Statutory Publications Office (see QR 3.9) can provide copies. They hold a complete set, with one or two gaps, from 1922. There is no complete set before 1922. There are also sets from 1922 to 1960 at the Public Record Office and from 1922 to 1980 at the British Library's Official Publications Library. Unpublished SIs are assigned a number in the main series, so gaps in the numerical sequence of published SIs on the shelf will appear. They are included in the monthly and annual lists of SIs prepared by HMSO, but not in the *Table of Government Orders* (on which see para 3.92 below). For further information on local SIs, see R.J.B. Morris 'Finding and Using Local Statutory Instruments' (1990) 11 *Statute Law Review* 28-47.

3.69   HMSO also publishes SIs in bound volume form (several pale blue volumes per year). These only appear some time in arrears. It is important to realise that the bound volumes do not include all the SIs that were originally published in individual form. Instruments revoked or spent within the year in which they were made and instruments classified as local (the second category above) are excluded. For this reason some libraries may keep and bind the loose SIs as well as or instead of taking HMSO's bound volumes. Otherwise individual SIs that were published but are not in the bound volumes can be obtained from HMSO. As explained below (paras 3.138-3.139) there are some kinds of subsidiary legislation that are not issued as SIs, for example certain types of Order in Council. Although they are not issued individually with the SIs and do not have an SI number, some are nonethless included in the bound

Figure 3.16

STATUTORY INSTRUMENTS

1992 No. 1751

GAS

The Gas (Modification of Therm Limits) Order 1992

Made - - - -	*14th July 1992*
Laid before Parliament	*16th July 1992*
Coming into force	*6th August 1992*

The Secretary of State, in exercise of the powers conferred on him (as respects article 2) by section 8A(1) of the Gas Act 1986**(a)** and after consultation with the Director General of Gas Supply and (as respects article 3) by section 2(2) of the European Communities Act 1972**(b)** being the Minister designated**(c)** for the purposes of that section in relation to units of measurement to be used for economic, health, safety or administrative purposes, and of all other powers enabling him in that behalf, hereby makes the following Order:—

Citation and commencement

1. This Order may be cited as the Gas (Modification of Therm Limits) Order 1992 and shall come into force on 6th August 1992.

Amendment of the Gas Act 1986

2. In the following provisions of the Gas Act 1986:—

    (a) section 4(2)(d) (duty of Secretary of State etc. to enable persons to compete effectively);

    (b) section 8(5)(b) (limitation of authorisation to premises a minimum distance from the main of a public gas supplier unless a specified rate of supply is exceeded of gas); and

    (c) section 14(4)(b) (provision for special agreements with customers for a minimum supply of gas),

for " 25,000 therms " there shall be substituted " 2,500 therms ".

Consequential amendment of the Gas (Metrication) Regulations 1992

3. For paragraph (5)(a) of regulation 3 of the Gas (Metrication) Regulations 1992**(d)** there shall be substituted the following paragraph:—

    "(5) With effect from 1st January 2000—

        (a) in the following provisions—

            (i) section 7(12) (definition of "relevant main "), and

            (ii) section 10(5) (limitation on public gas supplier's duty to supply),

    for " 25,000 therms " there shall be substituted " 732,000 kilowatt hours "; and

        (aa) in the following provisions—

            (i) section 4(2)(d) (duty of Secretary of State etc. to enable persons to compete effectively),

---

(a) 1986 c. 44; section 8A(1) was inserted by section 37 of the Competition and Service Utilities Act 1992 (c. 43), and section 4 was amended by paragraph 5 of Schedule 1 to that Act.
(b) 1972 c. 68.
(c) S.I. 1976/897.
(d) S.I. 1992/450.

Figure 3.17

(ii) section 8(5)(b) (limitation of authorisation to premises a minimum distance from the main of a public gas supplier unless a specified rate of supply is exceeded of gas), and

(iii) section 14(4)(b) (provision for special agreements with customers for a minimum supply of gas),

for " 2,500 therms " there shall be substituted " 73,200 kilowatt hours ";".

Tim Eggar
Minister of State,
14th July 1992   Department of Trade and Industry

EXPLANATORY NOTE

(This note is not part of the Order)

This Order varies the limit of 25,000 therms specified in sections 4(2)(d), 8(5)(b) and 14(4)(b) of the Gas Act 1986. The Order provides for the limits in those provisions to be reduced from 25,000 therms to 2,500 therms.

The Order also makes consequential changes to regulation 3(5) of the Gas (Metrication) Regulations 1992, S.I. 1992/450 in relation to sections 4(2)(d), 8(5)(b) and 14(4)(b). These regulations implement Council Directive No. 80/181/EEC (O.J. 1980, No. L39, 15.2.80, p.40), as amended by Council Directive No. 89/617/EEC (O.J. 1989, No. L357, 7.12.89, p.28), which establishes the units of measurement to be used throughout the Community. Regulation 3(5) specifies that the conversion of 25,000 therms into kilowatt hours becomes effective from 1st January 2000. The Order provides for the references to " 25,000 therms " and " 732,000 kilowatt hours " in regulation 3(5) to be replaced with a reference to " 2,500 therms " and " 73,200 kilowatt hours " in respect of those provisions mentioned above which are amended by this Order.

volumes of SIs issued by HMSO, appearing at the end of the last volume for the year. From 1961 the SIs in the bound volumes are arranged in numerical order. Before that date they are grouped by broad subject headings, with an index by number. As already mentioned the annual volumes go back to 1890, but there is an official consolidation, *Statutory Rules and Orders and Statutory Instruments Revised*, which includes the text of all instruments in force as amended at 31 December 1948 (there were two earlier consolidations, in 1889 and 1904). It is arranged by subject in 25 volumes.

3.70 A companion to *Halsbury's Statutes* is *Halsbury's Statutory Instruments*. It is arranged and is used in a similar way, but unlike *Halsbury's Statutes* which offers the complete text of the statutes, not every SI is reproduced in full text, though the publishers, Butterworths, offer a telephone ordering service to subscribers for the text of any SI not included. However, all SIs are listed and if not given in full text are summarised. It has 22 bound volumes arranged by topic, with instruments appearing chronologically within topics. The text where it is given is printed as amended and there are full annotations including case references, etc. Each topic is preceded by a general introductory note giving an overview. Individual bound volumes are reissued from time to time. There are two looseleaf volumes, a service volume containing updating apparatus and an 'Additional Texts' volume containing the full text of selected instruments issued since the relevant bound volume was last reissued. The looseleaf service volume includes a cumulative annual supplement which notes up the text of the bound volumes and summarises SIs since issued. After the annual supplement are the monthly surveys. Summaries of SIs are given in purely numerical order as they are published. A key arranged by topics of the main work and an index provide access to these. In addition to the two looseleaf volumes, there is a softback index volume reissued annually.

3.71 Rather than using either of the above, subject-based looseleaf encyclopedias are often the easiest way to lay hands on a SI. Likewise, for court rules, which are published as SIs, the practitioner will invariably go the *Supreme Court Practice*, the *County Court Practice*, or *Stone's Justices' Manual* as the case may be, rather than to the originals, unless they are extremely recent.

3.72 There are two electronic sources as well. Lexis has the full text of all SIs in force, and Justis offer the full text from 1987 on-line and on CD-ROM.

Finding SIs by title

3.73 The main consolidated index to SIs arranged alphabetically by title is in the index volume to *Halsbury's Statutory Instruments*. The SI number is given together with the topic (but not page number) in the main work where it appears. Note, however, that the alphabetical list does not include SIs in the 'Additional Texts' service volume.

3.74 *Halsbury's Laws* also has an alphabetical table in volume 53(2), but while extensive it will only of course include those SIs referred to in that work. The table does not give the SI number directly — it is necessary to look in the volume and paragraph referred to. From 1990 *Current Law* has included an alphabetical list for the year. The list for the current year is cumulated in each monthly digest, so it is only necessary to look in the latest one. The list for the whole year then appears in the yearbook. Before 1990 the yearbooks had a list arranged by the main digest headings, but within the headings alphabetically by title (the yearbooks from 1990 continue that practice in addition to the strictly alphabetical list, though confusingly both lists are headed 'Alphabetical Table of Statutory Instruments'). Some looseleaf encyclopedias have tables of the SIs included arranged alphabetically by title. There is of course no difficulty in searching Lexis and Justis by title. On Lexis choose the SI file from the ENGGEN library and search on the title segment, eg TITLE(DAIRY W/4 QUOTAS W/4 1991), which will retrieve the Dairy Produce Quotas Regulations 1991. On the Justis CD-ROM it is straightforward to pick distinctive words from the title as search terms. UKOP (United Kingdom Official Publications) on CD-ROM would be another way. It includes titles and other catalogue information (but not full text) of SIs since 1980 (including unpublished local ones). If none of these sources are available a subject search would be necessary.

Finding SIs by subject

3.75   *Halsbury's Statutory Instruments* is usually the best starting place, or alternatively a subject-based looseleaf encyclopedia. In *Halsbury's* look first in the consolidated index in the annual softback index volume. A reference to the volume number and page (together with the SI number) will be given. As with the *Statutes* there is always the possibility that an SI originally in the service volume has been incorporated into a bound volume of the main work reissued since the index was prepared. Having checked the main index, the most recent material can be found by looking in the index to the monthly surveys in the looseleaf service volume. An alternative, or a cross-check on the index, is to use the *key* to the monthly surveys rather than the index. Look under the same topic and volume number that you found in the main work, and any new SIs in that topic will be listed.

3.76   The *Index to Government Orders* published by HMSO in two volumes, like its equivalent for statutes, is not the place to look for the latest developments as it is usually at least two years out of date, but the way the information is set can be helpful. It is arranged by broad topics with sub-headings. Enabling powers are given at the top of each heading and the titles and numbers of the SIs made under them are listed. Where the enabling power has not been exercised a statement to that effect is given. See figure 3.18.

3.77   *Current Law* yearbooks and monthly digests summarise the provisions of SIs under the relevant heading. As explained more fully in chapter 4 on case law (para 4.75) there are cumulative indexes to the yearbooks, but if you are concerned only with recent developments it is probably easier to browse through the main body of the work.

3.78   Justis's SI database on CD-ROM is a very effective way of searching by subject. Although the database only goes back to 1987 in full text (back to 1980 for catalogue information only), where there is an important SI of earlier date there may be a later amending SI within the scope of the database that will lead you to the principal SI. Lawtel, though not giving the full text, indexes SIs and being updated daily is very current. Lexis is another possibility and operates in the same way as described for statutes. As there is not such a wide range of finding aids as there is for statutes, Lexis can be of greater utility in this context. Remember that, as with the statutes, each paragraph of an SI is retrieved as a separate item.

Figure 3.18 Index to Government Orders

INDEX TO GOVERNMENT ORDERS 1989

PHILIPPINES, REPUBLIC OF

Arbitration (foreign awards) *See* ARBITRATION, **1** (3)
Carriage by air *See* CIVIL AVIATION, **4**
Crimes in aircraft *See* CIVIL AVIATION, **7**
Designs *See* PATENTS, **3**
Merchant Shipping Acts *See* MERCHANT SHIPPING, **6** (2) (*a*) (4) (*a*) (i) (8) (9) (*a*), **11** (2)
Oil in navigable waters *See* MARINE POLLUTION, **5**
Patents *See* PATENTS, **3**
Trade marks *See* PATENTS, **3**

PHOTOGRAPHS

Persons detained in custody *See* REMAND CENTRES; **1** (3), **2** (3); YOUNG OFFENDER INSTITUTIONS, E. & W., **3**; YOUNG OFFENDERS' INSTITUTIONS, S., **3**
Prisoners *See* PRISONS, **2** (2), **3** (1)

PHYSIOTHERAPISTS *See* PROFESSIONS SUPPLEMENTARY TO MEDICINE

PICNIC SITES (BYELAWS) *See* LOCAL GOVERNMENT, E. & W., **8** (4)

PICTURE GALLERIES *See* MUSEUMS AND GALLERIES

PIECEWORK WAGES *See* WAGES COUNCILS

PIERS *See* HARBOURS, DOCKS, PIERS AND FERRIES

PILOTAGE

1. *Preliminary*
2. *Functions of competent harbour authorities*

3. *Winding up of existing pilotage organisation*
   Miscellaneous

1 Preliminary

(1) SUBORDINATE LEGISLATION

Under *Pilotage Act 1987* (*c. 21*) O. and regs. by Secy. of State to be by S.I. and (except O. made under ss. 1 or 33) subject to annulment on resolution of either House .. .. s. 30

(2) COMMENCEMENT OF ACTS

Power
1987   Secy. of State may by O. appt. (except for s. 27) day for coming into force of Act of 1987 Diff. days may be apptd. for diff. provns. or diff. ppses.
Pilotage Act 1987 (c. 21) s. 33 (2)

Exercise
1987/1306   Pilotage Act 1987 (Commct. No. 1) O. [apptg. 1.9.1987 for ss. 24, 25, 28, 30, 31, 32 (1)–(3), 33, sch. 1 paras. 1–4]
1987/2138   Pilotage Act 1987 (Commct. No. 2) O. [apptg. 1.2.1988 for rep. of s. 15(1)(i) of the 1983 Act]
1988/1137   Pilotage Act 1987 (Commct. No. 3) O. [apptg. 1.8.1988 for s. 29, and 1.10.1988 for remaining provns. except the repeal of provns. of the 1983 Act relating to the Pilotage Commn. pending its abolition]

(3) ADAPTATION OF ENACTMENTS, ETC.

Power
1987   Secy. of State may by regs. make transtl., consequential or incidental provn. (incl. rep. or amdt. of local enactment) .. .. *Ibid.* s. 32 (1)
Exercise
Power not yet exercised
Power
1987   Secy. of State may by O. make provn. as to operation of byelaws and other matters relating to pilots' benefit fund established under Act of 1983 .. .. *Ibid.* sch. 1 para. 4
Exercise
1987/2139   Pilotage Act 1987 (Pilots' National Pension Fund) O.

1359

Finding SIs by enabling Act

3.79 If you have a statute in front of you which contains a power enabling regulations or orders to be made, you may want to know whether the power has been exercised. When the power is delegated to a minister, it is usually stated expressly that the power is to be exercised by statutory instrument. However, some powers are not delegated to a minister but to the Crown itself. Such powers are usually expressed in the statute to be made by Order in Council — eg 'Her Majesty may by Order in Council direct that the provisions of this Act apply to any relevant overseas territory' — with no mention of statutory instruments. Do not be alarmed — such Orders in Council, because of the provisions of s 1(1) of the Statutory Instruments Act 1946, are in fact SIs like any other (though there can be Orders in Council which are *not* made under a statute and so are not SIs — see paras 3.138-3.139 below).

3.80 The best manual approach is to use *Halsbury's Statutes* and the *Current Law* statute citators. If you find the text of the particular section of the statute in *Halsbury's* as described in para 3.28, any SIs will be given in a note 'Orders made under this section' or 'Regulations made under this section'. As always, then check the annual cumulative supplement under the volume number and page of the main work, and then the equivalent section in the looseleaf noter-up. Depending on the date of the last noter-up, even more recent developments can be checked in the statute citator in the latest monthly digest of *Current Law*. Find the relevant statute by year and chapter number, then the SI number will be given against the section number if any have been made, eg

40. Education Reform Act 1988
   s.3, order 91/2567
   s.17, regs. 92/155-157

This shows that an order, SI no 2567 of 1991, was made under section 3 of the Education Reform Act 1988 (chapter 40), and that three sets of regulations, SIs 155, 156 and 157 of 1992, were made under section 17. If *Current Law* statute citators are used in preference to *Halsbury's* for checking SIs made before the current year, you will need to work back through the softback 1989- citator and the 1972-88 and 1947-71 bound volumes (note that in the 1947-71 volume the numbers given are not SI numbers as in the example above, but paragraph numbers to the *Current Law* yearbooks). If the Act in question is of long standing, working backwards, pausing to look at the SIs retrieved as you go, will ensure you do not have to bother with SIs listed in the earlier citators that in fact have since been revoked.

3.81 Another tip when doing research in this area is to bear in mind the table of SIs given at the front of each volume of *Halsbury's Statutes*, which consolidates in one list all the SIs mentioned in the annotations to each Act. It saves having to plough through the annotations to every section if you want all the SIs made under a particular Act or are uncertain which sections of the Act contain enabling provisions.

3.82 *Halsbury's Statutory Instruments* can also be used to find SIs by enabling Act, though not quite with the same particularity. In the looseleaf service volume is a table of statutes arranged chronologically. All this gives is a reference to the relevant topic. The introductory notes, which will refer to the relevant enabling legislation, for that topic can then be perused.

3.83 An alternative approach, but not offering such good currency, is to use the *Index to Government Orders*. On green pages at the front is a table of statutes which gives references to particular subject headings in the body of the work where the particular enabling powers and details of the orders made under them are set out. One noteworthy feature is that it includes those orders (few in number) that are not made in the form of SIs.

3.84 The above deals with manual sources but electronic sources if available may be as good or better. Lawtel in particular, because of its currency is an excellent method; the primary arrangement of SIs is under enabling Act. SIs on CD-ROM, bearing in mind its currency, also works and Lexis is another option, especially if speed is essential. Access the STATS file in the ENGGEN library and confine the search to the authority segment. For example to find all SIs made under the Merchant Shipping Act 1983 type: authority(merchant shipping w/6 1983).

Worked example

What SIs have been made under s 56 of the Merchant Shipping Act 1988? (The section enables orders to be made extending the Act, which relates to the registration of merchant ships, to overseas territories.)

1. *HALSBURY'S STATUTES*: MAIN WORK

3.85 Find the statute in the main work by looking in the alphabetical list in the 'Tables of Statutes and General Index' volume. The reference given is **39(S)**, Shipping 1. The **(S)** indicates a looseleaf current statutes service volume rather than a bound volume. In the binder including volume 39 material at page 1 of the Shipping title will be found the Act. Among the notes at the end of s 56 (on page 73) is the paragraph 'Orders in Council made under this section'. In this instance it merely says that at the time of going to press there were no orders.

2. *HALSBURY'S STATUTES*: ANNUAL CUMULATIVE SUPPLEMENT

3.86 Find the part covering volume 39, Shipping and Navigation. After the annotations to the bound volume 39 of the main work is a separate sequence headed **39(S)** covering annotations to the current statutes service material for that volume. The following entry will be found

Vol 39(S)   **SHIPPING AND NAVIGATION**

PAGE

Section 56

73n *Orders in Council under this section.* The Merchant Shipping Act 1988 (Cayman Islands) Order 1988, SI 1988/1841; the Merchant Shipping Act 1988 (Isle of Man) Order 1989, SI 1989/679; the Merchant Shipping Act 1988 (Bermuda) Order 1989, SI 1989/1334.

3. *HALSBURY'S STATUTES*: LOOSELEAF NOTER-UP SERVICE VOLUME

3.87   Again go to the material covering volume 39 and after the main sequence find the annotations to vol 39(S). A further SI, the Merchant Shipping Act 1988 (Bermuda) Order 1991, SI 1991/1703, is noted.

4. *CURRENT LAW*: STATUTE CITATORS IN LATEST MONTHLY DIGEST

3.88   The noter-up to *Halsbury's Statutes* was up to date to November 1991. Therefore it would be necessary at this date to go first to the December 1991 monthly digest. In the statute citator section in fact only the 1991 SI we already have found is listed. In the latest monthly part for 1992 a further SI is found. Only the number, 1991/2875, is given. That SI will be found on the shelf to be The Merchant Shipping Act 1988 (Guernsey) Order 1991, and, incidentally, it will be noted that though made in December 1991 — hence the 1991 number — it was not laid before Parliament (when it would have been published) until January 1992 — hence it was listed in the 1992 citator rather than the 1991 citator.

Finding amendments and revocations

3.89   *Halsbury's Statutory Instruments*, provided you follow the following three stages, should provide a check on any amendments or revocations up to the last monthly update. First the text or summary in the main work will give full details of amendments and revocations up to the date of its last reissue. Next check the annual cumulative supplement in the looseleaf service volume and lastly the *key* to the monthly surveys, both of which are arranged by the topic and volume number of the main work.

3.90   If the text has been found in a looseleaf encyclopedia, or on Lexis, it should be in its amended state as at the time of the last update. The *Current Law* legislation citator 1972-1988 contains a table of SIs affected from *1947* to 1988 (it is the statute citator part of the volume that starts in 1972). This table is updated to the pre-current year in the 1989- legislation citator (see figure 3.19). These are probably easier to use than *Halsbury's Statutory Instruments*. A table of SIs affected during the year is also included in the *Current Law* yearbooks, but there is no equivalent table in the monthly digests. However, there are entries for all SIs under the appropriate subject heading in the monthly digests and these usually indicate if the SI amends or revokes an earlier one. As amending SIs usually (though not invariably) have the same title as the principal SI, the alphabetical table of SIs in the latest monthly digest is another way of checking. For example the Diseases of Animals (Approved Disinfectants) Order is amended by an SI entitled the Diseases of Animals (Approved Disinfectants) (Amendment) Order.

3.91   If you have access to it, the Justis SI CD-ROM database is an excellent way of finding revocations and amendments, and if it can be supplemented by an on-line search it provides better currency than any of the printed sources. Use the number of the SI you wish to check as a search term.

3.92   The equivalent of the *Chronological Table of Statutes* for SIs is the *Table of Government Orders* (see figure 3.20) and its virtues and vices are similar. It will not help with amendments or revocations made in the last year or two but gives a

Figure 3.19   Current Law: *legislation citator*

STATUTORY INSTRUMENTS AFFECTED 1989–91

1989—cont.

485	revoked 90/199
491	revoked 91/1715
504	revoked 89/1964
507	amended 90/113
524	amended 91/585
526	revoked 90/384
527	revoked 91/466
528	revoked 91/467
529	revoked 89/619
533	amended 90/2486; 91/1476
534	amended 89/1034
535	revoked 91/871
536	revoked 91/870
537	revoked 89/1295
550	amended 90/1477
578	amended 89/1446
581	amended 89/2216; 90/2625; 91/1476
583	revoked 90/1205
590	revoked 90/428
590	amended 89/1430
597	revoked 91/383
600	revoked 89/717
602	revoked 90/2497
616	revoked 90/551
622	revoked 91/987
623	revoked 91/986
632	revoked 90/958
634	revoked 91/951
645	revoked 91/960
655	revoked 90/20
658	revoked 90/6
659	revoked 89/1767
660	revoked 91/5
670	amended 90/881; 90/1562
671	amended 90/1157
672	revoked 89/840
683	revoked 91/351
736	revoked 90/1989
741	revoked 90/691
744	amended 90/955
745	revoked 91/338
746	amended 90/2212
767	amended 89/1107
776	amended 90/1025
808	revoked 90/383
814	amended 90/778
816	amended 89/1303
823	amended 89/1951; 90/823; 90/2398
825	revoked 91/2567
835	amended 91/2136
837	amended 90/2625
847	revoked 91/2630
849	amended 90/1331
869	amended 89/1841; 89/2337; 91/1393; 91/1949; 91/2844
876	amended 90/2486; 91/1476
899	revoked 90/1697
902	revoked 89/1964
904	revoked 90/1281
910	amended 90/2486
945	amended 90/2625; 91/1476
948	amended 90/1905
949	amended 89/1611; 91/1025
950	amended 90/1203; 91/1228
954	amended 89/1136; 90/1109; 91/1278; 91/1537
955	amended 89/1032
980	revoked 90/1503
988	revoked 89/1293

1989—cont.

990	revoked 89/1294
991	revoked 89/1296
1004	revoked 89/2437
1007	revoked 89/1067
1008	revoked 89/1068
1009	revoked 89/1212
1009	amended 89/1069
1010	revoked 89/1070
1011	revoked 89/2510
1018	revoked 90/381
1019	revoked 90/379
1039	revoked 90/1380
1056	revoked 89/2318
1058	amended 89/2260; 90/145; 91/141; 91/1127
1060	amended 89/2363
1069	revoked 89/1212
1095	revoked 90/2623
1100	amended 89/2147; 90/1003; 91/2237
1105	amended 90/1456
1112	revoked 91/1522
1116	revoked 90/2384
1119	revoked 91/2768
1129	amended 91/201
1130	amended 90/1699; 91/1626
1131	revoked 90/1698
1133	amended 90/1346; 91/1495
1134	amended 90/1345; 91/1494
1139	amended 90/1433
1147	amended 89/1384; 91/1837; 91/2790
1156	amended 90/1629
1159	amended 89/1383
1174	revoked 89/1229
1176	revoked 89/1230
1202	amended 90/2487
1234	amended 90/706
1235	amended 90/1546; 91/1767
1236	amended 90/1548; 91/1831
1237	amended 90/1547; 91/1830
1238	amended 89/1262
1242	amended 90/1439
1244	amended 90/1440
1245	revoked 90/1441
1263	amended 90/880
1270	revoked 89/2376
1279	revoked 91/5
1281	revoked 90/20
1283	revoked 90/6
1287	revoked 90/549
1293	amended 89/2415; 90/2153
1295	revoked 89/1692
1297	amended 91/889; 91/1120; 91/1377; 91/1695; 91/2070
1299	amended 90/2552
1319	amended 89/1541; 90/1561; 91/1134; 91/1840; 91/2240
1321	amended 90/1657; 90/834; 90/835; 90/1549; 90/1657; 90/2208; 91/234; 91/503; 91/849; 91/1175; 91/1599; 91/2695; 91/2742
1332	revoked 90/1503
1334	revoked 91/1703
1349	revoked 89/2004
1350	amended 90/2594
1359	amended 90/778
1365	revoked 90/475
1373	revoked 89/2057
1384	amended 91/2790
1400	revoked 90/1696

complete historical conspectus from the earliest times, so can provide details of SIs affected before 1947 (thus outside the scope of *Current Law*) and details of when and how SIs that are no longer in force (so outside the scope of *Halsbury's SIs* or Lexis) were revoked. It is arranged by year and number and specifies whether an instrument has been amended (am.) or revoked (**r.**) or is spent, superseded or expired. Those wholly or partly in force are printed in bold; those not in force are printed in italic. Where there has been an amendment or revocation the authority is given. Note, however, that for pre-1949 instruments that are still wholly or partly in force, only amendments since 1948 are given; any earlier amendments will be shown as annotations to the text of the instrument as it appears in *Statutory Rules and Orders and Statutory Instruments Revised to December 31, 1948*, to which reference is given. Orders in Council before 1894, when the present numbering system began, are listed by date. Those orders not issued as SIs are also listed by date and appear after the numerical sequence for the year. However, local SIs that were not printed are not included; hence there are gaps in the numerical sequence (the gaps provide confirmation, though, that the instrument in question was indeed never printed).

3.93 For very recent developments, as mentioned earlier in connection with commencement orders, Lawtel, current journals, or HMSO's *Daily List* would have to be scanned. This is not scientific, but likely SIs can usually be spotted by title or subject matter. In the case of the *Daily List*, the number (but not the title) of any SI amended or revoked is given in the entry for each SI.

Worked example: finding amendments and revocations

Has the Child Abduction and Custody (Parties to Conventions) Order 1986 (SI 1986/1159) been amended or revoked?

1. *HALSBURY'S STATUTORY INSTRUMENTS*: MAIN WORK

3.94 See figure 3.21. Find the SI in the main work via the alphabetical table in the index volume or the chronological table in the service volume. It is in volume 4, title Children (Part 5). The volume is a 1992 reissue. The text is not given in full but the amendment note gives a long string of amending SIs. It will be noticed, though, that many of these SIs have themselves been subsequently revoked. Reading through the list it will be found that only two are still in force:

(xii) 1991/1461
(xvi) 1991/2870

For both it says 'listed ante'. This just means that you can find their titles by looking at the chronological list of SIs given at the start of Part 5 of the title Children. They are in fact the Child Abduction and Custody (Parties to Conventions) (Amendment) Order 1991 and the Child Abduction and Custody (Parties to Conventions) (Amendment No 4) Order 1991 respectively.

2. *HALSBURY'S STATUTORY INSTRUMENTS*: ANNUAL CUMULATIVE SUPPLEMENT

3.95 This will be found in the looseleaf service volume, and is arranged by the volume numbers of the main work. In this case, however, volume 4 of the main work has been reissued since the last cumulative supplement, so contains nothing further.

Figure 3.20 Table of Government Orders

1972

421 **Intermediate Areas and Derelict Land Clearance Areas O.**
art. 2, 4 sch. r., 1979/837

422 **Housing (Intermediate Areas) O.**

428 *National Insurance (Non-participation—Benefits and Schemes) Amdt. Prov. Regs.* r., 1972/1031

429 *General Medical Council (Registration (Fees) Regs.) O. of C.* r., 1978/1772

430 **Certificates of Arrest and Surrender (Royal Navy) Regs.**

431 *Civil Aviation (Notices) (Amdt.) Regs.* r., 1978/1303

432 *Sugar (Distribution Payments) (No. 3) O.* superseded, 1972/578

433 *Sugar (Distribution Repayments) (Amdt.) (No. 2) O.* superseded, 1972/579

434 *Composite Sugar Products (Distribution Payments—Average Rates) (No. 3) O.* superseded, 1972/580

435 **Agricultural Investment (Variation of Rate of Grant) O.**

436 *Income Tax (Small Maintenance Payments) O.* spent

437 **Commons Registration (Disposal of Disputed Registrations) Regs.**

438 **Smoke Control Areas (Exempted Fireplaces) O.**
sch. am., 1974/762

440 *Approved Expenditure (Housing Act 1969 Part II) O.* superseded, 1980/857

442 *Teachers' Superannuation (Family Benefits) (S.) Amdt. Regs.* r., 1977/1360

444 **Raising of the School Leaving Age O.**

445 *Colonial Air Navigation (Amdt.) O.* r., 1976/421

446 **Merchant Shipping (Confirmation of Legislation) (Queensland) O.**

447 **Merchant Shipping (Tonnage) (Overseas Territories) (Amdt.) O.**

448 *Second United Nations Conference on the Standardisation of Geographical Names (Immunities and Privileges) O.* spent

449 *Trucial States (Temp. Provns.) O.* spent

450 **Civil Aviation Act 1971 (Channel Is.) O.**

451 **Civil Aviation Act 1971 (Is. of Man) O.**
sch. Pt. II para. 10, 14 replaced, 1980/188

452 **Air Navigation (Jersey) O.**

453 *Air Navigation (Guernsey) O.* r., 1981/1805

454 *Air Navigation (Is. of Man) O.* r., 1979/929

455 *Air Navigation (Noise Certification) (Amdt.) O.* r., 1979/930

456 **Merchant Shipping (Light Dues) O.**
sch. 2 am., 1973/964, 1974/868, 1975/2194

457 *Housing (Improvement of Amenities of Residential Areas) (S.) O.* r., 1979/253

460 *Livestock and Livestock Products Industries (Payments for Scientific Research) O.* spent

464 **Transitional Relief for Interest and Royalties paid to Non-Residents (Ext. of Period) O.**

465 **Non-Residents' Transitional Relief from Income Tax on Dividends (Ext. of Period) O.**

466 *Residential Establishments (Payments by Local Authies.) (S.) Amdt. O.* superseded, 1974/169

467 *National Health Service (Appointment of Consultants) (S.) Regs.* spent

468 *Coal Industry (Borrowing Powers) O.* r., Coal Industry Act 1973 (c. 8)

469 *Coal Industry (Accumulated Deficit) O.* r., Coal Industry Act 1973 (c. 8)

470 **Herring (North Sea Fishing) Licensing O.**

471 **Herring (North Sea) Restrictions on Landing O.**

474 *National Health Service (Designation of London Teaching Hospitals) Amdt. (No. 2) O.* r., 1974/32

475 *National Health Service (Designation of London Teaching Hospitals) Amdt. (No. 3) O.* r., 1974/32

478 *Greater London Council (Sewerage Area) O.* spent

Figure 3.21   Halsbury's Statutory Instruments: *index volume and main work*

**CHILD ABDUCTION AND CUSTODY (PARTIES TO CONVENTIONS) ORDER 1986
SI 1986/1159**

NOTES
Authority   This Order in Council was made on 8 July 1986 under the Child Abduction and Custody Act 1985, ss 2, 13, Halsbury's Statutes, 4th edn Vol 6, title Children.
Commencement   1 August 1986.
Amendment   This Order in Council has been amended by: (i) SI 1987/163 (revoked) (ii) SI 1987/1825 (revoked) (revoking SI 1987/163); (iii) SI 1988/588 (revoked) (revoking SI 1987/1825); (iv) SI 1988/1083 (revoked) (revoking SI 1988/588); (v) SI 1988/1839 (revoked) (revoking SI 1988/1083); (vi) SI 1989/479 (revoked) (revoking SI 1988/1839); (vii) SI 1989/843 (revoked) (revoking SI 1989/479); (viii) SI 1989/980 (revoked); (ix) SI 1989/1332 (revoked) (revoking SI 1989/843); (x) SI 1990/1503 (revoked) (revoking SI 1989/980 and 1332); (xi) SI 1990/2289 (revoked) (revoking SI 1990/1503); (xii) SI 1991/995 (revoked); (xiii) SI 1991/1461, listed ante (revoking SI 1990/2289); (xiv) SI 1991/1698 (revoked) (revoking SI 1991/995); (xv) SI 1991/2624 (revoked) (revoking SI 1991/1698); and (xvi) SI 1991/2870 (listed ante) (revoking SI 1991/2624).
General   This Order in Council specifies for the purposes of the Child Abduction and Custody Act 1985, Halsbury's Statutes, 4th edn Vol.6, title Children, the Contracting States to the 1980 Hague Convention on the Civil Aspects of International Child Abduction, and to the 1980 Convention on Recognition and Enforcement of Decisions concerning Custody of Children and on Restoration of Custody of Children, as well as the territories to which those two Conventions extend. The Contracting States to the Hague Convention on the Civil Aspects of International Child Abduction are: the Argentine Republic; Australia; Austria; Belize; Canada (the territories of Ontario, New Brunswick, British Columbia, Manitoba, Nova Scotia, Newfoundland, Prince Edward Island, Quebec, Yukon Territory, Saskatchewan, Alberta and the Northwest Territories); the French Republic; the Federal Republic of Germany; the Hungarian People's Republic; Ireland; Israel; the Grand Duchy of Luxembourg; Mexico; the Kingdom of the Netherlands; New Zealand; Norway; the Portuguese Republic; Spain; Sweden; the Swiss Confederation; the USA; the Socialist Federal Republic of Yugoslavia. The Contracting States to the European Convention on Recognition and Enforcement of Decisions concerning Custody of Children and on Restoration of Custody of Children are: the Republic of Austria; the Kingdom of Belgium; the Republic of Cyprus; the Kingdom of Denmark; the French Republic; the Federal Republic of Germany; the Grand Duchy of Luxembourg; the Kingdom of the Netherlands; Norway; the Portuguese Republic; Spain; Sweden; the Swiss Confederation.

3. *HALSBURY'S STATUTORY INSTRUMENTS*: MONTHLY SURVEY — KEY

3.96 In the looseleaf service volume after the annual supplement will be found the monthly summaries arranged chronologically by SI number. After the summaries is the key, which is arranged like the supplement by volume number of the main work. Turning to volume 4, title Children (Part 5), further amendments and revocations will be found (see figure 3.22). Following these through it will be established that:

1991/2870 [ie (xvi) given above] was revoked by 1992/227

but

1992/227 was then itself revoked by 1992/803

Thus, at the date of the last monthly survey:

1986/1159 was still in force as amended by 1991/1461 and 1992/803.

4. *CURRENT LAW*: LATEST MONTHLY DIGEST

3.97 Find the alphabetical table of SIs in the latest monthly digest. All the amending SIs we have found have had the same title as the main instrument, ie Child Abduction ... etc (Amendment) Order. Looking under this title in the alphabetical list is a way of checking whether *Current Law* has picked up any more recent ones than *Halsbury's Statutory Instruments*. In this case it has not.

5. HMSO *DAILY LISTS*

3.98 Unless you have access to Lawtel, to be completely up to date, look through the list of SIs in every *Daily List* since the last update of *Halsbury's Statutory Instruments* for any SIs with a title Child Abduction ... etc. It is best to work backwards, starting with the most recent list. If you have Lawtel, it should be up to date to within the last day or so. In this case, the exercise, if carried out in June 1992, would have found one further SI, the Child Abduction and Custody (Parties to Conventions) (Amendment) (No 2) Order 1992 (SI 1992/1299), which amends 1986/1159 and revokes SI 1991/1461. The upshot at that date would thus have been that SI 1986/1159 was still in force as amended by SI 1992/803 and SI 1992/1299.

Commencements notified in the *London Gazette*

3.99 As already stated, it is the practice to print the date on which an SI comes into operation at its head, and indeed for SIs that are required to be laid before Parliament this is obligatory under s 4(2)(a) of the Statutory Instruments Act 1946. However, sometimes this is not possible because the operation of the SI is contingent on some future event of uncertain date. The commonest examples are SIs which implement in domestic law provisions of international treaties that are still subject to ratification, of which double taxation agreements probably form the most numerous class. An important recent example outside the field of double taxation was the Civil Jurisdiction and Judgments Act 1982 (Amendment) Order 1990 which extended the Brussels Convention to Spain and Portugal following their entry into the European Communities, but only came into force on the date they ratified the Convention. In such cases

Figure 3.22   Halsbury's Statutory Instruments: *key to monthly summaries in the looseleaf service volume*

AMENDMENTS AND REVOCATIONS

SI		SI		SI		SI	
1958/1991	revoked by	1992/2069		1988/2132	amended by	1992/2069	
1962/1591	revoked by	1992/2069		1988/2132	amended by	1992/2071	
1983/525	revoked by	1992/2069		1991/1395	amended by	1992/2068[1]	
1988/913	revoked by	1992/2071					

[1] In the title Matrimonial Law (Pt 2)

Part 5 GENERAL

INSTRUMENTS

SI

1992/227   Child Abduction and Custody (Parties to Conventions) Order 1992
1992/332   Children and Young Persons (Protection from Tobacco) Act 1991 (Commencement No 2) Order 1992
1992/803   Child Abduction and Custody (Parties to Conventions) (Amendment) Order 1992
1992/1200   Horses (Protective Headgear for Young Riders) Act 1990 (Commencement) Order 1992
1992/1201   Horses (Protective Headgear for Young Riders) Regulations 1992
1992/1299   Child Abduction and Custody (Parties to Conventions) (Amendment) (No 2) Order 1992
1992/1431   Child Support Act 1991 (Commencement No 1) Order 1992
1992/1714   Child Abduction and Custody (Parties to Conventions) (Amendment) (No 3) Order 1992
1992/1938   Child Support Act 1991 (Commencement No 2) Order 1992
1992/2644   Child Support Act 1991 (Commencement No 3 and Transitional Provisions) Order 1992
1992/2662   Child Abduction and Custody (Parties to Conventions) (Amendment) (No 4) Order 1992

AMENDMENTS AND REVOCATIONS

SI		SI	SI		SI	
1986/1159	amended by	1992/227	1991/1461	revoked by	1992/1299	
1986/1159	amended by	1992/803	1991/2870	revoked by	1992/227	
1986/1159	amended by	1992/1299	1992/227	revoked by	1992/803	

CIVIL DEFENCE
Vol 4 (1992 Issue)

INSTRUMENTS

None

AMENDMENTS AND REVOCATIONS

None

CIVIL RIGHTS AND LIBERTIES
Vol 4 (1992 Issue)

Part 1 RACE RELATIONS

INSTRUMENTS

SI
1992/619   Race Relations Code of Practice (Non-Rented Housing) Order 1992

AMENDMENTS AND REVOCATIONS

None

(HSIS—Issue **235**)   9

it is the practice to notify their entry into force in the *London, Edinburgh*, and *Belfast Gazettes*. This practice is apparently dictated by the Foreign and Commonwealth Office, without regard for the fact that few law libraries take the *London Gazette* and that it only has quarterly indexes. If you do use the indexes look under 'Foreign and Commonwealth Office'; for issues since the last index look through each one in the 'State Intelligence' section at the front and keep an eye out for the 'Foreign and Commonwealth Office'. But it may be easier just to telephone the Nationality and Treaty Department at the FCO.

EC legislation

Types of EC legislation

3.100   The terms primary and secondary legislation are sometimes applied to EC legislation, but they bear a slightly different meaning from those terms in the context of domestic legislation as described at that start of this chapter. Primary legislation refers to the treaty provisions contained in the treaties that established the three Communities — the European Economic Community (EEC), the European Coal and Steel Community (ECSC) and the European Atomic Energy Community (Euratom) — together with the treaties of accession by subsequent member states, the Single European Act (the treaty that started the 1992 ball rolling), and the various amending treaties. The treaty provisions can have direct effect and are capable of conferring individual rights enforceable in the UK courts without further enactment. Discussion of this form of legislation is deferred to chapter 5 where treaties in general are dealt with. Here we are concerned with secondary legislation, that is the legislation that emanates from the Council and the Commission of the European Communities. There are three main types: Directives, Regulations, and Decisions. The Council and the Commission also issue Recommendations and Opinions, but these are only a form of quasi-legislation and do not have binding force. This classification and terminology, however, while applying to legislation issued under the EEC and Euratom treaties — and so to the bulk of EC legislation — does not apply to legislation under the ECSC treaty; the differences will be mentioned below.

3.101   A Directive, without more, does not have direct effect but requires all the member states to enact domestic legislation within a certain period of time. A Directive may, however, acquire direct effect and confer rights on individuals if it is not implemented in domestic law within the specified period or if the purported implementing legislation is contrary to the Directive. Most Directives are implemented in the UK by means of SIs, the enabling power for the making of the SIs being the European Communities Act 1972. Exceptionally, if its importance warrants it, a Directive may be implemented by means of an Act. The Consumer Protection Act 1987, which implemented the Product Liability Directive 85/374, being one of the few examples. The ECSC equivalent of a Directive is a Recommendation, of which there are two kinds: 'general' and 'individual in character' (for some explanation of the difference see A.G. Toth *Oxford Encyclopaedia of European Community Law* vol 1).

3.102   Regulations, on the other hand, are directly applicable in that they do not require national implementing legislation. Indeed it can be contrary to EC law for a member state to enact its own legislation in an area provided for by a Regulation. This can give rise to the misconception that national legislation is of no relevance to

Regulations. In practice many Regulations require additional national provisions in relation to, for example, procedure and enforcement, and such legislation is perfectly permissible as long as it does not impinge on the substantive effect of the Regulation. In 1991 about 50 SIs were issued in connection with the implementation of Directives, whereas about 90 were concerned with Regulations. The ECSC equivalent of a Regulation is a 'general' Decision.

3.103 EEC and Euratom Decisions are akin to Directives — they require national implementing legislation and only have direct effect in the same circumstances as do Directives. But, unlike Directives, they are not of general application and are addressed to particular member states or particular persons or bodies. They are less numerous than either Regulations or Directives — about seven were implemented by SI in the UK in 1991. ECSC Decisions 'individual in character' roughly equate (see *Toth*, cited above, for distinction between individual and general ECSC decisions).

Numbering and citation

3.104 An EC Regulation is illustrated (see figure 3.23). The format is similar for other types of legislation. This is a Regulation emanating from the Council, but it might equally have been issued by the Commission. For simplicity of exposition the framework of numbering is first explained in terms of EEC and Euratom legislation; how ECSC material fits in will be described later (para 3.106). All the Regulations passed in each year are assigned a running number in one sequence and all the Directives and Decisions are assigned a number in another sequence (at any rate they were until the beginning of 1992 — as explained in para 3.105 below the position has been further complicated since then). To provide unique identification, the last two digits of the year are added to the number — after the number for the Regulations sequence and before the number for the Directives and Decisions sequence. For example, a Regulation passed in 1985 might be 534/85 and a Directive from the same year 85/143. Thus it is necessary to remain alert when dealing with those numbers in the annual sequence that could be mistaken for a year, eg Regulation 90/91 or Directive 76/84. Although all legislation has since 1967 emanated from the joint bodies of the three European Communites, in a formal citation it is the practice to add the abbreviation for the relevant Community, and also to specify whether it is Council or Commission legislation, eg:

> Council Directive 76/149/EEC
> Commission Regulation 87/1479/ECSC
> Council Decision 89/176/Euratom

3.105 In addition the date the legislation was made and the subject matter as it appears at the head of the text of the legislation may be given. As discussed below, the official text of legislation is published in the *Official Journal of the European Communities* L series. It is helpful and good practice to add the *Official Journal* (OJ) citation. For the latter it is usually sufficient to specify the issue number and year, or the particular date on which the issue was published (which is not the same as the date the legislation was made), but for completeness both may be given. Thus a completely comprehensive citation would be:

> Council Directive 82/471/EEC of June 30, 1982, Concerning Certain Products Used in Animal Nutrition (OJ No L213, 21.7.1982, p 8)

Figure 3.23

No L 205/2   Official Journal of the European Communities   22. 7. 92

COUNCIL REGULATION (EEC) No 2015/92
of 20 July 1992
amending Regulation (EEC) No 1432/92 prohibiting trade between the European Economic Community and the Republics of Serbia and Montenegro

THE COUNCIL OF THE EUROPEAN COMMUNITIES,

Whereas under Regulation (EEC) No 1432/92 (¹), trade between the European Economic Community and the Republics of Serbia and Montenegro is prohibited;

Whereas the United Nations Security Council adopted on 18 June 1992 Resolution 760 (1992), which allows under certain conditions the export to the Republics of Serbia and Montenegro of commodities and products for essential humanitarian need;

Whereas it is necessary to amend Regulation (EEC) No 1432/92 in order to allow under certain conditions the exports to the Republics of Serbia and Montenegro of commodities and products for essential humanitarian need;

Having regard to the Treaty establishing the European Economic Community, and in particular Article 113 thereof,

Having regard to the proposal from the Commission,

HAS ADOPTED THIS REGULATION:

Article 1

Regulation (EEC) No 1432/92 is hereby amended as follows:

1. Paragraph (a) of Article 2 shall be replaced by the following:

'(a) the export to the Republics of Serbia and Montenegro of commodities and products intended for strictly medical purposes and foodstuffs notified to the Committee established pursuant to Resolution 724 (1992) of the United Nations Security Council, as well as the export to these Republics of commodities and products for essential humanitarian need, which has been approved by the said Committee under the simplified and accelerated "no objection" procedure;'.

2. Article 3 shall be replaced by the following:

'Article 3

Exports to the Republics of Serbia and Montenegro of commodities and products for strictly medical purposes or for essential humanitarian need as well as foodstuffs shall be subject to a prior export authorization to be issued by the competent authorities of the Member States.'

Article 2

This Regulation shall enter into force on the day of its publication in the *Official Journal of the European Communities.*

It shall apply with effect from 19 June 1992.

This Regulation shall be binding in its entirety and directly applicable in all Member States.

Done at Brussels, 20 July 1992.

*For the Council
The President*
D. HURD

(¹) OJ No L 151, 3. 6. 1992, p. 4.

But for most practical purposes all that is needed is:

   Dir. 82/471 (OJ 1982 L213)

Indeed, if all you had was 82/471, it would still be traceable. However, a complication in the numbering introduced in 1992 means that in future that will no longer be the case. Whereas hitherto there have been just the two sequence of numbers — Regulations on the one hand, Directives and Decisions on the other — Directives and Decisions are now to have their own respective sequences: 92/22 could be refer to either of two documents unless 'Dir.' or 'Dec.' is specified.

3.106   Grasping the basic numbering structure for EEC and Euratom material outlined above is sufficient for most everyday purposes, but if you do encounter ECSC material it is as well to be on guard for its peculiarities. The table in the Quick Reference Guide (QR3.16) sets out the position. ECSC Recommendations and Decisions appear in the year/number sequence if they are 'individual'; if they are 'general' they appear in the number/year sequence. Speaking very loosely, the majority of ECSC Recommendations are in the year/number sequence together with EEC/Euratom Directives and Decisions; and the majority of ECSC Decisions are in the number/year sequence together with the EEC/Euratom Regulations.

3.107   The formal titles of EC legislation, in comparison to the titles of UK statutes and SIs, are usually the least used and least useful part of their citation on account of their length and unmemorability (eg Commission Directive on the Approximation of the Laws of the Member States Relating to Motor-Vehicle Headlamps which Function as Main-Beam and/or Dipped-Beam Headlamps and to Incandescent Electric Filament Lamps for such Headlamps). However, some legislation may be referred to colloquially or for convenience by some short title especially if it is well known or important, eg the Second Banking Directive, but the practice of doing so, without at some point giving a Directive number or OJ reference is to be deprecated (the Second Banking Directive, by the way, is Directive 89/646 OJ 1989 L386).

Sources for the text of EC legislation

Official Journal of the European Communities

3.108   Since 1967 the *Official Journal* has been published in two series, Legislation (L series) and Information and Notices (C series, for 'Communications'), and it is the former which is the official vehicle for promulgating Commmunity legislation. It follows from the continental model of issuing legislation in the form of official gazettes. Both series are published in the nine official languages. Most UK libraries will naturally only have the English version; one or two of the larger libraries, for example the Institute of Advanced Legal Studies, may also have the French version, but all versions are equally authentic. They are extremely voluminous, being published almost daily, so some libraries may keep back copies on microfiche.

3.109   When using them, two features can cause some puzzlement. First, some items are listed in bold with an asterisk, others are not; the latter are supposedly of lesser importance or short duration, usually on agricultural matters. Secondly, it is arranged in two sequences described as 'Acts whose publication is obligatory' and 'Acts whose publication is not obligatory'. Although the distinction does have legal significance, for practical purposes all you need to know is that the first sequence is number/year material (ie, for the EEC and Euratom, Regulations) and the second sequence is year/number material (ie, for the EEC and Euratom, Directives and Decisions).

3.110 As the *Official Journal* was not published in English before the accession of the United Kingdom, a special edition in several volumes was published in 1972 which translated all Community legislation then in force into English. A further special edition, containing material not included in the first, was published in 1974.

Encyclopedia of European Community Law: Series C

3.111 This ten volume looseleaf work published by Sweet & Maxwell contains the text of much (though by no means all) EC legislation in force. Series C contains the secondary legislation, which we are concerned with here. Series A contains the relevant UK sources and Series B the treaties. It is arranged by broad topic, with material filed chronologically within topics. The first volume contains comprehensive tables of treaty provisions, secondary legislation by number and cases. The last volume contains an index. As with some other very large looseleaf works, a hazard to be aware of is that the tables and index are not replaced in their entirety with every service issue but only consolidated from time to time. Separate supplementary tables and index will be found after the main sequence.

Butterworths European Law Service

3.112 This has recently commenced publication and reprints legislation in particular areas in pamphlet form which are kept in boxed sets. It promises to be a useful service (provided the booklets do not get lost), but at the time of writing it is too early to give a full evaluation.

Other printed sources

3.113 Another large looseleaf work, published by Graham and Trotman and the Office for Official Publications of the European Communities, is devoted specifically to EC legislation generated in pursuance of '1992', *Completing the Internal Market of the European Community: 1992 Legislation*; it reproduces in facsimile the relevant parts of the *Official Journal*. Commercial publishers in other member states have produced works similar to Sweet & Maxwell's *Encyclopedia* in their own languages.

Electronic sources

3.114 The volume and complexity of EC legislation make electronic sources come into their own. The Community's own database Celex, however, is not for the fainthearted. More user friendly is the version provided on the Justis system available on CD-ROM and on-line or the version provided on Lexis. Both of these rely on information supplied by Celex, which suffers from time lags. This and other aspects of its production may improve with the recent transfer of responsibility for Celex from the Administrative Directorate to the Office for Official Publications of the European Communities. In the meantime Justis have taken to keying in themselves from the *Official Journal* some material not yet available in full text on Celex. Not a source of the text but mentioned here with electronic sources because it is a very useful finding tool is SCAD on CD-ROM. This is the official EC bibliographical database and covers all legislation (except material listed in the contents of the OJ in light type) and many other materials. It is marketed in the UK by two different vendors with different search software, Context Ltd (the Justis host) and ILI, as EC Infodisk.

Finding known EC legislation

3.115 If you have an OJ reference, there should be no difficulty. If you only have a Directive or Regulation number, the best place to look is Butterworths' *European Communities Legislation: Current Status*. Another possibility are the tables at the front of the first volume of *Encyclopedia of European Community Law: C series*. For recent legislation remember to check the supplementary table. The monthly indexes to the *Official Journal*, which cumulate annually, also contain numerical lists. Celex, *Halsbury's Laws*, and, if you know how to convert the number into a Celex document number, the *Directory of Community Legislation in Force* are other possibilities. The main point to bear in mind when using any of these tables is the order in which the different categories of legislation are listed. The Quick Reference Guide sets this out (QR3.18).

3.116 If all you have is a title, such as Fourth Directive on Company Law, you will probably need to use Celex or SCAD which will allow text searching or to adopt a subject approach, as there is no general alphabetical table by title. But there is one useful short-cut that sometimes works if the legislation is of some importance, namely the legislation index in the *Legal Journals Index*. Where there have been journal articles on particular EC legislation, they will be entered in the legislation index in the form 'Commission Directive 90/388 on Competition in the Markets for Telecommunications Services' or 'Council Regulation 4064/89 on the Control of Concentration between Undertakings'. As this format means they file by number within each of the four permutations of heading — Council/Commission Directive/Regulation — you will need to browse through them to see if there is one with the title you are looking for (see para 2.25 on how the filing order works). It will obviously help if you know roughly when the legislation was made, as it is then that there is the greatest likelihood of there being an article.

Finding EC legislation by subject

3.117 The subject indexes to *European Communities Legislation: Current Status* and to the *Encyclopedia of European Community Law* are the main manual sources. But extremely useful for giving a quick snapshot of the main legislation in any particular area is the paperback, *Butterworths Guide to the European Communities*. Of large scale works there is also the T.M.C. Asser Institute's *Guide to EEC Legislation*, but it does not cover ECSC and Euratom legislation and is not as up to date. Electronic sources, though, are often the ideal solution. It is also worth remembering that many looseleaf subject encyclopedias now include EC materials; for example, about a third of Miller's *Product Liability and Safety Encyclopaedia* is devoted to EC materials. Vaughan's looseleaf textbook or *Halsbury's Laws* are also other possibilities. The EC produces its own indexes in the form of monthly indexes to the *Official Journal* and the *Directory of Community Legislation in Force and Other Acts of the Community Institutions*, which cumulates twice a year. But these are not particularly easy to use.

3.118 If it is specifically Single Market legislation that is required, it may be quicker to use the various sources devoted to this. Baker and McKenzie's *Single Market Reporter* is a very handy printed source, though it does not contain the actual text. Probably most useful of all is the Department of Trade and Industry database Spearhead which is available on-line via Profile or Justis. It is also available on the Justis Single Market CD-ROM with other sources. Euroscope produced by Coopers and Lybrand is another on-line source.

Finding amendments and repeals

3.119   This process has been greatly simplified by Butterworths' *EC Legislation: Current Status*, which lists all EC legislation chronologically by number and indicates whether it is still in force or whether it is has been amended (see figure 3.24). It is reissued every year in two bound volumes and has interim softback supplements. Its publishers, Butterworths, also offer a telephone enquiry service. The *Encyclopedia of European Community Law* could also help. It either reprints the legislation incorporating amendments or indicates amending legislation in the annotations. Electronic sources are another possibility; the Quick Reference Guide suggests some search strategies (QR3.22). The *Directory of Community Legislation in Force* is the official publication that is supposed to provide this information and indeed it is reasonably up to date being issued twice a year. The main difficulty is finding the legislation concerned in volume 1, which is arranged by broad subject. Volume 2 contains an alphabetical index, and also a numerical list, but the latter is in form of Celex document numbers, which are Directive and Regulation numbers rejigged into a form that is unintelligible to the uninitiated.

Finding UK implementation of EC legislation

3.120   Butterworths *EC Legislation: Current Status* has recently acquired a stable companion, the *EC Legislation Implementator* (see figure 3.25), which like its sister publication has greatly simplified a previously fraught area. It only covers implementation in the strict sense of implementation of Directives, not UK legislation relating to Regulations. It includes as an appendix the Commission's annual report on implementation in all member states, which for each Directive simply says 'Yes' or 'No' against each member state, not giving the actual references to any legislation, and indicates if 'No' whether proceedings have been initiated. Like other Butterworths European services, there is a telephone enquiry service, which updates the twice yearly hard copy. For Single Market legislation, Spearhead is the best source, especially as, if the legislation has not been implemented, the government contact name given may be able to advise on when implementation is likely. Lexis or the Justis CD-ROM databases of SIs would be another approach, as the Regulation or Directive will be cited in the text of the implementating SI. The number of the Regulation or Directive would be the best search term. Celex, on the record for each Directive, has a field for national implementation, and the information is also given separately in sector 7, but is woefully incomplete — though it may be a starting point for finding implementing legislation in other member states.

Local and Personal Acts

3.121   A separate Parliamentary procedure is available to enact legislation that affects only a particular locality, person or body. A distinctive feature of this procedure is that rather than being initiated by an MP, as is public legislation, the Bill is promoted by the person or body interested. The resulting Acts are known collectively as Local and Personal Acts. That is not to say there cannot be Public

Figure 3.24   EC Legislation: Current Status

86/146

86/127 [Dec (EEC,ECSC)]
(OJ L86 31.3.86 p221)

Internal Agreement on the measures and procedures required for implementation of the Third ACP-EEC Convention

86/129 [Cm Dec (EEC)]
(OJ L101 17.4.86 p32)

amending 75/271

86/130 [Cm Dec (EEC)]
(OJ L101 17.4.86 p37)

laying down performance monitoring methods and methods for assessing cattle's genetic value for purebred breeding animals of the bovine species

86/131 [Cm Dec (EEC)]
(OJ L101 17.4.86 p40)

amending 83/471

86/132 [Cm Dec (EEC)]
(OJ L101 17.4.86 p41)

amending 83/355

ssd in part 88/165

86/133 *[Cm Dec (ECSC)]*
(OJ L101 17.4.86 p42)

derogating from 1/64; amending 85/496

ssd 86/532

86/134 *[Cm Dec (ECSC)]*
(OJ L101 17.4.86 p43)

derogating from 1/64

spent

86/136 *[Cl Dec (EEC)]*
(OJ L106 23.4.86 p34)

authorising the extension, for the period from 2.5.86 to 2.11.86, of the sea fisheries agreement between Spain and Angola

spent

86/137 *[Cl Dir (EEC)]*
(OJ L106 23.4.86 p35)

authorising certain member states to defer further the application of 77/780

spent

86/138 [Cl Dec (EEC)]
(OJ L109 26.4.86 p23)

concerning a demonstration project with a view to introducing a Community system of information on accidents involving consumer products

1   am 90/534
2   r 90/534
3   r 90/534
4   r 90/534
AnI   am 90/534
AnII   r 90/534

86/139 *[Cm Dec (EEC)]*
(OJ L108 25.4.86 p58)

concerning certain protective measures relating to African swine fever in the Netherlands

rpld 86/368

1   *am 86/150, 86/302*
2   *am 86/150, 86/302*
3   *am 86/150, 86/302*
An   *am 86/302*

86/140 *[Cm Dec (EEC)]*
(OJ L108 25.4.86 p59)

amending 85/331

ssd 87/444

86/141 [Cm Dec (EEC)]
(OJ L112 29.4.86 p32)

authorising certain member states to provide derogations from 77/93

86/142 *[Cm Dec (EEC)]*
(OJ L112 29.4.86 p34)

on STM licences for milk and milk products from 3 to 7 March 1986

spent

86/145 *[Cm Dec (EEC)]*
(OJ L112 29.4.86 p37)

amending 85/632

rpld 86/448

86/146 *[Cm Dec (EEC)]*
(OJ L112 29.4.86 p39)

amending 83/421

ssd 86/486

Figure 3.25   EC Legislation Implementator

Butterworths EC Legislation Implementator

Directive Number	Title/OJ Reference	Target Date	UK Legislation
82/368	Council Directive (EEC) 82/368 amending 76/768 on the approximation of the laws of the Member States relating to cosmetic products OJ L167 15.6.82 p1	1.1.83	SI 1984/1260 The Cosmetic Products (Safety) Regulations 1984 SI 1985/2045 The Cosmetic Products (Safety) (Amendment) Regulations 1985 (implement 84/415 which amends 82/368)
82/434	Commission Directive (EEC) 82/434 on the approximation of the laws of the Member States relating to methods of analysis necessary for checking the composition of cosmetic products OJ L185 30.6.82 p1	31.12.83	SI 1983/1477 The Cosmetic Products (Amendment) Regulations 1983 SI 1984/1260 The Cosmetic Products (Safety) Regulations 1984 SI 1989/2233 The Cosmetic Products (Safety) Regulations 1989 SI 1991/447 The Cosmetic Products (Safety) (Amendment) Regulations 1991 (implement 90/207 which amends 82/434)
82/471	Council Directive (EEC) 82/471 concerning certain products used in animal nutrition OJ L213 21.7.82 p8	30.8.82	SI 1984/51 The Feeding Stuffs (Amendment) Regulations 1984 SI 1986/177 The Feeding Stuffs Regulations 1986 (implement 82/471 as amended by 84/443,85/509) SI 1986/1735 The Feeding Stuffs (No.2) Regulations 1986 (implement 82/471 as amended by 84/443, 85/509) SI 1988/396 The Feeding Stuffs Regulations 1988 (implement 82/471 as amended by 86/530) SI 1989/2014 The Feeding Stuffs (Amendment) Regulations 1989 (implement 88/485 which amends 82/471) SI 1991/1475 The Feeding Stuffs (Amendment) Regulations 1991 (implement insofar as they relate to medicinal products 89/520, 90/110 which amend 82/471) SI 1991/2840 The Feeding Stuffs Regulations 1991 (implement 82/471 as amended by 85/509, 3768/85, 86/530, 88/485, 89/520, 90/439)

General Acts that are of only local or limited application; for example the British Railways Board (Finance) Act 1991 and the Severn Bridge Act 1992 are both Public General Acts. The difference lies in the procedure by which they are enacted.

3.122 Local and Personal Acts were very numerous in the nineteenth century; there were many more than the Public General Acts. They were used particularly in relation to boroughs, railway and canal companies, and the enclosure of common land. On the personal side, they were one important method of obtaining a divorce before it became available in the secular courts in 1857, and they were the only way of obtaining naturalisation before 1844. Their numbers have since declined and the modern Local Acts have usually been employed in connection with the powers and constitutions of bodies such as local authorities, statutory companies and universities, and to enable works to be carried out for railways, light rapid transit systems, harbours and marinas. In future their number will decline considerably further as new procedures have been introduced by the Transport and Works Act 1992 to authorise such works to be carried out without additional legislation. On the personal side, these Acts are now extremely rare. They have been used to enable the marriage of persons within the prohibited degrees of affinity, eg stepmother and stepson, but with the passing of the Marriage (Prohibited Degrees of Relationship) Act 1986 these will become even fewer.

3.123 The current position, then, is that there are three separately numbered series of Acts of Parliament: Public General, Local, and Personal, though the latter two are bound together and share a common title page. Local and Personal Acts are sometimes referred to collectively as Private Acts because they both start life as Private Bills (not to be confused with Private *Members'* Bills — Public Bills introduced by backbenchers rather than ministers) and both are enacted by a similar Private Bill procedure. But there is a great risk of confusion here because until 1948 those Acts that are now called Personal were in fact called Private; the equivalent of the current three series were thus Public General, Local, and Private. Broadly speaking this triumvirate goes back to 1798, though it is only since 1870 that the Acts printed in these three series conform to the modern classification. Before 1798 (and since 1539), there were only two series, Public and Private, but many of the so-called Public Acts were in fact passed via the equivalent of the Private Bill procedure and would today be classified as Local or Personal Acts: they merely included a clause deeming them to be Public Acts in order to meet the requirements then in effect as to judicial notice. The classification and printing of Acts in the nineteenth century before 1870, and throughout the eighteenth century, is extremely fraught. If help is ever needed reference should be made to the introduction to the Law Commission's *Chronological Table of Local Legislation* (discussed further below at para 3.130), Maurice F. Bond *Guide to the Records of Parliament* (HMSO, 1971) pp 97-101, and Sheila Lambert *Bills and Acts: Legislative Procedure in Eighteenth Century England* (Cambridge University Press, 1971).

Anatomy and citation

3.124 Their appearance and citation are much the same as Public General Acts. The main difference is that instead of the chapter number being given in arabic numerals, Local Acts have the chapter number in lower case roman numerals and Personal Acts have the chapter number in *italic* arabic numerals. Confusion can sometimes arise with nineteenth century Local Acts because well over a hundred were issued each year and the abbreviation 'c.' for chapter can be mistaken for the roman numeral 'c'. Thus it is safer in this context to use the abbreviation 'ch.' for chapter.

Sources for the text of Local and Personal Acts

3.125   Only the largest law libraries, such as the Law Society, the Inns of Court, and the British Library Official Publications Library have major sets of Local and Personal Acts, and indeed it is only since 1922 that every single Act has been officially printed. Before then some were only privately printed. In the early period all that may exist is the printed Bill rather than the Act itself. The modern Local and Personal Acts are issued by HMSO individually as Queen's Printer's copies in the same way as Public General Acts, but there are no official annual bound volumes — tables, indexes and a title page are supplied for libraries to bind their own sets from the loose Acts.

3.126   There are at present virtually no other sources. Interestingly, *Current Law Statutes Annotated* have now decided to include Local and Personal Acts. This only started in 1991, but if continued it will mean that Local and Personal Acts will be much more widely available than hitherto. Otherwise *Halsbury's Statutes* includes most of those relating to London. Volume 26 is devoted to the title London, but some are placed in other titles; for example the Port of London Acts are in the title Ports and Harbours in volume 34. Lexis also includes Acts relating to London and also the Lloyds Acts. *Statutes in Force* includes about half a dozen of general interest and the very occasional item may be reprinted in looseleaf encyclopedias — the Lloyds Acts, for instance, are reproduced in the *Encyclopedia of Insurance Law*.

Finding by title

3.127   There used to be no alphabetical lists purely by title for Local and Personal Acts, except for those in each annual volume. However, the House of Lords Private Bill Office in 1991 completed the preparation of an *Alphabetical Index to the Local and Personal Acts 1850-1988*. This is not published but copies of the typescript (amounting to some nine bound volumes) have been deposited in various libraries, including the Law Society, the Inns of Court, the Supreme Court Library, and the Law Commission. Its usefulness is greatly enhanced by the provision of cross-references from keywords such as the names of places and persons where they are not the first word of the title. Outside its dates of coverage and if a year or approximate year is not known, there is still no means of tracing a Local or Personal Act purely by its title - a search by subject matter is necessary.

Finding by subject

3.128   Because of its keyword cross-references the above typescript *Alphabetical Index* will probably now be the first place to look in those libraries that have it. However, the main published tool is the *Index to Local and Personal Acts* (HMSO) which covers 1801 to 1947. A *Supplementary Index* was published in 1967 which covers 1948 to 1966. There is no consolidated index thereafter, only the indexes in each annual volume. The *Index* is arranged by a dozen or so broad categories, such as Railways, Canals, Local Government. Within each category there is an alphabetical listing, the entry element usually being the name of the place, person or company. The only other modern tool if you happen to be looking for Acts connected with the enclosure of common land — a very numerous class of Local Act — is W.E. Tate

A Domesday of English Enclosure Acts and Awards (University of Reading Library, 1978) which is arranged by county but has a full place name index.

3.129   There are some older indexes. Thomas Vardon's *Index to the Local and Personal and Private Acts 1798-1839* published in 1840 is superseded by the HMSO *Index* except for the three years at the start of its coverage, but George Bramwell's *Analytical Table of the Private Statutes*, published in two volumes, 1813-1835, goes back to 1727. It is also worth remembering, as mentioned above, that many Acts before 1798 which appear to be merely local were technically Public Acts. *Statutes at Large* prints the titles of such Acts and includes them in its index, but does not include the full text. *Statutes of the Realm* does include the text and indexes them, but that set only covers up to 1714.

Finding amendments and repeals

3.130   For the early period and for any very recent changes this is problematic, but the bulk of amendments and repeals can now be traced through two sources. The first is the *Chronological Table of Local Legislation* prepared by the Law Commission. It is not published as such, but the typescript has been deposited in most of the libraries having significant collections of local legislation. This table was prepared by examining all local legislation passed from 1925 to 1973 and noting the effect of this legislation on all local legislation passed since 1798. Thus it does *not* include any amendments or repeals made by legislation passed before 1925. It is arranged by chapter number. Before 1925 only legislation that has been affected is included; from 1925 to 1973 all legislation is listed whether affected or not. One of the quirks of Local Acts is that they are quite frequently amended by SI. Such effects are also noted if the SI was a published one — no effects of unpublished local SIs are included.

3.131   From 1974 (hence the cut-off date of 1973 for the Law Commission's project) amendments and repeals to Local Acts are listed in the main *Chronological Table of the Statutes* (the two black volumes published by HMSO). There are tables of those Local and Personal Acts, of whatever date, that have been affected since 1974 and all Local and Personal Acts passed since 1974, whether affected or not, at the end of volume two, after the main sequence of Public General Acts (see figure 3.26).

3.132   These two sources thus give a complete picture for the period 1925 to within the last two years or so. A further check can also be made in the tables volumes of the HMSO annual bound sets of Public General Acts. An annual bound set may have been published since the last edition of the *Chronological Table of Statutes*. If so, this may take you forward another year. Among the tables is one of 'Legislation affected'. This lists those Public General and Local and Personal Acts that have been amended or repealed by any Act or SI passed in that year; they are listed chronologically by chapter number, Local and Personal Acts in each year coming after Public General Acts.

3.133   If one is checking on the status of a Local Act passed before 1925, another place to look is the *Index to Local and Personal Acts 1801-1947*. Although primarily a subject index, it does indicate repeals or partial repeals. All legislation from 1900 was checked for any effects on earlier legislation, and so for that period it is exhaustive. In addition some repeals made before 1900 are noted, but these are not

Figure 3.26   Chronological Table of the Statutes

```
            CHRONOLOGICAL TABLE OF THE STATUTES          1757

1885 (48 & 49 Vict.).
   c. i     ..  Local Govt., Board's Provisional Orders Confirmation
               Milford O. r. (saving)—Dyfed, 1987 (c. xxiv), s. 78 (2).
   c. viii  ..  Local Govt. Board's Provisional Orders Confirmation (Poor Law) (No. 6).
               Burton-upon-Trent Union O. r.—Staffordshire, 1983 (c. xviii), s. 78,
               sch. 5 pt. II.
   c. xi    ..  Local Govt. Board's Provisional Orders Confirmation (No. 2).
               Leek Order r.—Staffordshire, 1983 (c. xviii), s. 78, sch. 5 pt. II.
               Cambridge Order r.—Cambridge City Council, 1985 (c. xl), s. 15, sch. 2
               pt. II.
   c. xiii  ..  Runcorn Gas. r. (except ss. 24, 27, sch.) (Cheshire) (saving)—(Cheshire
               C.C., 1980 (c. xiii), s. 112, sch. 3.
   c. xviii .  East Surrey Water.
               ss. 8, 20–23 r.—S.I. 1978/1482.
   c. xix   ..  Blackburn Water. r. (except ss. 6–8)—County of Lancs., 1984 (c. xxi),
               s. 146 (2) (b), sch. 8 pt. I.
   c. xx    ..  Rickmansworth and Uxbridge Valley Water.
               s. 3 r. in pt.—S.I. 1982/1579.
   c. xxviii    East Surrey Water.
               s. 2 r. in pt.—S.I. 1989/2101 (L).
               5, 26, 55 r.—S.I. 1989/2101 (L).
   c. xxxv .    Fulwood Local Board.—r., County of Lancs., 1984 (c. xxi), s. 146 (2) (b),
               sch. 8 pt. I.
   c. lv    ..  Gas Orders Confirmation (No. 1).
               Middlewich Order (except ss. 22–24) r.—Cheshire C. C., 1980 (c. xiii),
               s. 112, sch. 3.
   c. lxiv  ..  Gas and Water Orders Confirmation (No. 2).
               Great Grimsby Gas Order r.—Humberside, 1982 (c. iii), s. 102 (2), sch. 8
               pt. II.
   c. lxvi  ..  Tramways Orders Confirmation (No. 1).
               Bradford and Shelf, and Shipley Orders r.—West Yorks., 1980 (c. xiv),
               s. 95, sch. 5.
   c. lxxxviii  London and Northwestern Railway
               s. 21 r. in pt.—British Railways, 1987 (c. xxix), ss. 11 (5) 47, sch. 2 pt. I.
   c. xci   ..  Hartlepool Headland Protection and Improvement.—r. (except ss. 13, 14)
               County of Cleveland, 1987 (c. ix), s. 43 (1), sch. 2 pts. I, II.
   c. xciii     Great Eastern Railway (Gen. Powers).
               s. 39 r.—Brit. Rlys (Liverpool Street Station), 1983 (c. iv), s. 26, sch. 3.
   c. cv    ..  Local Government Board's Provisional Order Confirmation (Municipal
               Corporation).
               Seaford O. r.—East Sussex, 1981 (c. xxv), s. 108, sch. 6.
   c. cvi   ..  Local Government Board's Provisional Orders Confirmation (No. 3).
               Widnes O. r.—Cheshire C. C., 1980 (c. xiii), s. 112, sch. 3.
               Leek O. (2) r.—Staffordshire, 1983 (c. xviii), s. 78, sch. 5 pt. II.
               Burnley O. r.—County of Lancs., 1984 (c. xxi), s. 146 (2) (b), sch. 8
               pt. I.
               Haverfordwest O. r. (with saving)—Dyfed, 1987 (c. xxiv), s. 78 (2), sch. 2,
               sch. 3 pt. II.
   c. cvii  .   Local Govt. Board's Provisional Orders Conf. (No. 7).
               Bournemouth O. r.—Bournemouth Borough Council, 1985 (c. 5), s. 71,
               sch. 4 pt. II.
               Ystradyfadwy and Pontypridd O. r. (Mid. Glamorgan)—Mid Glamorgan
               C.C., 1987 (c. vii), s. 56, sch. 2 pt. II.
   c. cviii     Local Government Board's Provisional Orders Confirmation (Poor Law)
               (No. 9).
               Hopton and Coton, &c. O. r.—Staffordshire, 1983 (c. xviii), s. 78, sch. 5
               pt. II.
   c. cx    ..  District of St. John Cowley. r. (saving)—S.L.(Reps.), 1977 (c. 18), ss. 1
               (1), 2, sch. 1 pt. XII.
   c. cxvii     Bootle-cum-Linacre (Fictitious Bonds).—r., County of Merseyside, 1980
               (c. x), s. 146 (3) (b), sch. 5.
   c. cxx   ..  Northwich Local Board. r. (except ss. 7, 8, 20–22) (Cheshire) (saving)—
               Cheshire C. C., 1980 (c. xiii), s. 112, sch. 3.
   c. cxxii     Southport Improvement. r. (except ss. 17, 126, 127)—County of Merseyside,
               1980 (c. x), s. 146 (3) (b), sch. 5.
   c. cxxiv     Bradford Waterworks and Improvement. r. (except ss. 7, 9, 10, 18) (West
               Yorks.) (saving)—West Yorks., 1980 (c. xiv), s. 95, sch. 5.
```

the result of systematic research and cannot be regarded as exhaustive. Thus for changes made before 1900 all one can do is hope for the best, and trust that any amending statutes will come to light when searching by subject.

3.134 For any very recent developments since the last edition of the *Chronological Table of the Statutes* or, if it is more recent than that, the latest annual bound set of Public General Acts, there is no alternative but to look through the individual Acts and hope that a likely looking title is apparent. To be completely thorough one would have to check for Public General Acts and SIs as well. Harbour Revision Orders, for example, which are issued as SIs, quite commonly amend earlier Local Acts. A Lexis search in the STATIS file should pick up any Public General Acts and non-local SIs that have amended a Local Act. Unfortunately where SIs amend Local and Personal Acts they are often local SIs which will not be on Lexis, and so the latest authoritative statement of all amendments and repeals is going to be as at the date of the last annual bound set of Public General Acts. In practice, however, a Local Act is usually only going to be referred to if the relevant body or local authority is the client or one of the parties, and they will almost certainly be aware of any very recent legislation affecting them.

Subsidiary legislation not published as statutory instruments

3.135 The definition of an SI as provided by the Statutory Instruments Act 1946, which introduced the term, is wide and accounts for the vast bulk of subordinate legislation. However, there are some kinds that fall outside its ambit. They are generally encountered only rarely, but when they are they can cause disproportionate difficulty. They are of six kinds: (1) those that can be described as perverse exceptions, (2) orders not made by the Crown or ministers, (3) prerogative or quasi-prerogative orders, (4) special procedure orders, (5) bye-laws and (6) traffic regulation orders.

Perverse exceptions

3.136 From time to time enabling legislation is passed that for no apparent reason provides that the subordinate legislation should be promulgated by some means other than SI. The best known example is the Immigration Rules made under the Immigration Act 1971, which are passed by way of a resolution of both Houses of Parliament and are published as House of Commons papers. Other examples are the Electricity Supply Regulations 1937, only recently revoked, Lord Chancellor's Instruments under the Public Records Act 1958 varying the 30-year rule, and Breath Test Device (Approval) Orders made under the Road Traffic Act 1988. As mentioned above (para 3.58) commencement orders under the Competition and Service (Utilities) Act 1992 were not issued as SIs simply because of a drafting error in the Act. This kind of material may be published in an ad hoc fashion by HMSO or the relevant body or government department, and may be included in looseleaf encyclopedias; the Lord Chancellor's Instruments mentioned above are available for inspection at the Public Record Office. If in doubt it is probably best to try to speak to the relevant official in the government department, who may be identified from the *Civil Service Yearbook*.

Orders not made by the Crown or ministers

3.137 The Statutory Instruments Act 1946 only applies to powers expressed to be delegated to the Crown or ministers of the Crown. Where it is expedient that the power should be exercised by some other official the enabling Act will usually deem the official to be a minister for these purposes in order that the resulting regulations may be published and treated as SIs. The Chief Registrar of Friendly Societies, for example, makes regulations under the Friendly Societies Acts as if he were a minister, and they are published as SIs. Sometimes, however, this is not considered appropriate. Perhaps the most familiar examples to lawyers are the various solicitors' practice rules made by the Council of the Law Society (with the concurrence of the Master of the Rolls) under the Solicitors Act 1974. Other examples are the regulations made by the Securities and Investment Board under the Financial Services Act. Bye-laws and traffic regulation orders could be said to be another illustration of this category, but they are dealt with separately below.

Prerogative or quasi-prerogative orders

3.138 The formal method by which some SIs are passed is by Order in Council — these instruments are signed at meetings of the Privy Council and like the Royal Assent to Acts the procedure is merely symbolic. However, not all Orders in Council are also SIs. Some are made in the exercise of those remaining prerogative powers that have not been usurped by statute rather than under enabling legislation. Constitutional orders affecting dependent states are the most common example. A rare but important example in the domestic sphere is the Civil Service Order in Council 1982 which regulates, or empowers the regulation of, the conditions of employment of civil servants. Strictly speaking these are not 'delegated' legislation.

3.139 As well as by Order in Council, the prerogative powers may be exercised by other species of instrument such as Royal Proclamations and Royal Warrants. In those areas where these were traditionally used but which are now governed by statute, the power delegated — in this case delegated to the Crown, not to a minister — may be expressed to be exercisable by one or other of these kinds of 'prerogative' instrument rather than by Order in Council. Since the Statutory Instruments Act only applies (in the case the Crown) where the statute confers a power expressed to be exercisable by *Order in Council*, these other species of instruments are not SIs. The Coinage Act 1971, for example, provides that new designs and denominations of coins are to be authorised by Proclamation. Thus, to summarise, there are two classes of this kind of 'not-SI' legislation:
(a)   Orders in Council (and other instruments) that are not made under statute at all, but under the prerogative powers of the Crown.
(b)   Instruments made by the Crown (as opposed to ministers) under statute where the statute says that the power is to be exercisable by some form of instrument other than an Order in Council.
These Orders in Council, Proclamations, Royals Warrants, etc that are not SIs are published in the *London Gazette*. As mentioned above (para 3.69), some are also published in the official *bound* volumes of SIs, appearing at the end of the last volume for the year after the SIs themselves and arranged by date (they are not numbered). The volume for 1972 illustrates the mixed bag one finds. It includes Royal Instructions concerning Hong Kong and the Cayman Islands, a Royal Warrant concerning war pensions, and a Proclamation made under the Emergency Powers Act 1920

declaring a state of emergency during the dockers' strike. The Civil Service Order in Council is reprinted in *Harvey on Industrial Relations and Employment Law* (Butterworths, looseleaf).

Special procedure orders

3.140 Certain categories of order, usually relating to the compulsory purchase for certain purposes of land owned by local authorities or statutory undertakers, are not made by means of a Local Act or by means of an SI, but undergo a special Parliamentary procedure and are subject to the Statutory Orders (Special Procedure) Acts 1945 and 1965. The resulting Statutory Orders may be printed and issued by HMSO along with SIs but they are not numbered. Because in most cases there are now much less convoluted ways of making compulsory purchase orders, they are very uncommon — the only such example in 1991 was The Great Yarmouth Outer Harbour Act 1986 (Extension of Time) Order 1991. How you would find one if you did not know it already existed I do not know.

Bye-laws

3.141 Bye-laws come in two varieties. On the one hand there are the bye-laws made by local authorities either under the general power in s 235 of the Local Government Act 1972 or under specific powers in a miscellany of statutes (lists of such powers are given as Appendix 6 in the *Encyclopedia of Local Government Law* and as Appendix 5 in *Cross on Local Government Law*), and on the other hand there are the bye-laws made by particular bodies, such as British Rail or London Transport, under their constituting legislation. For this material one is usually entirely reliant on the body providing the text in its accurate and up-to-date form. The extent to which local authorities are efficient in this varies. Model bye-laws exist to cover common eventualities to enable provisions to be similar from authority to authority.

Traffic Regulation Orders

3.142 Responsiblity for the regulation of roads and traffic is exercised by both the Secretary of State for Transport and by local authorities. Regulations made by the former will be in the form of SIs, albeit often local unpublished SIs. But the plethora of minor rules and regulations — parking, bus lanes, bus stops, one-way streets, no right turns, etc — are made by the latter under powers delegated by the Road Traffic Regulation Act 1984. The regime for making such regulations differs between London and outside London. Outside London they come in the form of Traffic Regulation Orders, usually obtainable from the county council. Inside London, they used to be made by the GLC in the form of Traffic Management Orders, which came in a proper numbered series not dissimilar to SIs. They are now made individually by each borough separately. As with bye-laws one is almost wholly reliant on the local authority or borough in providing an authoritative text. However, a notice (but not the text) of some of them may appear in advance in local newspapers or *London Gazette*. In the quarterly indexes to the latter the notices are under 'Road Traffic Regulation Act 1984'.

Quasi-legislation

3.143 The legal effect of quasi-legislation, miscellaneous material falling some-where between legislation proper and mere administrative rule-making, is illustrated by two well-known examples, the Highway Code and the Codes of Practice made under the Police and Criminal Evidence Act 1984. The breach of either does not give rise directly to any liability, but breach of the first can be used as evidence of negligence and breach of the second may render a confession inadmissible. There are many more examples of codes of practice, which may be made under statute or be purely voluntary agreements.

3.144 Goverment circulars are another common species of quasi-legislation. In some areas such as planning law, they assume almost as much importance as subsidiary legislation proper. Home Office circulars impinge heavily on such matters as prisons. They have also been very important in relation to the operation of magistrates courts. From the wide range of other kinds of quasi-legislation, one particular example worth mentioning is extra-statutory concessions made by the Inland Revenue. Naturally enough these cannot override a statutory provision, but in practice a mass of detailed regulation of taxation is made in this way. Longmans publish a looseleaf *Inland Revenue Practice and Concessions* and recent information may be found in *Simon's Tax Intelligence*.

3.145 Other important materials are the rule books of the various Self-Regulatory Organisations (SROs), such as LAUTRO and FIMBRA, that are recognised under the Financial Services Act. They are published in printed form (usually in looseleaf format) by the SROs themselves and may be reprinted in works such as the *Encyclopaedia of Financial Services*. But they are also available in an electronic version, C-Text, together with the Companies Acts and other related sources, supplied by Compliance. This is used by the bodies themselves and by some of the City law firms. It is regarded as being the most up-to-date source.

3.146 Other examples of quasi-legislative materials are Building Regulations Approved Documents (until 1986 these details were published in the SIs themselves but are now separate), British Standards, Accounting Standards, the Rules and Regulations of the Stock Exchange, and the Stock Exchange *Admission of Securities to Listing*. The latter are partly delegated legislation in category 2 above (para 3.135) in that they are made under the Financial Services Act, but they are also partly made simply pursuant to its Deed of Settlement.

3.147 No particular rules can be laid down for finding and using quasi-legislation. The most important kinds may be published by HMSO, but mostly it will be issued by government departments or the relevant bodies themselves. Looseleaf subject encyclopedias often include such material, as do some journals — the *Justice of the Peace*, for instance, often reprints Home Office circulars. The Quick Reference Guide gives a few other examples (QR3.31).

Legislative history and proposals for legislation

3.148 It is sometimes necessary to research how a particular statute or legislative provision came to be passed. Legislative history, the analysis of the passage of legislation through the legislature, in other jurisdictions, for example the United States, is an acknowledged tool for statutory interpretation. In England, there are much narrower limits on the extent to which the courts can look behind the statute itself. For example, until very recently it was not permissible to cite *Hansard* in court. The House of Lords decision in *Pepper v Hart* ([1993] 1 All ER 42) has now relaxed that ruling in some circumstances. Where a statute is ambiguous, obscure or led to an absurdity, the clear statements in Parliament of the minister or promoter of the Bill (together if necessary with such other Parliamentary material as is necessary to understand them and their effect) can be called in aid. There is also some leeway under the so-called mischief rule of statutory interpretation which allows reports which led to legislation, such as those from the Law Commission, to be referred to in order to identify the 'mischief' which the statute was intended to rectify. These two grounds for citing extra-statutory material thus remain narrow. But even if legislative history cannot be formally cited in court, advisers often wish to refer to it in order to gain reassurance and bolster their arguments. Academic researchers of course do not have the same constraints and often need to make use of such sources. These kinds of material are also needed when advising on proposed changes in the law that may be imminent as well as for retrospective research.

Statutes

The typical life-cycle of a new statute

3.149   Many new pieces of legislation start life as a goverment green paper, so called because they traditionally have green covers. Such papers are meant to be consultation papers and invite comments from interested persons or bodies. The Court and Legal Services Act 1990 was preceded by four green papers issued by the Lord Chancellor on different aspects of the legal profession. After the consultation period is over, the government will typically issue a white paper setting out their firm policy in light of comments received. If sufficiently important, the white paper may be debated in Parliament, either on the floor of the House or in a Select Committee.

3.150   Initial proposals for legislation, however, may not come directly from the government. The Law Commission is the official body charged with law reform, and their proposals go through the similar two-stage process of first being issued in a consultation paper (formerly called working papers) and then in a final report. It is often their practice nowadays to include the draft text of a Bill in the final report. The Law Reform Committee and the Criminal Law Revision Committee, though no longer active, were two other important official law reform bodies. Legislation may also have its roots in one-off reports, either emanating from a full-blown enquiry such as a Royal Commission (though this mechanism fell into disfavour during the Thatcher administration) or from smaller departmental or inter-departmental committees. Occasionally reports from outside bodies may be relevant. For example a report by the organisation Justice was highly influential in setting up the Ombudsman system. Much legislation, however, has no specific antecedents in the form of such reports. The matter may be non-controversial, for example a consolidating measure, or the matter is felt by the government to be too urgent, for example the dangerous dogs legislation rushed through in 1991 in the wake of some highly publicised injuries to children.

3.151   The description that follows is concerned with the procedure for Public Bills. There is an altogether different procedure for Private Bills (those that result in Local and Personal Acts), and there are further complications if a Bill is declared to be a 'Hybrid Bill', ie a Public Bill that effects a particular private interest. A Bill may be first introduced in either the House of Commons or the House of Lords, but will proceed through the same stages whichever House takes it first. Generally most government Bills introducing new policies originate in the Commons, as do all Finance Bills and Bills involving taxation. The Lords traditionally take first Bills concerned with the administration of justice or other matters that are within the ministerial responsibility of the Lord Chancellor and also usually consolidation Bills. Recently it has been the practice for one or two other substantial Bills to be introduced in the Lords in order to make best use of Parliamentary time and to lessen the backlog that can accumulate late in a session. Bills introduced by backbenchers as opposed to government ministers are called Private Members' Bills (not to be confused with Private Bills).

3.152   The order of proceedings in both Houses is First Reading, Second Reading, Committee Stage, Report Stage, Third Reading. When it has completed these stages in both Houses it finally returns to the first House for consideration of the amendments made by the other House. There are, however, some differences in practice and procedure between the Houses. In both Houses the First Reading is purely formal, and it is only after the First Reading that the Bill is printed. The Second Reading is again similar in both Houses, and is a general debate on the principles and purpose of the Bill. In the Commons, small non-controversial Bills are occasionally considered in a Second Reading Committee rather than on the floor of the House. In the Committee Stage the Bill is considered clause by clause and detailed amendments are moved. (The terminology here is that 'sections' in Acts are 'clauses' in Bills.) In the Commons the Committee Stage is usually taken by a Standing Committee. There are several Standing Committees (not to be confused with Select Committees) lettered A, B, C, etc to which Bills are assigned. The Committee Stage may sometimes be taken in whole or in part on the floor of the House — this is called, somewhat paradoxically, a Committee of the Whole House. This is usually reserved for matters of particular constitutional importance and for certain clauses of Finance Bills. An alternative to the usual Standing Committee or to a Committee of the Whole House is a Special Standing Committee. This innovation was introduced in 1980, but has been hardly used since. Its distinctive feature, which is a commonplace feature in other legislatures such as the American Congress, is that it is empowered to call outside witnesses and experts to give evidence. The Criminal Attempts Act 1981 followed that route, and Professor J.C. Smith among others spoke before it. In the Lords, by contrast, the Committee Stage is virtually always taken by a Committee of the Whole House. Only on very rare occasions is it taken by a Committee proper, which is called the Public Bill Committee. The Bill which became the Charities Act 1992 was a recent such occasion, it being necessitated by a shortage of time before the general election.

3.153   The Report Stage and the Third Reading in the Commons are often taken together in one sitting and there is only limited opportunity to make further amendments; the latter stage is often purely formal. In the Lords, although matters debated in committee theoretically should not be reopened, there is more leeway to introduce amendments at the Report Stage and Third Reading. Government amendments in response to criticisms in the earlier stages are often introduced at this late juncture. When a Bill that started in the Commons has completed its stages in the

Lords, the Commons consider the Lords' amendments. If they are not approved, they are sent back to the Lords, and theoretically they can yo-yo back and forth until agreement is reached. In practice an accomodation is reached through the 'usual channels', though very occasionally a Bill may be lost through lack of agreement — the Trade Union and Labour Relations (Amendment) Bill 1974-1975 went back and forth six times and was still not agreed by the time the session ended. If a Bill introduced in the Commons does not receive the agreement of the Lords, it can be reintroduced in the next session and under the Parliament Acts 1911 and 1949 receive Royal Assent without the further agreement of the Lords; but this ultimate expression of the supremacy of the Commons has only ever been invoked on four occasions, the most recent being the War Crimes Act 1991; it had not been used before that since the passing of the Parliament Act 1949 itself. The Parliament Act 1911 also allows for the immediate passing without the consent of the Lords of a Bill certified by the Speaker to be a 'money Bill', but in practice no Bill has received Royal Assent in this way. Once the Bill has completed all its stages it receives Royal Assent and becomes an Act (it is disappointing to learn that the Original Act is not signed by the Sovereign herself but by the Clerk of the Parliaments).

3.154   Depending on the size of the Bill the whole passage through Parliament may take some weeks — in the Lords there are mininum intervals that usually have to elapse between each stage — though in an emergency and with the acquiescence of MPs and peers a Bill may got through extremely quickly. A notorious example was the Official Secrets Act 1911, which, despite its draconian effect, was passed in a day with virtually no debate. In the Commons, debate may be curtailed by means of a 'guillotine' motion. A Public Bill that has not completed all its stages by the end of the Parliamentary session is lost in its entirety and has to be reintroduced afresh in the following session — partially completed Public Bills cannot be carried over from one session to the next (though there is provision for carrying over Private Bills and Hybrid Bills). For this reason the guillotine is sometimes a practical necessity, though the Opposition may view it more cynically. The researcher may be thus disappointed to discover that the particular section or sections they are interested in are not discussed at all in *Hansard*.

Finding pre-Bill proposals and reports

3.155   In chapter 6, the various tools for tracing Parliamentary and non-Parliamentary official publications are described. But for this particular category of material they are usually a long way round. The quickest way to find references to green papers, white papers, and other reports that preceded a particular statute is to look in *Current Law Statutes Annotated*. Details will be found in the general note at the beginning of the statute (see figure 3.27), or sometimes, if the statute embraces more than one area, in the general note to a particular part of the Act. Textbooks which discuss the statute will also often make reference to such papers and reports. If neither of those sources yield an answer, look at the Second Reading debate in *Hansard*. The minister in introducing the Bill will invariably mention the background to the legislation. If no specific report or paper is mentioned, it is fairly safe to assume that there was none.

3.156   If you are looking for a particular law reform proposal that has not yet been enacted or want to know whether there are any proposals in the offing, the above sources of course will not help. The place to look instead is the excellent publication produced quarterly by the Law Commission, *Law Under Review*, which collates all

Figure 3.27   Current Law Statutes Annotated

An Act to make provision for securing computer material against unauthorised access or modification; and for connected purposes.

[29th June 1990]

PARLIAMENTARY DEBATES
Hansard: H.C. Vol. 164, col. 390; Vol. 166, col. 1134; Vol. 171, col. 1287; H.L. Vol. 519, col. 230.

INTRODUCTION

Background to the Legislation
The Computer Misuse Act 1990 gives effect, with some modifications, to various changes to the law recommended by the Law Commission's Report No. 186, *Computer Misuse*, Cm. 819, published in October 1989. The Commission undertook an investigation of this area of law in the light of public concern over "the misuse of computers or computer systems by parties other than those entitled to use or control those computers, either by simply seeking access to the computers, or by going further and using the computers or amending the information in them for what may be a wide range of ulterior motives" (Law Com. No. 186, para. 1.1). The Report followed the publication of a Report by the Scottish Law Commission in 1987, which advocated the creation of a new offence in Scotland, of "obtaining unauthorised access to a computer": *Report on Computer Crime* (Scot. Law Com. No. 106, Cm. 174). During the period of the English Law Commission's deliberations, however, further urgency was given to the matter when the House of Lords confirmed the decision of the Court of Appeal quashing the convictions of the two defendants in *R.* v. *Gold*; *R.* v. *Schifreen* [1988] A.C. 1063, a case in which a freelance computer journalist and an accountant had taken advantage of slack computer security arrangements to gain unauthorised access to the Prestel system, a computerised public information service. They gained access to the system on numerous occasions, altered files, and left various messages in the

---

* Annotations by Martin Wasik, LL.B., Barrister, Senior Lecturer in Law, Manchester University.

18–1

the law reform projects currently being conducted by government departments and agencies, including the Law Commission itself. It gives full details of consultation papers and reports already issued and gives a contact name, which is particularly helpful for papers and reports not widely circulated and which are not available from HMSO. Not as comprehensive but covering Law Commission and other published reports is *Current Law*, which lists them in the monthly digests and yearbooks under 'Law Reform'. Green and white papers are also listed in the *House of Commons Weekly Information Bulletin*, and those lists are cumulated in the *Sessional Information Digest* for each year. The Law Commission in its annual report lists which of its reports have been adopted and which are still on the shelf.

Using Bills

3.157   Before elaborating further, clarification is needed on one terminological difficulty that is apt to cause confusion. There are two series of Bills, the series that is printed for and considered by the House of Commons and the series that is printed for and considered by the House of Lords. These are, logically enough, usually referred to as House of Commons Bills and House of Lords Bills respectively — and will be so referred to here. However, the term 'House of Lords Bill' is sometimes also used to refer to a Bill that was first *introduced* in the Lords. Such Bills are distinguished by having [HL] in square brackets after their title. They are nonetheless printed like any other Bill in the series of House of Commons Bills when they come to be considered by that House.

3.158   The Bills in each series are numbered through a session, the number for the Commons series being given in square brackets. Before the 1988/89 session, the numbering of the House of Lords series was given in round brackets; this only slight distinction made it difficult to tell a Commons Bill from a Lords Bill when looking at the cover or a citation. Now the Lords Bills spell it out, and are numbered HL Bill 1, 2 etc. Although 'HC' is not printed on them, it should be added when citing Commons Bills. For citation purposes it is of course essential to give the years of the session (rather than the year of publication) as well as the number of the Bill. In both Houses Bills are often reprinted at different stages, especially after the Committee Stage, incorporating the amendments made to date. These prints are assigned a new number. In the Commons the text of amendments tabled during the passage of a Bill are found in the 'Vote bundle', the daily compilation of papers issued to MPs, and are not issued by HMSO to subscribers to the Bills. Amendments tabled to Lords Bills, on the other hand, are issued with the Bills. Where quite a number of separate amendments have been tabled, they are gathered together and printed as a 'Marshalled list of amendments' shortly before the debate when they are to be considered. Sometimes on large Bills there may be more than one marshalled list. The marshalled lists bear the same Bill number as the print of the Bill to which they refer with the addition of an upper case roman numeral, eg HL Bill 45-I, HL Bill 45-II, etc. One curiosity in the numbering of Lords Bills to bear in mind is that before the 1986/87 session they were treated as House of Lords *papers*, and numbered as part of that series, not as a series on their own. The numerical sequence thus contained reports, committee minutes, accounts, etc intermingled with Bills.

3.159   To trace recent Bills, the best place to look is in the *House of Commons Weekly Information Bulletin*. The latest issue contains an alphabetical list of all Public Bills for the current session (see figure 3.28), which gives their numbers and shows what stage they have reached together with the dates of the preceding stages.

Figure 3.28   House of Commons Weekly Information Bulletin

COMPLETE LIST OF PUBLIC BILLS BEFORE PARLIAMENT THIS SESSION

The following is a list of Public Bills which have come before Parliament this session, with the exception of Order Confirmation Bills.

In order to save space, the list is in an abbreviated form. The title of the Bill is followed by the name of the Member and/or Peer sponsoring it. Under this, at the left hand margin, the letter denotes the type of Bill (see Legislation - General Notes). This is followed by the Bill number (or Bill numbers if it has been reprinted as amended, with the original first and the latest reprinting last). Then follow the dates of the various stages (eg 8.11 - 8 November). For further details relating to ballot Bills (type W) see Legislation - General Notes and inside front cover this issue.

An asterisk (*) means that proceedings were formal, with no debate.

ADOPTION OF ROADS (COMPULSORY PROCEDURES)   Mr J Hutton
    X)   Commons: (46)   1R: 25.6   (not printed)

AIRCRAFT NOISE (CONTROL)   Mr N Deva
    Y)   Commons: (68)   1R: 21.10   (not printed)

AIRPORTS (TOWN AND COUNTRY PLANNING)   Mr J Denham
    Y)   Commons: (61)   1R: 15.7   (not printed)

ARMED FORCES (LIABILITY FOR INJURY) [HL]   Lord Swinfen
    Z)   Lords: (5)   1R: 11.5   2R: 9.6

ASYLUM AND IMMIGRATION APPEALS   Mr K Clarke   (Government)
    A)   Commons: (69)   1R: 22.10

BANKRUPTCY (SCOTLAND)   Mr I Lang   (Government)
    A)   Commons: (6,62)   1R: 8.5   SGC: 4 & 8.6   2R: 17.6   Comm (1st Scot SC): 30.6-20.10

BOUNDARY COMMISSIONS   Mr K Clarke / Earl Ferrers   (Government)
    A)   Commmons: (11,42)   1R: 5.6   2R: 15.6   Comm: 22 & 23.6   Remaining stages: 30.6
         Lords: (24)   1R: 1.7   2R: 16.7   Comm: 20.10

BRITISH COAL AND BRITISH RAIL (TRANSFER PROPOSALS)   Mr M Heseltine / Earl of Caithness   (Government)
    A)   Commons: (1)   1R: 7.5   2R: 18.5   Comm (SC A): 4-18.6   Remaining stages: 29.6
         Lords: (22)   1R: 30.6   2R: 13.7

CARAVAN SITES (AMENDMENT)   Mr C Onslow
    W5)   Commons: (16)   1R: 10.6   *P2R: 5.2(1st)*   (not printed)

CARDIFF BAY BARRAGE (HYBRID)   Mr D Hunt   (Government)
    A)   Commons: ((6,94,91/92),4,56)   1R: 4.11.91   2R: 25.11.91   Select Comm: 21.1-26.2.92
                                Comm (SC A): 10.3.92   Motion to suspend proceedings: 16.3.92
                                Motion relating to Committee membership: 9.6.92   Comm (SC F): 23.6-7.7.92
                                Rep: 20.10

CARRIAGE OF GOODS BY SEA [HL]   Lord Goff of Chieveley / Mr R Page
    Z)   Lords: (12)   1R: 21.5   All stages: 15.6
         Commons: (48)   1R: 25.6   2R: 3.7*   Remaining stages: 10.7*
         Royal Assent (cap 50, 1992): 16.7

CHRONICALLY SICK AND DISABLED PERSONS (AMENDMENT)   Dr R Berry
    W19)   Commons: (30)   1R: 10.6   *P2R: 5.2(3rd)*   (not printed)

CIVIL RIGHTS (DISABLED PERSONS) [HL]   Baroness Lockwood
    Z)   Lords: (13,25,29)   1R: 1.6   2R: 15.6   Comm: 1.7   Rep: 15.7

CIVIL SERVICE (MANAGEMENT FUNCTIONS) [HL]   Earl Howe   (Government)
    A)   Lords: (17,34)   1R: 4.6   2R: 15.6   Comm: 7.7   Rep: 22.10

COMMONWEALTH OF EUROPE   Mr T Benn
    X)   Commons: (33)   1R: 17.6

COMMUNITY CARE (RESIDENTIAL ACCOMMODATION) [HL]   Baroness Cumberlege / Mrs V Bottomley
                               (Government)
    A)   Lords: (2)   1R: 7.5   All stages 21.5
         Commons: (9)   1R: 21.5   2R: 4.6   Comm (SC E): 16-25.6   Remaining stages: 1.7
         Royal Assent (cap 49, 1992): 16.7

Date of Royal Assent and chapter number are given for those that have been passed. The section which lists forthcoming business for the week will tell you whether it is likely to have been further debated since the date of the issue. Lawtel includes a daily updated list of progress of Bills and summarises the content of some, but it does not include the dates of the Report or Committee Stage, nor Bill numbers. Bills are included in HMSO's *Daily List*. *The Times* on its 'Politics and Government' page each Friday gives the next week's business in Parliament, as do other newspapers. There is a table of progess of Bills in the *Current Law* monthly digests, but it only gives the date of the latest stage. The flaw in this is that it does not indicate whether the Bill was introduced in the Commons or the Lords, so it does not actually tell you how much further it has to go. There is a similar table in *Halsbury's Law Monthly Review* (under the heading 'Parliament' in the main sequence). Although, like *Current Law*, it does not give details of the previous stages or a Bill number, it does at least say whether it has passed all its stages in the other house. Cross-references are also given to the issue of the *Monthly Review* where the contents of the Bill are summarised. Progress of Bills is also summarised in some of the legal weeklies, such as *New Law Journal* and *Solicitors Journal*. If you do not have access to the above sources or have difficulty, the Public Information Office at the House of Commons is always very helpful.

3.160   Much of the information in the *House of Commons Weekly Information Bulletin*, including the list of Bills, is consolidated each year in the *Sessional Information Digest*, which began in 1983/84. Older Bills may be traced through the various indexes to government publications and Parliamentary papers described in chapter 6.

3.161   If you are researching the history of a statute, the main purpose of looking at the Bill is to make sense of the Parliamentary debates, especially if you are trying to trace the derivation of a particular section. Not only the text but the numbering of a particular clause in a Bill will vary from print to print, and will almost certainly be different from the number given to the section when it finally emerges as an Act, so it is helpful to have the Bill to hand to identify the clause being referred to in the debates. Similarly, the Bills are necessary to identify the relevant debates when the particular provision was not in the original Bill but was introduced as an amendment.

Finding Parliamentary debates on Bills

3.162   The verbatim transcripts of proceedings are the *Parliamentary Debates: Official Report*, or *Hansard* (the name of the family of printers and publishers who produced it until it was officially taken over in 1908). It is true that since 1978 there has also been sound recording of both Houses, since 1985 televised recording of the House of Lords and since 1988 televised recording of the House of Commons; the tapes are preserved in the Sound Archive Unit of the House of Lords Record Office and are then transferred to the National Sound Archive after seven years. Nonetheless it is the printed *Hansard* that provides the authoritative record, and tapes cannot be used to overrule *Hansard*. There are three series of *Hansard*. The main two cover the Commons and Lords respectively. They are published daily and weekly in unrevised form, and then in bound volumes which may incorporate corrections (which can be proposed by members). As well as the oral proceedings themselves they contain the written questions to ministers and their answers. The third series, which started in 1919, covers those debates at the Committee Stage of Bills in the House of Commons that take place in a Standing Committee, rather than on the floor of the House. From the lawyer's point of view these are often the most useful because it is often only at the Committee Stage that a particular clause may be considered at all, but, unfortunately, because they are of less wide general interest (and are very expensive) they are less commonly available. They are issued in individual parts covering one sitting of a Committee, which will occupy either a morning or an afternoon. However, unlike the daily Commons *Hansard*, they are not printed overnight, and there can be some delay in their appearance. Eventually HMSO produces bound volumes for each Parliamentary session arranged by Standing Committee letter (A, B, C, etc). As well as the debates of the Standing Committees, minutes of their proceedings are published as House of Commons papers, but they are only formal documents and are not a subsitute for the debates themselves. On the rare occasions when the Lords take the Committee Stage not on the floor of the House but in a Public Bill Committee, the debates are published separately from the main *Hansard* in the same format as the Commons *Standing Committee Debates*. Some libraries may have back copies of *Hansard* on microfiche. From the 1988/89 session Commons *Hansard* (but not the Standing Committee debates) became available on CD-ROM.

3.163   *Hansard* is printed with two columns to the page, and it is the columns rather than the pages that are numbered. One source of possible confusion is that in the Commons *Hansard* there are separate sequences of column numbering for the debates themselves and for the written answers. The latter numbers are printed in italic. In the weekly parts the written answer sequence appears after each day's proceedings; in the bound volumes the written answers are all brought together in the second half of the volume. The Lords *Hansard* used to have just one sequence of column numbering, but from the 1990/91 session they have adopted the Commons practice of having a separately numbered sequence for written answers. However, they helpfully (unlike the Commons) prefix the italic numbers with 'WA'. It should also be noted that in both series slight discrepancies in the column numbering can occur between the unrevised daily and weekly parts and the revised bound volumes.

3.164   One of the easiest ways to find debates on a recent Bill is to look in the *House of Commons Weekly Information Bulletin* for the current session or the *Sessional Information Digest* for previous recent sessions. In the list of Public Bills the dates (though not the precise column numbers in *Hansard*) of all the debates are given (see figure 3.28). An alternative and equally straightforward route, if you are looking for debates on a Bill that has been enacted, is to look at the general note at the start of the text of the Act in *Current Law Statutes Annotated*, where full references to all the debates are given. Lawtel will also give the dates of debates on recent Bills. *Hansard* on CD-ROM is another route but will not cover the Lords stages.

3.165   There are printed indexes to *Hansard* itself. In the Commons they are issued fortnightly. In the Lords they are issued weekly, but there is also a separate cumulative index that comes out eight or nine times a year. In both series of *Hansard* there is an index for each bound volume and then a cumulative index for the whole session in the last bound volume of the session, though in the case of the Commons there has recently been a long delay in producing it. In these printed indexes entries will be found under the title of the Bill. Where a stage of a Bill was purely formal and there was no debate (eg First Reading) the column number is asterisked. Debates are also indexed on Polis (Parliamentary On-line Information System), its coverage of legislative debates beginning on 3 November 1982.

3.166   If you need to look at older debates, you will find that before 1909 the Lords and Commons debates were issued as one series. It was only in 1909 when they were taken over officially and published by HMSO that the debates were completely verbatim. The fullness and quality of coverage before then becomes more variable the earlier one goes. Although from about 1841 *Hansard* (which has its origins in the series produced by Cobbett from 1803) was the only general series of debates (there are numerous later short compilations, and compilations on particular subjects), before then there were various other series produced as commercial ventures, and also retrospective compilations (of which Cobbett's *Parliamentary History 1066-1803* is the best known). A full annotated bibliography of these is: David Lewis Jones *Debates and Proceedings of the British Parliaments: a Guide to the Printed Sources* (HMSO, 1986. House of Commons Library document; no 16).

Statutory instruments

3.167   SIs by definition only receive limited Parliamentary scrutiny, so legislative background on them is sparse. There are four possible routes for making an SI. Which is followed depends on the provisions of the enabling legislation. The most exacting route, which is reserved only for the most important kinds of SI, is the affirmative resolution procedure. The instrument is considered in draft and is only made if approved by both Houses. Two minor variations on this are that the instrument may first be made and take immediate effect, but will cease to have effect unless approved by both Houses within a stated period, or it may be made first but only come into effect after an affirmative resolution of both Houses. The second route is the negative resolution procedure. A draft is laid before Parliament and becomes law automatically after a certain period has elapsed unless negative resolutions are passed within the stated period. Again there is a variation on this: the instrument may first be made and come into effect immediately but will be annulled if a negative resolution is passed within the stated period. Thirdly, there may only be a requirement that once the instrument has been made it is laid before Parliament. There is no opportunity for debate or to prevent its passing, though members of Parliament are thus theoretically alerted to its existence and could ask questions of the minister responsible. Lastly, there may not be even a requirement to lay it before Parliament.

3.168   Instruments subject to affirmative or negative resolution procedure may be issued in draft by HMSO. In appearance a draft is identical to an SI proper except that it has not at that stage been allocated a number, and 'Draft Statutory Instruments' appears at its head. Unlike a Bill, when a draft instrument is considered amendments cannot be tabled — the whole instrument passes or fails in its entirety. Even for affirmative resolution instruments the amount of Parliamentary time allocated for debate is very restricted, and many negative resolution instruments are not debated at all. In the House of Commons, debates may take place on the floor of the House or in a Standing Committee on Statutory Instruments. The latter is generally used for less controversial measures and its function is purely that of debate, the necessary resolution itself being passed by the House. In the House of Lords the debate will be on the floor of the House. The Parliament Act 1911, incidentally, does not apply to delegated legislation, so in theory the Lords could block an instrument indefinitely, but in practice this does not happen. Any debates will be found in the Commons and Lords *Hansard* using the indexes (or Polis), or in the Standing Committee debates. The fact that an instrument has been referred to a Standing Committee will be recorded and indexed in the Commons *Hansard*, but the Standing Committee debates are most easily identified by browsing through the section listing individual issues of the debates in the first part of the HMSO monthly or annual catalogues. Each issue of the debates, covering a single sitting (limited to one and a half hours), is devoted to a particular instrument or group of related instruments, the titles of which, usually but not always under the word 'Draft', form the entry point in the catalogue; they are *not* indexed in the alphabetical index at the back of the catalogues. Minutes, as opposed to verbatim debates, of the Standing Committee are published as House of Commons papers. Even before *Pepper v Hart* ([1993] 1 All ER 42), the House of Lords had referred to Parliamentary debates to ascertain legislative intent with regard to an SI implementing an EC Directive - *Pickstone v Freeman* [1989] 1 AC 66. The precise reasoning in that case, which sought to distinguish the position of an SI from that of an Act, was subject to some comment at the time. Presumably now, if the criteria in *Pepper v Hart* are met, a debate on an SI may be cited in court without having to rely on that reasoning.

3.169 The other form of Parliamentary scrutiny is through the Joint Committee (of both Houses) on Statutory Instruments. All SIs that are laid, and all those *general* SIs that are not required to be laid are brought to its attention; local SIs receive no scrutiny. The Committee is not able to look at the merits or policy of the measure but is supposed to act as a watchdog for any impropriety in form or content. They have powers to draw to the attention of Parliament any instrument which for example levies a tax, has restrospective effect, appears to be ultra vires its enabling legislation, or is defectively drafted. In practice the Committee relatively seldom makes a formal reference to Parliament but seeks adjustments directly from the government department concerned. The minutes of the Committee are published both in the House of Commons papers and in the House of Lords papers, though they seldom shed light in the way that a debate would. Those instruments which would not be within the competence of the House of Lords (eg relating to financial matters) are not scrutinised by the Joint Committee but by the Select Committee on Statutory Instruments — a House of Commons Committee consisting of those Commons members who sit on the Joint Committee (their minutes are obviously only published as House of Commons papers). Finding the minutes relating to consideration of particular SIs in HMSO catalogues is not easy. The minutes and reports are entered straightforwardly enough under either 'Joint Committee ...' or 'Select Committee ...' as the case may be in the main alphabetical sequence of the monthly and annual catalogues, but the reports are just listed as for instance 11th report, 12th report and so on; it is then necessary to look through all the reports for the session (though the date the SI was laid will give some guidance as to when in the session to look). Where particular instruments were considered in detail the title may be given in the entry for the minutes, but some minutes refer to several instruments.

EC legislation

3.170 The complexities of the EC legislative process and its resulting documentation mean that only a superficial account can be attempted here. *Butterworths Guide to the European Communites* provides useful, at-a-glance, information on the institutions and other matters. There are also a number of detailed guides to EC documentation, of which Ian Thomson's *The Documentation of the European Communities: a Guide* (Mansell, 1989) is particularly useful. A helpful table from that work showing the legislative stages and corresponding documentation is reproduced (see figure 3.29). The most important species of pre-legislation documentation are the COM documents, which contain proposals for legislation together with an explanatory memorandum. They are identified by year and running number. When they come into the public domain the COM number is suffixed by 'final' to distinguish them from earlier drafts that may have circulated internally, eg COM(80) 139 Final. COM documents are available at a number of libraries which are designated European Documentation Centres or Depositories (see QR 9.9); other libraries may take them on subscription. The text of the proposal, but without the explanatory memorandum, is published in the *Official Journal* C series (Information and Notices) — as opposed to the L series containing adopted legislation. The C series also contains other related documentation as shown in the table. For full research European Parliament reports and debates may also be needed.

3.171 Tracing proposals for legislation is best done through electronic sources. It is probably wise to check as many as possible. If, as is quite likely, it is specifically Single Market legislative proposals that are of interest, probably the best starting point is one of the specialist tools in this field such as the Justis Single Market CD-ROM (see para 3.118). Otherwise the SCAD database available on CD-ROM (available either from Context who market the various Justis products or ILI who market SCAD as EC Infodisk) could be looked at first. The Celex database, on CD-ROM or on-line, also contains preparatory material — it is in sector 5. A further very useful addition to the materials available in CD-ROM is the *Official Journal* C series, which is now being put out by Justis. Polis, if available, will include the material received by the House of Commons Library. COM and other consultative documents received are listed in the *House of Commons Weekly Information Bulletin*. In general it is probably sensible advice for a lawyer who is unfamiliar with EC documentation to seek specialist advice. This could take the form of contacting the information offices of the European Commission and of the European Parliament in London and elsewhere, though the volume of enquiries they have to deal with may not make this practicable if the matter is urgent. For solicitors, the Law Society Library is a designated Relay Centre to field enquiries that would otherwise go the Commission Information Office and has specialist staff. Many university and public libraries which are European Documentation Centres will also have knowledgable librarians. There are also designated Euro Info Centres aimed at information for businessmen (see the list of addresses at QR 9.9). In the case of proposals connected with Single Market legislation, the official responsible for implementation in the relevant government department may be able to help — they can be identified from the Spearhead database (on Justis's Single Market CD-ROM or on-line via Profile) or you could try the *Civil Service Yearbook*. Solicitors in some of the large firms will have the advantage of Brussels branch offices, which have their ears to the ground, to consult.

3.172 A further area that may require research, and which is not covered by Ian Thomson's book, is consideration of proposed EC legislation at Westminster. While national parliaments do not have a direct role in passing EC legislation, their scrutiny can have a strong influence on governments when the proposals come before the Council of Ministers. Scrutiny of EC proposals differs somewhat between the House of Commons and House of Lords, and unlike consideration of Bills is not a sequential and co-ordinated process. Although there may be co-operation between the two Houses, they largely proceed independently and may or may not consider the same legislation. In the House of Commons the Select Committee on European Legislation, which like other Select Committees is composed primarily of backbenchers, considers proposed legislation first. Its role is not so much to consider the merits but to consider whether the proposals raise questions of legal or political importance and

Figure 3.29   EC legislative stages and documentation

EC Legislative stages	Related documentation
1. Commission sends *proposal* to Council	1.
2. Council seeks *Opinion* of European Parliament (EP) and, where appropriate, the Economic and Social Committee (ESC)	
3. EP considers legal base of proposal	
4. EP Committee adopts *report*, with or without amendments	2.
5. EP in plenary session considers report on *first reading* and (a) rejects Commission proposal, or (b) agrees to proposals with amendments (Opinion in legislative resolution), or (c) agrees to proposal without amendment (Opinion in legislative resolution)	3.
6. ESC gives *Opinion*	4.
7. Commission considers amendments, and may within one month accept or reject them or withdraw proposal and resubmit it including some or all amendments	5.
8. Within no time limit Council adopts *Common Position*, and can accept EP amendments, or reject them, unless Commission has submitted a modified proposal. The Common Position is sent to EP	
9. At *Second Reading* Council's Common Position is referred to the EP Committee which made the first report	
10. EP Committee recommends to the EP Plenary Session (a) rejection of Common Position, or (b) acceptance of Common Position with amendments, or (c) acceptance of Common Position without amendments	6.
11. Within three months of receiving Common Position EP adopts one of these recommendations	7.
12. Commission may, within one month, re-examine the Common Position and include some or all EP amendments; it then forwards the re-examined proposal to Council	
13. Within three months the Council must adopt the re-examined proposal by qualified majority. Unanimity is required to amend the re-examined proposal	
14. Proposal becomes law	8.

EC legislative procedure: related documentation
1. COM Document (text of proposal and explanatory memorandum) or *Official Journal* 'C' Series (text of proposal only)
2. EP Report: Series A (European Parliament Session Document) (explanatory section and proposed text of Opinion)
3. *Official Journal: Annex* (debates of the EP in Plenary Session). *Official Journal* 'C' series (text of Opinion)
4. CES opinions and reports or *Official Journal* 'C' series
5. As no. 1
6. As no. 2 (Opinion on Common Position)
7. As no. 3
8. *Official Journal* 'L' series

Reproduced from Thomson *The Documentation of the European Communities: a Guide* (Mansell, 1989)

to recommend whether they should be considered further by the House. If it recommends further consideration it further recommends whether this should be by way of a debate on the floor of the House or in the European Standing Committee. These recommendations are by and large followed by the government in organising the business of the House. The reports of the Select Committee of which there quite a number in each session are published as House of Commons papers and the particular documents considered in each report are usually listed in their titles. A frustrating feature of this is that documents under consideration are not identified by COM Doc numbers, but by a separate Council of Ministers reference number. Debates on the floor of the House, which are reserved for the more important proposals and to which only a relatively small amount of Parliamentary time can be devoted, will appear in the main *Hansard*, and debates in the European Standing Committee appear separately in the *Standing Committee Debates*.

3.173 In the House of Lords the relevant Committee is called the Select Committee on the European Communities; the distinction in its title from the Commons committee is indicative of its slightly different role. As well as considering particular documents it also considers broader policy areas; and as well mere scrutiny of documents it fully investigates the merits of proposals. It is regarded as one of the most important Lords committees, and this is reflected in its manpower and expertise. Their reports, which can be quite substantial, are published as House of Lords papers, and almost always receive a full debate on the floor of the House.

3.174 Tracing whether a particular proposal has been considered, however, is not all that easy. House of Commons Select Committee reports are included in the main sources that index Parliamentary papers: UKOP on CD-ROM, Index to House of Commons papers on CD-ROM, Polis, HMSO on-line database, HMSO monthly and annual catalogues, HMSO in print on microfiche. Of these, electronic sources offer the best chance: key words from the titles of the documents being reported on can be searched for, as these are usually included in the title of the report. Unfortunately it is not possible to search on COM Doc number except on Polis, because as mentioned above the number for the document under consideration which is given in the title of the Committee report is a separate Council of Ministers reference number. Debates on the floor of the House can, with some perseverance, be traced through the indexes to *Hansard*; if the CD-ROM version is available so much the better. Finding particular Standing Committee debates is rather more difficult. The House of Commons Public Information Office may be able to help using Polis; otherwise it would be a question of looking through the issues of the debates for a period after the Select Committee had recommended further consideration. In the House of Lords, consideration of particular documents may be buried in a report covering a wider topic, but the sources above (except HC papers index on CD-ROM) will retrieve what Select Committee reports there are. Debates on Select Committee reports are entered in the printed indexes to House of Lords *Hansard* under the title of the report not under the Committee nor (usually) under the general heading European Community. Lords *Hansard*, unfortunately, is not yet available on CD-ROM.

Worked example: full-scale statute law research

3.175 During 1992 your client has been opening a chain of high street retail outlets. A distinctive feature of these premises are awnings over the shop fronts which match the company's standard colour scheme — garish purple with pink spots. He is concerned about whether he needs planning permission. He has had problems with the planning authorities in the past over previous business ventures, when balloons and flags flying from his premises were thought to amount to advertisements. In particular he wants to know if it makes any difference whether the name of the company is on the awnings or not. Research the relevant legislation and any background material relevant to the legislation.

Getting started: *Halsbury' Statutes*

3.176 With this kind of problem the quickest way to get started is often to go straight to a large looseleaf work, for example in this case the *Encyclopedia of Planning Law* or *Butterworths Planning Law Service*. They will certainly need to be consulted for double-checking and for background information at some stage, but here for the purposes of illustration a systematic approach using *Halsbury's Statutes* is described first.

1. Halsbury's Statutes: main work

3.177 Using the general index or by browsing along the shelf find the main volume dealing with planning, which is volume 46 'Town and Country Planning' (1990 reissue). The index to the volume under advertisement control takes you to ss 220-225 of the Town and Country Planning Act 1990. S 220 provides for regulations controlling the display of advertisements. S 222 provides that:

> Where the display of advertisements in accordance with the regulations made under s 220 involves development of land—
> (a) planning permission for that development shall be deemed to be granted by virtue of this section ...

The meanings of 'advertisement' and 'development' are clearly of importance here. The annotations to s 222 refer you to s 55 for the definition of 'development' and to s 336(1) for the definition of 'advertisement'. The latter reads:

> 'advertisement' means any word, letter, model, sign, placard, board, notice, device or representation, whether illuminated or not, in the nature of, and employed wholly or partly for the purposes of, advertisement, announcement or direction, and (without prejudice to provisions of this definition), includes any hoarding or similar structure used, or adapted for use, for the display of advertisements, and references to the display of advertisements shall be construed accordingly;

A typical statutory definition which looks set to cause us problems in deciding whether it covers awnings.

If the awnings fall within the section, we are also going to need the relevant regulations. The annotations to s 220 state:

> Up to August 1990 no regulations had been made under this section, but, by virtue of the Planning (Consequential Provisions) Act 1990, s 2 post, the Town and Country Planning (Control of Advertisements) Regulations 1989, SI 1989/670, as amended by SI 1990/881, have effect as if so made.

It transpires that the 1990 Act is a consolidating Act, and the notes to s 220 give references to the previous legislation from which it derives, the Town and Country Planning Act 1971. In the case of such Acts it is common to have consequential and transitional provisions to keep in force for the time being regulations made under the previous legislation. It is sometimes provided for by a specific section in the consolidating Act, sometimes by means of SIs made under the Act, or, in the case, as here, of very large and complex measures, by means of a separate Act.

Having found the position as at 1990 we need to check on whether there have been any further amendments to the sections we are interested in, namely ss 55, 220-225, 336(1), and any further regulations.

2. Halsbury's Statutes: annual cumulative supplement

3.178   Going to the relevant part covering volume 46 we find that there has been no change to the sections of the 1990 Act, but the regulations under s 220 have been further amended by SI 1990/1562.

3. Halsbury's Statutes: looseleaf noter-up

3.179   Under volume 46 we find that since the last annual cumulative supplement both s 55 and s 336(1) have been amended by the Planning and Compensation Act 1991. Reference to the statute in vol 46(S) is given, ie the looseleaf Current Statutes service volumes. In the noter-up s 55 of the 1990 Act was stated to be amended by s 13(1) of the 1991 Act. On turning to s 13(1) we find that in fact in this case the amendent of the definition of 'development' is to do with demolition and is not material here. The noter-up gives several sections which amend s 336(1). Working through them we quickly come to s 24 which indeed amends the definition of 'advertisement' by inserting in it 'awning, blind'.

At this stage we have got all the material as at the date of the last issue of the noter-up to *Halsbury's Statutes*: ss 55 and 220-225 of the 1990 Act as passed, s 336(1) of the 1990 Act as amended by s 24 of the 1991 Act, and the regulations SI 1989/670 as amended by SI 1990/881 and SI 1990/1562.

Very recent developments

1. Any further amendments to the statutes?

3.180   Look in the statute citator of the last monthly part of *Current Law* for the 1990 Act. Of the sections we are interested in, s 336 features:

s. 336 amended 1992 c. 14 sch. 13

This proves to be a false alarm: go the Public General Acts for 1992 and chapter 14, which turns out to be the Local Government Finance Act 1992; schedule 13 merely amends the definition of 'Local authority' in s 336.

2. Any further regulations?

3.181   Go to the service volume of *Halsbury's Statute Instruments*, find 'Town and Country Planning' (as we have already found, this is the title used by *Halsbury's*) in the key to the monthly summaries. SI 1989/670 and its amending legislation has been revoked by SI 1992/666. In the monthly summaries this SI will be found to be the Town and Country Planning (Control of Advertisements) Regulations 1992.

Double-check that this is indeed the latest SI by looking in the statute citator in the latest monthly part of *Current Law* under s 220 of the 1990 Act. You could also look in the alphabetical table of SIs under 'Town and Country Planning' or in the subject index. Nothing further is found, and in fact in this case *Current Law* had not yet picked up the 1992 regulations.

Is the legislation in force yet?

3.182   In this case it is crucial to know not only whether all the legislation that has been found is in force yet but exactly when. For the regulations, this is straightforward: the summary in *Halsbury's Statutory Instruments* or the SI itself will show that the 1992 regulations came into force on 6 April 1992. For the Acts check first the latest edition of *Is it in Force?* The 1990 Act came into force on 24 August 1990, but as at 31 December 1991 s 24 of the 1991 Act was not yet in force. However, by going to the Dates of Commencement table in either the latest monthly part of *Current Law* or in the looseleaf noter-up volume of *Halsbury's Laws* a more recent commencement order, SI 1992/665, will be found which brought s 24 into force also on 6 April 1992. As they relate to each other it is not surprising to find that both the regulations and s 24 of the 1991 Act came into force on the same day.

Background to the legislation

3.183   The reasons for the introduction of s 24 and the specific inclusion of awnings and blinds in the definition of 'advertisement' are clearly going to be of interest, especially for deciding the position of any awnings erected before 6 April. ·

1. Current Law Statutes Annotated

3.184   The annotations to s 24 of the 1991 Act show that the changes were foreshadowed in a consultation paper *Efficient Planning* (July 1989) and that there had been two conflicting judicial decisions on canopies or awnings. To find further details of the consultation paper, the best place to look would be UKOP on CD-ROM, as this includes both HMSO publications and departmental publications not published by HMSO. If you did not have access to that, a search of the annual HMSO catalogue (or *HMSO in Print* on microfiche) would show that it did not seem to be an HMSO publication. It would then be necessary to check Chadwyck Healey's *Government Publications Not Published by HMSO* or a late 1989 issue of the Law Commission's *Law Under Review*.

2. Looseleaf encyclopedias

3.185   The *Encyclopedia of Planning Law* gets a black mark here. It prints the text of the 1990 Act as amended by the 1991 Act, but its commentary fails to pick up the change in the definition of advertisement. The main commentary on the defintion of advertisement is in the annotations to s 220 but it cites the unamended definition and the case law on it. The text of the amended definition is correctly given at s 336(1), but there is no commentary on it at that point.

Butterworths Planning Law Service had not yet taken account of the 1991 Act, but its section on the control of advertisements does draw attention to the general guidance on the 1989 regulations given in Department of Environment circular 15/89. The text of the circular will be found in the circulars division of the *Encyclopedia of Planning Law*. The Department of the Environment, as it happens, usually have their circulars published by HMSO and so it could also be obtained from them — it is listed in the 1989 HMSO catalogue. As that circular relates to the old regulations you would want to know whether there is a similar circular covering the 1992 regulations. A look through the Department of the Environment section of the HMSO monthly catalogues will reveal that a circular, 1992/5, was indeed issued in March 1992. If that had not been found the best way to be sure would have been to ring the Department of the Environment. To find the right official use the *Civil Service Yearbook*. If you have access to the CD-ROM version a search using the terms planning and advertisement would take you straight to the right place, but looking through the entry for the Department of the Environment in the ordinary version the following entry is not hard to find

Planning, Rural Affairs and Heritage

...

SPECIALIST PLANNING APPEALS

...

Grade 7

A F Hockin

Planning control over outdoor advertising and advertisement appeal decisions; Advertisement Control Officers; awards of appeals' costs

Enquiries: 0272 218577

Bills and Parliamentary debates

3.186   To find the Bill and debates look in the complete list of Public Bills in the *House of Commons Sessional Information Digest* for 1990-1991. The following entry will be found:

PLANNING AND COMPENSATION [HL] Baroness Blatch/Mr M Heseltine (Government)

(A) Lords: (10,25,31,100) 1R: 15.11 2R:27.11 Comm: 17,29.1 & 4,7.2 Rep: 19 & 21.2 3R: 28.2 CA: 1.7
Commons: (98,151) 1R: 28.2 2R:12.3 Comm(SC F): 21.3-30.4 Rep: 16.5 & 19.6 3R: 19.6
Royal Assent (cap 34, 1991); 25.7

This shows that it was a government Bill — the letter (A) means this, though it is also denoted 'government' — introduced first in the House of Lords, Baroness Blatch and Michael Heseltine being the ministers responsible.

The Bill numbers for the Lords are 10, 25, 31, and 100; and for the Commons 98 and 151. It started in the Lords on the 15 November 1990 and had its Third Reading there on 28 February 1991. It completed its Commons stages on 19 June 1991, and the Lords considered the Commons amendments (CA) on 1 July 1991.

3.187 Looking at the Bills it will be found that the clause that was to become s 24 was in the Bill from the beginning and started as clause 20. The various prints of the Bill and the numbering of the clause is as follows:

Lords Bill:
10: As first printed for Second Reading — cl 20
25: As amended in Committee — cl 20
31: As amended on Report — cl 20
100: Commons amendments

Commons Bill :
98: As first printed for Second Reading, ie as amended on third reading by the Lords — cl 20
151: As amended by Standing Committee — cl 23

Looking through the marshalled lists of amendments with the Lords Bills for each stage, it will be found that in fact an amendment to cl 20 was tabled by Lord Norrie at the Committee Stage that would have inserted into the definition of advertisement not only 'awning, blind' but also 'colour scheme'. This is very interesting, because the debate on the amendment, though not passed, might shed light on the question of whether our client's awnings by virtue of the colour scheme alone, without the name of the company on them, would constitute an advertisement.

3.188 The debates themselves may be found from the dates given in the *Sessional Information Digest* given above. Alternatively the volume and column numbers could be found from the general note to the Act in *Current Law Statutes Annotated*. Polis would also take you there, but there was not yet a sessional index to the bound volumes of *Hansard*. The debates likely to be of greatest value are the Second Reading debate, and the debate on the amendment in the Committee Stage. Baroness Blatch does refer to cl 20 in her opening speech (Vol 523 col 906), but does not shed much further light, saying only that it is for the purpose of removing doubt. At the Committee Stage on cl 20 — which will found only by flicking throught the pages of that stage — Lord Norrie makes an interesting speech, pointing out that the colour schemes are a form of advertisement and that doubts have been expressed by the Department of the Environment itself in the report of a working party in 1985. The minister, in reply, says that where there is a symbol, trademark or logo as well as the colour scheme, as there usually is, it would be an advertisement in any case. If there was none it would probably be caught by other planning controls, being a 'development'.

3.189 In the Commons there is no specific reference to cl 20 in the Second Reading debate, but in the Standing Committee debates (which, it will be remembered, are a separate series from Commons *Hansard*) an identical amendment, as proposed by Lord Norrie, is debated. This will only be found by looking at the front cover of each daily part of the Standing Committee debates on the Bill until cl 20 is spotted. The government minister offers a similar explanation. Mr Win Griffiths, the proposer, before withdrawing the amendment tellingly concludes (Standing Committee F, 18 April 1991, col 204):

I am grateful to the Minister for explaining how he considers the existing law can deal with the problem to which the amendment relates. Unfortunately, local planning authorities cannot call in aid in a court room remarks that are made in the Chamber or in a Committee when they are arguing about the interpretation of specific legislation. They cannot repeat Ministers' interpretations of the law if the judge interprets it differently.

That, as the law stood, was true. But of course, since *Pepper v Hart* ([1993] 1 All ER 42), that is no longer necessarily so. Notwithstanding Lord Mackay's dissenting speech in that case, which drew attention to the risks of increasing the costs of litigation, in future it will be not merely an incurious lawyer who does not fully research the background in *Hansard*; it may also be an incautious one.

4. Case law

Introduction

4.1 Finding and using legislation, as the last chapter indicated, may have its intricacies, but at least the extent of the material is reasonably finite. If you are looking for a statute in force, it is likely to be in the three or four shelves of books that comprise *Halsbury's Statutes*. Even the SIs, which seem to be published in daunting numbers, occupy only a few stacks in the law library. Law reports, on the other hand, represent a quantity of material of a different order of magnitude — only the largest law libraries contain anything approaching the complete corpus of published law reports. This fact puts effective legal research skills at a premium. The problem is compounded by the English common law doctrine that the force of a legal decision does not depend on it being reported. Hence this chapter is headed 'Case law', not simply 'Law reports', and a section below (paras 4.18-4.26) is devoted to the problems of using unreported cases.

The doctrine of precedent

4.2 Case law acts as a source of law through the mechanism of the doctrine of precedent. This topic is catered for at length both in introductory works on the English legal system and as a matter of scholarly debate in academic books and journals, and a potted account will not be attempted here. But it does have two practical implications for legal research. The first is the importance of noting which court made a decision. This is not simply a matter of being familiar with the hierarchy of the courts and realising that a decision of the House of Lords is worth rather more than one from a county court. It is also important in assessing the chances of a particular court not following one of its own decisions, because the rules on the application of the doctrine of precedent on this point vary from court to court. The House of Lords Practice Statement [1966] 1 WLR 1234 and the Court of Appeal (Civil Division) guidelines in *Young v Bristol Aeroplane Co* [1944] KB 718 are only the most obvious examples. In the Divisional Court, for instance, there may be different practices depending on whether it is exercising its appellate jurisdiction or its supervisory jurisdiction — see Ian McCleod 'Precedent in the Divisional Court' (1990) 87(17) LSG 24, commenting on *R v Leeds County Court, ex p Morris* [1990] QB 523. It should be added that, apart from the court, it is worth noting the judge, especially when faced with apparently conflicting decisions at the same level. The decisions of some judges, both from the past and sitting now, carry more weight than those of others, though assessing this factor can only be a matter of experience.

4.3   The second implication is the importance of obtaining the fullest report, where there is a choice. It is not always apparent what a case does decide — to use the jargon, what the *ratio decidendi* is — especially where there is more than one judgment. A notorious illustration of the sport 'Hunt the *ratio*' was provided by the five judgments of the House of Lords in *Chaplin v Boys* [1971] AC 356 (a reading of the headnote is sufficient to appreciate the problem). Reports in the newspapers or journals often cannot include all of the reasoning or all the judgments, and older reports vary greatly in their length. Even where it is clear what a case decides, there may be incidental arguments and reasoning that are of persuasive value. Using case law is not a matter of arithmetic, simply totting up the binding precedents on either side, but a fluid process of analysis and persuasion. Reliance on a short report may deprive you of valuable ammunition.

Which cases are reported?

4.4   It is worth looking briefly at how it is decided to report a case. The decision is in the hands of the editor of the series of law reports, not in the hands of the judge, though the judge, or indeed counsel, can suggest that a case is worth reporting. Carol Ellis QC, editor of *The Law Reports*, has described their policy:

> To merit reporting, a case must either introduce a new principle or new rule of law, materially modify an existing principle of law or settle a doubtful question of law. Also included are questions of interpretation of statutes and important cases illustrating new applications of accepted principles. Thus, a case which depends on its own particular facts is not reportable. — (1975) 6 *Law Librarian* 5.

Because by their nature they more often meet the above criteria, and because of the weight accorded them by the doctrine of precedent, the decisions of the House of Lords and Court of Appeal feature most in the law reports as a percentage of cases heard. Virtually all the 80 or so cases that the House of Lords hears each year are reported, while only a small proportion of the thousands of first instance cases in the High Court are reported. However it should be realised that, apart from *The Law Reports*, most law reporting is in the hands of competing commercial publishers, and so the rigorous and apparently objective policy outlined above is not the end of the story. Economic limitations can determine whether a case, particularly one of only specialist interest, sees the light of day. Conversely, some series may include cases which in truth add nothing new, but which are included to give the impression of better coverage than their rivals. New series of law reports continue to start up, while others cease publication.

The range of law reports

Modern series

General series

4.5 *The Law Reports*, already mentioned above, head the list. Although not a commercial publication, neither are they a government one (though HMSO do publish one or two law reports, eg *Reports of Tax Cases* and *Immigration Appeals*). They are published by an independent body, the Incorporated Council of Law Reporting, which has charitable status (a fact that was itself the subject of a law report), and they are the nearest we have in England to 'official' law reports. They started in 1865 with funds from the Inns and the Law Society at a time when law reporting had become an unmanageable free-for-all, a situation to which some might think we have come full circle. Their title, with its definite article, may falsely imply that there are no other law reports (and for that reason can cause confusion in speech), but correctly reflects their pre-eminence. They are the most authoritative reports because the judge is given an opportunity to check the text before publication. They are also the only reports to include a summary of the argument of counsel, which, though not a source of law as such, is a useful adjunct. For these reasons, and because of their consequent general availability, they should be cited in preference to other reports where there is a choice (certainly in court — *Practice Direction (Law Reports: Citation)* [1991] 1 WLR 1, reiterated in *In re D (a Minor) (Adoption Order: Conditions)* [1992] 1 FCR 461, Times, 30 January 1992).

4.6 The organisation of *The Law Reports* follows the structure of the courts, and the different series within it mirror the rationalisation and amalgamations that have taken place since 1865, so today there is a series for each division of the High Court: Queen's Bench, Chancery and Family. Decisions of the House of Lords and Privy Council appear in the *Appeal Cases*. Decisions of the Court of Appeal, however, do not have a series of their own but appear in the series for the division in which the case originated. If the case is appealed to the House of Lords, publication of the report of the case in the Court of Appeal is sometimes delayed so that it can appear instead in the *Appeal Cases* alongside the judgment of the House of Lords. The table (figure 4.1) indicates the precursors of the modern series and how they evolved. It also indicates the modes of citation, which are subtly, but crucially, different for each series (citation in general is dealt with in more detail at para 4.28 below). Note that the loose parts of the *Chancery* and *Family* reports are issued together, and will only go into their separate series on the shelf on being bound.

4.7 The Incorporated Council also publish the *Weekly Law Reports*. The weekly parts form three volumes each year. The contents of volumes 2 and 3 provide advance publication, for the sake of currency, of judgments that are destined to appear in *The Law Reports* proper. Volume 1 contains reports deemed to be of less importance and which are not subsequently included in *The Law Reports*. This arrangement means that each weekly part is in two halves with separate pagination, the first half containing volume 1 cases, and the second half containing, depending on the time of year, either volume 2 or volume 3 cases.

4.8 The *All England Law Reports* published by Butterworths is the other major general series and like the *Weekly Law Reports*, with which it competes, it is

Figure 4.1

Law Reports   39

TABLE OF THE LAW REPORTS

The mode of citation is given in brackets. In the first, second and third columns, dots (. . .) are put where the number of the volume would appear in the citation. In the fourth column square brackets([ ]) are put where the year would appear in the citation.

1866–1875	1875–1880	1881–1890	1891–present
House of Lords, English and Irish Appeals (L.R. ... H.L.)			
House of Lords, Scotch and Divorce Appeals (L.R. ... H.L.Sc. or L.R. ... H.L.Sc. and Div.) Privy Council Appeals (L.R. ... P.C.)	Appeal Cases (...App.Cas.)	Appeal Cases (...App.Cas.)	Appeal. Cases ([ ]) A.C.)
Chancery Appeal Cases (L.R. ... Ch. or Ch. App.) Equity Cases (L.R. ... Eq.)	Chancery Division (...Ch.D.)	Chancery Division (...Ch.D.)	Chancery Division ([ ]) Ch.)
Crown Cases Reserved (L.R. ... C.C., or, ... C.C.R.)	Queen's Bench Division (...Q.B.D.)		
Queen's Bench Cases* (L.R. ... Q.B.)		Queen's Bench Division (...Q.B́.D.)	Queen's (or King's) Bench Division ([ ] Q.B. or K.B.)†
Common Pleas Cases (L.R. ... C.P.)	Common Pleas Division (...C.P.D.)		
Exchequer Cases‡ (L.R. ... Ex.)	Exchequer Division (...Ex.D.)		
Admiralty and Ecclesiastical Cases (L.R. ... A. & E.) Probate and Divorce Cases (L.R. ... P. & D.)	Probate Division (...P.D.)	Probate Division (...P.D.)	Probate Division ([ ]P.) Since 1972 Family Division ([ ]Fam.)

* Note that there is also a series called Queen's Bench Reports in the old reports (113–118 E.R.).
† After 1907 this includes cases in the Court of Criminal Appeal, later the Court of Appeal, in place of the previous Court for Crown Cases Reserved.
‡ Note that there is also a series called Exchequer Reports in the old reports (154–156 E.R.).

Reproduced from Glanville Williams *Learning the Law* (11th edn, Stevens, 1982)

published in weekly parts forming three (or recently four) bound volumes a year. The overlap of coverage with the *Weekly Law Reports* is considerable but by no means total. It also aims at greater timeliness in publication.

Specialist series

4.9   Apart from these general series, there is a proliferation of subject-based reports. Some are long-standing, such as *Lloyds Reports* (which cover commercial and shipping law), *Reports of Tax Cases*, and *Reports of Patent Cases*, and go back to the end of the last century. Others, such as the *Planning, Property and Compensation Reports* and the *Road Traffic Reports*, are of respectable middle age. The majority, though, have started in the last 10 years or so, and there are few areas not covered — *Medical Law Reports*, *Administrative Law Reports*, *Re-insurance Law Reports* and *Pension Law Reports* are just some of the more recent examples. Not all, though, are destined for longevity. *Butterworths Trading Law Cases* ceased publication after only three years in 1988, and *Palmer's Company Cases* stopped competing with two other company law reports from rival publishers. These reports often fill a need and may contain cases not reported elsewhere, but there is considerable overlap and duplication both with other rival specialist series and with general series. For legal research this can be both a boon and a bore. The more places in which a case can be found the better the chances of having available at least one report of it. On the other hand, if you wish to be thorough, you may need to check that you have the best and fullest report.

Journals

4.10   Many of the legal periodicals carry law reports. The general journals, such as the *New Law Journal*, *Law Society's Gazette* and *Solicitors Journal* carry short reports, many of which will subsequently be reported more fully. The *New Law Journal* was formed in 1967 from the merger of two much older titles, the *Law Journal* and the *Law Times*, and these two periodicals carry a substantial number of reports and go back to the nineteenth century. The latter series sometimes causes confusion on two counts. First it is not to be mistaken for the *Times Law Reports*. Secondly, from 1859 the reports are bound in a separate series *Law Times Reports* (New Series) giving quite full reports, though the periodical itself still continued to carry short notes of cases. The reports proper are sometimes cited as LT, rather than more specifically, and correctly, as LTR. The *Justice of the Peace*, which is still current, has a similar arrangement. Full reports appear as the *Justice of the Peace Reports*, cited as JP, while the periodical, the *Justice of the Peace*, carries briefer notes of cases, cited as JPN.

The specialist journals also frequently carry reports which can be very useful. Some, like those in the *Estate's Gazette* on property matters and in the *Construction Law Journal* are full-length reports, and are often not reported elsewhere. Others are briefer notes. The reports in the *Criminal Law Review* and in *Family Law* deserve special mention, though they are brief, because of the expert commentary given on each case. *Legal Action* is a source of unreported cases at county court level in housing and social welfare law.

Newspapers

4.11   The most up to date sources for law reports are the newspapers. *The Times* has been providing law reports since 1884 and until recently (except for a very brief excursion by *The Guardian* in the 1960s) had a monopoly. Indeed it still leads the field and has the advantage that its reports are supplied by reporters from the Incorporated Council. Their monopoly was first dented by *The Financial Times* which has carried highly regarded reports, concentrating on commercial matters, since 1982, but it was the launch of *The Independent* that opened the field up. Their decision to carry law reports led to *The Guardian* and *The Daily Telegraph* following suit. *The Daily Telegraph* has since fallen by the wayside, but the other two continue, with *The Independent* arguably having the leading edge in terms of quantity and quality of coverage. *The Independent* also carries once a week a page of very brief 'Case summaries' prepared by the reporters of the *All England Law Reports*. There is a good deal of overlap between the newspaper reports, but the overlap does not necessarily occur on the same day. Many of the cases will get reported more fully, but many do not. Until 1950 this was not a problem as the reports in *The Times* were reissued in a proper series of numbered bound volumes, *The Times Law Reports*. In the 1980s Professional Books undertook a similar venture, but for copyright reasons they were only for sale abroad. We had to wait until 1990 for a Scottish publisher to reintroduce this sensible practice on a proper footing. They are issued in monthly parts, fully indexed, by A. & T. Clark. *The Financial Times* in conjunction with the publishers Kluwer attempted an even more ambitious project, which was not simply to reprint the reports as they had originally appeared in the paper, but to publish subsequently the full text of all the judgments. Unfortunately this proved to be uneconomic and only ran from 1986 to 1988, with two retrospective volumes for 1982. Apart from the above, it is therefore necessary to use the collections of cuttings kept by most law libraries in various shapes and forms. If such a cuttings file is not available, reference will need to be made to the papers themselves. Large libraries may keep back files, often on microfilm, or nowadays on CD-ROM. The text of some of the newspapers is also available on some on-line services (see para 8.27). The newspapers themselves are also occasionally needed for a case reported as a news item rather than as a law report proper. A pre-1950 reference to *The Times* cited by day of publication rather than a volume number in *The Times Law Reports* points to such a case.

EC reports

4.12 EC law can no longer be regarded as a specialist area, and indeed cases from the European Court of Justice at Luxembourg are included selectively in the various English series described above (including from time to time *The Law Reports* themselves), but there are two main series in this area. The official series is the *European Court Reports* (ECR), and for this reason they should be cited in preference where there is a choice (at any rate before the Court itself). All cases are reported but since 1989 some may only appear in summary form. Most libraries will only have the English version, but they are published in all the official languages of the Community and the authentic text is that of the language of the case (there are rules as to which language the language of the case is to be where more than one member state is involved, but it is stated on the report). However, publication is currently at least two years behind. The other main series, the commercially published *Common Market Law Reports* (CMLR), is indispensable, not only for filling the time lag before the *European Court Reports* appear, but also because it includes, as well as the judgments of the Court itself, Commission decisions and decisions of national courts, include those in the United Kingdom, relevant to EC law. The American-based *Common Market Law Reporter* published by CCH may also be on the shelves in some libraries. Both ECR and CMLR are available on-line either via Justis or Lexis. The

Justis Celex CD-ROM also includes the full text of those reported in the ECR, but only summaries of those awaiting publication (in which case '0000' is given against the page reference for ECR). As well as the ECR, the Court does issue typescript versions of judgments in advance, which some libraries may take and which will be the only source for cases not yet in CMLR either. A fortnightly summary of proceedings, again in mimeographed format, is another source of information. The 'operative' part of the judgment, though not the full text, is also published in the *Official Journal of the European Communities* C series, as are various Court notices.

4.13   When using EC cases it is useful to be aware of some differences from English cases and also of some aspects of procedure before the Court. Cases may be heard by a full court, with up to 13 judges, or in a 'Chamber' with no fewer than three judges. As decisions are by simple majority, there is always an uneven number of judges. The most marked difference from English cases is that there is only a single judgment and there cannot be dissenting opinions; this can make interpretation of judgments, especially from a full court in a controversial case, somewhat fraught. One of the judges who will hear the case is appointed judge-rapporteur when the case is first registered, and he oversees preliminary matters and is also responsible for drafting the judgment.

4.14   The other aspect which is particularly foreign to the English lawyer is the role of the Advocate-General. There are currently six Advocates-General appointed to the Court, and one will be assigned to each case. To quote from Lasok and Bridge *Law and Institutions of the European Communities* their function is threefold:

> to propose a solution to the case before the Court; to relate the proposed solution to the general pattern of existing case law; and, if possible, to outline the probable future development of the case law.

The Advocate-General's submission is in the form of an 'opinion'. It is not binding on the Court but is highly influential and where the Court adopt the reasoning they may only give a relatively brief judgment. The opinions are published in the ECR — before 1985 after the judgment, from 1985 in front of the judgment. They are also issued individually in advance in mimeographed form in the same way as the judgments. As well as opinions and judgments, the other species of document to appear in the ECR are orders of the Court. These are decisions usually concerned with procedural matters or interim measures. Another feature that becomes apparent when using ECJ reports, is that the Court frequently joins cases which relate to the same issue; several case numbers will then be attached to a single ECR reference. Although it does not affect use of the material, a further aspect of procedure before the Court that is alien to the English way of doing things is that almost all of the proceedings are conducted on paper; the oral hearing plays only a small part.

4.15   Although the description above has been in terms of the European Court of Justice, since the 1 November 1989 there has also been the Court of First Instance (CFI) to consider. This was created with the intention of lessening the load on the main Court. It hears three main types of case: staff cases (ie disputes with employees of the Community bodies themselves), certain cases brought by undertakings under the European Coal and Steel Community treaty, and certain competition cases brought by private parties. It does not hear references for preliminary rulings from national courts under article 177 nor cases brought by member states or the EC institutions themselves. Appeals on points of law only lie to the ECJ itself. They are reported in the ECR, which is now officially entitled *Reports of Cases Before the Court of Justice and the Court of First Instance*, but often only in summary form; and they may also of course appear in CMLR and elsewhere.

Older reports

Nominates

4.16 Before the Incorporated Council of Law Reporting was founded in 1865, the pattern was for reports to be issued by commercial publishers under the name of a particular law reporter who usually covered a particular court. Because these reports are known by the reporter's name, they are referred to as nominate reports. This form of reporting has its origins as far back as the sixteenth century when the reports usually circulated in manuscript. The first reports were mostly printed retrospectively; it is only with Durnford and East's *Term Reports* at the end of the eighteenth century that contemporaneous reports published in serial parts, as we now know it, first began. Few libraries hold complete sets of all the various nominate reports that were published from around 1585 to 1865. Instead most libraries will have the *English Reports* which reprinted most of the nominate reports. The reports are collected together by court. The 178 volumes were originally published in 1900-1932, but there has recently been a facsimile reprint by Professional Books. As this is the form in which they are most commonly used, the pre-1865 nominate reports are often, if loosely, referred to as 'The English reports'. Another venture to make available the materials in the nominate reports in manageable form was the *Revised Reports* published in 149 volumes from 1891 to 1917. They differ in three important respects from the *English Reports*. First they only cover cases from 1785. Secondly, the arrangement is strictly chronological and only one report of a particular case appears. Thirdly, the reports are heavily edited to produce the 'best' report. The *English Reports* in contrast cover the full time span (and even include some cases from the Year Books, on which see further below), reprint the cases as they appeared, and include collateral series covering the same cases. The consequence is that the *Revised Reports* are little used and are not acceptable as a formal citation. However, they do include cases from some series not in the *English Reports* and if the original nominates for those series are not available they may be better than nothing.

Year Books

4.17 Pre-dating the nominate reports are the Year Books, so called because they are anonymous compilations arranged chronologically by regnal year and law term. Their function originally appears not to have been to record precedents as such, but to act as educational tools through which developments in the law were discussed. They are mainly of interest to legal historians, but from time to time cases from them are cited. For example in *Midland Bank Trust Co Ltd v Green (No 3)* [1982] Ch 529 five Year Book cases were adduced on the point of whether the tort of conspiracy could apply to husband and wife. They date from medieval times up to the sixteenth century. They were among the earliest law books to be printed, but the standard edition, though arguably the least reliable, is the so-called Maynard edition, published 1678 to 1680, which is available in a modern facsimile reprint. Some of them have been the subject of modern scholarly editions by the Selden Society, the Ames Foundation, and in the Rolls series. Some have never been printed and are only in manuscript. They are in Law French and are cited by regnal year, term and plea number. In the unlikely event of having to use them, further guidance will be found in *Manual of Law Librarianship* (ed Elizabeth Moys, 2nd ed, Gower, 1987) pp 282-284.

Unreported cases

4.18   Except in magistrates courts, a record either on tape or in shorthand is made of proceedings in most cases. Where a judgment is given *ex tempore*, as often happens in cases at first instance, this will be the only record of the judgment. The recording of proceedings is contracted out by the Lord Chancellor's Department to private firms. The availability of transcripts from these recordings is described below, but why might an unreported case be needed?

Why needed?

4.19   Usually of course transcripts are only of interest to the parties themselves, for example if an appeal is being contemplated. Unreported cases have two main kinds of use for others. The first is where a case is needed as an authority but is not available in the law reports, either because it has simply been passed over — opinions on what is reportable can vary, and editors are not infallible — or because of a time lag in reporting. The other type of application is where cases are sought not as authorities, but as illustrations of trends in judicial decision-making, especially in those areas where judges have wide discretion, such as quantum of damages, financial provision and other dispositions in family cases, and sentencing. Finding recent examples of what the courts have decided can give reassurance to advisers even though the decisions are in no way binding precedents. Other applications include researching an unusual fact situation to see if any other cases like it have been heard, examining the track record of particular judges, barristers or solicitors, and checking what litigation a particular firm or individual has previously been involved in.

Availability

4.20   The main problems with unreported cases are first finding that a case exists and secondly obtaining a copy. There are three main sources: Lexis, permanent reference copies, and the shorthand writers themselves. A full table setting out at a glance the sources for the various courts is given in the Quick Reference Guide (QR4.17), but a general description is given here.

LEXIS

4.21   This service has transformed the availability of unreported cases, and many lawyers who are otherwise sceptical of computers acknowledge that this is a compelling reason to subscribe to it. However, it is important to be aware of its exact scope — there is a tendency, because of the publicity it has received, to assume that if a case is unreported, it must be on Lexis. First, while the main database of reported cases goes back to 1945, transcripts date only from 1980. Secondly, while it is comprehensive for the House of Lords, Privy Council, Court of Appeal (Civil Division) and certain defined categories of High Court case, many High Court cases are only included if they have already been noted in one of the journals that are scanned. Having said that, Lexis is the only way of finding unreported cases by subject or if only incomplete details are known. It will also be the only source for the text of unreported cases more than six years old that are not among those kept as permanent reference copies, as explained below. There are one or two practical points to bear in mind when searching Lexis for unreported cases. Unlike law reports, transcripts have no headnote or apparatus, so your search strategy may be different. You can if you wish confine a search to unreported cases only, or alternatively exclude them (see QR4.36). It should also be remembered that if an unreported case is subsequently reported, the report is substituted for the transcript (unless the report is one of the few series that Lexis does not cover, eg *British Company Law Cases*, in which case the citation is added but the text remains that of the transcript).

PERMANENT REFERENCE COPIES

4.22   Copies of unreported judgments are available for reference for only a limited number of courts. These are the House of Lords, Privy Council, Court of Appeal (Civil Division) from 1950, Court of Appeal (Criminal Division) from 1989, Employment Appeal Tribunal and Immigration Appeal Tribunal, Official Referees Court (part of the Queen's Bench Division) from 1991 (reserved judgments only), and the Patents Court (part of the Chancery Division) from 1970. The Court of Appeal (Civil Division) transcripts from 1950 to 1980 have also been published on microfiche by HMSO.

4.23   As virtually all House of Lords cases are now reported, access to the original judgments is usually only needed for extremely recent cases not yet reported or only reported in the newspapers (where they usually appear within a day or two), or for old cases that for some reason were not reported. The Judicial Office of the House of Lords will supply copies of judgments either individually or on subscription. Some libraries may get copies in this way. Another source, and the main source for old materials, arises from the fact that each side in an appeal to the House of Lords has to prepare in advance a written summary of their arguments, called the 'printed case'. These, together with other documents such as transcripts of the case in the courts below and documentary evidence, are produced in multiple copies for the use of the law lords, officials and the parties during the hearing. By a long-standing arrangement, each year surplus copies of these documents, together with the judgments, are deposited in a few libraries. The Privy Council operates a similar system.

4.24   Except for the patent cases, the remainder of the transcripts mentioned above are kept at the Supreme Court Library (in the Queen's Building in the Royal Courts of Justice). It is somewhat surprising that this practice began so recently. The retention of the Court of Appeal (Civil Division) transcripts was on the initiative of Lord Evershed, then Master of the Rolls, who had found himself in the unsatisfactory position of being bound by decision of the Court of Appeal 15 years earlier which was unreported and for which only slender details could be unearthed — *Gibson v South American Stores* [1950] Ch 177. The usefulness of the material in the Supreme Court Library is limited in so far as it can only be consulted in person and there are no subject indexes. The HMSO microfiche edition has improved the availability of the Court of Appeal (Civil Division) transcripts, but that too has no subject index. However, some help in finding unreported judgments of the Court of Appeal (Criminal Division) by subject matter is the *Criminal Appeal Office Index*. This summarises selected cases on law, procedure and sentence, some of which may subsequently be reported but some of which may not. It is published three times a year as a supplement to *Archbold*. It cumulates through the year, the last issue of the year being permanent. It is also available as a database on the Justis on-line service. This has the advantages of being able to search the whole database from 1982 in one go, of being able to search free text of the summaries, and of being more up to date than the printed version. The patent cases are kept at the British Library's Science Reference Library (address at QR4.21), and only cases more than six years old may be photocopied.

SHORTHAND WRITERS

4.25 Having a transcript made specially is expensive, and even where one is already made charges for copies are high. However, there is now an element of competition, and tapes may be transcribed by any authorised transcriber who cannot charge more than a prescribed maximum. To order a transcript full details of the case will need to be known and tapes are usually only kept for the last six years. Different firms cover different courts. The table in the Quick Reference Guide shows who to contact.

Use in court

4.26 A final word on transcripts concerns their use in court. In the early days of Lexis, the Court of Appeal and House of Lords became tetchy because they feared it would open the floodgates and a mass of unreported decisions would be cited before them. The comments on the subject from Lord Diplock in *Roberts Petroleum Ltd v Bernard Kenny Ltd* [1983] 2 AC 192 at 200-202 were themselves subject to some criticism at the time, and these fears have proved largely unfounded. Nevertheless, it remains the case that in the House of Lords counsel, to cite an unreported case, must seek prior leave, which will only be granted on the assurance that it contains a relevant point of law not to be found in a reported case — *House of Lords Practice Directions and Standing Orders* (January 1992 ed) para 16.7. There are no such formal requirements in other courts, but — and this, it seems to me, is the answer to Lord Diplock — it is unwise advocacy to cite an irrelevant case, be it reported or unreported. Beldam LJ recently criticised the excessive citing of even reported cases which were merely examples when the principles had been authoritatively stated in a limited number of leading cases — *R v Sheffield Stipendiary Magistrate, ex parte Stephens* Times, 16 March 1992.

Anatomy of a law report

4.27 Most full law reports follow the pattern illustrated, which is taken from *The Law Reports* (see figure 4.2). (1) At the head are the names of the parties, the dates of the hearing and the judge or judges. (2) There follows catchphrases, which are used for indexing, and (3) the headnote. The headnote is compiled by the reporter and is his most significant contribution. It has to summarise succinctly and accurately the issues in the case, what was held and any significant comments made in passing (*obiter dicta*). (4) Lists of cases cited in the judgment and in argument are provided. (5) At this point a summary of the pleadings and of the facts may be given, or it may be that it is merely indicated where in the judgment the facts are to be found. (6) The names of counsel are given, and, in *The Law Reports*, a summary of their argument. (7) Preceding the judgment there may appear the words 'Cur. adv. vult.', which means that the judgment was reserved, as opposed to being given immediately in court at the conclusion of the proceedings (one technique sometimes used to play up the weakness of an unfavourable authority is to point out that is was unreserved). (8) After the judgments themselves and any consequent orders of the court, are (9) the

Figure 4.2

ROST v. EDWARDS AND OTHERS

[1989 R. No. 189]

1990   Jan. 22, 23. 29;   Popplewell J.
       Feb. 1

Parliament—Privilege—Proceedings in Parliament—Libel action by Member of Parliament against newspaper—Newspaper article alleging failure to register interests in Register of Members' Interests—Member not appointed to committees of House—Whether appointment of chairman and members "proceedings in Parliament"—Whether evidence relating to registration of interests privilege of Parliament—Bill of Rights 1688 (1 Will. & Mary, sess. 2, c. 2), art. 9[1]

The plaintiff, a Member of Parliament and a consultant to two organisations concerned with energy, brought an action for libel arising out of an article published in a national newspaper which he alleged meant that he was improperly seeking to sell privileged and confidential information obtained by him as a member of the House of Commons Select Committee on Energy to Danish companies. The plaintiff wished to call evidence that as a result of the article he had been de-selected from membership of the Standing Committee of the Electricity Privatisation Bill and had not been appointed chairman of the Select Committee on Energy. He further sought to adduce evidence as to the criteria for registration in the Register of Members' Interests, the nature of his consultancies and reason why he had not registered his interest. The defendants, the journalist, editor and publisher of the article in the newspaper, wished by way of justification to rely on the failure to register.

On the question whether the evidence related to proceedings in Parliament:—

Held, (1) that the appointment of a chairman and membership of a committee of the House formed part of the proceedings of Parliament; that even though the plaintiff merely wished to adduce such evidence as evidence of fact without any critical examination of the appointments, such evidence fell within the privileges of Parliament and could not be adduced without the authority of Parliament as they were matters that questioned proceedings in Parliament within the meaning of article 9 of the Bill of Rights 1688 (post, pp. 474H—475E).

Dingle v. Associated Newspapers Ltd. [1960] 2 Q.B. 405 and *Church of Scientology of California v. Johnson-Smith* [1972] 1 Q.B. 522 applied.

Blackshaw v. Lord [1984] Q.B. 1, C.A. distinguished.

(2) That since the Register of Members' Interests was a public document, the court would not be astute to find a reason for ousting its jurisdiction and, therefore, unless and until Parliament enacted that the register was privileged, the court would not rule against the admission of evidence of the practice and procedure for the registration of members' interests in that register; and that, therefore, the parties were entitled to adduce evidence of whether the plaintiff should have registered an interest therein (post, p. 478A–F).

The following cases are referred to in the judgment:

Attorney-General of Ceylon v. De Livera [1963] A.C. 103; [1962] 3 W.L.R. 1413; [1962] 3 All E.R. 1066, P.C.

Blackshaw v. Lord [1984] Q.B. 1; [1983] 3 W.L.R. 283; [1983] 2 All E.R. 311, C.A.

Bradlaugh v. Gossett (1884) 12 Q.B.D. 271

Church of Scientology of California v. Johnson-Smith [1972] 1 Q.B. 522; [1971] 3 W.L.R. 434; [1972] 1 All E.R. 378

Dingle v. Associated Newspapers Ltd. [1960] 2 Q.B. 405; [1960] 2 W.L.R. 430; [1960] 1 All E.R. 294

Jay v. Topham (1689) 12 St. Tr. 821

Parliamentary Privilege Act 1770, In re [1958] A.C. 331; [1958] 2 W.L.R. 912; [1958] 2 All E.R. 329, P.C.

Pickin v. British Railways Board [1974] A.C. 765; [1974] 2 W.L.R. 208; [1974] 1 All E.R. 609, H.L.(E.)

Reg. v. Paty (1704) 2 Ld. Raym. 1105

Reg. v. Secretary of State for Trade, Ex parte Anderson Strathclyde Plc. [1983] 2 All E.R. 233, D.C.

Stockdale v. Hansard (1839) 9 Ad. & El. 1

Williams v. Reason (Note) [1988] 1 W.L.R. 96; [1988] 1 All E.R. 262, C.A.

No additional cases were cited in argument.

ACTION.

By a writ dated 17 January 1989 and a statement of claim served on 17 February 1989 the plaintiff, Peter Rost M.P., claimed damages for libel contained in an article which appeared on the front page of the issue of "The Guardian" dated 15 February 1988, written by the first defendant, Robert Edwards, a journalist. The second defendant, Peter Preston, was the editor and the third defendant, Guardian Newspapers Ltd., was the publisher of the newspaper. In addition, the plaintiff sought an injunction to restrain the defendants from publishing or causing to be published the same or any similar libel of him.

During the trial, submissions were made to Popplewell J. for rulings on whether evidence of membership of committees of the House and the practice of Members of Parliament registering their interests in the Register of Members' Interests (H.C. 115) was inadmissible as being the subject of Parliamentary privilege. After the initial submissions were made, when it became clear that a question of Parliamentary privilege might be involved, the hearing was adjourned so that questions could be submitted to the Attorney-General and his assistance requested.

The facts are stated in the judgment.

Sir Nicholas Lyell Q.C.,S.-G. and *Philip Havers* for the Attorney-General. The basis of Parliamentary privilege is, first, the right of Parliament to be the sole arbiter of what is said and done in Parliament and secondly, the right of free speech in Parliament so that Members of Parliament may conduct themselves there without fear of legal consequences: see Article 9 of the Bill of Rights 1688. A Member of Parliament cannot be sued for what he says in Parliament or for what he does in the course of or in connection with proceedings in Parliament

Richard Hartley Q.C. and *Andrew Caldecott* for the plaintiff. The principles sought to be extracted by the Solicitor-General from the cases he cited have no application to the instant case because of the factual basis on which those cases depended. Although the courts appeared to have given a wide interpretation to the word "questioned", in fact it was used in the context of "attributing an improper motive" or "adversely questioning" and not used synonymously with "examining". If the Bill of Rights had intended to prevent any discussion about what was said in Parliament the word "impeach" would not have been used. All the cases cited involved some criticism either of individual Members of Parliament or the Houses of Parliament as a whole. Thus in *Bradlaugh v. Gossett*,

Cur. adv. vult.

1 February. POPPLEWELL J. read the following judgment. In this case the plaintiff is claiming damages for a libel arising out of an article published by "The Guardian" newspaper on 15 December 1988. The first defendant is a journalist, the second defendant is the editor and the third defendant is the publisher of the newspaper.

At the material time the plaintiff was a Member of Parliament and a member of the House of Commons Select Committee on Energy. He

In the result, I conclude that claims for privilege in respect of the Register of Members' Interests does not fall within the definition of "proceedings in Parliament," and accordingly I rule that it is open to the plaintiff to give the evidence that he seeks to do in relation to the registration of members' interests and it is open to the defendants to challenge that evidence.

Finally, may I say how grateful I am to all concerned for the very great assistance that has been given to the court.

Ruling accordingly.

Solicitors: Peter ˙Carter-Ruck & Partners; Lovell White Durrant; Treasury Solicitor.

[Reported by MISS GERALDINE FAINER, Barrister-at-Law]

names of instructing solicitors. (10) The final item is the name of the law reporter. Traditionally, for the case to be an authority that could be cited in court, a report had to be authenticated by a barrister, so this qualification appears after the reporter's name. Since 1 April 1991, when s 115 of the Court and Legal Service Act 1990 came into force, it may also be a solicitor. Although it is of small importance, the curious may wonder why in *The Law Reports* sometimes the full name of the reporter is given, and sometimes only initials. The answer is that full-time reporters of the Incorporated Council, whose appointment is approved by the court, have the privilege of using just their initials, whereas supernumerary reporters or those in training but not yet appointed give their full names.

Citations

4.28   The standard form of citing case references is: name of case (printed in italics or underlined) — year — volume number — abbreviation for the series — page number — and, optionally, the court. For example:

Derry v Peek (1989) 14 App Cas 337, HL
Lloyd v McMahon [1987] 1 All ER 118, CA

Square and round brackets

4.29   The above examples also illustrate the convention on the use of round and square brackets for the year. Some series adopt a volume numbering that runs consecutively throughout the series so that the volume number can uniquely identify the volume on the shelf. The year is only given for added information and is given in round brackets. Other series, either have no volume numbers or only use volume numbers within a year, in which case the year is the primary means of identification and appears in square brackets.

Technically, a round bracket date should refer to the date of judgment, not the date of publication of the report. This can cause confusion when a report is not published until some time later, particularly where the date of publication has been printed on the cover or lettered on the spine. The case of *B v B* decided in 1979 was reported in volume 3 of the *Family Law Reports*, and so is correctly cited as (1979) 3 FLR 187. On looking at the shelf, the reader might be a little puzzled to see that this series did not start until 1980 and volume 3 was published in 1982. In the case of square bracket dates (which necessarily have to reflect the date of publication), it is the practice (or should be) to add a round bracket date as well if there is a disparity. An extreme example was *Palmer v Young*, a case from the seventeenth century. It was only for a case in 1903 that counsel unearthed manuscript details of it. It was successfully relied upon and got included as a note to the case in question. The citation, correctly if curiously, is therefore (1694) [1903] 2 Ch 65n.

4.30   Unreported cases are cited just by name, court and date of judgment; for the sake of clarity 'unreported' can be added:

Burke v Hare 12 July 1990 ChD Patent Court (unreported)

Abbreviations

4.31 Law reports are universally cited by an abbreviation rather their full title. The standard guide for deciphering abbreviations is the *Index to Legal Citations and Abbreviations* by Donald Raistrick published in 1981 (a new edition, published by Bowker Saur, is due in 1993). A quotation from an experienced law librarian given in the foreword to this work strikes a chord: 'They cause more trouble than almost anything. They're supposed to save time. But they don't'. Raistrick has alleviated the problem, but they can still be a cause of aggravation even to the experienced lawyer.

To minimise the aggravation, three things need to be borne in mind when using *Raistrick*. The first is to be alive to the context of an abbreviation. Many different series share the same abbreviation, but the application of common sense will usually point to the right one. For example, FLR as well as standing for *Family Law Reports*, as in the previous paragraph, can equally stand for *Financial Law Reports*, the Australian *Federal Law Reports*, the Indian *Federal Law Reports*, the *Federal Law Review*, the *Fiji Law Reports* or the *University of Florida Law Review*. *Raistrick* gives coverage dates for particular series, and this is usually the main clue in distinguishing identical abbreviations. Secondly, at the time of writing *Raistrick* is now over 10 years old, so do not be surprised if the abbreviation for a recent report is not in it; even when the new edition is out it will naturally suffer from creeping obsolescence. Lastly, one needs a grasp of the filing order of the abbreviations, which is not transparently obvious. A page is illustrated (see figure 4.3). There are two main sequences. First come initials on their own: A.A., A.B., A.C. etc. Then come part-words sharing the same root: Ab., Ab.Ca., Ab.Eq.Cas. etc. The added complication is abbreviations linked with an ampersand (&). These come at the end of the sequence with same initial letter or the same initial part-word, as the case may be: A.A., A.B., A.Z., A.& A., A.& B., Aa., Ab. Ab.& A., Ac., Ac.B., Ac.D., Ac.& A., etc. A useful feature of *Raistrick* is that for the nominate reports cross-references are given to the appropriate volumes of the *English Reports* and *Revised Reports*.

4.32 For abbreviations too recent to be included in *Raistrick* the table of abbreviations in the monthly parts and yearbooks of *Current Law* are the best source. *The Digest* also includes a good list (in the front of vol 1(1) and in the cumulative supplement), as do *Halsbury's Laws* and Osborne's *Law Dictionary*. Many textbooks helpfully include tables of abbreviations of works cited. In the case of elusive citations it is worth checking the source, as occasionally authors may cite non-standard sources and assign them their own abbreviation. For example the abbreviation D.C.C. would be meaningless, unless one knew that it came from Gadsen's *Law of Commons*, where it is used to refer to a collection of Decisions of the Commons Commissioners held in the Arts and Social Sciences Library, University College Cardiff.

4.33 *Raistrick* makes a point of including as many variant abbreviations for the same series as possible. It is therefore of no assistance if you are approaching the problem from the other end and wish to know what abbreviation to use if you yourself are citing a case. The problem is solved for many modern series of reports because they print the preferred form of citation on the reports themselves. For older series, the *Manual of Legal Citations* published by the Institute of Advanced Legal Studies provides some recommendations. Part I (1959) covers the British Isles, and part II (1960) the Commonwealth.

Figure 4.3   Raistrick *Index to Legal Citations and Abbreviations*

163

K

K. Kammer (Ger.) Chamber, division
Kenyon's Notes of Cases King's Bench (96 ER) 1753–1759
Keyes' Court of Appeals Reports (40–43 New York)
King
Kotze's High Court Reports, Transvaal (S.Afr.) 1877–81
Wetboek van Koophandel (Neth.) commercial code
K.B. King's Bench
Kommanditbolaget (Ger.) Limited partnership
Koninkijk Besluit (Neth.) Royal Decree
Law Reports King's Bench. 1901–52
KBA Kansas Bar Association
K.B.B. Kentucky Bench and Bar. 1975–
K.B.C. King's Bench Court
K.B.D. King's Bench Division
K.B.Div'l.Ct. King's Bench Divisional Court
K.B.J. Kentucky Bar Journal. 1971–4
Kentucky State Bar Journal. 1936–71
K.B.U.C. Upper Canada King's Bench Reports
K.C. King's Counsel
K.C.R. Kansas City Law Review. 1932–8
Reports tempore King (25 ER) 1724–33
The University of Kansas City Law Review. 1938–63
The University of Missouri at Kansas City Law Review. 1964–8
K.F. Gold Coast Judgments and the Masai Cases by King-Farlow (Ghana) 1915–17
KG Kammergericht (Ger.) Appeal Court, Berlin
Kommanditgesellschaft (Ger.) Limited partnership
K.Ga.A. Kommanditgesellschaft auf Aktien (Ger.) Limited partnership on share basis
K.H.C.D. Kenya High Court Digest
K.I.R. Knight's Industrial Reports. 1966–75

K.L.G.R. Knight's Local Government Reports. 1903–
K.L.J. Kentucky Law Journal. 1912–
K.L.R. Kathiawar Law Reports (India)
Kenya Law Reports. 1919–
K.L.T. Kerala Law Times (India) 1948–
KO Konkursordnung (Ger.) Bankruptcy
K.S. King's Sergeant
KVO Kraftverkehrsordnung für den Güterfernverkehr mit Kraftfahrzeugen (Ger.) Regulation of carriage of goods by motor vehicles
KWG Reichsgesetz über das Kreditwesen (Ger.) Law on credit operations
K.W.I.C. Keyword-in-context
K. & B. Kotze & Barber's High Court Reports (Transvaal. S.Afr.) 1855–88
K. & B.Dig. Kerford & Box. Victorian Digest
K. & E.Conv. Key & Elphinstone, Conveyancing. 15ed. 1953–54
K. & F.N.S.W. Knox & Fitzhardinge's New South Wales Reports
K. & G. Keane & Grant's Registration Appeal Cases. 1854–62
K. & G.R.C. Keane & Grant's Registration Appeal Cases. 1854–62
K. & Gr. Keane & Grant's Registration Appeal Cases. 1854–62
K. & J. Kay & Johnson's Vice Chancellors' Reports (69–70 ER) 1854–58
K. & O. Knapp & Ombler's Election Cases. 1834–35
K. & R. Kent & Radcliffe's Law of New York, Revision of 1801.
K. & W. Kames and Woodhouselee's Dictionary (Scot.) 1540–1796
K. & W.Dic. Kames and Woodhouselee's Dictionary (Scot.) 1540–1796
Ka.A. Kansas Appeal Reports
Kam. Kames' Remarkable Decisions Court of Session (Scot.) 1716–52

Kam.Eluc. Kames, Elucidations of the Laws of Scotland
Kam.Eq. Kames. Principles of Equity
Kam.L.Tr. Kames. Historical Law Tracts (Scot.)
Kam.Rem. Kames' Remarkable Decisions, Court of Session (Scot.) 1716–52
Kam.Sel. Kames' Select Decisions (Scot.) 1752–68
Kam.Sel.Dec. Kames' Select Decisions 1752–68
Kames Kames' & Woodhouselee's Dictionary of Decisions (Scot.) 1540–1796
Kames Dec. Kames & Woodhouselee's Decisions, Court of Session 1540–1796
Kames Dict.Dec. Kames & Woodhouselee's Dictionary of Decisions, Court of Session (Scot.) 1540–1796
Kames Elucid. Kames' Elucidations of the Laws of Scotland (Scot.)
Kames Eq. Kames' Principles of Equity (Scot.)
Kames Sel.Dec. Kames' Select Decisions (Scot.) 1752–68
Kan. Kansas Supreme Court Reports. 1862– Kansas
Kan.App. Kansas Appeals Reports
Kan.B.Ass'n.J. Kansas Bar Association Journal
Kan.C.L.Rep. Kansas City Law Reporter. 1888
Kan.City L.Rev. Kansas City Law Review. 1932–38
Kan.Civ.Pro.Stat.Ann. Kansas Code of Civil Procedure
Kan.Crim.Code & Code of Crim.Proc. Kansas Criminal Code and Code of Criminal Procedure
Kan.Dig. Hatcher's Kansas Digest
Kan.Jud.Council Bul. Kansas Judicial Council Bulletin
Kan.L.J. Kansas Law Journal. 1885–7
Kan.Law. Kansas Lawyer. 1895–1911
Kan.Sess.Laws Session Laws of Kansas
Kan.St.L.J. Kansas State Law Journal
Kan.Stat. Kansas Statutes
Kan.Stat.Ann. Kansas Statutes Annotated
Kan.U.C.C.Ann.(Vernon) Vernon's Kansas Statutes Annotated, Uniform Commercial Code
Kan.U.Lawy. Kansas University Lawyer. 1895–96

Kan.Univ.Lawy. Kansas University Lawyer. 1895–96
Kans. Kansas Supreme Court Reports. 1862–
Kans.App. Kansas Appeals Reports
Kans.S.B.A. Kansas State Bar Association
Kansas L.J. Kansas Law Journal. 1885–7
Kar. Indian Law Reports. Karachi Series. 1939–47
Pakistan Law Reports. Karachi Series. 1947–53
Kar.L.J. Karachi Law Journal (India) 1964–
Katch.Pr. Law Katchenovsky. Prize Law. 2ed. 1867
Kashmir L.J. Kashmir Law Journal (India) 1929
Kashmir Law Journal (India) 1962–
Kauf.Mack. Kaufmann's Edition of Mackeldey's Civil Law
Kay Kay's Vice Chancellors' Reports (69 ER) 1853–4
Kay Ship. Kay. Shipmasters and Seamen. 2ed. 1894
Kay & J. Kay and Johnson's Vice Chancellors' Reports (69–70 ER) 1854–8
Kay & John. Kay and Johnson's Vice Chancellors' Reports (69–70 ER) 1854–8
Kay & Johns. Kay and Johnson's Vice Chancellors' Reports (69–70 ER) 1854–8
Ke. Keen's Rolls Court Reports (48 ER) 1836–38
Keane & G.R.C. Keane & Grant's Registration Appeal Cases. 1854–62
Keane & Gr. Keane & Grant's Registration Appeal Cases. 1854–62
Keat.Fam.Sett. Keatinge. Family Settlements. 1810
Keb. Keble's King's Bench Reports (83–84 ER) 1661–79
Kebl. Keble's King's Bench Reports (83–84 ER) 1661–79
Keble Keble's King's Bench Reports (83–84 ER) 1661–79
Keen Keen's Rolls Court Reports (48 ER) 1836–38
Keen Ch. Keen's Rolls Court Reports (48 ER) 1836–38
Keil. Keilwey's King's Bench Reports (72 ER) 1496–1578
Keilw. Keilwey's King's Bench Reports (72 ER) 1496–1578
Kellwey Keilwey's King's Bench Reports (72 ER) 1496–1578
Keith Ch.Pa. Registrar's Book, Keith's Court of Chancery (Pennsylvania)

Published by Professional Books, 1981

Citation of European Court of Justice cases

4.34 In same way that *The Law Reports* reference for a case should be cited in preference to references from other series, ECJ cases should be cited by the official *European Court Reports* reference, though as with English cases it is helpful to cite alternative references as well. The name of the case cited should be that which appears as the running head on the report in the ECR (though many publications follow various variants — see para 4.61 below), and the case number should be given as well. Each part and volume of the ECR is now printed in two sequences with separate pagination distinguished by a roman numeral I or II, the first covering the ECJ itself, and the second the Court of First Instance. Examples of official citations would thus be:

> Case C-286/88 *Falciola v Comune di Pavia* [1990] ECR I-191
> Case T-38/89 *Hochbaum v Commission* [1990] ECR II-43

Since 1989 when there have been the two courts, the case numbers are prefixed by C and T respectively. Case numbers are also sometimes suffixed with 'R', which signifies cases concerned with applications for interim relief, or 'A', which is added to the original case number if there are additional applications from the same applicant.

The range of finding aids

4.35 Lexis and *Current Law*, as we saw in the last chapter, are not just tools for case law, but it is in this area that they are at their most powerful and useful. There are also tools specifically devoted to finding case law, of which *The Digest* is the leading example. Except for cases in the last month or so and for cases only reported in the newspapers, it is rare for a case to be neither on Lexis, nor in *Current Law*, nor in *The Digest*.

Lexis

4.36 This contains the full text of nearly all reported English decisions since 1945, together with, as already mentioned, many unreported decisions from 1980. *Reports of Tax Cases* go back to 1875. In addition it has cases from many other jurisdictions, the American database being the most comprehensive. European Court cases are also fully covered. It is usually current to the last three or four weeks. The sheer size of the database can give one a sense of security that, within its date limits, a search will be truly comprehensive. Such a sense of security is usually justified, but it is always worth keeping at the back of one's mind the fact that there are theoretically one or two gaps, though, since 1980 at any rate, these are in practice minimised by the transcript coverage. The main gaps are, first, notes of cases in journals which are not scanned for transcript purposes, eg *Legal Action*; secondly, pre-1980 cases picked up by *Current Law* but not otherwise reported; and lastly some recent specialist series of reports, the following being examples: *Banking Law Reports, British Company Law Cases, Family Court Reporter, Medical Law Reports, Palmer's Company Cases, Pensions Law Reports*, and *Planning Appeal Decisions*. However, the list of materials included is always being reviewed, and a full list of the contents of the libraries is issued annually.

Even if one can afford to carry out most of one's research using Lexis, it is still important to have a thorough grasp of manual tools. For practitioners, when weighed against the cost of their time, it is usually extremely cost-effective, but sometimes it would be using a sledgehammer to crack a nut, and apart from the possibility of gaps in its coverage mentioned above, you may need to go back before 1945.

4.37 The mechanics of using Lexis either on a dedicated terminal or on a PC are straightforward and will not be described here, but it is inadvisable to use the system without training — indeed Butterworths (Telepublishing), who market the system, will not permit access to new users unless they undertake one of their training sessions. The inexperienced user will not damage the system but they might damage their wallet — the main cost element is incurred on entering each new search so aborting incorrectly formulated searches and starting again can be expensive. Most large firms of solicitors have the system, and there are special arrangements for small firms, for barristers through Lincoln's Inn and Inner Temple libraries and on some circuits, and for academic users. It should be emphasised, though, that it is a commercial service and it is not possible to obtain access even for a one-off search unless you are a subscriber.

Current Law

4.38 This publication indexes and provides summaries of most reported cases. (It also includes occasional unreported cases, usually ones with unusual facts from the Crown or county courts — after the name of the case the name of the barrister or solicitor who reported it to *Current Law* is given with the phrase 'ex relatione'.) As it name implies it is geared to recent materials, and this is reflected in its structure — monthly parts, which are cumulated into separate yearbooks — but it does go back to 1947, and its indexes and citators cumulate over substantial spans, making a useful general tool. A new departure from 1992 is a CD-ROM version, which contains in one database all the yearbooks from 1986. This will potentially be very useful, though it is too early to give a full assessment. One unusual feature of it, however, is that as well having the data from the printed version in computer-searchable form, the printed pages have been scanned, so that the results of a search when printed out on a laser printer look exactly like the original rather than as a run-of-the-mill computer printout. One feature of *Current Law* that used to cause some confusion was that until 1990 it was published in two versions. One called *Current Law* contained only English material; the other, called *Scottish Current Law,* included all the English material in the main version but with the addition of a supplement of Scottish materials. From 1991 the two versions have been integrated. A noticeable side effect has been the increased awareness of, and demand for, Scottish authorities by English lawyers. A sister publication covering materials from countries throughout Western and Eastern Europe, *European Current Law,* was launched in 1992, though full coverage of European Communities law relevant to the UK is still to be found in *Current Law* itself.

The Digest

4.39 This provides access to the whole body of case law that might be still be of value, whatever its date. In approximately 40 volumes arranged by subject brief summaries are given not only of all relevant English case law but also of selected Scottish, Irish, Commonwealth and European cases. It is kept up to date in three ways. First, when there is sufficient new material to warrant it, particular volumes are reissued in revised form (hence it is important to be aware of the date of the volume you are using). Secondly, there is an annual cumulative supplement. Thirdly there are continuation volumes (identified by letters, A, B, etc rather than volume numbers), which contain in permanent form material that would originally have appeared in the annual supplement. Apart from the main work, the supplement and the continuation volumes, there are consolidated tables of cases and a consolidated index. Originally called *The English and Empire Digest* it has been through two complete editions prior to the current one. For very obscure old material it is occasionally necessary to refer to these as material may have been excised in the course of revision.

4.40 The presentation and layout of *The Digest* has been greatly improved in the more recently reissued volumes, but the appearance of older volumes can be a little daunting. Two points need explanation. One is that the Scottish, Irish and Commonwealth cases (which appear in smaller print) had a separate sequence of numbering even though they were interspersed with the English cases throughout the volume. To distinguish the two, the paragraph numbers of the small print cases had an asterisk. Secondly in the table of cases the number referred to used to be the page number not the paragraph number — an eagle eye was needed to browse through the page to find the case. The modern volumes, though retaining the smaller print for the Commonwealth cases, have just one sequence of numbering and the tables refer to those numbers.

Other finding aids

Daily Law Reports Index

4.41 The *Daily Law Reports Index* is an excellent publication that started in 1988 and makes the searching of the plethora of reports that appear in the daily newspapers more manageable. It covers *The Times*, *The Independent*, *The Financial Times*, *The Guardian* and recently *Lloyds List* and *The Scotsman* too. It also covered *The Daily Telegraph* during the period it carried law reports. It is now published weekly (it used to be fortnightly), so has better currency than *Current Law*, and is the place to finish off any piece of research for the very latest developments. The weekly parts are cumulated quarterly and annually, and the annual volumes remain of permanent value as quite a number of newspaper reports of lesser importance are neither reported more fully nor are they always digested by *Current Law*. It is also available in an electronic version, which some firm and other libraries may have, or it can be searched for you by the publishers for a fee (currently a minimum of £20 per quarter of an hour). The electronic version, of course, has more powerful retrieval facilities and enables the entire database back to 1988 to be accessed in one search.

Legal Journals Index

4.42 The *Legal Journals Index* is a sister publication to the *Daily Law Reports Index*. Its main application, tracing articles, has been covered in Chapter 2, but it can be useful for tracing cases especially very recent ones, as it indexes reports and notes of cases as well as articles proper. As described above, there are many reports in journals that do not appear elsewhere. Even where the reference is to an article about a case rather than a report of a case, this may still be of use as the article may well throw up related cases. It is monthly, but publication is usually slightly ahead of *Current Law*. It goes back to 1986 and like its sister publication is available electronically. As mentioned in chapter 2, from 1993 there is a separate *European Legal Journals Index*.

Lawtel

4.43 Lawtel, a viewdata system available via BT's Prestel service, is another useful service for recent cases (it has several other features apart from its coverage of cases). It is updated daily with summaries of reports from the newspapers, so in terms of currency has the edge on the printed version of the *Daily Law Reports Index*, and also includes a range of cases from the major series of law reports.

The Law Reports Index

4.44 *The Law Reports Index* is a widely used tool. Prepared by the Incorporated Council of Law Reporting, it is issued in pink parts three times a year, with an on-going cumulation which eventually forms a permanent cumulation covering 10-year periods. The main caveat on using it is that its title is misleading. It is neither an index to just *the* (official) *Law Reports* nor to *all* law reports. Apart from *The Law Reports*, the *Weekly Law Reports* and the *Industrial Cases Reports*, which are the reports prepared by the Incorporated Council, it covers: *All England Law Reports*, *Criminal Appeal Reports*, *Lloyd's Law Reports*, *Local Government Reports*, *Road Traffic Reports*, *Tax Cases* and *Tax Case Leaflets*. References to reports in these other series are only given in the main subject index if the case does not appear in one of the Incorporated Council's own titles, though parallel citations to them are provided in the tables of cases reported and considered. *The Law Reports Index* does therefore cover all the major series and often that may be all that is needed. The structure of the cumulations is also in some ways easier to use than *Current Law* and some of its tables of particular materials judicially considered are not to be found in other publications. Nonetheless, because there are so many series that it does not cover, it would be rash to rely on *The Law Reports Index* alone for any in-depth research. The precursor of *The Law Reports Index* was *The Law Reports Digest* with coverage back to 1865.

Halsbury's Laws

4.45 *Halsbury's Laws*, as we saw in Chapter 2, is always a good starting point for any research. The main work, though not a digest of cases as such, will lead you to most of the relevant case law on a subject, and in the table of cases citations are sometimes found that are not in *The Digest*. But apart from the main work are the *Monthly Reviews* which are filed in the service volume. These are similar to *Current Law*'s monthly digests, with which in many ways they compete. However it is unusual to find cases in it that have not been picked up by *Current Law*, except for cases on quantum of damages in personal injury cases, where, particularly recently, it has made an effort to cast its net widely.

Indexes to particular series

4.46 Lastly, to be borne in mind are indexes and tables to particular series. The table of cases to the *English Reports* is particularly useful for finding pre-1865 cases by name and saves time battling with *The Digest*. The *All England Law Reports* regularly produce cumulated tables and indexes, as do some specialist series of reports. They are usually just a convenient shortcut and not a substitute for systematic research, but occasionally they can solve problems that the other sources described above cannot. For example the *All England Law Reports* index is one of the few that list cases by defendant as well as by plaintiff.

EC case law finding aids

4.47   Apart from the above sources, there are some finding aids devoted to EC case law. The two most useful printed sources are the *Gazetteer of European Law*, prepared by Neville March Hunnings, editor of the *Common Market Law Reports*, and *Butterworths EC Case Citator and Service*. The first is in two volumes and indexes the case law of both the European Court itself and of national courts up to 1983 by name, number and subject. It also includes in effect a citator in a section called 'Case search'. From 1989 there has been a monthly version of the *Gazetteer* called *Case Search Monthly*, which cumulates in an annual volume. As well as all the access points provided by the *Gazetteer* it includes a legislation citator called the 'Law tracker'. Unfortunately at the time of writing, there remains a gap in this service between 1984 and 1988. The Butterworths publication provides a variety of entry points and provides complete coverage in respect of timespan but is confined to ECJ cases. Despite its title it does not note up cases that have been cited in later cases as does the *Gazetteer*'s 'Case search'. There is an official digest to EC law, *Digest of Case Law Relating to the European Communities*, in looseleaf form, but it is neither complete nor very up to date. The T.M.C. Asser Institute have also published a *Guide to EC Decisions*. Apart from these manual sources, there is Celex, which includes ECJ case law as well as legislation, and is available on-line and on CD-ROM via Justis. Lexis includes the full text of ECR, CMLR, and the text of decisions from the mimeographed advance judgments. Also worth mentioning for recent material and current awareness rather than for retrospective research is the *European Court of Justice Reporter*, a monthly digest of all ECJ cases published by Sweet & Maxwell.

Finding cases by name

4.48   A very common problem is that you can remember the name of case but not its citation. Or it may be that you have one citation but want to find out whether it is reported in another series of reports, either because the volume is not on the shelf (stolen from the library, on the senior partner's desk) or because it might be more fully reported elsewhere. Or it may just be that the citation you have proves to be inaccurate.

Variety and forms of case name

4.49   Although most cases are named in the form of *Smith v Jones*, it is worth being familiar with the other common and uncommon forms of case name for two reasons. First, it helps if you know under which element the name is entered in tables and indexes (though this is usually fairly apparent). Secondly, and more importantly, it can throw light on the subject and date of the case if you do not already know them. As discussed below, this is often useful in choosing the best place to start your search.

The following are examples of different forms of case name, with the usual entry element in bold.

4.50

Donoghue v Stevenson

The usual form in civil cases, ie Plaintiff v Defendant (Pursuer v Defender in Scottish cases), or Appellant v Respondent. Names of firms looking like personal names can sometimes cause confusion: '**John** Fox v Bannister King' in *Current Law*, but '**Fox** (John) (a firm) v Bannister King' in the *All England Law Reports* index.

Cross-references from the names of defendants, if that is all you know, are only given in a minority of sources, which include *All England Law Reports* indexes, *Daily Law Reports Index*, and *Index to the Times Law Reports* (see the list in the Quick Reference Guide, QR4.3).

4.51

R v Hunt

The usual form in criminal cases. There are two small pitfalls. In most modern tables of cases, this form of name comes at the beginning of the letter R, but in some older tables it is listed as 'Rex' or 'Reg', filing after cases beginning 'Ra'. Secondly, although 'R' is the filing element in most general sources, specialist criminal law works often use just the name of the defendant.

The new student or inexperienced librarian on hearing the name of the case in formal parlance, 'The Crown against Hunt', is advised not look it up under 'C'.

4.52

R v Secretary State for the Home Department, ex parte Hosenball

The usual form of name for cases in the Divisional Court of the Queen's Bench Division by way of judicial review (as here) or by way of case stated from magistrates or Crown Courts (in which case the name of the court will be given as defendant). The name given 'ex parte' is that of the applicant, and as these cases are often known by that name, some indexes provide cross-references from it.

The names of ministers can sometimes cause problems. In this case the name, quite reasonably, might be cited verbally or in print as 'R v Home Secretary', though that is not its official name.

4.53

Ex parte Rees

This form of name is usually where the report is on a point raised only at a hearing of one party in the absence of the other party, and the case does not proceed to trial between the parties, typically nowadays cases on application for leave to apply for judicial review. Although the name of the applicant is always used as the entry element, there is always the possiblity of editorial error, as in the 1990 *Current Law* which has two cases under '**Ex** parte'.

4.54

Attorney-General, ex relator Tilley v Wandsworth Borough Council

The form of name in a relator action (a form of obtaining relief in public law matters through the Attorney-General, used before the introduction of the current form of judicial review in 1977, though not formally abolished). A case in this form is likely to be on administrative law before 1977.

4.55

Re Taylor

This form of name crops up most commonly, though by no means exclusively, in the area of wills and probate, where the name of the case is that of the deceased because the executors or administrators who have brought the case before the court are not parties as such. Likewise the three examples below.

In the goods of Parker
Re Potter's Will Trusts
In the estate of Potticary

4.56

Re a Company No 0003843 of 1986

There is no basic difficulty with such company law cases, other than the fact that they are a strain on the eye when perusing tables of cases (and a strain on the memory if one does not have a pencil immediately to hand).

4.57

Re S (A minor) (Care Proceedings: Wardship Summons)

In family cases, for reasons of confidentiality, the full name is often not given. The modern practice is to give the subject-matter of the case in parentheses to help distinguish cases, but it can be an uphill struggle if one does not know the qualifying terms with precision. In older cases where they are not provided, one can only rely on a date to differentiate.

4.58

Practice Direction (Commercial Court: Urgent Matters)

These are not case reports as such, but are published in the law reports. As they are very numerous, the same problem of knowing the precise form of name arises. Although this species of report is most commonly in the form of 'Directions', to lure the unwary there are also 'Practice *Notes*', 'Practice *Statements*', and from the House of Lords '*Procedure* Directions'.

4.59

*The **Goring***

This is the name of a ship, which is often the preferred form of name of shipping cases. Most indexes provide cross-references from the case in 'Plaintiff v Defendant' form to the name of the ship (or from the ship to the plaintiff if that is entry point editorially preferred).

4.60

***Bayer** AG v Winter (No 2)*

A case may be reported when the court decides a preliminary issue or interlocutory matter. If the same case is also subsequently reported on another point — the issue at trial or another interlocutory matter — then it will bear the same name but a number is added, as here, to distinguish the two. Numbers are not used to distinguish a case reported at first instance from the same case reported on appeal — if necessary the abbreviation for the court, eg QBD, CA, or HL, is added after the name. Matters get complicated when separate interlocutory points and the substantive case each get appealed, possibly up to the House of Lords, in turn. The Spycatcher case and the International Tin Council litigation were notorious examples — tracing all the different reported points and stages in tables of cases will induce a headache.

European Court of Justice cases

4.61   The names of ECJ cases can cause problems, which is why it is helpful to have the official ECJ case number as well and in some sources cases are listed by number rather than name. But if name is what you have got, bear in mind the following. Where the case is solely a reference for a preliminary ruling under article 177 from a national court of a member state, then the name is usually that of the case as it was in the national court. For references to the ECJ from the English courts, it may thus be in any of the forms above; for references from other national courts a wide of variety of often impenetrable looking names will arise. In cases where the applicants or defendants are member states and the Commission of the European Communities, tables of cases vary as to the entry element and the form of the name of member states. There may be the following permutations, with the form used in the ECR themselves given first:

> **Commission** or **Commission** of the European Communities or **EC** Commission or **European** Commission
> **Belgium** or **Kingdom** of Belgium
> **Denmark** or **Kingdom** of Denmark
> **France** or **French** Republic
> **Germany** or **Federal** Republic of Germany
> **Greece** or **Hellenic** Republic
> **Ireland** or **Republic** of Ireland
> **Italy** or **Italian** Republic
> **Luxembourg** or **Grand** Duchy of Luxembourg
> **Netherlands** or **Kingdom** of the Netherlands
> **Portugal** or **Portuguese** Republic
> **Spain** or **Kingdom** of Spain
> **United** Kingdom or **UK** or **Great** Britain

Often in addition to the parties a popular name or name of the subject-matter is used, especially for cases between the Commission and member states where there are numerous examples under the same parties, for example:

Re **Low-fat** cheese: EC Commission v Italy (C-210/89)

Or the subject-matter may added after the name of the parties:

EC Commission v United Kingdom: Re Tachographs

If you yourself are citing an ECJ case, as noted above (para 4.34) you should use the form of name as it appears on the running head of the report in the ECR.

Choosing a starting point and following through

4.62   The best place to start looking depends largely on how recent a case you think it is. If you know that, it can be an added advantage to know what it is about (which you usually will), because an obvious shortcut for cases that are not too recent is to look in the table of cases in a standard work: if you have a procedural point look in *The White Book*, if you have a landlord and tenant point look in *Woodfall*. Knowing the subject-matter is also of course indispensable if you have a case with a common name and you are to recognise it when you find it. The form of name alone, as given in the examples above, can sometimes tell you immediately that you are dealing with say a shipping case or a family case. The names of the parties themselves can also help: an insurance company is likely to be involved in an insurance case, a construction company in a building case. The names may also be an early warning signal that you are not dealing with an English case at all. For example a company name followed by 'Pty Ltd' points to an Australian case.

4.63   Assuming you have not been able to take advantage of the shortcut of looking in a textbook, the best way to illustrate a more systematic approach is to take the commonest eventuality: an English case reported in the last few years rather than the last few days. Undoubtedly the best starting point is the *Current Law Case Citator*. The fact that it is picking up cases cited during the coverage period as well as cases reported during the period increases your chances of success. As explained in the worked example below, in some instances you may still be one step away from finding the citation itself but in others you are given it directly. To be thorough, however, you will need to check the two bound volumes, the paperback supplement, and the cumulative table in the latest monthly digest. *The Digest* is probably the next place to look, but is less satisfactory than *Current Law* as a starting point since it is a three-step process to arrive at the citation itself. On the other hand, *The Digest* provides much greater historical coverage and the initial search is limited to just two places, the consolidated table of cases and the table of cases in the cumulative supplement. If reasonably certain that the case is pre-1865, rather than looking in *The Digest*, it is usually rather simpler and quicker to look in the table of cases to the *English Reports* (the reprint of the nominates).

4.64   *The Law Reports Index* is best spurned for this type of problem, unless it happens to be readily at hand and you are confident that you have a mainstream case. (The only cases to be found in *The Law Reports Index* that are not generally indexed in *Current Law* are the dismissals by the Appeal Committee of leave to appeal to the House of Lords, which are noted in the *Weekly Law Reports* — but all these contain is one line dismissing the petition.) Lexis is of course likely to give you the answer quickest of all, but for a basic enquiry like this it is probably an expensive way of doing things unless you are in tearing hurry and money is no object.

4.65   If you have not found the case in *Current Law* or *The Digest*, a double-check in *Halsbury's Laws* would be sensible. You will need to look in the consolidated table of cases, the annual cumulative supplement and the current service volume. There-after the possibilities are that you have a case that is very recent, very old, very obscure, not English or not reported. If you have access to Lawtel or an in-house database such as the Law Society Library's, you will be able to check for recent cases in the newspapers up to the last day or two. Alternatively, the *Daily Law Reports Index* will bring you up to the last week: look in the cumulative 'Parties Index' in the binder of weekly parts, in any quarterly parts, and in the annual volumes. The case index in the latest monthly part of the *Legal Journals Index* is also worth checking, as its currency is slightly better than the *Current Law* monthly digests and it will pick up the case if it has been in the *New Law Journal, Law Society's Gazette, Criminal Law Review* or other journal.

4.66   If by this stage you have still not found the case, you ought to be suspicious. Consider whether the spelling of the names could be wrong, whether the parties have been given the wrong way round, whether it is not an English case at all, or whether it might be unreported. If you think it is not English, look at some of the sources suggested in chapter 7. If it might be unreported, this is the point to consider a Lexis search. The other possibility, which will usually be apparent from the context, is that it is an old case that has somehow slipped the net of *The Digest*. Double-check in the table of cases to the *English Reports* and look in superseded editions of the table of cases to *The Digest* (if they are available) — in the course of revision some cases do get excised.

If you are sure that a case exists with a name *something* like the name you have, but you have failed completely to find it by name, the only course is do a subject search and hope you recognise it when you see it.

Finding EC cases by name or number

4.67   The above sources will include references by name but there are also alphabetical tables (including both applicant and defendant) in the *Gazetteer of European Law* and *Case Search Monthly*. The references there are to the two main sequences where the case reference will be found: ECJ cases arranged by their official number and a list of decisions of national courts arranged by its own numbering system. *Butterworths EC Case Citator* has a table by applicant, and also a separate table by nickname (which may be the defendant in some cases); the main sequence is by ECJ case number. The primary arrangement of the T.M.C. Asser Institute *Guide to EC Decisions* is also by ECJ number and it too has a parties index including both applicants and defendants. The electronic sources will do this as well of course — search strategies are suggested in the Quick Reference Guide (QR4.4-4.5).

Worked examples of finding cases by name

1. Using Current Law case citators

4.68   The illustration (see figure 4.4) shows a page from the 1977-88 volume. There is also a volume covering 1947-76, and an annually updated volume going from 1989 to the pre-current year.

A This case is one reported (and digested by *Current Law*) during the coverage period of the volume. Full citations to the reports are given, in this case to the *Weekly Law Reports, Solicitors Journal* and *All England Law Reports.*
      References at the right-hand margin are also given to the paragraph numbers in the *Current Law* yearbooks where the case is digested and where it has been considered in a later case.

B This case has been *cited* during the coverage period. The full case reference is given because it was reported before 1947 and will not be digested in *Current Law* itself.

C This case has again been cited during the coverage period, but unlike case B the full case reference is *not* given here because it is after 1947 but outside the coverage period of this particular volume: look in the 1947-71 volume of the citator to find the full case references.

D This case is one that has been reported both at first instance and in the Court of Appeal. The references for the Court of Appeal are given first — CA comes after them before the semi-colon — and the case in the Chancery Division (whose decision was affirmed) is given second.

2. Using the Current Law monthly digests

4.69   The table of cases in each monthly part cumulates the tables in the previous parts in that calendar year. Like the citators it covers both cases reported and cases cited (see figure 4.5).

A This case is printed in capitals in the table of cases, indicating a case digested during the year rather than simply cited. There are references to two monthly parts. The first is where a report from *The Times* has been picked up. The second is where it has subsequently been reported more fully in the *Weekly Law Reports*; the digest for the second is also fuller than the first. But note that a second reference will only be given if the subsequent report appears in *The Law Reports*, the *Weekly Law Reports*, or the *All England Law Reports*; citations to other subsequent reports are only picked up at a later stage in the annually published case citator volume.

B The name for case B is printed in lower case, and so is a case cited during the year. The case cited will be found in the body of the digest for the case at the paragraph given.

3. Using The Digest

4.70   The consolidated table of cases will contain all the cases except those in the cumulative supplement. The reference is to the volume number of the main work, not the case itself (see figure 4.6). Turn to the table of cases in the volume given. In

Figure 4.4   Current Law: *case citator*

CASE CITATOR 1977–88   **HAR**

Hang Wah Chong Investment Co. *v.* Att-Gen. of Hong Kong [1981] 1 W.L.R. 1141;
(1981) 125 S.J. 426, P.C. .... *Digested* 81/**2728**
Hanid, July 29, 1988, Criminal Injuries Compensation Bd. .... *Digested,* 88/**1144**
Haniel Handel GmbH, *Re* [1987] 1 C.M.L.R. 445, E.C. Commission .... *Digested,* 87/**1508**
Hanif (Hoosha Kumari) *v.* Secretary of State for the Home Department [1985] Imm.A.R.
57, Imm.A.T. .... *Digested* 86/**1683**
Hanily *v.* Minister of Local Government and Planning (1947–51) .... *Applied,* 88/385
Hankey *v.* Clavering [1942] 2 K.B. 326 .... *Considered,* 88/2011: *Distinguished,* 79/1586
Hanks *v.* Ace High Productions [1978] I.C.R. 1155; [1979] I.R.L.R. 32; (1978) 13 I.T.R.
524, E.A.T. .... *Digested,* 79/**898:** *Applied,* 84/1242: *Considered,* 83/1245
Hanks *v.* Ministry of Housing and Local Government [1963] ....*Applied,* 79/2634; 85/2604
Hanlon *v.* Fleming [1981] I.R. 489. Fire Supreme Ct .... *Digested,* 83/**1682**

A   Hanlon *v.* Hanlon [1978] 1 W.L.R. 592; (1977) 122 S.J. 62; [1978] 2 All E.R. 889, C.A. ......*Digested,* 78/**1616**:
            Considered, 79/141**5**

Hanlon *v.* Law Society [1981] A.C. 124; [1980] 2 W.L.R. 756; (1980) 124 S.J. 360;
[1980] 2 All E.R. 199, H.L.; affirming [1980] 1 All E.R. 763, C.A. .... *Digested,* 80/**1664**:
Considered, 81/1347, 1604; 83/1857; 84/1994: *Applied,* 83/2194; 84/1994; 85/1988:
Distinguished, 83/2183; 87/2295

B   Hanna, The (1866) L.R. 1 A. & E. 283 .... *Applied,* 84/**3163**
Hanna *v.* Chief Constable of the Royal Ulster Constabulary [1986] 13 N.I.J.B. 71 .... *Digested,* 87/**2847**
Hanna *v.* Commissioner of Valuation, VR/16/1983, N.I. Lands Tribunal .... *Digested,* 85/**2456**
Hannaford *v.* Selby (1976) 239 E.G. 811 .... *Digested,* 77/**2498**
Hannaford & Burton *v.* Polaroid Corp. *See* Solavoid Trade Mark.
Hannah Blumenthal, The. *See* Paal Wilson & Co. A/S *v.* Partenreederei Hannah
Blumenthal; Hannah Blumenthal, The.

C   Hannam *v.* Bradford Corporation [1970] .... *Applied,* 77/**2307**:
            Considered, 78/2997, 82/464; 85/79: *Referred to,* 85/9**1**

Hannam *v.* Mann [1984] R.T.R. 252, C.A. .... *Digested,* 84/**2293**
Hannan *v.* TNT–IPEC [1986] I.R.L.R. 165, E.A.T. .... *Digested* 86/**1276**
Hannibal (E.) & Co. *v.* Frost (1988) 4 BCC 3, C.A. .... *Digested,* 88/**307**
Hannible *v.* Bridge (1976) 6 Fam. Law 176, C.A. .... *Digested,* 77/**1560**
Hanning *v.* Maitland (No. 2) [1970] .... *Applied,* 88/2112: *Followed,* 79/2160
Hanno (Heinrich) & Co. B.V. *v.* Fairlight Shipping Co; Hanse Schiffahrtskontor GmbH *v.*
Andre S.A.; Kostas K., The [1985] 1 Lloyd's Rep. 231 .... *Digested,* 85/**3180**
Hans Just I/S *v.* Danish Ministry for Fiscal Affairs (No. 68/79) [1981] 2 C.M.L.R. 714;
[1981] E.C.R. 501, European Ct. .... *Digested,* 82/**1152**
Hansa Nord, The. *See* Cehave N.V. *v.* Bremer Handelsgesellschaft mbH; Hansa Nord,
The.
Hansen *v.* Harrold [1894] 1 Q.B. 612 .... *Referred to,* 77/2740

D   K., decd., *Re* [1986] Fam. 180; [1985] 3 W.L.R. 234; (1985) 129 S.J. 364; [1985] 2 All
E.R. 833; (1985) 16 Fam.Law 19; (1985) 135 New L.J. 655; (1985) 82 L.S.Gaz.
2242, C.A.; affirming [1985] Ch. 85; [1985] 2 W.L.R. 262; (1985) 129 S.J. 132;
[1985] 1 All E.R. 403; [1986] 1 F.L.R. 79; (1985) 15 Fam.Law 129; (1985) 82
L.S.Gaz. 1335 .... *Digested,* 85/**3848**

Figure 4.5   Current Law: *cumulative table of cases in monthly parts*

CUMULATIVE TABLE OF CASES

D. v. D. (ACCESS: CONTEMPT: COMMITTAL), Jan 386
D. (A MINOR) (CHILD: REMOVAL FROM JURISDICTION), Re, Jul 418
D. & F. Estates v. Church Commissioners, Mar 378
D. & F. Estates v. Church Commissioners for England, Jul 445
D., Re, Aug 192
D.B. DENIZ NAKLIYAN TAS v. YUGOPETROL, Apr 139
D.H., Re, Jan 193
DAILY v. ETABLISSEMENTS FERNAND BERCHET, Apr 244
DAISYSTAR v. TOWN AND COUNTRY BUILDING SOCIETY, Feb 372, May 368
DALE v. BRITISH COAL CORP. (NO. 1), Jul 380
DALE v. BRITISH COAL CORP. (NO. 2), Jul 382
DALBY v. TOOGOOD, Jan 193
DALGLEISH v. LOTHIAN AND BORDERS POLICE BOARD, Jul 821
DALGLEISH v. ROBINSON, Feb 532
DALLAS v. H.M. ADVOCATE, Apr 527
DALLHOLD ESTATES (U.K.) PTY. v. LINDSEY TRADING PROPERTIES, May 291
DANBROGIO v. KNOWSLEY BOROUGH COUNCIL, Jul 194
DANSK DENKAVIT v. SKATTEMINISTERIET (C-200/90), Aug 545
DANSK PELSDYRAVLERFORENING v. E.C. COMMISSION (T-61/89), Jul 642
DARBO v. D.P.P., Aug 111
DARBY v. MARCONI ELECTRONIC DEVICES, May 176
DARLINGTON BOROUGH COUNCIL v. DENMARK CHEMISTS (FORMERLY PLANSWEEP), Aug 291
DARROCH v. STRATHCLYDE REGIONAL COUNCIL, May 571
Daubney v. Daubney, Apr 145
Davidson v. Quirke, Aug 82
Davis Contractors v. Fareham District Council, Feb 51
DAVIS v. CITY & HACKNEY HEALTH AUTHORITY, Feb 285
DAVISON v. THE POST OFFICE, Apr 114
Davstone Estate's Leases, Re, Manprop v. O'Dell, Feb 274
Davy v. Spelthorne Borough Council, Apr 2, Jul 474
DAVY OFFSHORE v. EMERALD FIELD CONTRACTING, Feb 409, Mar 461
DAWSON v. DOONAN, MORRIS, O'NEILL & CO., Feb 643
DE AZEVEDO (MOREIRA) v. PORTUGAL (No. 11294/84), Apr 163
De Dampierre v. De Dampierre, Mar 368, 406, 622, Jun 736
De Fontenay v. Strathclyde Regional Council, Feb 679
DE FREITAS v. D.P.P., Jul 507
De Lassalle v. Guildford, Feb 59

372 **Leave to appeal—from determination by single Lord Justice—incorrect exercise of discretion—whether leave would be granted**

[Supreme Court Act 1981 (c.54), s.54(6).]
Section 54(6) of the Supreme Court Act 1981, which prohibits any appeal to the Court of Appeal from the determination by a single Lord Justice of an application for leave to appeal, was not limited by the *Scherer* principle, whereby the jurisdiction of the appellate court was not ousted if the judge had not exercised his discretion on a proper basis (*Scherer v. Counting Instruments* [1986] C.L.Y. 2572 distinguished).
DAISYSTAR v. TOWN AND COUNTRY BUILDING SOCIETY, *The Times*, February 14, 1992, C.A.

368 **Court of Appeal—leave to appeal—refusal by Single Lord Justice—whether full court has jurisdiction to entertain appeal from refusal**

[Supreme Court Act 1981 (c.54), s.54(6).]
A full Court of Appeal has no jurisdiction to hear an appeal against the refusal by a single Lord Justice of leave to appeal.
As' applications for leave to appeal in respect of three High Court decisions were refused by a single Lord Justice. As sought to appeal to the full Court of Appeal, on the ground that in dismissing one of the applications, the single judge had taken into account a matter which did not relate to it.
Held, refusing leave to appeal, that s.54(6) of the 1981 Act denies the full court jurisdiction to entertain an appeal from a single Lord Justice, even on the ground that the single judge, in reaching his decision, has failed to exercise his discretion properly or at all (*Racal Communications, Re* [1980] C.L.Y. 273, *Aden Refinery Co. v. Ugland Management Co.* [1986] C.L.Y. 91 applied; *Anisminic v. Foreign Compensation Commission* [1969] C.L.Y. 1866, *Scherer v. Counting Instruments (Note)* [1986] C.L.Y. 2572 distinguished).
Per curiam: if, through mischance, a single judge has in truth never reached a decision on the application before him, s.54(6) of the 1981 Act does not apply.
DAISYSTAR v. TOWN AND COUNTRY BUILDING SOCIETY [1992] 1 W.L.R. 390, C.A.

59 **Title to land—warrant offered to induce exchange—whether collateral contract—whether enforceable**

[Law of Property (Miscellaneous Provisions) Act 1989 (c.34), s.2.]
Where a contract for the sale of land was in two parts and awaiting exchange, an offer by the vendor to warrant the state of his title to induce the purchaser to exchange could amount to a collateral contract, outside the requirements of s.2 of the Law of Property (Miscellaneous Provisions) Act 1989.
Solicitors for V and P signed a contract in two parts for the sale of a house. The day before the due date for exchange, V's solicitor wrote to P's solicitor that he was still awaiting up-to-date office copy entries from the Land Registry recording V's title. On the due date of exchange V's solicitor enclosed a letter with V's part of the contract, confirming that contracts had been exchanged conditionally on the basis that the office copy records would show V as proprietor, and P's solicitor accepted and forwarded his part of the contract on that basis. V's title was accepted when office copy records later became available. P did not pay the price and V sued for specific performance. P asked for leave to defend on the grounds that the contract for sale did not comply with s.2 of the Law of Property (Miscellaneous Provisions) Act 1989.
Held, granting V specific performance, that s.2 of the 1989 Act required that the terms for sale of land had to be set out at length, and since the terms of the letters were not referred to in the parts of the contract which were exchanged, they did not satisfy the requirements of s.2. However, V's solicitor's letter was an offer of a warranty that V would be shown in the register as the proprietor, and the offer and its acceptance by P in exchanging contracts was a collateral contract independent of the contract of sale and outside the provisions of s.2 (*De Lassalle v. Guildford* [1901] 2 K.B. 215 applied).
RECORD v. BELL [1991] 1 W.L.R. 853, Baker, Q.C., sitting as a High Court Judge.

example **A** the table of cases in volume 11 gives a page number (see figure 4.7). Scan the page to find the case. Example **B** is a New Zealand case (N.Z.) not an English case. The table of cases in volume 6 refers to paragraph number, not a page number. Being a Commonwealth case the number is preceded by an asterisk and will be found among the small print cases (see figure 4.8).

The cumulative supplement is arranged according to the volume numbering of the main work. From the table of cases go to the section covering the volume given (see figure 4.9). The paragraph numbers in each section are followed by the letter a, b, etc to distinguish them from the equivalent paragraph numbers in the main work. At the paragraph in the supplement the case with its reference is digested. Note that the table of cases in the cumulative supplement (unlike the consolidated table of cases) enters 'R v' cases under the defendant.

4. Using Lexis

4.71   Select the ENGGEN library and the CASES file.

(a)   Cases with a distinctive name, eg *Junior Books v Veitchi Co*

     Type: name(Junior Books)

(b)   Cases with a common name, eg *Smith v London Borough of Lewisham* — use a proximity search:

     Type: name(Smith w/6 Lewisham)

or combine with another element, eg date:

     Type: name(Johnson) and date aft 1990

Note all the above examples are searching just on the segment of the case containing its name. A search without specifying the name segment will retrieve the case itself but also all other cases in which it has been cited. For this type of enquiry it would thus not usually be the most economical approach, but it is a way of finding cases, provided of course they have been cited, that are not otherwise on the database, for example pre-1945 cases.

Finding cases by subject

4.72   The best way to tackle subject searching depends on your objective. You may be engaged on a major piece of research requiring an exhaustive list of authorities. You may, on the other hand, need only a quick overview of the leading cases. You may be familiar with the area and only want to check for any recent developments. Or, as often happens, you can remember a case but not its name. A pathway for an exhaustive piece of research is suggested here, but can be adapted as appropriate for these other needs.

As discussed in the opening chapter, before starting your search it is well worth while getting clear in your own mind the likely legal issues and areas of law involved, and running through the possible terms that might be used and then considering broader and narrower terms and synonyms.

Figure 4.6   The Digest: *consolidated table of cases volume*

GUTHRIC   416

Guthric v Muntingh (1829) (S AF) **42 Ship**
Guthrie, Re, Trustees, Exors & Agency Co of New Zealand Ltd v Gutrie (1925) (NZ) **50 Wills**
Guthrie, Re (1924) (CAN) **50 Wills**
Guthrie, ex p (1822) **4(2) Bkpcy**
Guthrie, ex p (1824) **4(2) Bkpcy**
Guthrie v Abool Mozuffer (1871) **16 Courts**
Guthrie v Abul Mazaffar (1871) (IND) **12(1) Contr**
Guthrie v Armstrong (1822) **1(2) Agcy; 29 Insce**
Guthrie v Baker (AUS) **17 Damgs**
Guthrie v Canadian Pacific Ry Co (1900) (CAN) **38 Rys**
Guthrie v Clark (1886) (CAN) **40 S Land**
Guthrie v Cochrane (1846) (SCOT) **34 Mines**
Guthrie v Crossley (1826) **5(2) Bkpcy**
Guthrie v Fisk (1824) **4(1) Bkpcy; 45 Stats**
Guthrie v G & SW Ry Co (1858) (SCOT) **3 Arbn**
Guthrie v Lister (1866) **12(1) Contr**
Guthrie v McCrindle (1949) **31 L&T**
Guthrie v Ogilvie, Dykes, etc (1830) (SCOT) **1(2) Agcy; 44 Solrs**
Guthrie v Stewart (SCOT) **31 L&T**
Guthrie v Walrond (1883) **11 Confl; 23 Exors**
Guthrie v Walroud (1874) **23 Exors**
Guthrie v WF Huntting Lumber Co Ltd (1910) (CAN) **36(1) Negl**
Guthrie v Wilson (SCOT) **30 Intox**
Guthrie v Wood (1816) **25 Fraud Conv**
Guthrie, Craig, Peter & Co v Brechin Magistrates (1888) (SCOT) **38 Pub Hlth**
Guthrie, R v (1870) **14(2) Crim**
Guthrie, R v (1877) (CAN) **22(2) Evid**
Guthrie, R v (CAN) **19 Eccl**
Guthrie & Co, Re, ex p Bank of Australasia (1884) (NZ) **35 Mtge**
Guthrie & Co, Re, ex p Bank of NZ (1884) (NZ) **6 B of Exch**
Guthrie & Co, Re (1884) (NZ) **36(2) Prtnrs**
Guthrie's Case (1898) (NZ) **9(1) Coys; 9(2) Coys**
Guthrie's Exor v Guthrie (1945) (SCOT) **50 Wills**
Guthrie's Trustees v Ireland (SCOT) **30 Intox**
Gutieres, In the Goods of (1869) **11 Confl**
Gutierrez, Re (1879) **4(1) Bkpcy**
Gutierrez, ex p (1879) **4(1) Bkpcy**
Gutierrez, ex p (1880) **4(1) Bkpcy**
Gutkin v Winnipeg City (1933) (CAN) **28(4) Infts**
Gutman, R v (1904) (AUS) **25 Gaming**
Gutsch, Re (1959) (CAN) **28(3) Infts**
Gutsch, ex p (1959) (CAN) **8(2) Comwlth**
Gutsch, ex p (1960) (CAN) **8(2) Comwlth**
Gutschmidt, R v (1939) (CAN) **14(2) Crim**
Gutsell v Reeve (1935) **32 Limit of A**
Gutsole v Mathers (1836) **3 Auct; 32 Libel**
Gutta Pecha Corpn, Re (1900) **10(2) Coys**
Gutta Percha & India Rubber Co of Toronto's Applns, Re (1909) **47(2) Trade Mks**
Gutta Percha & Rubber (London) Ltd (no 789,574) Appln, Re (1935) **47(2) Trade Mks**
Gutta Percha Corpn Ltd, Re (1899) **9(1) Coys; 10(1) Coys**
Guttenberg v R (1905) (S AF) **15 Crim**
Guttenberg v R (1906) (S AF) **14(2) Crim**
Gutter v Locrofts (1592) **31 L&T**
Gutter v Tait (1947) **3 Bailmt**
Gutteridge v Munyard (1834) **31 L&T**
Gutteridge v Smith (1794) **6 B of Exch**
Gutteridge v Stilwell (1883) **23 Exors**
Gutteridge, R v (1851) **15 Crim**
Gutteridge (Doe d) v Sowerby (1860) **1(2) Agcy**

Guttierez, In the Goods of (1869) **11 Confl**
Guttridge, R v (1840) 9 C & P 228 **14(2) Crim**
Guy, Re (1887) **5(2) Bkpcy**
Guy v Brady (1885) (CAN) **1(2) Agcy; 3 Barr**
Guy v Brown (1600) **11 Comns**
Guy v Brown (1601) **19 Easmt**
Guy v Churchill (1887) **44 Solrs**
Guy v Churchill (1888) **5(1) Bkpcy**
Guy v Churchill (1889) **1(2) Agcy**
Guy v Ferguon Syndicate Co Ltd (1892) (NZ) **9(1) Coys**
Guy v Goudreault (1864) (CAN) **12(1) Contr**
Guy v Gower (1816) **44 Solrs**
Guy v Grand Trunk Ry Co, Re (1884) (CAN) **13 Corpns**
Guy v Gregory (1840) **32 Libel**
Guy v Guy (1840) **28(4) Infts**
Guy v Guy (1910) (NZ) **37(1) Perps; 50 Wills**
Guy v Guy and Foster (1900) **27(3) H&W**
Guy v Kearney (1842) (IR) **6 B of Exch**
Guy v Livesey (1618) **27(1) H&W**
Guy v M'Carthy (1886) (IR) **23 Exors**
Guy v Newson (1833) **17 Deeds**
Guy v Nichols (1694) **12(2) Contr**
Guy v Sharp (1833) **50 Wills**
Guy v Shulhan (1962) (CAN) **27(1) H&W**
Guy v Walker (1892) **37(2) Pract**
Guy v Waterlow Bros & Layton Ltd (1909) **9(2) Coys**
Guy v West (1808) **7 Bounds&F**
Guy (WJ) & Son v Glen Line Ltd (1948) **42 Ship**
Guy Butler (International) Ltd v Customs & Excise Comrs, Customs & Excise Comrs v Guy Butler (International) Ltd (1976) **49 VAT**
Guy Mannering, The (1882) **42 Ship**
Guy-Pell v Foster (1930) **12(2) Contr; 26 Guar**
Guyana and Trinidad Mutual Life Insurance Co Ltd v RK Plummer and Associates Ltd (1988) (TRINIDAD & TOBAGO) **12(2) Contr**
Guyer v R (1889) **25 Game; 45 Stats**
Guyer Oil Co Ltd, Golden Eagle Oil & Gas Ltd and Husky Oil (Alberta) Ltd v Fulton & Gladstone Petroleum Ltd (1973) (CAN) **47(1) Trade**
Guyer's Application, Re (1980) **26 Hghys**
Guyot v Thomson (1894) **12(1) Contr; 17 Deeds; 36(3) Pats**
Guyot, R v (1927) (CAN) **22(2) Evid**
Guyot & Vigouret & Award made by Gosselin, Re (1919) (CAN) **3 Arbn**
Guyot-Guenin & Son v Clyde Soap Co (1915) (SCOT) **2 Aliens**
Guyton & Rosenberg's Contract, Re (1901) **50 Wills**
Guzak and Guzak v McEwan (1965) (CAN) **27(1) H&W**
Guzerat Spinning & Weaving Co v Girdharlal Dalpatram (1880) (IND) **9(1) Coys**
Guzzala Hanuman v R (1902) (IND) **15 Crim**
Guzzo, R v (CAN) **21 Estpl**
GW Bates & Co v J & P Cameron & Co (1855) (SCOT) **8(1) Carr**
GW Golden Construction Ltd v Minister of National Revenue (1966) (CAN) **28(1) Inc T**
GW Murray & Co Ltd (1934) (CAN) **5(1) Bkpcy**
GW Ry Co, ex p, Re Foster v GW Ry Co (1882) **37(2) Pract**
GW Ry Co v Bater (1922) **37(2) Pract**
GW Young & Co Ltd v North British and Mercantile Insurance Co, GW Young & Co Ltd v Scottish Union and National Insurance Co (1907) **37(1) Pldg**

Figure 4.7   The Digest: *table of cases in volume of main work—reference to page number*

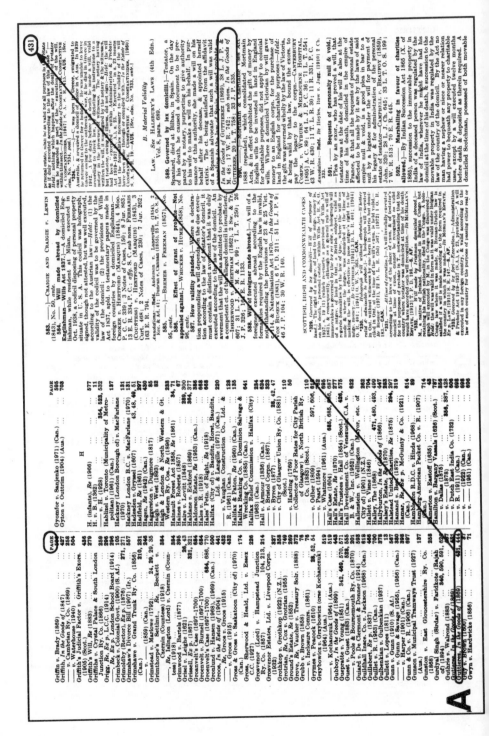

Figure 4.8   **The Digest:** *table of cases in volume of main work—reference to paragraph number*

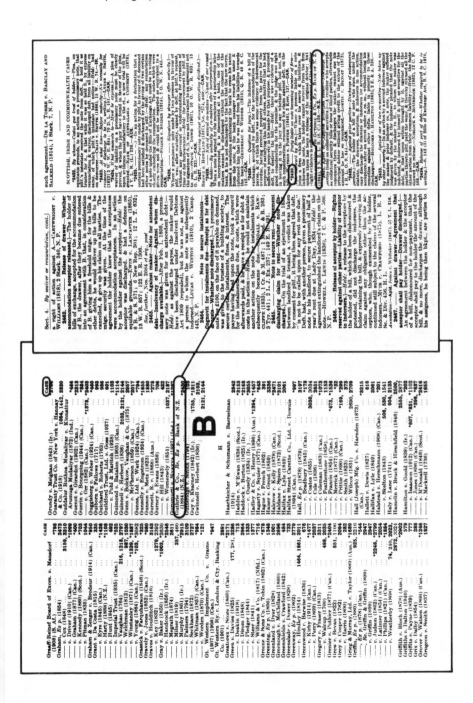

Figure 4.9   The Digest: *cumulative supplement*

Table of Cases

Vol 26—Hire Purchase and Consumer Credit

Part 1—Consumer credit

5148 Apld UCB Leasing Ltd v Holton (1987) 137 NLJ 614

5151A *Advertisement—Willingness of credit company to give credit* JENKINS v LOMBARD NORTH CENTRAL PLC [1984] 1 All ER 828, (1984) See Continuation Vol G

5155a *Execution of the agreement—Improper execution—Whether liability existing* The defendant, in relation to a hire purchase agreement on a car, gave a false address and was subsequently convicted of evading a liability by deception, with intent to make default on any existing liability to make a payment, contrary to the Theft Act 1978, s 2(1)(b). On appeal, he contended that as the total amount payable had been left blank on the hire purchase agreement with the car dealer, according to the provisions of the Consumer Credit Act 1974, s 61(1), the agreement was improperly executed. Under s 65 of the Act, such an improperly executed agreement was enforceable only on the order of the court, and there was not an existing liability to make a payment. *Held*, the fact that the agreement was unenforceable without an order of the court did not mean that there was no existing liability. The object of s 65 was that if the agreement was not properly completed, one of the remedies of a disappointed contractor for enforcing his liability was removed from him, in that he could not retake possession under the hire purchase agreement. The defendant's argument was untenable and the appeal would be dismissed.

R v MODUPE (1991) 135 SJ 249, (1991) Times, 27 February, CA

5156a *Form and content of agreement* LOMBARD TRICITY FINANCE LTD v PATON (1989) See Continuation Vol H

5168 Apld (dictum Diplock LJ) R v Crown Court at Knightsbridge, ex p Marcrest Ltd [1983] 1 All ER 1148; Sturolson & Co v Weniz (1984) 272 Estates Gazette 326 **Consd** Antoniades v Villiers [1988] 2 All ER 309

5174a *Default—Recovery of amount outstanding* Where a creditor seeks to recover sums outstanding under a regulated consumer credit agreement as a result of the debtor's default, judgment should be entered for the full outstanding amount owed by the debtor without any allowance for the rebate of unearned charges for credit to which the debtor may be entitled on early settlement by virtue of ss 94(1) and 95(1) of the Consumer Credit Act 1974, since under regs 4 and 6(1) of the Consumer Credit (Rebate on Early Settlement) Regulations 1983 the effect of the debtor's potential entitlement to a rebate is to reduce his indebtedness at the data of payment, and not at the date of judgment, by enabling him to discharge his indebtedness by a payment which may be less than 100p in the pound depending on when he discharges it. However, for the protection of the debtor the judgment for the full outstanding amount should be indorsed with a notice drawing

Often in practice you have gone to a textbook or *Halsbury's Laws*, looked up a few of the cases mentioned, and then some of the cases cited in those cases, so that a preliminary list of authorities begins to build up. This is certainly a useful and practical approach because it gives a feel for what is likely to be relevant and clarifies the object of the search. But it tends to involve duplication of effort, and so, according to taste, it may be better to start on the systematic approach from the word go.

The systematic approach

4.73 The systematic approach has three stages which usually proceed with diminishing returns. The initial stage is the main trawl which will yield the bulk of the references. The second stage is to check for any very recent cases in the last few days or weeks. And the last stage is to note up all the cases you have found so far to double-check whether there have been cited in any other cases you have missed. A fourth stage, either if you have found very little or if you have the time and resources to go to town, would be to repeat the whole process with sources from other jurisdictions — Commonwealth materials if the topic is a common law one, or possibly European materials if it is EC related.

Stage one: the main trawl

4.74 For stage one, Lexis is unquestionably the best starting place. Apart from cost and availability, the only proviso to that might be where the area of law is wholly unknown to you, in which case you might consider an initial search in manual sources (or a textbook) to familiarise yourself with the terminology that is likely to be used.

Before starting your Lexis search, jot down a search strategy. There are four basics to this strategy. First, start with a broad search — you can subsequently narrow it at no extra cost using the 'Modify' facility, but you cannot subsequently broaden it without incurring a new search charge. Secondly, think of as many synonyms has possible. Thirdly, remember to truncate words which may appear with different endings, eg COMPENSAT! will retrieve COMPENSATE, COMPENSATED, COMPENSATES, COMPENSATING, COMPENSATION, COMPENSATORY. Fourthly, when searching for two terms that appear in conjunction use the proximity facility (W/) rather than entering them as a phrase, if there is a chance that the two terms might be grammatically separated, eg BREACH OF CONFIDENCE would not retrieve 'a breach by the commission of its statutory duty of confidentiality'.

If you do not have access to Lexis, you will have to rely mainly on *Current Law* yearbooks and *The Digest*. Even if you have done a Lexis search *The Digest* may be needed for older cases and for Commonwealth cases, and even the *Current Law* yearbooks, particularly before 1980 when there are no transcripts on Lexis, may throw up the odd case. If you have done a Lexis search, or after you have found a few cases in *Current Law* or *The Digest*, it is worth pausing to look at the cases you have found in order to gauge what further material is likely to be relevant, and see whether any leading cases, which will summarise the main authorities, are apparent.

4.75 There are two ways of using the *Current Law* yearbooks for subject searching. One is to use the cumulative indexes that are to be found in the yearbooks for 1971 (covering 1945-1971), 1986 and 1989, and the annual indexes thereafter. The hazard with this approach is that the indexing practice and terminology has changed over the years, so while the annual indexes may be internally consistent, when they are merged in the cumulative indexes they may not be. The other approach is to look through the body of each yearbook under the heading applicable. This, however, is only safe when the topic is self-contained and readily falls under a specific heading, eg 'Patents' or 'Income tax'. To be safe it may be necessary to follow both methods, which can be very time-consuming. A portion of this drudgery will be removed by the CD-ROM version which covers the yearbooks since 1986 in one database. When using the cumulative indexes the references are to yearbook and paragraph number, eg 84/1976 refers to paragraph 1976 in the yearbook for 1984 (*not* paragraph 84 in the 1976 yearbook).

4.76 *The Digest*, in contrast, only involves looking in two places — the main work and the cumulative supplement. The recently reissued consolidated index to the whole work will usually take you straight to the right paragraph number (unlike its predecessors which were very inadequate). Alternatively, simply browse along the shelf looking for a likely main topic and then, having found the right volume, look through the contents pages for the topic. When you have finished with the main work check the corresponding section in the cumulative supplement, which will give summaries of recent cases and also refer you to material from earlier supplements that has been transferred to one of the continuation volumes.

Stage two: very recent developments

4.77 Stage two is to catch any very recent developments — the supplement to *The Digest* is only annual. If you have not already done so, check the latest monthly digests of *Current Law*. The latest part includes a cumulative index to all the preceding parts for that year, but as with the yearbooks you may need or prefer to browse through the body of the entries for each month. Lawtel will cover even more recent developments. It may also be worth flicking through any recent parts of law reports that have been published since the last monthly part of *Current Law*, especially if there is a recognised specialist series for the particular area.

4.78 The other two tools for very recent developments are the *Daily Law Reports Index* and *Legal Journals Index*, though a retrospective search of these is also wise if you wish to be sure of being comprehensive. They both use the same system of subject indexing, which is rather different from other sources. Each item is assigned a number of key words, and the entries are repeated under each key word in rotation. Thus the case of *R v Independent Television Commission, ex p TSW Broadcasting Ltd* appears three times in the key word index in the *Daily Law Reports Index* under:

JUDICIAL REVIEW. Licensing. Television
LICENSING. Television. Judicial review
TELEVISION. Judicial review. Licensing

The terms are strictly controlled and are assigned from a thesaurus, which sets out the relationships between broader, narrower and related terms. Cross-references between these terms are not given in the indexes themselves, but a printed copy of the thesaurus is available separately and may be available in some libraries. It is thus important when using these two indexes to search on the most specific term first and then think of possible broader terms. For example in the case given above, the term used is 'Television' not 'Broadcasting'.

Both these sources, as already mentioned, are available in electronic form, and for subject searching this does have notable advantages over the printed version. For one thing the thesaurus itself is accessible. It is also possible to 'explode' the thesaurus so that one search embraces all the terms at each level and sub-level in a hierarchy, without having to key them all in laboriously using 'OR' connectors. But the main advantage is the ability is search on words that are not index terms, particularly in the case of the *Daily Law Reports Index* words that appear in the quite lengthy summaries of each case.

4.79 Having completed stages one and two of your search, the final step is to check whether any of the cases you have found have been cited in other cases. Such cases are likely to be on the same subject (though not necessarily — the case may have been cited on an altogether different point) and it ensures that what you have found is still good law. The tools for doing this, citators, are treated in a separate section below (para 4.85-4.91) as their use is not confined to subject searching.

If time is short

4.80 The systematic approach above can be adapted according to how much time you have and how much prior knowledge of the subject you have. But if you do not need to be completely comprehensive and you have very little time probably the two best places to try are *The Law Reports Index* or the cumulated index to the *All England Law Reports*. The latter will cover all the mainstream case law from 1936 until the last year or so, while the former allows you to concentrate on just the last 10 or 20 years and will cover some specialist areas like industrial law or tax law. These two sources will be in virtually every law library, but another excellent alternative for this kind of search if it is available to you is the CD-ROM version of the *Weekly Law Reports*. You can do a Lexis-type search without the attendant search costs. If time is short and the above sources retrieve a lot of cases, do not try to look them all up, but pick one at the highest level of court which is also recent — nine times out of ten all the relevant authorities will already have been assembled there.

Worked examples

Using Current Law yearbooks to find recent cases

4.81

How many cases on Anton Piller orders have been digested since 1986?

1. 1990 YEARBOOK

The index at the back covers 1990 only. Under 'Anton Piller orders' is one case — 90/3546. Details of the case will found at paragraph 3546.

2. 1989 YEARBOOK

The index at the back covers the yearbooks from 1987 to 1989. Under 'Anton Piller orders' seven cases are given: 87/2883, 89/2886, 2887, 87/2884, 89/2888, 87/2889, 87/2885. These cases are in the 1987 and 1989 yearbooks at the paragraphs given. The section of the yearbook they are in is 'Practice (Civil)'. If instead of using the index, you browse through all the entries in the 'Practice (Civil)' section in each yearbook, one more case will be found that is not in the index — 88/2837, which is headed with the catchphrases 'Discovery — use of documents — Anton Piller order — committal proceedings'.

3. 1986 YEARBOOK

The index at the back covers all the yearbooks from 1972 to 1986. If you look up 'Anton Piller orders' all that you will find is three cases from 1980. But remember that the indexing practice changed after 1986. Anton Piller orders, except for the three 1980 cases which seem to be aberrations, in fact appear in this index as a sub-heading of 'Practice'. This lists two cases from 1986, 86/2563-4, together with earlier cases.

This is a good example of where the CD-ROM version would show its potential.

Using The Digest to find older cases

4.82

What cases are there on treasure trove?

Go to the consolidated index volumes. Under the heading 'Treasure trove' in the P-Z volume the following entries will be found:

> concealing **15** *Crim* 8723, *6428
> general rule **11** *Const L* 943, 944, *597
> inquest on **13** *Crnrs* 1726
> *jura regalia* **11** *Const L* 836

Go to the volumes of the main work and paragraphs listed, remembering that the asterisked paragraphs are the small print Commonwealth cases. In the main work you will find cross-references given to other entries in the same volume or other volumes. These entries should already have been picked up in the consolidated index, but you may notice that some paragraph numbers do not correspond to those given in the index. The reason for this is that there may been a reissue of the volume referred to. Here volume 15 was reissued after volume 11 was last published; hence the references to volume 15 in volume 11 may no longer be accurate. However, at the back of the new volume 15 is a 'Reference Adaptor' which gives in the left column the old paragraph reference and in the right the new one. Check against this to confirm that the consolidated index did pick up all the references.

Go to the annual cumulative supplement. The main references to treasure trove were those in volume 11 so check the section in the cumulative supplement under 'Volume 11 — Constitutional law' and look for paragraphs 943 and 944. Two more recent cases on treasure trove will be found and are numbered 944a and 944b. Full details are not given but you are referred to continuation volumes F and H. These are both again arranged by volume number and topic as in the main work.

Finding cases on quantum of damages for personal injuries

4.83   Cases on the substantive law of damages and of negligence will be found in the sources listed above but advisers often need to know what the 'going rate' is for the amount of damages awarded for particular injuries, which is in the discretion of the court. Such cases are not precedents and turn on their facts so are not the subject of conventional law reports, but published information is available.

The basic tool is the looseleaf work *Kemp and Kemp: Quantum of Damages in Personal Injury and Fatal Accident Claims*, published by Sweet & Maxwell. Butterworths also publish a work, *Personal Injury Litigation Service* by Goldrein and De Haas, which gives full coverage of the substantive law and procedure, but also includes a section on quantum awards. There are two other sources which should be consulted mainly, but not exclusively, for recent cases. The monthly reviews which form part of the service to *Halsbury's Laws* are particular strong on quantum cases. The monthly reviews are filed in their own binder with *Halsbury's Laws*, and contain the full details of the cases (under the head 'Damages'), but in the separate looseleaf noter-up volume is a cumulative table by injury (eye, leg, etc) with brief details of the amount of the award which acts as a source of quick reference and as a key to the monthly reviews. The monthly reviews are cumulated as the *Halsbury's Laws Annual Abridgment*. There is a similar service in *Current Law*, though it may not necessarily cover the same cases. The awards are summarised in each monthly digest and in the yearbooks under the heading 'Damages', but in the latest monthly part there is a cumulative table similar to that in the *Halsbury's Laws* monthly reviews. Lawtel also offers a table by type of injury, which is an option from the decisions menu.

Finding cases in which particular words or phrases have been judicially considered

See chapter 2, paras 2.47-2.50.

Finding EC cases by subject

4.84 Often the most precise way to find EC cases on a topic is to search by a particular treaty provision or legislative provision that might have been considered, rather than by subject terms; sources that index cases by legislation are described below (para 4.98). But if you do need to search by subject-matter, Justis and Lexis if you have access to them are usually the most effective approach; some search strategies are suggested in the Quick Reference Guide (QR4.14). Of the printed sources the *Gazetteer of European Law* and *Case Search Monthly* are more fully indexed by subject than the *Butterworths EC Case Citator* whose 'key phrase/sector' index only covers selected cases that have 'substantially contributed to EC law', though it does not have the gap in timespan of the former. Vaughan's *Law of the European Communities* at the end of each subject division usefully gives lists of relevant cases. There is an alphabetical subject index to the T.M.C. Asser Institute's *Guide to EC Court Decisions* but that work is not updated very frequently. The official publication *Digest of Case Law Relating to the European Communities* is probably a last resort. For recent cases and current awareness there are *European Current Law* and *European Court of Justice Reporter*. *Current Law* itself also covers some ECJ cases, as does *The Digest*, and of course the sources for English cases above will cover cases in the English courts relevant to EC law.

Following up cases: citators

4.85 It is important to know whether a particular case you are using has been cited ·in a later case. Its authority may have been strengthened by being expressly approved by a higher court; on the other hand, it may have been overruled. Between these two extremes there are various gradations of citation. They are usefully set out in the front of the cumulative supplement to *The Digest* with explanations of their meaning which should be referred to. The main terms are: applied, approved, considered, disapproved, distinguished, doubted, explained, extended, followed, not followed, overruled, and referred to. The subtle distinctions in meaning between these terms epitomise the fluid way in which the doctrine of precedent is applied in practice. As has already been mentioned, citators are also an excellent way of doing a subject search, if you already know of a leading case. If you have a recent case a citator may tell you if it has been appealed.

4.86 By far the most comprehensive way of following up citations is to use Lexis. Even apart from its transcript coverage, it will almost invariably find more citations than the printed citators. Simply formulate the name of the case as your search request, eg CANDLER W/5 CRANE will retrieve all cases in which C*andler v Christmas Co* has been cited. The case itself will of course be among the cases retrieved (if it is within the scope of the database) but being by definition the earliest case of those retrieved it will be at the end of the list.

4.87 The *Current Law* case citators have already been described in connection with finding cases by name. Remember that you will need to look in the two hard bound volumes covering up to 1988, the softback supplement and the cumulative table of cases in the latest monthly digest. Refer to the worked examples at para 4.68 cases **A, B,** and **C** and at para 4.69 case **B**.

4.88 The *Current Law* citators only go back to 1947, though of course they cover earlier cases *cited* since then. The best source for earlier coverage is *The Digest*. Find the case by name as described earlier. At the foot of the entry is a section 'Annotations' which gives other cases in which it has been cited. Further annotations will be given in the cumulative supplement. *The Law Reports Index* and its precursor *The Law Reports Digest* have tables of cases judicially considered (not to be confused with the separate tables of cases reported) which can be useful in addition or instead of *Current Law* and *The Digest*. There is a table of cases judicially considered in the consolidated tables to the *All England Law Reports* if that is all that is to hand, but it only covers citations in the All ER to other cases reported in the All ER.

4.89 The new monthly and annual published version of the *Times Law Reports* includes a table of cases judicially considered, as did the *Index to the Times Law Reports* published by Professional Books from 1982. Both will contain citations not picked up by *Current Law*. The printed version of the *Daily Law Reports Index* unfortunately does not have such a table, but a search of the electronic version will pick up any cases mentioned in the summaries of the cases indexed. The CD-ROM version of the *Weekly Law Reports* would also certainly be worth a try.

4.90 If you are a barrister you may also have the benefit of another system, which some of the Inn libraries provide, but which few other libraries, if any, do nowadays (because it is an exceptionally tedious task), namely the physical noting up of the volumes themselves. The references for later cases are written in red ink at the head of the report that has been cited! *The Law Reports* used to have a similar system, whereby they issued sticky labels bearing the references for subscribers to stick into their own copies at the relevant point.

4.91 Finally, a useful source if you have been unable to find any cases in the above and wish to try your luck with Commonwealth authorities, or if you are doing in-depth research where Commonwealth authorities might be relevant, is the *Australian and New Zealand Citator to UK Reports*, which gives English cases cited in the Australian and New Zealand courts. The main volume up to 1972 only covers those English cases reported in the main series, and its coverage of pre-1865 cases is confined to those that appear in the *All England Law Reports* reprint series, but the annual cumulative supplement thereafter is wider in scope.

Finding cases that cite EC cases

4.92 As with English cases, electronic sources are by far the most effective method. A search example using Lexis is given in the Quick Reference Guide (QR4.11), or Justis on-line or on CD-ROM could be used. Either the name or the number can be used as a search term. The main printed source is the *Gazetteer of European Law* supplemented by *Case Search Monthly* in the 'Case Search' section, though you need to know the case number (which can be traced through the alphabetical index if you have only the name). A useful feature is that the citations are graded in importance, the citations providing the most extensive consideration being given in bold, and mere mentions in italic. *Butterworths EC Case Citator*, as mentioned, does not currently perform this function. The English citator sources described above will of course catch ECJ cases cited in the English courts. The search example in the Quick Reference Guide (looking for cases that cite Case 79/83 *Harz v Deutsche Tradax GmbH*) while retrieving 16 cases in the EURCOM library on Lexis, retrieves a further nine in the ENGGEN library.

Finding cases on legislation

4.93 Even in those areas that are statute-based and not governed by common law, case law remains important as a source of interpretation and construction. As well as the statutes themselves, SIs are also judicially considered from time to time.

For both statutes and SIs Lexis, as for case citations, is the most powerful tool. Formulate your search by taking words or phrases from the title of the legislation and combine them if necessary with the section number. For example to search for cases in which section 7 of the Employment Act 1990 was considered type:

Employment w/4 1990 w/15 7

Note that it is generally inadvisable to search on 'section' or 's' or to try to limit the search to a particular sub-section.

4.94 Although offering only a fraction of the coverage of Lexis, because it similarly provides full text retrieval, the *Weekly Law Reports* on CD-ROM are well worth checking, if Lexis is not available (or affordable), in addition to the printed sources mentioned below. The *Current Law* yearbooks on CD-ROM, in theory should not yield anything on statutes not found in the manual statute citator since, if the provision is of sufficient significance to be mentioned in the digest to the case, it is going to be picked for the citator, but it may be worth double-checking by this method. On the other hand it will be more useful for citations of SIs since those are not covered by the printed citator.

4.95 The two main manual sources for statutes are the annotations to *Halsbury's Statutes* and the *Current Law* legislation citators. These give case references as well as noting amendments and repeals to the statutes themselves, as described in the last chapter. If you need to look at case law before 1947 (which will not be covered by *Current Law*) or for case law on statutes no longer in force (which will not be in the current edition of *Halsbury's Statutes*), there is a table of statutes judicially considered in *The Law Reports Digest*.

4.96 *The Law Reports Index*, as the latter work is now called, also has such a table. But where it scores over *Current Law* is that it also has a table of SIs judicially considered. The section on SIs in the *Current Law* legislation citators, unlike its section on statutes, does not note up case law.

The Law Reports Index, it should be noted, has four other useful citators that are often overlooked: standard forms of contract judicially considered, overseas enactments judicially considered, European Community enactments judicially considered, and international conventions judicially considered.

4.97 If you are looking for cases on SIs, the other main source is *Halsbury's Statutory Instruments*, which includes some cases in the annotations. There are also four other places to try. The consolidated tables to the *All England Law Reports* go furthest back. Subsidiary legislation judicially considered is split between six different tables: Rules of the Supreme Court, County Court Rules, Matrimonial Causes Rules, Bankruptcy and Insolvency Rules, Other Rules, and Regulations. The *Daily Law Reports Index* has a table of legislation considered, which includes not only statutes and SIs but also EC legislation and treaties, as does the index to the *Times Law Reports*.

4.98 Although *The Law Reports Index* and the *Daily Law Reports Index* include EC legislation considered, the best place to look for cases on EC legislation is again Justis or Lexis. Of printed sources the *Butterworths EC Case Citator* is the most useful: it includes full listings by treaty provision, regulations, directives and decisions. The 'Law tracker' section of *Case Search Monthly* would be a cross-check, though it means looking through the parts and annual volumes and only goes back to 1988 — the *Gazetteer of European Law* does not have an equivalent section. The table of legal provisions in the T.M.C. Asser Institute *Guide to EC Court Decisions*, if available, is another possibility. For recent cases, especially those from national courts in other member states, *European Current Law* could be checked: regulations, directives and decisions are in fact included in the table headed 'Treaty provisions referred to'.

4.99 Cases which consider Local and Personal Acts do not arise that often, but if you need to research this, those tools described above that include Local and Personal Acts judicially considered, as well as Public General Acts, are listed in the Quick Reference Guide (QR4.15).

Worked example: full-scale case law research

4.100   Find as many cases as possible on the writ *ne exeat regno*. (If you were unfamiliar with this, you might start with a law dictionary which would tell you that it is prerogative writ usually issued from the Chancery Division to restrain a person, such as an absconding debtor, from leaving the kingdom.)

1. Lexis

4.101   The search request 'Exeat Regno' in the CASES file in the ENGGEN library will retrieve at least 15 cases (of which 4 are unreported), the earliest being in 1968. This would take less than two minutes to do. Compare the time and the results using the manual sources below.

2. *Current Law*

4.102 Nothing will be found in the 1990 or 1991 yearbooks or the latest monthly parts, but three cases are listed in the 1987-89 index in the 1989 yearbook under:

Practice (Civil)
    writ
        ne exeat regno
87/1748 *Thaha v Thaha* (1987) 17 Fam Law 234
87/3137 *Allied Arab Bank v Hajjar* [1987] 1 FTLR 455
88/2963 The same case as above but with a fuller digest based on the report at
    [1988] 2 WLR 942

4.103   As this last case at the time it was digested was only in the *Weekly Law Reports*, you might wish to find the subsequent *Law Reports* reference, it being a volume 2 case. The *Current Law* case citator 1977-88 gives the answer — [1988] QB 787. But you will also find an illustration of the hazards when the same case is reported at different stages of litigation, hazards to which even *Current Law* can succumb. The citator lists two cases by that name as follows:

Allied Arab Bank v Hajjar Digested 88/2905; Not followed 88/3404
Allied Arab Bank v Hajjar (No. 2) Digested 88/3405

Our case on the *ne exeat regno* point is the first one, and was heard at an interlocutory stage before Legatt J. The second case is at trial before Hirst J, and is reported on an entirely different point, the tort of conspiracy. However, it transpires that the case also went to the Court of Appeal on yet another point — Hirst J's order concerning a Mareva injunction — which is also reported. *Current Law* has got comprehensively confused. The paragraph number given against the first case is in fact for the Court of Appeal decision. The correct paragraph numbers for the *ne exeat regno* decision in the 1987 and 1988 Yearbooks are omitted altogether, and the decision not followed in case 88/3404 is not the first but the second.

4.104   Proceeding to the 1972-86 index in the 1986 yearbook, *ne exeat regno* is not indexed as such — there is only a string of references to writs in general. This will mean looking through the body of each yearbook for the entries on writs in the 'Practice' section. There is one case in 1986:

86/2724 *Al Nahkel for Contracting and Trading v Lowe* [1986] 2 WLR 317

And one in 1985:

85/2747 *Lipkin Gorman v Cass* The Times, 29 May 1985

4.105 At this point it would be worth looking at the cases you have retrieved so far. A perusal of those cases will reveal that they all apply *Felton v Callis* [1969] 1 QB 200, which appears to be the leading case in the area and furthermore that there have been no other reported cases since. So instead of ploughing on through yearbooks it is worth looking at it. This indeed proves to be a leading case which shows that prior to 1968 the last reported case was in 1957 and before that in 1893, and gives extensive citations to earlier authorities.

3. The Digest

4.106 As there is clearly a lot of old authority on this subject, *The Digest* is definitely going to be needed even if you have done a Lexis search. In the consolidated index the subject appears straightforwardly enough under 'Ne Exeat Regno'. Virtually all the references given are to the same region of the title Equity in volume 20. Five pages of cases will be found there, including several Commonwealth ones. A double-check in the equivalent section in the cumulative supplement only picks up those cases already noted from *Current Law*.

4. Daily Law Reports Index

4.107 No entries will be found in the key word index under 'ne exeat regno' and the cases under 'Writs' do not seem to be relevant. If you were uncertain whether you were looking under the right terms, it would be worth looking in the *Legal Journals Index*. It uses the same system of key words but also includes cross-references to the preferred form of heading. You will find that for 'Ne Exeat Regno' the index uses the terms 'Writs' and 'Arrest'. Therefore the conclusion that there have been no newspaper reports since 1988 seems valid.

5. Legal Journals Index

4.108 The subject index does not pick up any additional cases — it only lists some journal reports for the cases we have already found, but it will also be seen that there are several articles commenting on the *Al Nahkel* and *Allied Arab Bank* cases. An inspection of the longest of them — (1987) 103 LQR 246 — pays dividends. In only the second footnote an unreported case from 1985 is given — *Yui Wing Construction* — which would only otherwise have been found on Lexis. And a further perusal reveals a further two unreported cases in 1976 and 1982 at footnote 21. There is also extensive citation of early authorities, not all of which are in *The Digest*.

6. Double-checking

4.109   As the case involves civil procedure, one obvious place to look, and where in real life one may well have started, is *The Supreme Court Practice*. The notes to Order 45 r 1 give several references, though not to anything we have not already found. *Halsbury's Laws* — the main volume, the annual cumulative supplement, and the looseleaf noter-up — also covers the same ground, though until one has looked one does not know that.

4.110   The other method of double-checking to is look up the leading cases we have found in the case citators. No further references are revealed in the English ones, but interestingly the *Australian and New Zealand Citator to UK Reports* does show that *Felton v Callis* was cited in a New South Wales case in 1975, which suggests a further trip round Commonwealth authorities might be worth while.

4.111   Lastly, to illustrate that there is always more than one way to approach a problem, one should ask whether there is any legislation involved in the subject-matter. If so, *Halsbury's Statutes* and the legislation citators might throw up some cases. Here it will have been noted that one of the issues in *Felton v Callis* was how the remedy tied in with s 9 of the Debtors Act 1869, and some of the cases (though in this instance none we have not already found) could be tracked down that way.

European Convention on Human Rights case law

4.112   As an appendix to this chapter, some guidance on this increasingly important area is offered. At the risk of stating the obvious, it should be appreciated that the European Convention on Human Rights is a product of the Council of Europe, which is an entirely separate organisation from the European Communities. There are currently 25 member states and its headquarters are in Strasbourg. Unlike EC law the European Convention on Human Rights is not part of our domestic law — yet — so treatment of it was not included with the earlier materials in this chapter. The relationship of the European Convention on Human Rights and domestic law is touched on in the next chapter on treaties, to which reference should be made (para 5.2). Apart from its technical relevance in the context of statutory interpretation as described there and despite its non-incorporation, its general significance for the English lawyer, both academic and practising, is evidenced by the fact that reports of some cases appear in the newspaper law reports and are digested in *Current Law* and *The Digest* (and indexed in the *Daily Law Reports Index*). Although deriving from separate institutions, the Convention is also of increasing significance in relation to EC law in so far as the Court of Justice of the European Communities applies the Convention in deciding the scope of general principles of Community law, and in so far as those EC member states that have incorporated the Convention into their domestic law apply it in their own courts.

4.113   There are three separate bodies involved in deciding whether there has been a breach of the Convention. The European Commission of Human Rights considers applications initially. Their first task is to decide on the admissibility of the application; the large majority of applications are rejected at this stage on the grounds, for example, that national remedies have not been exhausted, or that the wrong alleged is not within the scope of the Convention. If the application is found to be admissible, the Commission has then to establish the facts and try to reach a 'friendly settlement'. If a settlement is not reached a report is made giving an opinion on the merits of the case. This report is communicated to the Committee of Ministers (ie the foreign ministers of each member state, though much of the business is conducted by deputies) of the Council of Europe. Within three months the case may be referred — by the Commission, by the Committee of Ministers, or by a state (though not by an individual applicant) — to the European Court of Human Rights, who then finally make a judgment on the case. If it is not referred to the Court, under article 32 of the Convention, the final decision rests with the Committee of Ministers, who adopt a resolution, which usually accords with the majority opinion of the Commission as there is no further investigation of the merits, as there would be in the Court. The Committee of Ministers also have the role, under article 54 of the Convention, of supervising the execution of judgments of the Court and their own decisions.

4.114   This process thus generates four main species of case law: *decisions* of the Commission on admissibility, *reports* of the Commission on the merits, *judgments* of the Court, and *resolutions* of the Committee of Ministers. In addition, the Commission make reports in respect of friendly settlements, stating the facts and the outcome, and the Committee of Ministers may adopt resolutions with respect to the enforcement of judgments of the Court or its own decisions. Of these the judgments of the Court are the most important and the least numerous — there have only been about 250 to date; they are all published. Reports of the Commission on the merits, which are of the next importance, are published straightaway if the case is referred to the Court. If the case is not referred to the Court, the report remains confidential, other than to the parties, until the Committee of Ministers have either decided there has been a violation, in which case publication is delayed until the expiry of the time-limit placed on the defaulting party for compliance, or decided there has not been a violation, in which case publication is usually immediate. Decisions on admissiblity are very numerous and only a selection of the most significant are made widely available. Reports of the Commission on friendly settlements are mainly of interest for the remedies and compensation agreed. Resolutions of the Committee of Ministers being largely formal are the source likely to be needed least.

4.115   Reports of Court judgments are usually identified by the names of the parties (though they also bear a case number), as are reports from the Commission (which also bear the application number). However most admissibility decisions of the Commission only bear the application number, not the names of the parties. Resolutions of the Committee of Ministers are also only identifed by number, prefixed with 'DH', eg DH (92) 8 — the eighth human rights resolution of 1992.

Sources for the text of European human rights case law

4.116   Probably the most widely available is the commercially published *European Human Rights Reports* (EHRR), which covers judgments of the Court, reports of the Commission, and occasional other documentation such as Rules of Procedure; it started publication in 1979 and is also loaded on Lexis. However, for judgments of the Court, the official series is *Publications of the European Court of Human Rights: Series A: Judgments and Decisions*. Each judgment is assigned a volume number. There is an accompanying series, *Series B: Pleadings, Oral Arguments and Documents*, which bear the same volume number. Because there are long delays in the publication of judgments in *Series A*, advance copies of individual judgments are issued as mimeographed typescripts (in A4 format with grey covers). The official version of the Commission publications since 1975 has been *Decisions and Reports* (cited DR) — before then it was called *Collection of Decisions*. This contains reports on the merits and a selection of admissibility decisions. Like the Court judgments, the Commission reports are issued in advance (A4 with pale blue covers). The full text of admissibility decisions are entered on the database maintained in Strasbourg. Printout from this and also on-line access is made available to official depositories in member states. In the UK, this is the British Institute of International and Comparative Law (BIICL), based in the same building as the Institute of Advanced Legal Studies in London. Resolutions of the Committee of Ministers are published individually in mimeographed typescript (usually only one sheet) then again individually in printed form. They are held by the BIICL, if not elsewhere.

4.117 The texts of selected admissibility decisions and of Committee of Ministers resolutions are included in the *Yearbook of the European Convention on Human Rights*, published under the auspices of the Council of Europe. It also includes, though only in summary form, selected Court judgments and Commission reports. Its publication, however, is seriously in arrears. The most up-to-date source of information on case law, though again only in summary form, is the press releases issued by the Court, Commission and Committee of Ministers. These form the basis of the *Human Rights Case Digest* published six times a year by the British Institute of Human Rights (based at King's College, London). The Council of Europe also publish *Information Sheets*, which are misnamed in so far as they are thick pamphlets in the Council's A4 mimeographed style; they again include case material in summary form covering several months.

Finding European human rights case law

4.118 As mentioned, *Current Law*, *The Digest* and the *Daily Law Reports Index* do cover this to a limited extent. In *Current Law* cases will be found under the heading 'Human rights' in the body of the yearbooks and monthly parts. Pending reissue of volume 26 of the main work, they are only in continuation volumes G and H and the cumulative supplement of *The Digest* under the title 'Human rights' with volume 26 material. In the *Daily Law Reports Index* they will be listed in the key word index under 'European Convention on Human Rights' and usually also by specific Article number under that title in the legislation index. All three will also list cases by name. Often the easiest way is via textbooks on the subject, of which there is quite an array. The main manual in-depth tool is the *Digest of Strasbourg Case-law Relating to the European Convention on Human Rights*. This collates all the case law by Convention article number and has various alphabetical and numerical tables. The orginal five bound volumes covered 1955 to 1982; there are now looseleaf updates but they are still very behind. There are cumulative indexes covering volumes 1 to 20 and 21 to 40 of the Commission's *Decisions and Reports*, which comprise indexes by subject, by state subdivided by application number, by application number, and by Convention article number. It is to be hoped that a cumulative index to volumes 41 to 60 is promptly published as soon as volume 60 is reached. A useful entry point to the main case law by subject-matter, though again supplementation has become rather slow, is the *Stock-taking on the European Convention on Human Rights: a Periodic Note on the Concrete Results Achieved Under the Convention*, published in mimeographed form by the Commission. The Lexis version of the *European Human Rights Reports* would also certainly be a possibility, especially for searching by names of other cases considered — a type of information not very well covered in the manual sources.

4.119 Apart from these sources, the only alternatives are to look in individual volumes of *European Human Rights Reports*, Commission *Decisions and Reports*, *Yearbook of the European Convention on Human Rights*, and *Human Rights Case Digest*. Of these the *European Human Rights Reports* is the only one to include a table in each volume of cases judicially considered. The Commission and the Court also each publish an annual *Survey of Activities*, which apart from giving statistical information may provide other information somewhat sooner than the *Yearbook*. Finally, apart from holding the text of sources not widely available and having access to the Strasbourg database, the British Institute of International and Comparative Law maintain some internal indexes and may be able to offer assistance (address and telephone number at QR9.3).

5. Treaties

Reasons for researching treaties

5.1 In looking at how and why an English lawyer may use international treaties, it is necessary to appreciate the way in which English common law views them. The important distinction here is between treaties that have been expressly incorporated into domestic law and those that have not. In some jurisdictions, treaties (or some classes of treaty) can take effect in domestic law once they have been ratified without further legislation — they are said to be self-executing; in the United Kingdom direct or indirect Parliamentary approval must be given by means of a statute or SI.

5.2 However, this is is not to say than an unincorporated treaty can never have domestic legal consequences. For the purposes of statutory interpretation it is assumed that Parliament would not pass legislation contrary to the obligations of the Crown under international law. If there is an ambiguity in a UK statute in an area covered by an international treaty that has been ratified by the United Kingdom, the courts can invoke the treaty provisions to resolve it. The European Convention on Human Rights is perhaps the most prominent illustration. As is well known, though ratified by the United Kingdom this has not been enacted in domestic law and direct redress is only available via the European Court of Human Rights in Strasbourg; yet the courts here have been increasingly prepared to cite it. The leading authority on the use of the Convention by the courts is the House of Lords decision in *R v Secretary of State for the Home Department, ex parte Brind* [1991] 1 AC 696. The decision made clear the limits to citing the Convention: the Convention's provisions on freedom of expression may have seemed fully germane to a challenge to the Secretary of State's decision under statute to ban terrorist broadcasts, but as there was no ambiguity in the statute the provisions could not be invoked. The decision also appeared to rule out the use of the Convention as a weapon in judicial review proceedings: to treat the Convention as necessarily a 'relevant consideration' that ought always to be taken into account by administrative decision-makers would be to incorporate it into domestic law by the back door. However, the Court of Appeal has subsequently applied *ex parte Brind* where there was not an ambiguity in a statute but an ambiguity in the common law, thus allowing them to invoke the Convention to resolve previous conflicting decisions of courts of co-ordinate jurisdiction (on whether a local authority as a corporate body can sue for libel): *Derbyshire County*

Council v Times Newspapers Ltd [1992] 1 QB 770. Interestingly, in that case, Balcombe LJ points out that the Convention has also been used by the courts in considering the principles upon which it should exercise a discretion, eg whether or not to grant an interlocutory injunction — *Attorney-General v Guardian Newspapers Ltd* [1987] 1 WLR 1248 at 1296 and 1307; and that even where the law is certain the courts may still 'when appropriate' consider whether the United Kingdom is in breach of the Convention, as the Divisional Court agreed to do in deciding the scope of the offence of blasphemy in *R v Chief Stipendiary Magistrate, ex parte Choudhury* [1991] 1 QB 429 at 449. The *Derbyshire County Council* case was heard on further appeal to the House of Lords (The Times, 19 February (1993)), but they decided the point without finding any need to rely on the Convention.

5.3   The distinction between unincorporated and incorporated treaties, however, is heavily qualified in the case of the European Communities treaties. Under Community law treaty obligations are not only directly applicable in the sense of binding states without those states enacting domestic legislation, but also may (depending on the European Court's view of the particular provision) have direct effect in the sense of conferring rights on individuals either vis-a-vis a state (so-called vertical direct effect) or vis-a-vis other individuals (so-called horizontal direct effect). The United Kingdom has coped with this novel regime by incorporating Community law in general into domestic law by means of statute — the European Communities Act 1972 — but, by that Act, permitting future treaty obligations to be given effect in the domestic law without further legislation. The full ramifications of this are still being explored.

5.4   International treaties, whether incorporated into domestic law or not, are also of course of interest to academics and students researching public international law, and to practitioners on the rare occasions on which disputes come before international tribunals. Unincorporated treaties will also be of interest to practitioners in giving advice, in the same way that Bills and white papers are, if there is a likelihood of their being adopted in the near future. For example the UK signed the UNIDROIT Convention on International Factoring in 1990 and its enactment, at the time of writing, is only awaiting the availability of Parliamentary time. Even if the UK has not incorporated a treaty, or indeed even if it has not signed it, the practitioner may be interested in it if an international transaction involves a country that has. For example, as more countries adopt it, the UN Convention on Contracts for the International Sale of Goods assumes increasing importance, even though the UK is not a signatory.

Terminology and citation

5.5   Treaties may be bilateral, made between two states, or multilateral, made between several states. International organisations may (depending on their constitution) also enter into treaties with states — the European Communities, for example, do so frequently. Although here the expression 'treaties' is being used generically to describe all international agreements, the documents themselves come with a wide range of labels which are generally interchangeable and have no legal significance. 'Convention' is perhaps the commonest term in the multilateral sphere. On the other hand, many workaday bilateral agreements are called 'Exchanges of Notes' as this is how they are executed. Covenants, pacts, charters, agreements, declarations are other terms. 'Protocol' may also be encountered as a term for a treaty like any other, but nowadays it is used particularly for agreements that amend or supplement a principal treaty, as with the seven protocols that have been added to the European Convention on Human Rights since it was originally made in 1950. In using international legal materials another species that may be encountered are model laws prepared by international organisations. They are not treaties, but are mentioned here should they be confused with them. They may be drafted and agreed between participating members like treaties and have the similar aim of promoting international uniformity in the law, but they are not binding on states, merely offering a model to follow if states choose to enact them in their own law. The most well-known example is the UNCITRAL (United Nations Commission on International Trade Law) Model Law on International Commercial Arbitration, which, in the United Kingdom, is to be adopted in Scotland but has been rejected for England and Wales.

5.6　Citation of treaties is not especially formalised. The main elements are the title, the date of signature, and, in the case of multilateral treaties, the place of signature. The formal titles of treaties that appear on their face are frequently abbreviated colloquially or for convenience. In some cases the popular title takes over from the title proper except in the most formal citations, as has happened with the European Convention on Human Rights which is technically entitled the European Convention for the Protection of Human Rights and Fundamental Freedoms. With such well-known treaties it is possible to get away without citing the date, but usually it is essential in order that they be may be traced easily. The place of signature for multilateral treaties — usually the place where an international conference to draft and agree the treaty has been held — is not always a crucial element for identifying a treaty, but it assumes particular importance when, as often happens, it becomes transposed into the treaty's popular title. The Convention on Jurisdiction and Enforcement of Judgments in Civil and Commercial Matters, signed at Brussels on 27 September 1968, is widely known simply as the Brussels Convention. This is all very well if the context is clear (or in the few cases where it has virtually assumed official status, like the Treaty of Rome), but otherwise a reference to the Geneva Convention, the New York Convention, or the Hague Convention is as helpful as being referred to King Henry — there are rather a lot of them. The numbered provisions of a treaty — the equivalent of sections in an Act — are usually termed articles.

Sources for the texts of treaties

5.7　If the treaty has been incorporated into domestic law, the text is often going to be readily available because the modern practice is to append it, if possible, as a schedule to the statute or SI. One-off treaties will usually be enacted by statute, but where there are frequent agreements in a particular area, for example double taxation, an enabling statute will allow them to be given effect by SI. The title of the statute or SI may follow more or less closely the title of the treaty — for example, the Brussels Convention mentioned above is to be found in the Civil Jurisdiction and Judgments Act 1982. On the other hand, the only clue may be the broad subject-matter of the Act: the Convention Relating to the Carriage or Passengers and their Luggage by Sea is to be found in the Merchant Shipping Act 1979. However, sometimes the treaty will be enacted merely by reference to the official text without incorporating it as a schedule. This is usually on the grounds of length, which can be a problem particularly where there is a multi-lingual parallel text. The Convention Concerning International Carriage by Rail 1980, for example, runs to almost 400 pages and so was not reproduced in the International Transport Conventions Act 1983 which gave effect to it.

5.8   The official text of treaties that the United Kingdom has ratified is the *United Kingdom Treaty Series*. They are published by HMSO as command papers (on which generally see chapter 6 paras 6.9-6.10), and so bear a command paper number as well as a *Treaty Series* number. In libraries they may be kept together as a series or kept with other command papers. In the latter eventuality, as explained at para 6.11, the command papers may be arranged by their number or by broad topic in sessional volumes of Parliamentary papers. For citation purposes the command paper number is the most important element, but the *Treaty Series* number is helpful to have as well. An example is shown in figure 5.1. The command paper number is given in the bottom left hand corner.

5.9   Some treaties which the United Kingdom has not ratified are also officially published by HMSO because of their international importance or because the United Kingdom may have signed but not yet ratified them. These are also command papers, but instead of appearing in the *Treaty Series* they are assigned to a Foreign and Commonwealth Office 'Miscellaneous Series' if they are multilateral or to particular country series if they are bilateral. These series have their own numbering, but it is almost invariably the command number that is used for citation purposes. If the treaty is subsequently ratified, it is reissued in the *Treaty Series*.

5.10   The *United Kingdom Treaty Series* started in 1892. Before that date they appear as command papers among the sessional volumes of Parliamentary papers and in the *British and Foreign State Papers*; there is considerable overlap between the two sources, but some treaties are only to be found in one of them. The latter series, compiled by the Foreign Office, began in 1812, and contained other international materials as well as treaties. It continued publication until 1968, and so for the period from 1892 until then there is also considerable duplication with the *Treaty Series* (for fuller details of its history and contents see Nigel Smith 'British and Foreign State Papers' (1986) 17 *Law Librarian* 64-66).

5.11   If you do not have access to these primary sources, bear in mind that the text of important treaties may be reprinted as appendices to practitioners' works in the relevant field. There are also a number of subject collections of treaty materials. For example, CCH publish a looseleaf collection, *British International Tax Agreements*, and the *British Shipping Law* series published by Stevens includes the four volumes of *International Maritime Law Conventions* edited by Nagendra Singh. In the same field as the latter, with the added advantage of being looseleaf, is the *Ratification of Maritime Conventions*, published by Lloyds of London Press, which includes the full texts as well as the ratification information. The American-based looseleaf specialists Oceana have been especially active in publishing collections of materials of international interest in particular fields, such as commercial arbitration, telecommunications, multinational corporations, environmental law, law of the sea, human rights and terrorism. Diamond's *International Tax Treaties of all Nations* is an Oceana publication that deserves particular mention, as do, in the same field, the publications of the International Bureau of Fiscal Documentation, based in Amsterdam. For students of international law, there are Ian Brownlie's collections *Basic*

Figure 5.1

The International Convention was previously published as Miscellaneous No. 23 (1972) Cmnd. 5002.

INTELLECTUAL
PROPERTY

Treaty Series No. 63 (1990)

International Convention

further revising the Berne Convention for the Protection of Literary and Artistic Works of 9 September 1886

Paris, 24 July 1971 as amended on 2 October 1979

[The United Kingdom instrument of ratification was deposited on 29 September 1989 and the Convention and amendments entered into force for the United Kingdom on 2 January 1990]

Presented to Parliament
by the Secretary of State for Foreign and Commonwealth Affairs
by Command of Her Majesty
October 1990

LONDON : HMSO

£6·60 net

Cm 1212

Documents in International Law and *Basic Documents on Human Rights* (Oxford University Press).

5.12 Under article 102 of the United Nations Charter 1945 all treaties made by members of the UN are to be registered with its Secretariat 'as soon as possible'. They are then published in the *United Nations Treaty Series*. Although it will contain UK treaties, it is most likely to be needed for treaties to which the UK is not party. However, whether due to delays in deposit by member states or bureaucratic inefficiency in the Secretariat, the series is lamentably in arrears: there is currently an arrears of about eight years. For this reason, *International Legal Materials* published in periodical form by the American Society of International Law is invaluable; it issues the text of many treaties very swiftly, though it cannot be comprehensive (incidentally, the full text from 1980 is available on Lexis).

5.13 The precursor to the *United Nations Treaty Series* was the *League of Nations Treaty Series*, founded in the hope that by means of registration and publication, secret treaties, which were seen as one of the evils leading to the Great War, would be eradicated. Before 1919, though there was no similar universal series, there were a number of compilations, commercial treaties naturally being covered most thoroughly. Hertslet and Martens are the two best-known compilers. However, a monumental work that has recently completed publication is the *Consolidated Treaty Series* which aims to be as complete a collection as possible of treaties from all these disparate sources for the period 1648 until the foundation of the League of Nations in 1919. It is arranged by date, though there are some appendix volumes containing material omitted from the main work.

5.14 Many countries produce their own equivalents of the *United Kingdom Treaty Series* for treaties to which they are party. These are most likely to be needed for treaties which the United Kingdom has not ratified and which have not yet appeared in the *United Nations Treaty Series* and which are not of sufficient significance to be picked up by *International Legal Materials*, typically bilateral treaties.

Texts of EC treaties

5.15 The treaties that established the Communities, the treaties of accession, and subsequent amending treaties are widely available from a variety of sources, apart from those already mentioned. The Official Publications Office of the EC produces a collection in two bound volumes, which are reissued from time to time. The English language version comes, as do all English language official publications of the EC, in distinctive purple covers. Sweet & Maxwell's *Encyclopedia of European Community Law* contains the treaty material as part B of the service. The main treaties are also included in similar works produced by other publishers, often with substantial commentary, such as Smit and Herzog *The Law of the European Economic Community* (New York: Matthew Bender, 1976-) and the *Common Market Reporter* published by CCH. There are also selections of treaty material designed for student use such as *Sweet & Maxwell's European Treaties* (now rather out of date) or Rudden and Wyatt's *Basic Community Laws* (Oxford: Clarendon Press). Any new provisions will be published first of all in the *Official Journal of the European Communities*.

5.16 Not to be confused with the treaties establishing and regulating the Community itself, are the treaties entered into *by* the Community. These are first published in the L series of the *Official Journal*, but there is also an official multi-volume compilation *Collection of the Agreements Concluded by the European Communities* — another purple manifestation. A third source, which may be more convenient, especially for recent treaties not yet in the latest edition of the purple *Collection*, is the HMSO version. All the EC treaties are published by HMSO as command papers but they are also numbered within each year in a 'European Communities' series which runs parallel to the *United Kingdom Treaty Series* and to the 'Miscellaneous series' already mentioned. With all European materials there is always the risk of confusing documentation relating to the European Communities with that relating to the Council of Europe; in this case the HMSO 'European Communities' treaty series should not be confused with the *European Treaty Series* which is a Council of Europe publication.

Tracing treaties

5.17   For United Kingdom treaties the basic finding aid is the *Index of British Treaties*. Originally published by HMSO in 1970 in three volumes under the editorship of Clive Parry, it covered all treaties from 1101 to 1968 (or as nearly all as was practically possible given the time span and the inherent problems in defining a 'treaty'). A very welcome fourth volume covering 1969-1988 and updating the previous volumes was published in 1991; the opportunity was also taken to reissue with it the first three volumes on microfiche, which is helpful for any library that originally failed to acquire them. The main form of arrangment of the index is chronological by date of signature. Exhaustive bibliographical references are given to virtually all possible sources, such as *United Kingdom Treaty Series* number, command number, volume and page number in sessional sets of Parliamentary papers, *United Nations Treaty Series*. However, because it commenced publication after the *Index*, references are not given to the *Consolidated Treaty Series* for pre-1919 treaties. Understandably enough, it also does not go to the lengths of including references to statutes which have treaties annexed as schedules or to books which are not ostensibly collections of treaties. Cross-references are given to later amending treaties, as are, for multilateral treaties, the parties at the time of publication of the index (supplemented to 1988 by volume 4). There are subject indexes in volumes 3 and 4. These are each in three sequences: multilateral treaties arranged by subject, bilateral treaties by country subdivided by subject, and bilateral treaties by subject subdivided by country.

5.18   There are indexes produced from time to time to accompany the *United Kingdom Treaty Series*, but as they are not consolidated they are less useful. As the *United Kingdom Treaty Series* and the other related series issued by the FCO are published by HMSO as command papers, they will also be listed in the various catalogues of government publications discussed in chapter 6. Note that in the monthly and annual HMSO catalogues the main entries are listed under 'Treaties' in three sequences: multilateral, European Communities and 'United Kingdom' (ie bilateral).

5.19   For multilateral treaties, whether or not the United Kingdom is a party, the standard work is Bowman and Harris *Multilateral Treaties: Index and Current Status* (originally published by Butterworths, supplements now issued by the University of Nottingham Treaty Centre). Although it does not claim to be absolutely comprehensive, it covers the vast bulk of treaties likely to be encountered in practice. The primary arrangement is again chronological. Full references to sources of the text and other apparatus are provided (see figure 5.2). After the main sequence is a separate table, easily overlooked, giving a chronological list of treaties that have not been provided with their own main entries but which are referred to in the notes, amendments or other sections of the main entries. At the back are a subject index and a word index. The main work was first published in 1984, but since then there have been annual cumulative supplements which contain in their first half additional treaties (including some pre-1984 treaties originally omitted) and then in the second half updating material arranged by the treaty number in the main work.

5.20 Less widely available, less up to date, and less easy to use than either of the above two sources, but with a wider scope than either is the *World Treaty Index* by Peter H. Rohn (2nd ed, Santa Barbara, Ca.: ABC-Clio Information Services, 1985). Its coverage is from 1900-1980, and it includes information on some post-1919 treaties that are not in the *League of Nations* or the *United Nations Treaty Series*.

5.21 The *United Nations Treaty Series* has its own indexes which cumulate quite wide spans (as does the *League of Nations Treaty Series*). Each includes a chronological index and an alphabetical index. The United Nations also produce a monthly list *Statement of Treaties and International Agreements Registered or Filed and Recorded with the Secretariat*. An alphabetical index cumulates through the calendar year. Although produced in monthly issues, its publication is at least a year in arrears.

5.22 Tracing pre-1919 treaties, especially non-British treaties, has been greatly simplifed by the *Consolidated Treaty Series*. There are 12 volumes of indexes to the 231 volumes of the main work. There is a party index, subdivided chronologically within each country, and a general chronological index, which covers all treaties other than those dealing with colonial and postal matters; the latter, because they are particulary numerous and generally of less significance, have their own chronological index in order to make the main index easier to use.

Checking status and parties

5.23 Apart from tracing treaties by subject-matter or date, as described above, the most usual research problem is finding out whether a treaty is in force yet and who the parties to it are. Some treaties become binding on the contracting parties as soon as they have all signed them, but the commonest method of entry into force is by subsequent ratification by the individual states. Which organ of state is empowered to ratify varies from state to state. In the United Kingdom, it is the Crown — treaty-making is a prerogative power, so is not a matter requiring Parliamentary approval, though as a matter of practice treaties subject to ratification are laid before Parliament as least 21 days in advance. Treaty-making is also, of course, one of the prerogative powers that are beyond the jurisdiction of the courts. In the United States, in contrast, for some kinds of treaty the President requires approval of two thirds of the Senate for ratification.

5.24 Ratification, though, may not be the end of the story. The treaty may provide, in analogous fashion to the commencement provisions of statutes, for a certain period to elapse after ratification before entry into force. Although, if there is no contrary

Figure 5.2   Bowman and Harris *Multilateral Treaties: Index and Current Status*

1972

TREATY 592   CONVENTION FOR THE CONSERVATION OF ANTARCTIC SEALS

CONCLUDED	11 **Feb** 72, London
LOCATION	UKTS 45(1978), Cmnd 7209; 29 UST 441, TIAS 8826; 11 ILM 251; 77 RGDIP 555; Kiss 272
ENTRY INTO FORCE	11 Mar 78. Later acceptances effective 30 days after deposit: Art 13
DURATION	Unspecified. Denunciation permitted on 30 Jun of any year, by giving notice on or before 1 Jan of same year. Other parties may then withdraw on same date by giving notice to that effect within 1 month of notification of the first denunciation: Art 14
RESERVATIONS	No clause
AUTHENTIC TEXTS	E F R S
DEPOSITARY	UK
OPEN TO	States participating in the Conference on the Conservation of Antarctic Seals, and others invited to accede with consent of all parties: Arts 10, 12
PARTIES (11)	ARGENTINA* 7 Mar 78; BELGIUM 9 Feb 78; CHILE* 7 Feb 80; FRANCE 19 Feb 75; JAPAN 28 Aug 80; NORWAY 10 Dec 73; POLAND 15 Aug 80; SOUTH AFRICA 15 Aug 72; UK 10 Sep 74; USSR* 8 Feb 78; US 19 Jan 77
TERRITORIAL SCOPE	No clause. Declared applicable; UK - Channel Is, Isle of Man
SIGNATORIES	AUSTRALIA 5 Oct 72; NEW ZEALAND 9 Jun 72
NOTES	The present Convention regulates the killing of Antarctic seals by nationals or vessels of the parties' nationality or flag. See also the relevant measures agreed under the 1959 Antarctic Treaty (treaty 390) and the 1979 Conservation of Antarctic Marine Resources Convention (treaty 779). And see on the conservation of seals, the 1957 Interim Convention on Conservation of North Pacific Fur Seals, 314 UNTS 105, 8 UST 2283, TIAS 3948; 8 Ruster 3716, as amended and extended in 1963, 1969, 1976, and 1980. This establishes the North Pacific Fur Seal Commission. Parties: Canada 16 Sep 57; Japan 20 Sep 57; USSR* 14 Oct 57; US* 30 Aug 57. In force 14 Oct 57.

TREATY 593   CONVENTION FOR THE PREVENTION OF MARINE POLLUTION BY DUMPING FROM SHIPS AND AIRCRAFT

CONCLUDED	15 **Feb** 72, Oslo
LOCATION	UKTS 119(1975), Cmnd 6228; JOF 21 May 74; 1974 RTAF 38; 55 Vert A 725; 11 ILM 262; 78 RGDIP 901; 2 Ruster 530; Kiss 266
ENTRY INTO FORCE	7 Apr 74. Later acceptances effective 30 days after deposit: Art 23
DURATION	Unspecified. Denunciation permitted on 1 year's notice after the Convention has been in force for that party for 2 years: Art 24
RESERVATIONS	No clause
AUTHENTIC TEXTS	E F
DEPOSITARY	Norway
OPEN TO	States invited to participate in the 1971 Oslo Conference on Marine Pollution. Other states may accede by unanimous invitation of the parties: Art 22
PARTIES (13)	BELGIUM 28 Feb 78; DENMARK 28 Jul 72; FINLAND 2 May 79; FRANCE 7 Mar 74; GFR 23 Nov 77; ICELAND 27 Jun 73; IRELAND 25 Jan 82; NETHERLANDS 29 Sep 75; NORWAY 2 Jun 72; PORTUGAL 30 Jan 73; SPAIN 14 Jun 73; SWEDEN 13 Sep 72; UK 30 Jun 75
TERRITORIAL SCOPE	No clause
AMENDMENTS	1983 Protocol, Misc 12(1983), Cmnd 8942 (amends Arts 8,19,22 and Annex IV). Not in force
NOTES	The parties to this regional Convention (applying to the North Sea and North East Atlantic) agree to harmonise their policies and introduce measures to prevent pollution of the sea by dumping from ships and aircraft. Poland and the USSR were invited to participate in the Convention but declined. A Commission (the Oslo Commission) based on London has been established to administer this Convention. See also the 1972 London Dumping at Sea Convention

358

Published by Butterworths 1984. Supplements issued by the University of Nottingham Treaty Centre.

provision, multilateral treaties only come into force when all the parties have ratified, many modern multilateral treaties provide for entry into force as soon as a certain number of parties (or certain specified parties) have ratified. Here it should be appreciated that it is in the nature of an international treaty that it can only bind those states that have actually ratified it; if they have not, it is immaterial that they were signatories and that it is otherwise in force.

5.25 A further complication is that, if the treaty so allows, a state may not ratify it in its entirety but may make reservations, ie exclude particular articles from its undertaking. The parties to a treaty are not necessarily static either. States which were not original signatories may subsequently accede to it; and, if the treaty permits it, or if there exists one of the recognised grounds for termination, a state may withdraw from it. The duration of a treaty may not be indefinite. It may state on its face that it is to operate only for a limited period or it may be expressly superseded by a later treaty, but problems, analogous to the implied repeal of statutes, can arise where a later treaty between the same parties is inconsistent with an earlier treaty. These problems can be exacerbated by changes in the constitutional or geographical identity of states — the reunification of Germany and the fragmentation of the rest of Eastern Europe provide ample contemporary illustration. This area is governed by the doctrine of state succession, for whose intricacies the reader is referred to standard works on public international law.

5.26 As it is in the context of multilateral treaties that the problems of status and parties usually arise, *Bowman and Harris* (see para 5.19 above) is the most useful work in this field (see figure 5.2). Among the annotations to each treaty there are sections covering: entry into force, duration, reservations, parties, and signatories. Either the date that the treaty came into force or the requirements for entry into force are given. 'Duration' will indicate any specific provisions as to expiry and also whether denunciation is permitted. Which articles, if any, may be derogated from by reservation are stated. The 'parties' are those that have 'accepted' the treaty, whatever the method of acceptance is, be it definitive signature, ratification, accession or otherwise. The 'signatories' section, however, lists only those parties that have signed but not ratified (or otherwise accepted). If such parties subsequently accept, in the next edition of the cumulative supplement their names are transferred from the 'signatories' section to the 'parties' section. Under both headings an asterisk against the name of a country indicates that it has made a reservation; a double asterisk that it has withdrawn the reservation.

5.27 The *Index of British Treaties* gives similar information to *Bowman and Harris* and will cover bilateral treaties as well — provided of course that the United Kingdom is a party. It is less up to date, however; but bear in mind that the first three volumes can be updated to 1988 by using volume 4. The most up-to-date printed source for British treaties is the *Supplementary List of Ratifications, Accessions, Withdrawals, etc* prepared by the Foreign and Commonwealth Office. It is issued four times a year, and, though roughly six months in arrears, may be more up to date than the latest cumulative supplement to *Bowman and Harris*. It forms part of the *United Kingdom Treaty Series*, so is published by HMSO and each issue has its own treaty series number and command paper number. The drawbacks to using them are that the issues are not cumulative and the entries are arranged simply by broad subject heading. Having checked these printed sources, the safest way to make sure that you have the latest information is to telephone the Treaty Records section of the Nationality, Treaty and Claims Department of the Foreign and Commonwealth

Office; they are usually very helpful — their number will be found in the *Civil Service Yearbook.*

5.28   If you are dealing with a non-British treaty and *Bowman and Harris* does not help, the only recourse is the UN publication *Multilateral Treaties Deposited with the Secretary-General: Status as at 31 December* .... This annual publication is needless to say hopelessly out of date — it is currently published at least two years in arrears. One useful feature, however, is that as well as information on date of entry into force and parties, it often includes the actual text of any reservations. Depending on how frequently they are updated, an alternative source might well be looseleaf subject compilations of treaty materials; the Lloyds publication, *Ratification of Maritime Conventions*, for example, aims to give this type of information as well as just the texts.

Preparatory materials

5.29   As a brief coda to this chapter on treaties, it is worth mentioning that preparatory materials — the equivalent of white papers, Bills, and *Hansard* — are often of particular interest. Minutes of negotiations, proceedings of international conferences, and successive drafts of the treaty are often published and are of use not only for the academic study of international law but also as aids to interpretation in the event of a dispute that comes before an international tribunal such as the International Court of Justice. Although the text of the treaty, as in statutory interpretation, has primacy, these materials, which are generally known as *travaux préparatoires*, are often liberally referred to. There are no hard and fast rules about the form of publication, if they are published at all, but they will usually emanate from the international organisation concerned. Selections may be reprinted by commercial publishers — Oceana often include this kind of material in their looseleaf collections, such as *New Directions in the Law of the Sea.*

6. Other official publications

When are official publications needed?

6.1 Legislation, case law and treaties are lawyers' primary sources: why should they need to look at other official publications? There are four main applications:

— legislation or quasi-legislation not issued as statutes or SIs
— proposals for law reform and background to existing legislation
— judicial or quasi-judicial material not published as law reports
— material relevant to research into government activities that impinge on the law or its administration

The nature of the first two, which are probably the most important, have already been covered in chapter 3 on legislation, to which reference should be made (see paras 3.135-3.174). In so far as treaties are the equivalent of legislation in the international sphere, the brief mention of *travaux préparatoires* in the last chapter (para 5.21) can also be regarded as a species of the second category above. The last two categories will be expanded on a little here.

Quasi-judicial material

6.2 'Quasi-judicial' denotes decisions that are a halfway house between full-blown judicial precedent and arbitrary adminstrative rulings. As with quasi-legislation they can most easily be defined by example rather than by any underlying principle, though the jurisprudence of natural justice in the context of judicial review has imported some order to this field. Examples at the top end of the scale bordering on judicial decision-making are ministers' and inspectors' decisions in planning matters, Lands Tribunal decisions on rating and valuation, and Commissioners' decisions in the field of social security. Although on matters of law they are subject to the decisions of the higher courts and will often turn on their particular facts, they are of considerable importance to practitioners in ascertaining current practice and advising accordingly. Their affinity with case law is such that they have their own series of 'law reports' — the above three examples will found in for instance the *Planning Appeal Decisions*, *Rating and Valuation Reporter* and *Reported Cases of the Social*

Security Commissioner. For this reason these examples at the top end of the scale are really in the province of chapter 4 on case law — and indeed the above series are covered by such finding aids as *Current Law*.

6.3   Moving slightly down the scale we have, for example, the decision-making bodies who nowadays have wide reaching powers in connection with the regulation of companies and commercial activity and whose determinations are often of wider significance than the case in hand. Monopolies and Mergers Commission investigations and Office of Fair Trading reports come within this category. As well as the separately published full reports, summaries appear in the annual report of the Director of Fair Trading. Department of Trade investigations and the statements and rulings of the Panel on Take-overs and Mergers are important too.

6.4   Various public bodies, who are obliged to issue annual reports, take the opportunity to clarify their practice by highlighting particular cases they have had to deal with. Perhaps the two referred to most often by practitioners are the Charity Commissioners reports and the reports of the Criminal Injuries Compensation Board. The former contain decisions on charitable status — the 1991 report for instance includes the decision on whether the objects of the Margaret Thatcher Foundation were educational in the charity law sense — and the latter summarise awards made for different kinds of injury, and so act as a kind of *Kemp & Kemp* in this field.

6.5   The reports of the Ombudsman, or to give him his formal title, the Parliamentary Commissioner for Administration, are another important source. When the office was first set up reports of all cases investigated were published; nowadays select cases only are published (four times a year), but they continue to provide valuable guidance on what may amount to maladministration and when redress may be available. As well as the reports themselves useful supplementary information can also be obtained from the reports of the House of Commons Select Committee on the Parliamentary Commissioner for Administration which monitors his activities (and also now those of the Health Services Commissioner). As well as the original Ombudsman, parallel offices have been set up, either under statute or voluntarily, as watchdogs on various non-governmental public services, such as banking, insurance, building societies, and legal services. Their annual reports can similarly offer guidance in the event of a dispute in these fields.

6.6   As well as these regular publications, reports of one-off inquiries may be of wider interest than just to those involved. Official reports into air, sea, or rail accidents, for example, may give valuable background information on safety standards and procedures in the event of a lawyer having to act in similar circumstances. Another example is illustrated by a recent case in the Family Division — *Re E (Child Abuse: Evidence)* [1990] FCR 793. There the court was highly critical of social workers and police officers who had not followed nor even read the guidelines in child abuse cases set out by Butler-Sloss LJ in the Cleveland Report (Cm 412).

6.7   Although current materials are the most needed, from time to time older items may have to be consulted. Two illustrations indicate that the scope of materials of possible relevance is not narrow. The decisions of the Industrial Assurance Commissioner were published as House of Commons papers and continue to be cited in the footnotes to *MacGillivray and Partington on Insurance Law*. The Royal Commission on Market Rights and Tolls, whose reports were published from 1889 to 1891, collected a vast range of material on ancient franchises and other matters that are still referred to in the current edition of *Pease and Chitty's Law of Markets and Fairs*.

Research into law-related government activities

6.8   The kinds of material in this area are those likely to be used more in connection with academic research than as aids to the practitioner. One obvious example would be statistical information, such as the *Criminal Statistics* and *Judicial Statistics*. The police, the Crown Prosecution Service, prisons, the probation service, the administration of the courts and immigration are all areas where various official publications are produced, whether in the form of annual reports, particularly studies, or statistics. The House of Commons Home Affairs Committee is particular active in producing material in these kinds of areas. In chapter 3 the use of *Hansard* in connection with the background to Bills was discussed, but it serves also as a repository of factual information because it contains ministers' answers to Parliamentary questions both written and oral, which may be of value to the researcher, as may be general non-legislative debates. If only for prurient rather than scholarly reasons, the reports of the Review Body on Top Salaries, which include judicial salaries, are often asked for.

Types of official publications

Parliamentary papers

6.9   There are three series of Parliamentary papers other than Bills and *Hansard*: command papers, House of Commons papers and House of Lords papers. Command papers are presented to Parliament by ministers, technically by command of Her Majesty. Typical examples are government white papers and reports of Royal Commissions. House of Commons and House of Lords papers, while naturally enough covering material emanating from Parliament itself, such as reports and minutes of Select Committees, are wider than that. For example many quangos and other external bodies are required to present annual reports to Parliament and these may be House of Commons papers. But the distinctions between the series are not very meaningful to the average user, and so predicting which materials will be found in the command papers, which in the House of Commons papers, and which will not be Parliamentary papers at all can be done with little precision. The Quick Reference Guide gives examples of the most commonly encountered publications and which category they fall into (QR6.5). In the case of annual reports of public bodies a useful work, which tells you (among other things) whether they are published by HMSO, by the body itself or are not published at all, is *Public Bodies* prepared by the Office of the Minister for the Civil Service (part of the Cabinet Office) and published annually by HMSO.

6.10   Command papers began in 1833 and have been published in six separately numbered series since then, the new series being started to avoid the numbers exceeding four digits. To distinguish the six series, a different form of the abbreviation for the word 'Command' has been used, the very first series having a number only. It thus essential to note and cite the precise form of the abbreviation. The coverage of the six series is as follows:

1833-1869	1 — 4222
1870-1899	C 1 — C 9550
1900-1918	Cd 1 — Cd 9239
1919-1956	Cmd 1 — Cmd 9889
1957-1986	Cmnd 1 — Cmnd 9927
1986 to date	Cm 1 -

6.11   House of Commons and House of Lords papers are separately numbered in each Parliamentary session, which in modern times, unless disrupted by a general election that year, runs from November. It is thus necessary to cite the years of the session, not merely the calendar year of publication. The following is the correct form:

HC 129 (1974-75) or HL 174 (1984-85)

Libraries which take a complete set of Parliamentary papers will usually keep the recent ones filed as the three separate series. However, traditionally, and a few libraries may continue the practice, a set of sessional volumes for each House would be bound up, with the material rearranged according to subject-matter rather than numerically. Title pages and indexes were officially prepared and pagination assigned to each volume. Some libraries may have physically added the pagination or may have allowed it to remain merely notional. The order of the material in these sets, which amounted to anywhere between 30 and 100 volumes for each session, would be: bills, accounts and papers, and the reports from committees, etc. The index volume for each session translated command paper or House paper number into the appropriate volume and page numbers. As all command papers and many of the other papers are presented to both Houses of Parliament the sessional sets for each House contain much of the same material though they are not identical. If there is no reference to the contrary, a citation to a sessional set will be to the House of Commons version. A citation to a sessional set would look like:

PP (1894-1895) XXIV, 247

The roman numerals are the volume number, the arabic the page number. The House of Commons paper number or command number may cited too.

6.12   It should be mentioned that as well as the hard copy version, the Parliamentary papers are published on microfiche by Chadwyck-Healey. As well as the current papers issued monthly (so a little in arrears of the printed version), they have almost completed a large-scale retrospective version: all of the nineteenth century papers and the early twentieth century papers have been available in this form for some time and the remainder of the twentieth century will be completed in due course. A project to reprint the nineteenth century papers rearranged by subject was started by the Irish University Press but never completed; some libraries may have the papers in this form (large dark green volumes).

Non-Parliamentary publications

6.13   As mentioned, there are no hard and fast rules for knowing whether a governmental document is published in the Parliamentary papers or not. Even reports of inquiries and commissions which one expects always to appear as command papers can catch one out — for example both the Roskill Fraud Trials Committee report and the Andrews report on the government legal service were published as one-off items. HMSO are responsible for publishing many departmental items as well as Parliamentary papers, but there is an increasing trend for government departments to publish their own material themselves. But again there is no way of predicting whether or not an item will be an HMSO publication. The Nugee Committee report, which the Landlord and Tenant Act 1987 was based on, was not a command paper nor an HMSO publication, but was issued by the Department of Environment.

Since 1980 non-HMSO government publications have also been published on microfiche by Chadwyck-Healey in connection with their *Catalogue of Government Publications not Published by HMSO*.

Tracing official publications

Manual sources

6.14   HMSO produce monthly catalogues of their publications, including Parliamentary papers, Bills and Acts (but not SIs) and these are cumulated into annual catalogues. Before 1966 the annual catalogues were collected together in five-year groups with continuous pagination and a consolidated index. The publications issued by HMSO each day appear in the *Daily Lists*, which act as a source of information between monthly catalogues, though it is necessary to browse through each list to locate a particular item. (Unlike the monthly and annual catalogues they also include SIs and draft SIs.)

6.15   In the monthly and annual catalogues Parliamentary papers and Bills are listed first in their respective numerical sequences. There then follows a list arranged alphabetically by body responsible. Parliamentary papers are included here as well as in the numerical sequence. Publications from Parliamentary committees are entered in the alphabetical sequence strictly by title, eg under 'Select Committee on European Legislation' (the House of Commons committee) or 'Select Committee on the European Communities' (the House of Lords committee). The monthly catalogues have indexes which cumulate through the year. They include the names of chairmen of committees as well as subjects (as have the annual catalogues in recent years). The monthly catalogues have page numbers that run from issue to issue, and it is these that are referred to the index, rather than the particular month.

Figure 6.1 shows an entry from the 1991 HMSO annual catalogue with entries in both the numerical sequence of House of Lords papers and in the alphabetical sequence under the name of the Committee. Figure 6.2 shows that both entries are indexed under 'Medicinal products: patent protection', 'Oliver' (the chairman of the committee) and 'Patent protection: medicinal products'. Figure 6.3 shows the title page of the report itself; the paper number is in the bottom lefthand corner.

6.16   As many committee reports are best known by the name of the chairman, HMSO also produce a separate quarterly and annual listing by chairman. To find any government publication (not just HMSO ones) before 1982 by chairman the place to look is the four volumes of *British Government Publications: an Index to Chairmen and Authors* compiled by Stephen Richard (Library Association, 1974-1982), whose coverage goes back to 1800.

Figure 6.1   HMSO Annual Catalogue

10 *House of Lords papers. Session 1991-92*

House of Lords papers. Session 1991-92

Her Majesty's most gracious speech to both Houses of Parliament: delivered on Thursday, 31st October 1991. – [2], 4, [2]p.:30 cm.: 0 10 499992 6 *£1.45*

[ECC-i] Progress of scrutiny, 12 November 1991. – Select Committee on the European Communities. – 17p.: 30 cm. – 0 10 497892 9 *£3.95*

[ECC-ii] Progress of scrutiny, 26 November 1991. – Select Committee on the European Communities. – 14p.: 30 cm. – 0 10 497992 5 *£3.95*

[ECC-iii] Progress of scrutiny, 17 December 1991. – Select Committee on the European Communities. – 18p.: 30 cm. – 0 10 498092 3 *£3.95*

(1) Roll of the Lords spiritual and temporal. – 44p.: 30 cm. – 0 10 400192 5 *£7.00*

(3) Social security, Northern Ireland: consolidation of certain enactments relating to social security in Northern Ireland: Lord Chancellor's memorandum. – House of Commons papers 10. – 12p.: 30 cm. – 0 10 400392 8 *£2.35*

(4) 1st report, session 1991-92. – Committee of Selection. – The Lord Aberdare (chairman). – 4p.: 30 cm. – 0 10 400492 4 *£1.30*

(5) 1st report [session 1992-92]: patent protection for medicinal products with evidence. – Select Committee on the European Communities. – The Lord Oliver of Aylmerton (chairman of Sub-committee E). – 22, 25p.:ill., tables: 30 cm. – Evidence taken before Sub-committee E (Law and Institutions). – 0 10 400592 0 *£6.90*

(6) Amendment made on 11th November 1991 to the standing orders relating to public business. – 2p.: 21cm. – Relates to Standing Order 62. – 0 10 400692 7 *£0.60*

(9) 2nd report, session 1991-92. – Committee of Selection. – 4p.: 30 cm. – 0 10 400992 6 *£1.30*

(13) 1st report from the Select Committee on the House of Lords' Offices: session 1991-92. – Select Committee on the House of Lords Offices. – 4p.: 30 cm. – 0 10 401392 3 *£1.30*

(15) 3rd report, session 1991-92. – Committee of Selection. – 2p.: 30 cm. – 0 10 401592 6 *£0.70*

(17) Special report from the Select Committee on the Severn Bridges Bill. – Select Committee on the Severn Bridges Bill. – The Lord Ampthill (chairman). – [6]p.: 30 cm. – 0 10 401792 9 *£1.90*

(18) 1st report from the Select Committee of the House of Lords on Procedure of the House, session 1991-92. – Select Committee of the House of Lords on Procedure of the House. – 2p.: 30 cm. – 0 10 401892 5 *£0.70*

(23-I) 1st report, session 1991-92: Social Security Contributions and Benefits Bill [H.L.], Social Security Administration Bill [H.L.], Social Security (Consequential Provisions) Bill [H.L.], Social Security Contributions and Benefits (Northern Ireland) Bill [H.L.], Social Security Administration (Northern Ireland) Bill [H.L.], Social Security (Consequential Provisions (Northern Ireland) Bill [H.L.]. – 1: Report. – Joint Committee on Consolidation Bills. – House of Commons papers 140-I. – [8p.]: 30 cm. – 0 10 480192 1 *£1.90*

(24) Radioactive substances: consolidation of certain enactments relating to radioactive substances: Lord Chancellor's memorandum. – House of Commons papers 148. – 7p.: 30 cm. – 0 10 402492 5 *£1.90*

(25) 2nd report from the Select Committee on the House of Lords' Offices session 1991-92. – Select Committee on the House of Lords' Offices. – [7]p.: 30 cm. – 0 10 402592 1 *£1.90*

(30-i) Minutes of evidence taken before the Select Committee on Science and Technology, Sub-committee I: safety aspects of ship, design & technology: Thursday 7 November 1991: United States Coast Guard. – Select Committee on Science and Technology. Sub-committee I. – The Lord Carver (chairman). – p. 235-245: 30 cm. – 0 10 480292 8 *£4.50*

(30-ii) Minutes of evidence taken before the Select Committee on Science and Technology, Sub-committee I: safety aspects of ship design and technology, Thursday 14 November 1991: the Nautical Institute. – Select Committee on Science and Technology. Sub-committee I. – The Lord Carver (chairman). – p. 246-260: 30 cm. – 0 10 480392 4 *£4.50*

Select Committee on the Avon Light Rail Transit (Bristol City Centre) Bill [H.L.]

Special report from the Select Committee on the Avon Light Rail Transit (Bristol City Centre) Bill [H.L.]. – The Lord Elibank (chairman). – [2], 10p.: ill.: 30 cm. – House of Lords papers 43. – 0 10 404391 1 *£3.10*

Select Committee on the British Waterways Bill [H.L.]

Special report from the Select Committee on the British Waterways Bill [H.L.]. – 20p.:: 30 cm. – House of Lords papers 73. – 0 10 407391 8 *£5.25*

Select Committee on the Darlington Borough Council Bill [H.L.]

Special report from the Select Committee on the Darlington Borough Council Bill [H.L.]. – The Lord Quinton (chairman). – 8p.: 30 cm. – House of Lords papers 60. – 0 10 406091 3 *£1.45*

Select Committee on the European Communities

1st report [session 1991-92]: patent protection for medicinal products with evidence. – The Lord Oliver of Aylmerton (chairman of sub-committee E). – 22, 25p.:ill., tables: 30 cm. – House of Lords papers 5. – Evidence taken before Sub-committee E (Law and Institutions). – 0 10 400592 0 *£6.90*

3rd report, [session 1990-91]: a new structure for Community railways. –

Report. – The Lord Shepherd (chairman Sub-committee B), The Lord Ezra (chairman Sub-committee B). – 34p.: 30 cm. – House of Lords papers 11-I. – Evidence was taken before Sub-committee B (Energy, Transport and Technology). – 0 10 480991 4 *£7.95*

[Vol. 2: Evidence]. – The Lord Shepherd (chairman Sub-committee B), The Lord Ezra (chairman Sub-committee B). – 34, 167p.: 30 cm. – House of Lords papers 11. – Evidence was taken before Sub-committee B (Energy, Transport and Technology). – Incorporates paper 11-I. – 0 10 401191 2 *£19.80*

4th report, session 1990-91: working time: with evidence. – The Baroness Lockwood (chairman of Sub-committee C). – 16, 83p.: 30 cm. – House of Lords papers 12. – Evidence given before Sub-committee C (Social & Consumer Affairs). – 0 10 401291 9 *£13.50*

5th report, [session 1990-91]: Conference of Parliaments of the European Community: report. – 11p.: 30 cm. – House of Lords papers 20. – 0 10 402091 1 *£3.80*

6th report [session 1990-91]: correspondence with ministers. – The Baroness Serota (chairman) The Lord Shepherd (chairman Sub-committee B). – 43p.: 30 cm. – House of Lords papers 21. – Correspondence October 1990 to January 1991. – 0 10 402191 8 *£8.70*

7th report [session 1990-91]: non-food uses of agricultural products: with evidence. – The Lord Middleton (chairman of Sub-committee D). – 41, 219p.: ill., tables: 30 cm. – House of Lords papers 26. – Evidence taken before Sub-committee D (Agriculture & Food). – 0 10 402691 x *£22.75*

8th report [session 1990-91]: European agreements with Poland, Hungary and the Czech and Slovak Federal Republic: with evidence. – The Lord Aldington (chairman of Sub-committee A). – 128p.: tables: 30 cm. – House of Lords papers 35. – Includes written & oral evidence submitted to Sub-committee A (Finance, Trade & Industry & External Relations). – 0 10 403591 9 *£18.45*

9th report [session 1990-91]: conduct of the Community's external aviation relations: with evidence. – The Lord Oliver of Aylmerton (chairman of Sub-committee E), The Lord Lowry (chairman). – 128p.: 30 cm. – House of Lords papers 39. – Evidence submitted to Sub-committee E (Law & Institutions). – 0 10 403991 4 *£19.65*

Figure 6.2 HMSO Annual Catalogue

Figure 6.3

HOUSE OF LORDS SESSION 1991–92
1st REPORT

SELECT COMMITTEE ON
THE EUROPEAN COMMUNITIES

PATENT PROTECTION
FOR MEDICINAL PRODUCTS

WITH EVIDENCE

Ordered to be printed 12 November 1991

LONDON: HMSO
£8.90 net

(HL Paper 5)

6.17 Another useful tool for finding HMSO material is *HMSO in Print*, published on microfiche and cumulated every quarter. As it is a guide to what is in print, it is not an exhaustive bibliographical list, but it is a way of searching a large body of material at one go, rather than having to plough through annual catalogues. HMSO also produce sectional lists from time to time which cover publications available on particular subjects.

6.18 The HMSO *Daily Lists* and the monthly catalogues include a selection of material from international organisations, such as the European Communities, the United Nations, and the Council of Europe, which HMSO sells on an agency basis though not published by them. These materials do not reappear in the annual catalogue, but have their separate annual catalogue, the *Agency Catalogue* formerly called the *International Organisations Catalogue*.

6.19 Although the sources mentioned above are suitable for finding recent Parliamentary papers, there are separate indexes to these which may need to be consulted, especially for older papers. There are three consolidated indexes covering 1801 to 1852, 1852 to 1899, and 1900 to 1949 respectively; thereafter two decennial consolidations of the annual sessional indexes have appeared. However, the two nineteenth century indexes have now been superseded by the mammoth subject catalogue produced by Peter Cockton in connection with Chadwyck-Healey's microfiche edition of the nineteenth century papers. This hard copy catalogue is to be supplemented by a keyword index on fiche.

6.20 Finding material from *Hansard*, such as Parliamentary questions and non-legislative debates, by manual means is no different from finding debates on Bills as described in chapter 3 (paras 3.164-3.165), so nothing further will be added here, except a reminder that written questions and answers have their own sequence of column numbering.

6.21 Material published by departments rather by HMSO was notoriously difficult to trace until Chadwyck-Healey started to publish their work, accurately if somewhat awkwardly entitled, *Catalogue of Government Publications Not Published by HMSO*, which started in 1980. As mentioned all the publications listed are also available on microfiche.

Electronic sources

6.22 The most useful source other than for the most recent material and superior to any manual source is the CD-ROM product UKOP (United Kingdom Official Publications). This joint venture by HMSO and Chadwyck-Healey aims to get the best of both worlds by combining HMSO's catalogue data (including its agency publications) with Chadwyck-Healey's data for publications not published by HMSO to get a truly comprehensive collected catalogue of official publications. Its coverage goes back to 1980 and is updated quarterly within four weeks of the latest quarter, each update being an entire cumulation of the database. The search software, as with most CDs, provides very flexible searching, and, unlike some CDs, is user-friendly. Terms from a full complement of fields, such as title, chairman, subject, date, can be searched using conventional techniques such as Boolean logic and truncation. A more limited range of the main fields can be simply browsed through A to Z. There is a wide variety of display formats and options for downloading records.

6.23   HMSO also make their own catalogue data available on-line, via both the on-line host Dialog and the British Library's Blaise service. Although it does not have the non-HMSO publications, it is slightly more up to date than the UKOP CD, being updated monthly, and it goes back slightly further, to 1976.

6.24   As well as UKOP, Chadwyck-Healey also now produce a CD-ROM index covering only the House of Commons Parliamentary papers, ie command papers, House of Commmons papers, and House of Commons Bills. Although it has no particular advantage over UKOP, it is issued free to the subscribers of the microfiche edition of the papers and is a great improvement on the previous microfiche indexes. One difference from UKOP is that the *Index of House of Commons papers* derives from the Polis database (see para 6.25 below), which uses its own specially constructed thesaurus for subject headings, and so the entries for the same material may differ in this respect from the entries on UKOP; this is likely to have little impact in practice on retrieval. It started with the 1991/92 Parliamentary session and is issued twice a year.

6.25   Polis, the Parliamentary on-line information service, was set up by the House of Commons Library and the its main users are within the Palace of Westminster and government departments, but it is available to external users. The main coverage was originally material in *Hansard* and Parliamentary papers, but its scope has gradually been expanded. It is most useful as an index to *Hansard*, and Parliamentary questions in particular. It is also updated daily, though there can be slight time lags. But otherwise it is not very easy to use and the other sources mentioned will usually be preferable. Bear in mind also that the Public Information Office at the House of Commons will, within reason, answer enquiries using it, so a telephone call to them may be the simplest solution. The earliest material on it, House of Commons Parliamentary Questions, dates from 1980; details and dates of coverage of other material are given in the Quick Reference Guide (QR6.1).

6.26   The retrieval of material from *Hansard* is destined to be greatly simplified by the recent appearance of the CD-ROM version, again published by HMSO in collaboration with Chadwyck-Healey. Retrospective coverage goes back to the 1988/89 session, with each subseqent session being on a separate disk. For the current session there are intermediate cumulating disks issued after the Christmas and Easter recesses. As well as the full text of *Hansard* itself the indexes are included too, allowing for subject searching as well as free text searching. Searches can also be limited by date, MP, debate title, and column numbers. Results of searches are divided into the categories debates, written questions, and oral questions. The CD also contains a separate database of MPs, giving details of party, constituency, parliamentary career and so on. At the moment, however, the CD version only covers the House of Commons offical report: the House of Lords and Standing Committee debates are not yet available in this form.

Getting hold of official publications

6.27   Individual HMSO publications can of course be purchased through them if they are in print (or a photocopy obtained if out of print), and individual microfiche of non-HMSO publications can be bought from Chadwyck-Healey. Practitioners will have access to the resources available through firm libraries, the Law Society, and the Inns. Most university of libraries will have extensive holdings of official publications whether in special collections or arranged with other materials. Large public libraries may also stock them. In London, Westminster Central Reference Library and the Guildhall Library are particularly well equipped. The Official Publications and Social Sciences Service of the British Library is the major national resource and though (pending the opening of the new British Library building in St Pancras) much material is outhoused, the open access collections at the British Museum site are more extensive than sometimes assumed. Although access arrangements vary, the libraries of the goverment departments themselves, on the principle of going to the horse's mouth, should not be overlooked. The House of Commons and House of Lords Libraries themselves, unless you happen to be a Member of Parliament or by good fortune a peer of the realm, are not open, but in exceptional circumstances personal access to the resources of the Public Information Office of the House of Commons is permitted with advance permission, and the House of Lords Record Office which contains the archives (including printed records) of both Houses has a public search room. The place to check on government libraries and many other sources of information on official publications is the *Guide to Libraries and Information Units in Government Departments and other Organisations* prepared and reissued at frequent intervals by the British Library Science Reference and Information Service. On specifically Parliamentary materials, the House of Commons Public Information Office also issue a useful guide, *Access to Parliamentary Resources and Information in London Libraries*. The Quick Reference guide includes a list of European Documentation Centres and other sources of EC official publications (QR9.9).

7. Law outside England and Wales

When non-English law might be needed

7.1   There are three main types of research that might involve non-English law, and each may entail a different approach. The first is the not uncommon situation where the practitioner encounters a matter involving a foreign element. International trade, international financial transactions, off-shore trusts, international commercial arbitration and so on are the staple of City lawyers. Procedural matters are important too: forum shopping and the reciprocal enforcement of judgments being examples. But any practitioner may get a case involving perfectly everyday circumstances where the only complication is that they occur to a British citizen abroad, or to a foreign citizen here: having an accident, buying and selling property, getting divorced, dying, committing a crime, paying tax. And of course in this context abroad may, depending on the circumstances, mean Scotland, Northern Ireland, the Channel Islands or the Isle of Man. Unless an English lawyer happens also to have the relevant legal qualifications, it will often be necessary to instruct a local lawyer. But even if that is done, the English lawyer may well want background and clarification to make best use of any local advice; or, it may be that the information sought is only incidental and can be found without the need to go to a local lawyer.

7.2   The second application is in using cases from other jurisdictions that may have persuasive authority in the English courts. Although not binding on English courts, the decisions from the other common law countries — the United States, Canada, Australia and New Zealand being the most important — can be, and frequently are, cited. Such American and Commonwealth cases are typically used where English authorities on a point are controversial, contradictory, weak or lacking altogether. For this reason such cases may assume greater importance in argument before the appellate courts. Like English authorities, the weight attached to an American or Commonwealth case will depend on the level of the court and the reputation of the judge or judges. To the traditional canon of common law case law, now also have to be added decisions of national courts from member states in matters of EC law. Although for this kind of research the primary materials needed are the law reports themselves, legislation, textbooks, and journal articles from the relevant jurisdiction may be needed to make sense of the law surrounding the reported decision, and,

193

importantly, to ensure that the decision does not turn on a statute or precedent that expressly departs from English law.

7.3 The third application is what can be described as pure comparative research. This will usually be in the nature of academic research, where comparative law has a rich and long tradition. But it may impinge on the practitioner in so far as law reform proposals, particularly from the Law Commission, are often based on research into the law of other countries.

For the sake of completeness, two further scenarios should also be mentioned. The first is appeals from Commonwealth courts to the Judicial Committee of the Privy Council. English lawyers are less likely to get involved in these than they once were for two reasons. First, the number of countries which still retain this means of final appeal is steadily diminishing; Hong Kong, New Zealand and the Commonwealth Caribbean islands now provide the bulk of the business — Australia and Malaysia for instance have only recently abolished such appeals, while other countries, such as Canada, did so long ago. Secondly, the appeals are increasingly conducted by lawyers from their own countries. Nonetheless English firms of solicitors may act in such cases and English counsel may be instructed. A number of English lawyers voluntarily act in death penalty cases from the Caribbean, especially Jamaica, which has a notoriously high number of prisoners awaiting execution on death row. Clearly in such cases the English lawyer would need to be acquainted with the relevant law which may or may not be the same as English law.

7.4 The other possibility is that English counsel is instructed to act before a court in another jurisdiction because of a lack of suitably qualified local counsel. The main example is Hong Kong, though as mentioned below (para 7.98), these (lucrative) briefs have now been somewhat curtailed.

7.5 This chapter can only give a brief outline of materials that may be of use if you are in any of these situations and only covers those jurisdictions most likely to be encountered by the English lawyer. For many of the larger jurisdictions detailed legal research manuals exist to which reference can be made.

General comparative sources

7.6 Before looking at particular parts of the world, it is worth bearing in mind that there is quite a range of general materials comparing the law in a number of jurisdictions, though much of it relates to business and commercial law because that is where the biggest market for such publications lies.

Books and periodicals

7.7 For the quick enquiry into the nature of a particular foreign legal system the entries in the *Oxford Companion to Law* are often a useful starting point; more detail will be found in the academic work by Rene David, *Major Legal Systems in the World Today* (3rd ed, Sweet & Maxwell, 1985). Greater detail still will be found in the multi-volume looseleaf work *Modern Legal Systems Cyclopedia* (Buffalo, NY: W. Hein).

7.8 Remarkably useful for basic factual enquiries is the international law digest volume of the huge American annual law directory *Martindale-Hubbell*. It covers about 64 countries of the world. Each country only gets about 10 to 15 pages, but they are in small print and a lot of information, in the form of A to Z topics, is crammed in (see figure 7.1). Canadian law, both federal and provincial, gets much fuller treatment, and a whole separate volume is devoted to the digest of United States law.

7.9   A major new looseleaf publication that promises to offer one-stop shopping for the lawyer needing information on foreign law is the *International Encyclopaedia of Laws*, being issued by the Netherlands-based legal publishers, Kluwer. It is claimed that it will cover all major fields of law from all round the world; it remains to be seen how comprehensive it will be and how frequently the information is updated. The *International Encyclopedia of Comparative Law* (Tubingen: Mohr, 1971-) started publication over 20 years ago and is still not yet complete. Its scholarly approach and lack of any updating mechanism makes it likely to be of most use for academic research.

7.10   More practical are looseleaf compilations of the law of various countries on various topics such as those produced by the American-based publishers Oceana. They have full coverage of business law, for example *Digest of the Commercial Laws of the World*, but they cover other areas, for example *Transport Laws of the World*. J. O. von Kalinovski's vast *World Law of Competition* (New York: Matthew Bender, 1979-) is another American product, but English publishers produce similar comparative compilations in some fields; for example Barry Spitz *Tax Havens Encyclopedia* (Butterworths), Nigel Harris *The Use of Offshore Jurisdictions* (Longman), *International Trust Precedents* (Longman), *International Corporate Procedures* (Jordans). The International Bar Association is active in producing works (published in this country by Graham and Trotman) on procedural matters; for example, *Trial and Court Procedures Worldwide*, *Pre-trial and Pre-hearing Procedures Worldwide*, and *Enforcement of Foreign Judgments Worldwide*. The Law Library of the Library of Congress produces a number of valuable reports on foreign law.

7.11   The indexes to periodicals described in chapter 2 can be used. Comparative articles from British journals picked up by *Legal Journals Index* are likely to be of particular use as being written from an English perspective, but the *Index to Foreign Legal Periodicals*, briefly mentioned in chapter 2, will give a much fuller range of material, though most of the articles will not be in English. The other leading work, which has the advantage of being confined to material in English, is the *Bibliography of Foreign and Comparative Law Books and Articles in English* (Oceana, 1955-) originally edited by Charles Szladits. The leading comparative law journal published in this country is the *International and Comparative Law Quarterly*, issued by the British Institute of International and Comparative Law, who also publish the fortnightly *Bulletin of Legal Developments*.

Legislation

7.12   Finding the legislative sources of foreign countries has been revolutionised by a new three volume looseleaf work *Foreign Law: Current Sources of Codes and Basic Legislation in Jurisdictions of the World* (Littleton, Colorado: Rothman, 1989-) by Thomas H. Reynolds and Arturo A. Flores. It lists each country's codes, main compilations of laws, and official gazettes, and then gives a subject listing of the main laws operative in a particular area, together with any sources of English translations of the particular laws. A general introduction to the legal system of

Figure 7.1   Martindale-Hubbell

SWITZERLAND LAW DIGEST

Revised for 1993 edition by

PESTALOZZI GMUER & PATRY, of the Zurich and Geneva Bars.

(C.C. indicates Civil Code; C.O. indicates Code of Obligations.)

ABSENTEES:

If for reasons of absence a person of age (see topic Infants) cannot act in urgent matter nor designate representative, furthermore if property is not taken care of because person is continually absent with unknown abode or because of uncertainty as to heirs entitled to inheritance, curator (Beistand, curateur, curatore) is appointed by guardianship authority. (C.C. 392, point 1; 393, points 1 and 3; 548, subsection 1). See topics Death; Executors and Administrators, subhead Official Administrators of Estate.

Escheat.—Dividends subject to five years statute of limitations. Title to movables lost by abandonment only when coupled with intention to waive title. Estate passes to canton or municipality of last domicile of intestate decedent only if no grandparents or their issue survive.

ACKNOWLEDGMENTS AND OTHER PUBLIC AUTHENTICATIONS:

Publicly authenticated documents (Öffentliche Urkunde, acte authentique, atto pubblico) are of two kinds: (a) ordinary authentication, attestation or certification of facts by public officials, which include attestation of genuineness of a signature mostly based on acknowledgment by signing person (Beglaubigung, legalisation, autenticazione), and other certifications, e.g., as to conformity of copy with original, correctness of extract from document or register, etc., and (b) execution of publicly authenticated act or instrument by public official pertaining to legal relevant declarations of private persons.

Publicly authenticated documentations of all kinds provide full proof of facts evidenced but proof of incorrectness does not require special form. (C.C. 9).

Signature of blind person must be authenticated. (C.O. 14, 1085). All cantons have provisions for ordinary authentication of signatures or of other facts. Formal requirements of such ordinary authentications are within domain of cantonal law.

Form of publicly authenticated instrument is prescribed by federal law for validity of many legal acts of private law. (See topic Frauds, Statute of.) Inasmuch as federal law does not have pertinent provisions, as for matrimonial property contracts (C.C. 181); public wills (C.C. 499-503), inheritance pacts (C.C. 512), certain contracts of guaranty or of suretyship (C.O. 493), formal requirements for publicly authenticated instruments left to cantonal law (C.C. Final Title, 55). Authenticating person must make sure that instrument expresses true intention, and that it complies with formal requirements of federal or cantonal law.

Authenticating persons for ordinary authentications and/or publicly authenticated instruments are designated by cantonal law; in certain instances (e.g., civil status officers) within framework of federal law. These are notaries, judges, clerks of courts, mayors, clerks of municipalities or districts, special officials, sometimes private persons authorized to perform certain public authentications and insofar as to act as officials. See topic Notaries Public.

Signature of authenticating persons may be legalized, usually, but not always, directly by Chancellery of State of canton where person functions. Signature of that person may be superlegalized by Federal Chancellery in Berne, or by Swiss embassies or consulates abroad.

Switzerland is party to Convention for exemption of foreign public deeds from certification concluded in The Hague on Oct. 5, 1961, providing for "Apostille". See International Conventions section.

ACTIONS:

All actions must be brought before courts, with exception of summary, administrative procedures for collection of debts. See topic Collection of Debts and Bankruptcy.

Action is commenced in Switzerland when first procedural step is taken, such as conciliation procedure before justice of peace. Civil procedure is cantonal. Service of process is effectuated by courts, not by parties. Service of process for foreign proceedings must go through diplomatic channels and cannot be accomplished by Swiss lawyers. American lawyers may apply to local U.S. Consular Office in Switzerland for information. See topic Depositions and Discovery.

Swiss courts have judicial notice of foreign law but may in disputes of financial interest impose burden of proof on parties. If content of foreign law is unascertainable, Swiss law applies.

Limitation of.—See topic Limitation of Actions.

ADMINISTRATION:

See topic Executors and Administrators.

ADOPTION:

Adoption in Switzerland is governed by Swiss law unless to serious detriment of child it is not recognized in country of domicile or citizenship of adopting person or spouses.

Only a single person over 35 or spouses over 35 or whose marriage has lasted for more than five years may adopt another person who must be at least 16 years younger. (C.C. 264a-265). Adoptee, if capable of discernment, must consent and, if a minor or a person who has been placed under guardianship, parents or guardianship authorities must also consent. (C.C. 265-265d). Without consent of spouse no person can adopt or be adopted. Adoption is granted by competent authority at domicile of adopting person(s). (C.C. 268). Adoptee may take new name. Adoptee becomes adoptor's child and loses legal relationship to natural parents except to parent with whom adoptor is married. (C.C. 267). Adoption by Swiss citizen does not convey Swiss citizenship, unless adopted person is minor. (C.C. 267a).

AGENCY: See topic Principal and Agent.

ALIENS:

Conflicts.—International jurisdiction, private international law and recognition and enforcement of foreign decisions, to extent not covered by Switzerland's numerous international treaties, are governed by Private International Law Statute. It covers also international bankruptcy and international arbitration.

Foreign Citizens need residence permit; for gainful activity, also work permit. Temporary personnel, such as technicians or industrial workers also need work permits, unless they only come for few days as consultants. Trainees need temporary permits. No tourist visa is necessary for nationals of many countries; for U.S. citizens, valid passport suffices. All foreigners must register with police after specified stay in Switzerland.

From Nov. 1, 1991 till Oct. 31, 1992 nationwide only 8,006 permits could be granted to new immigrant foreign workers to be employed by private or public employers with specific cantonal and federal quotas. Permits are usually granted for one-year periods. Normally, immigrant may not change employer, profession or canton during first year. Most work permits are granted by cantons with consent of federal administration in Berne. Applications concerning exceptional cases involving national interest, scientific research and professional qualifications not found in Switzerland are handled by federal administration directly. Special rules apply to seasonal workers, trainees, "au pair" maids and other short-term workers. Regulations are very detailed and subject to yearly renewal.

"Central register of resident aliens" is kept. In exceptional cases, addresses of aliens may be disclosed to foreign authorities or to private persons, e.g., if it appears that alien is going into hiding in Switzerland.

Aliens may vote by mail in foreign elections if foreign law so provides.

Corporations Owned or Controlled by Aliens.—See topics Immovable Property, subhead Acquisition by Nonresidents; Corporations, subhead Share Corporation, catchline Alien Shareholders; and Foreign Investments.

European Economic Area.—If Switzerland joins, law will be liberalized in steps (see topic Treaties).

ARBITRATION AND AWARD:

International arbitration (where one party is non-Swiss) commenced before or after Jan. 1, 1989 is governed by Federal Private International Law Statute. If parties have chosen arbitration rules, these govern appointment, challenge and removal of arbitrators exclusively. Arbitral Tribunal rules on its own jurisdiction. Parties or Arbitral Tribunal choose procedure and applicable law freely. Assistance of state courts available, also for interim measures. Challenges of award may be totally excluded if both parties are non-Swiss, otherwise challenge only as in New York Convention on the Recognition and Enforcement of Foreign Arbitral Awards of June 10, 1958. Zurich Chamber of Commerce Arbitration is frequent in international contracts.

Domestic arbitration in all cantons except Luzern is governed by Concordat of Mar. 27, 1969.

Switzerland is party to New York Convention of 1958.

ASSIGNMENTS:

Applicable Law.—Law chosen by assignor and assignee, with respect to obligor only with obligor's assent, otherwise law applicable to obligation. Form of assignment governed by law applicable to contract providing for assignment.

Assignability.—Obligations are assignable without obligor's assent, unless not permissible by law, agreement, or nature of legal relationship. Obligor may not raise defense that assignment of obligation was excluded by agreement, if third person has become obligee in good faith based on written acknowledgment of indebtedness which does not mention its unassignability. (C.O. 164).

Instrument Transferring Title.—Assignment must be in writing; but promise to assign need not be in writing. (C.O. 165).

Notice.—Validity of assignment does not depend on notice to obligor. However, obligor in good faith without notice of assignment is validly discharged if obligor performs to former obligee. (C.O. 167).

Delivery of Evidence.—Assignor must deliver to assignee any document pertaining to obligation and other proof which assignor has. (C.O. 170).

Effect.—Rights connected with obligation pass ipso iure to assignee, unless inseparably connected with assignor's person. (C.O. 170).

Warranty.—In case of assignment for valuable consideration assignor warrants existence of claim at time of assignment, but warrants solvency of obligor only if so agreed. In case of assignment without valuable consideration, assignor is not even liable for existence of claim. (C.O. 171).

Defenses of Obligor.—In addition to special defenses against assignee, obligor has all defenses against assignor (and former assignors), provided such defenses existed at time obligor learned of assignment (C.O. 169); obligor has also defenses pertaining to validity of assignment or previous assignments.

ASSOCIATIONS:

Associations for noneconomic or economic purposes may be created in various forms either by agreement or incorporation.

Associations by agreement include various forms of partnerships. See topic Partnerships. Corporate bodies are legal entities (juristische Personen, personnes morales,

See Topical Index in front part of this volume.

SWZ – 1

each country is also given and major English language works on its law are mentioned. Being an American work it omits the United States.

7.13 One of the problems of using foreign legislation, if you can get access to it, is that of course it will not necessarily be in English. Some of the looseleaf works described above may give extracts of legislation in translation, but there are number of works that reproduce the full text as well as, or instead of, providing commentary. Oceana Publications, for example, have a series of *Commercial, Business and Trade Laws* of various countries in addition to their *Digest of Commercial Laws of the World*. Graham and Trotman in this country have produced translations of business laws from Middle East countries. Rothman publish the *American Series of Foreign Penal Codes*, though be careful of their date. The International Labour Office publish a *Legislative Series* covering labour laws. Blaustein *Constitutions of the Countries of the World* (Oceana) in a large number of looseleaf volumes is the definitive source for constitutional material.

Law reports

7.14 Apart from the Commonwealth and Europe, dealt with below, there are relatively few sources that bring together decisions of the courts of different countries. *World Intellectual Property Reporter* (BNA, Washington), *Lloyds Arbitration Reports*, and *International Litigation Procedure* (Sweet & Maxwell) are the main examples that come to mind.

Other jurisdictions in the British Isles

Scotland

7.15 Historically, the Scottish legal system developed separately from the English common law, taking its roots instead from continental Roman-based civil law. However, it has been heavily anglicised because since 1707 its legislation has emanated from Westminster and its final court of appeal in civil cases has been the House of Lords.

7.16 As was noted in chapter 3, some Acts of Parliament, for example on taxation, apply to the whole of the United Kingdom, while others may apply to Scotland only. Even where Scotland has separate legislation, its provisions may be very similar to the equivalent statute for England and Wales except for translating technical terms or making adjustments for differences in procedure. A particular problem is that new legislation, even where it is the ultimate intention for Scotland and England to be similarly treated, may not be introduced into the two jurisdictions simultaneously. Scotland may be treated as a guinea pig and be subject to the new regime first (as happened with the poll tax), or Scotland may as an afterthought receive the benefit of an English statute some time later. Many statutes applying to Scotland only will bear the same title as the related English statute simply with the addition of 'Scotland' in parentheses; for example there was a Housing Act 1988 and a Housing (Scotland) Act 1988. On the other hand they may appear in another guise; for example parallel provisions to the Courts and Legal Services Act 1990 were applied to Scotland, together with a whole range other unrelated measures, by the Law Reform (Miscellaneous Provisions) (Scotland) Act 1990.

7.17   The adoption of a strict doctrine of precedent in Scotland was only a nineteenth century development made under English influence. But now case law is treated in Scotland as a similar source of law. The decisions of the House of Lords in Scottish appeals are binding on the Scottish courts. As no Scots judges were appointed to the Judicial Committee of the House of Lords until 1866 and they have only been in a small minority since, the influence of English legal principles has been strong. As a result the same law may apply in Scotland as in England, even where there is no statutory provision. *Donoghue v Stevenson* after all was a Scottish appeal, as was, to take a more recent example in the law of negligence, *Smith v Littlewoods Organisation Ltd* [1987] AC 241. The decisions of the other English courts are not binding in Scotland but may be highly persuasive, and the reverse applies in England, particularly where an identical statutory provision has to be construed. Scottish decisions on quantum of damages in personal injury cases and on sentencing, as in England, do not operate as binding precedents but may provide useful illustrations for the English lawyer as much as for the Scottish lawyer.

7.18   If further background is required the standard work is David M. Walker *The Scottish Legal System* (6th ed, Edinburgh: W. Green, 1992); *The Scottish Legal Tradition* by M.C. Meston and others (new ed, Edinburgh: The Saltire Society and The Stair Society, 1991) is useful too. David Walker is also the author of the *Oxford Companion to Law*, so due weight is given to Scottish entries in it. Before outlining materials relevant to Scottish legal research, attention is drawn to fuller treatments elsewhere:

   Valerie Duffy *Legal Research in Scotland* (Hebden Bridge: Legal Information Resources, 1992)(Guides to legal research; no. 4)
   Dawn D. Mackey *How to Use a Scottish Law Library* (Edinburgh: W. Green, 1992)
   'Scots law': chapter 15 *in* Robert Logan (ed) *Information Sources in Law* (London: Butterworths, 1986)
   'Scots law': chapter 8 *in* Jean Dane and Philip A. Thomas *How to Use a Law Library* (2nd ed, London: Sweet & Maxwell, 1987)

References to Scottish materials will also be found at the appropriate points throughout the *Manual of Law Librarianship* (ed E.M. Moys, 2nd ed, Aldershot: Gower, 1987).

Textbooks and journals

7.19   Walker's *Scottish Legal System*, cited above, although not containing a formal bibliography is a source for a wide range of bibliographical information on Scottish books. There has recently been a marked increase in the output of Scottish legal textbooks and up-to-date treatments of many subjects are available. Both the publishers Butterworths and the Scottish arm of Sweet & Maxwell, W. Green, have been particularly active, and the list of the Scottish publisher T. & T. Clark has expanded. The major event in Scottish legal publishing, however, has been the production of *The Laws of Scotland: Stair Memorial Encyclopaedia* by the Law Society of Scotland in conjunction with Butterworths. This aims to be the equivalent of *Halsbury's Laws* for Scotland, the last similar venture, Green's *Encyclopaedia of the Laws of Scotland*, not having been updated since 1952. Begun in 1986, its 25 volumes are nearing completion. A looseleaf service volume keeps up to date the volumes that have already appeared and a softback consolidated interim index has been issued. As well the *Stair Encyclopaedia* and textbooks proper, the reports of the Scottish Law Commission (published by HMSO) can provide valuable expositions of the existing law in areas where reform is under consideration.

7.20   Scottish journal articles should be straightforward to trace. The following are the main titles, all of which are indexed in *Legal Journals Index*:

Journal of the Law Society of Scotland (full text also on Lexis from 1990)
Juridical Review
SCOLAG (Scottish Legal Action Group)
Scots Law Times
Scottish Law Gazette
Scottish Planning Law and Practice

Legislation

7.21   As pointed out in chapter 3, *Halsbury's Statutes* does not cover Acts or parts of Acts applying to Scotland only, so *Statutes in Force*, which does, comes into its own. *Current Law Statutes Annotated*, also described in chapter 3, includes Scottish statutes from 1991; before then they will be found in the separate edition, *Scottish Current Law Statutes Annotated*. The unannotated text as passed will of course also be available in the official HMSO edition of Public General Acts. A useful looseleaf compilation of statutory materials of use to the practitioner and arranged by subject is the *Parliament House Book*. *Is it in Force?*, despite bearing the colours of *Halsbury's Statutes* and often shelved with it, does include Scottish statutes, as do the *Current Law* statute citators. Bear in mind that before 1707 Scotland had its own Parliament; the Acts of the Parliaments of Scotland have a separate table in the second volume of the *Chronological Table of Statutes* — if the text of such statutes is needed reference should be made to one of the detailed guides already listed. Lexis is of little use; since 1980 parts of UK Acts applicable to Scotland are not actually deleted from the database as they were before then and amendments to those parts are included, but Acts wholly applicable to Scotland are not included.

Law reports

7.22   The main series of reports, equivalent to *The Law Reports,* is the *Session Cases* (some Scottish appeals to the House of Lords will also be in the English *Appeal Cases*). However, they suffer from a severe time lag in publication. To give greater timeliness and wider coverage two major series have recently appeared under the auspices of the Law Society of Scotland, *Scottish Civil Law Reports* and *Scottish Criminal Case Reports*. The case reports in the *Scots Law Times* are roughly equivalent to the *Weekly Law Reports*: they are proper full-length reports appearing weekly. *Green's Weekly Digest* aims at providing even greater currency — summaries of a very wide range of cases are included, a selection of which are subsequently reported fully in the *Scots Law Times*.

Of the English national newspapers *The Times* is the main one to carry cases from the Scottish courts, a practice that has now been adopted by *The Scotsman*; fortunately these are both covered by the *Daily Law Reports Index*. For older series of reports reference should be made to one of the specialist guides, but there is a pattern similar to England of nominate reports — and in fact before 1907 the *Session Cases* are divided into, and cited by, series identified by reporter.

7.23   Finding Scottish case law in the English law library has been made simpler by the inclusion since 1991 of Scottish material in *Current Law*. Before 1991 there was a separate edition *Scottish Current Law* (with associated *Scottish Current Law Yearbooks*, *Scottish Current Law Case Citators*, and *Scottish Current Law Statutes Annotated*) which contained all the English material, but with a Scottish supplement; this edition was not as widely available as the standard edition in English libraries. In the monthly digests and the yearbooks under the new arrangement, the Scottish material in the body of the work is still listed separately, coming at the end after Northern Ireland material. In the cumulative index to the monthly digests and in the index to the yearbooks the paragraph numbers of the Scottish entries are suffixed by 'S'. A particular hazard to be aware of in using *Current Law* for Scottish cases is its treatment of cases from *Green's Weekly Digest*. There are three points here. First, cases from *Green's Weekly Digest* are included only in the monthly parts *not* in the yearbooks. Secondly, only a very brief headnote is given, not a digest like other entries. Thirdly, although they are included in the cumulative subject index to the monthly parts, the names of the cases are *not* included in the cumulative table of cases.

7.24   The other main manual source is the *Digest*, described in chapter 4; Scottish cases are among the small print sequences. There are number of digests and indexes to older Scottish cases, such as the *Scots Digest*, the *Faculty of Digest* and, going back to 1540, *Morison's Dictionary of Decisions*.

7.25   Lexis, though limited for legislation, is useful for Scots case law, especially if your library does not run to holding the reports in printed form; unreported cases are included too. They are in the CASES file in the SCOT library (not the ENGGEN library); the contents are listed in the Quick Reference Guide (QR7.5).

7.26   When using Scottish cases, it is useful to have an idea of the various courts. In outline the following are the main courts. The superior civil court is the Court of Session which is divided into the Inner House which is roughly equivalent to the Court of Appeal (Civil Division) and the Outer House which hears cases at first instance and is roughly equivalent of the High Court. The Outer House sits in two Divisions of three or four judges. Cases in the Outer House are heard before a single judge. In criminal matters the superior court is the High Court of Justiciary. It sits both as an appellate court equivalent to the Court of Appeal (Criminal Division) and on circuit with a single judge to try serious crimes similarly to Queen's Bench Division High Court judges hearing serious cases on circuit at Crown Courts. The main inferior court is the sheriff court which has a civil jurisdiction similar to county courts, and in criminal matters tries less important cases on indictment before a jury as in Crown Courts before circuit judges or recorders, and also summarily. In the towns or cities that are burghs there are also the equivalent of magistrates courts.

Northern Ireland

7.27   The books by Dane and Thomas and by Logan, cited above in connection with Scots law (para 7.18), both also contain chapters on Irish law. The output of secondary literature, though still fairly modest, has been burgeoning since the setting up in 1980 of SLS Legal Publications to produce works specifically devoted to Northern Ireland law. Some modern books, for example those by Wylie on land law and conveyancing, cover both Northern Ireland and the Republic. The *Northern*

Ireland Legal Quarterly is the main periodical and of high quality. Articles from this and other British journals will be picked up by the *Legal Journals Index*. From January 1993 there is also *Irish Legal Journals Index*, produced by the publishers of the *Legal Journals Index*, Legal Information Resources Ltd. For earlier periodical literature reference should be made to the *Bibliography of Periodical Literature Relating to Irish Law* by Paul O'Higgins (Belfast: Northern Ireland Legal Quarterly, 1966; Supplements 1973, 1983).

7.28 The complexity of legislation for Northern Ireland reflects the complexity of the constitutional arrangements. The current position, which, except for a brief period between 1973 and 1974, has prevailed since the end of March 1972, is that most statutes that apply to Northern Ireland only are made by Order in Council and are issued as United Kingdom SIs: they take the form of and are passed as delegated legislation at Westminster but are in substance the equivalent of primary legislation. They bear an SI number but are not included in the official bound volumes of SIs; instead they are filed by a separate NI number (the equivalent of a chapter number for an ordinary statute) in binders labelled Northern Ireland statutes.

7.29 In addition to the Northern Ireland statutes there are some United Kingdom statutes that extend to Northern Ireland in the same way that some extend to Scotland; in the absence of any provision to the contrary an Act passed by the Westminster Parliament is presumed to extend to Northern Ireland, but in practice an express provision at the end of the Act will indicate whether or not it so extends either wholly or in part. Usually such statutes are ones that apply to other parts of the United Kingdom as well, but some apply to Northern Ireland only; these will have 'Northern Ireland' in their title (*before* the word 'Act'), for example the Social Security (Northern Ireland) Act 1975 or the Judicature (Northern Ireland) Act 1978. The reason these are not made by Order in Council as Northern Ireland statutes is that even before 1972 there were certain matters reserved for the Westminster Parliament and not within the legislative competence of Stormont, and it is those matters that are still the subject of Westminster statutes — the Westminster Orders in Council have only replaced the Stormont statutes.

7.30 Statutes were passed at Stormont by the Parliament of Northern Ireland from 1921 to 1972, and Measures (only four) were passed there between 1973 and 1974 during the brief legislative life of the Northern Ireland Assembly. The titles of Acts that emanated from Stormont are distinguishable from those that emanated from Westminster: the former all have the word 'Northern Ireland' *after* the word 'Act', for example the Land Registration Act (Northern Ireland) 1970. In addition some statutes passed by the Parliament of Ireland at Dublin before 1800 are still in force, as are of course some statutes passed at Westminster from 1800 to 1920. The *Statutes Revised, Northern Ireland* contain all the above material as at 31 March 1981 *except* United Kingdom statutes passed at Westminster since 1920 that extend to, or apply only to, Northern Ireland. The latter are included in *Statutes in Force*, the Public General Acts and *Current Law Statutes Annotated*. *Halsbury's Statutes* gives annotations as to the extension of UK statutes to Northern Ireland, but only includes the full text of selected UK statutes that apply only to Northern Ireland. HMSO Belfast produce indexes and chronological tables to the Northern Ireland statutes from time, and there is an annual cumulative supplement to the *Statutes Revised, Northern Ireland* issued in A4 format (the work itself, though in looseleaf binders, has not been updated so far).

7.31   Some United Kingdom SIs made under United Kingdom Acts that extend to Northern Ireland will likewise extend to Northern Ireland, but the vast bulk of subsidiary legislation for Northern Ireland is issued as an entirely separate series *Northern Ireland Statutory Rules and Orders* by HMSO Belfast. An index to these is published from time to time.

7.32   The official law reports are the *Northern Ireland Law Reports*. These suffer from delay; since 1971 the *Northern Ireland Judgments Bulletin* in mimeographed form has provided advance publication, but this series has only be more widely available since 1985. In the earlier years of the province decisions of the Northern Ireland courts were also published in series of law reports emanating from Dublin such as the *Irish Law Times Reports*. The Incorporated Council of Law Reporting for Northern Ireland have published an *Index to Northern Ireland Cases 1921 to 1970* (with supplement to 1975). The *Northern Ireland Law Reports* from 1945 and unreported cases from 1984 are on Lexis in the NILAW library.

7.33   *Current Law*, in a separate section sandwiched between European Communities and Scotland, covers all the above material including subsidiary legislation, as does the *Bulletin of Northern Ireland Law*.

Isle of Man

7.34   The practitioner is most likely to encounter Manx law in the context of companies, trusts and insurance on account of the island's status as a tax haven. Much of the legal literature will accordingly be found in specialist books and journals on offshore jurisdictions and tax planning, rather than in specific works devoted to the law of the Isle of Man, which are very few in number. One of the few recent works on the Isle of Man alone is *Trusts, Tax and Estate Planning Through the Isle of Man* by John Glasson and others (Key Haven Publications, 1989). There is also a recent book by Jane Bates, *Isle of Man Companies Act* (Sweet & Maxwell, 1992). A bibliography of Manx legal literature is included in W. Twining and J. Uglow *Law Publishing and Legal Information: Small Jurisdictions of the British Isles* (Sweet & Maxwell, 1981) (see also *Chloros*, cited below — para 7.42).

7.35   The island is able to pursue in its own fiscal policies because it is not part of the United Kingdom and has its own legislature, the Tynwald, which has a long history. Nonetheless it is a dependency of the United Kingdom, which acts on behalf of the island in external matters such as foreign affairs and defence, and Acts of Tynwald receive Royal Assent. Not all legislation, however, is made by the Tynwald. Many Acts of the United Kingdom Parliament extend, with the consent of Tynwald, to the Isle of Man. The normal procedure for this is different from the way United Kingdom statutes are extended to Scotland and Northern Ireland. Instead of simply incorporating an extension provision directly into the statute, an enabling power is inserted under which an Order in Council can be made (often incorporating certain local adaptations and modifications) after the consultative process has been completed. Such Orders in Council are United Kingdom SIs. The Isle of Man is not a member of the European Communities as such but has a special arrangement under Protocol 3 of the United Kingdom's treaty of accession so that it is treated as part of Europe for the purposes of customs and the free movement of goods. Although it has its own indigenous legal traditions based on Norse customary law, modern Manx law largely follows English common law as well statute law.

7.36   Access to primary legislation is provided by two publications: the *Subject Guide to the Acts of Tynwald including Alphabetical and Chronological Lists of the Acts*, revised annually, and the *Subject Guide to, and Chronological Table of, Acts of Parliament Extending or Relating to the Isle of Man*, the second edition of which is up to date to 31 March 1992. The new edition of the latter was consequent upon the Statute Law Revision (Isle of Man) Act 1991 which removed over 800 obsolete Acts of Parliament applying to the Isle of Man from the statute book. There is no modern consolidation of the Acts of Tynwald, though some individual acts such as the Companies Act are reprinted from time to time. The *Subject Guide*, however, makes it easy enough to find ones way about the annual volumes of Acts. There is a *Subject Guide and Chronological Table to Subordinate Legislation*, but it was last revised in 1981. Enquiries on obtaining copies of primary materials, particularly subordinate legislation which is issued in the form of government circulars and is not widely available outside the island, should be directed to the Central Reference Library, Government Buildings, Douglas, Isle of Man. The Attorney General's Chambers may also be able to offer advice.

7.37   The *Manx Law Reports*, which go back to 1972, are published by Law Reports International in Oxford, and have cumulative tables from time to time. There is also *A Book of Precedents: a List of Constitutional and Privy Council Judgments Affecting the Isle of Man from 1523 to 1986* compiled by Judy Thornley (Government Printer, 1987).

7.38   Finally an indispensable tool for all aspects of the law of the Isle of Man is the *Manx Law Bulletin*, prepared by the Attorney General's Chambers since 1983. It contains case notes and summaries of Acts of Tynwald (together with bills and questions in Tynwald), subordinate legislation and applicable United Kingdom statutes, all with their commencement dates; occasional articles are included too.

Channel Islands

7.39   The Channel Islands have a similar constitutional status to the Isle of Man and similar importance as tax havens. However, their legal systems derive from Norman law, the islands having originally been part of the Duchy of Normandy. As a consequence the customary law adapted from the old Norman *coutumes* is still a source of law, together with legislation and the decisions of the courts. There is also the consequence that much of the materials, especially the older ones, are in French. The Channel Islands comprise the two bailiwicks of Jersey and Guernsey each with their own legislatures, courts, and government. Alderney and Sark are dependencies of Guernsey, but are distinct jurisdictions with their own legislatures and legal customs.

7.40   The name of the body that is both legislature and government is 'The States' in three of the four jurisdictions; in Sark it is 'The Chief Pleas'. The position of the islands vis-à-vis the European Communities is similar to the Isle of Man: they are not member states but are treated as being within the Communities for the purpose of customs and the free movement of goods (but not the free movement of persons and services).

7.41   As in the Isle of Man, the usual means nowadays of extending United Kingdom statutes to the Channel Islands is by Orders in Council issued as United

Kingdom SIs. But whereas the Acts of Tynwald receive Royal Assent, the primary legislation of the States is sanctioned by Her Majesty by Orders in Council; these orders are made in the exercise of the prerogative power and so should not be confused with Orders in Council that are United Kingdom SIs (see para 3.138). The States can also legislate in certain areas without Royal sanction, either under general powers given by Order in Council (for example the power given to the Jersey States to make 'Regulations' of no more than three years duration) or in Guernsey under a residual common law power to legislate.

7.42   General guidance on the legal literature of the Channel Islands may be found in the *Bibliographical Guide to the Law of the United Kingdom, the Channel Islands and the Isle of Man* edited by A.G. Chloros (2nd ed, Institute of Advanced Legal Studies, 1973) — the Channel Islands are not covered by *Twining and Uglow*. Tolley's publish an annual *Taxation in the Channel Islands and the Isle of Man*. The accountants KPMG Peat Marwick, who have offices on both of the main islands, regularly issue booklets on such matters as banking, finance, investment and insurance in the islands. Again it should be emphasised that one must bear in mind comparative works and journal articles rather than assume there is no secondary literature to speak of on the islands.

Jersey

7.43   *The Jersey Law of Trusts* by Paul Matthews and Terry Sowden (2nd ed, Key Haven Publications, 1990) has valuable introductory matter as well as covering the subject in its title; it is one of the few modern works on the law of Jersey. The Jersey branch of the Institute of Directors has recently issued a useful booklet on *Guidelines for Jersey Directors* in the wake of the new Companies (Jersey) Law 1991. The constitutional position of the island is described at length in *A Constitutional History of Jersey* by F. de L. Bois (States' Greffe, 1972).

7.44   The *General Index of Legislation* is an index to all Jersey legislation, both primary and secondary, in force as 31 December 1990. The primary legislation has been issued as 'Laws' since 1979, before which the series was entitled *Recueil des Lois*. The Income Tax (Jersey) Law 1961 is reprinted as amended in looseleaf form. The other series, which has been published since 1939, is called Regulations and Orders.

7.45   This series contains four species of legislation: (1) regulations of three years' duration made under general powers; (2) reglations (or sometimes 'rules') of indefinite duration made by the States under powers in particular laws; (3) acts of the States which are the form of instrument used, for example, for commencement orders and for incorporation of treaty provisions; and (4) orders made by committees of the States (ie ministries) under powers in laws. Unlike the laws, which are numbered only within each year, regulations and orders have a reference number that runs from year to year and so is now well into four digits.

7.46   Before 1950 no reasoned judgments in the English style were given by the Royal Court of Jersey, so there are no proper law reports before that date. The only published guide was a *Table des Decisions*, which acted as a kind of digest of unreported decisions filed at the Royal Court. From 1950 a more English approach to precedent was adopted and reports appeared as *Jersey Judgments* published locally until 1984 when they were superseded by the *Jersey Law Reports* published by Law

Reports International in Oxford. Note that the latter series has an index and tables volume described as covering 'The Jersey law reports' from 1977 to 1986: in fact it is the *Jersey Judgments* that it covers from 1977 to 1984. The *Table des Decisions* already mentioned began in 1884 and continued to 1963. It was resuscitated for one further volume covering 1964-1978 published in 1980; unlike its predecessors this volume was mostly in English and its purpose was simply to note decisions *not* reported in the *Jersey Judgments*.

Guernsey

7.47   *The Constitution and Law of Guernsey* by Sir John Loveridge (La Société Guernesiaise, 1975) is a very useful booklet on the legal system in general. There is very little indeed written specifically on the law of Guernsey. The Guernsey Financial Services Commission have recently produced the *Guernsey Company and Trust Law Handbook* (edited by D.E. Thompson); they also produce various brochures on the financial services industry which may provide some background.

7.48   The primary legislation is called 'laws' though the series on its spine and covers is called *Orders in Council* (formerly *Recueil d'Ordres en Conseil*) because that is how they are enacted; an example of a formal title is thus: 'Order in Council ratifying a Projet de Loi [ie a Bill] entitled The Conditions of Employment (Guernsey) Law, 1985'. The other main series of legislation is called 'ordinances of the States' (formerly Ordonnances), which include original legislation made by the States not requiring Royal sanction and delegated legislation made by the States under laws. Before 1948 the Royal Court of Guernsey also had legislative powers. These were transferred to the States except in the case of defence regulations and rules of the court itself, which continue to appear in a series *Orders of the Royal Court*. In addition, the committees of the States make delegated legislation in the form of statutory instruments. Both Alderney and Sark similarly have their own *Orders in Council* and *Ordinances*. In certain areas Guernsey applies its legislation to Alderney, eg The Alderney (Application of Legislation) (Supplementary Benefit) Ordinance 1990, which is Guernsey Ordinance No XXXVI of 1990 applying Ordinance No XXXV.

7.49   Since 1965 judgments of the Court of Appeal of Guernsey and some other judgments have been printed. Since 1985, however, the main source of information on cases has been the *Guernsey Law Journal* which provides summaries, as it does of all legislation (including Alderney and Sark); occasional articles also appear in it. This publication makes finding Guernsey material considerably easier than it is for Jersey. Copies of the materials summarised are available from The Greffe.

Other common law jurisdictions

Republic of Ireland

7.50   The number of modern textbooks devoted to the law in the Republic have been increasing, thanks in particular to the Roundhall Press, Butterworths (who have taken over Professional Books' strong Irish list) and Sweet & Maxwell's *Irish Law Texts* series. The catalogues of these publishers provide a mini-bibliography of what is available. There is also a useful description of textbooks in the chapter on Irish law in *Information Sources in Law*. That work and *Dane and Thomas* (both cited above at para 7.18) in general give excellent coverage of sources of Irish law to which reference should be made. The Republic is of course also a full member state of the European Communities so its law is of interest from that point of view as well as being another common law jurisdiction. The Centre for European Law based at Trinity College Dublin produces a valuable series of publications.

7.51   The *Legal Journals Index* does not extend to journals published in the Republic, but a companion service, *Irish Legal Journals Index*, started in January 1993 and covers the dozen or so titles published in Ireland as well as articles from English journals on Irish law. The *Gazette of the Incorporated Law Society* and the *Irish Law Times* are the two main professional journals. The *Irish Jurist* is the leading academic journal, though it also contains material of use to the practitioner such as an annual digest of decisions and a list of legislation. Other specialist journals are also appearing. The periodical literature up to 1981 is covered by the bibliography by O'Higgins, already cited (para 7.27).

7.52   The official edition of the statutes, the *Acts of the Oireachtas*, are published in loose parts as they are passed and in annual bound volumes. There is no current consolidation of the text but there is a consolidated index covering 1922-1982. Since 1984 the official edition has been supplemented by the commercially produced *Irish Current Law Statutes Annotated*, which is similar to its English counterpart though in looseleaf format. Secondary legislation is in the form of statutory instruments as in England, though they are now only published in loose form, the official bound volumes having stopped in 1981. There is an eight volume index to the statutory instruments covering 1922-1979.

7.53   The two main current law reports series are the long-standing official *Irish Reports*, which emerged out of the previous Irish series produced by the Incorporated Council of Law Reporting, and the more recently established *Irish Law Reports Monthly* (1980-). However, there is considerable reliance on unreported cases. From 1976 all the written judgments of the superior courts are distributed in typescript form to various libraries and bodies. Indexes to these, known as 'Pink lists', were prepared and are currently issued as a supplement to the *Gazette of the Incorporated Law Society*. The Irish Association of Law Teachers prepared a consolidation of the pink lists, *Index to Irish Superior Court Written Judgments 1976-1982*. The published reports are indexed in the *Irish Digest* published in roughly decennial spans up to 1983. Selected Irish cases also appear in the English *Digest*.

United States

7.54   Not suprisingly, given the size of the legal literature, the size of the legal profession and the emphasis traditionally placed on legal research in American legal education, there are a quite a number of detailed American publications on legal research. The three leading works are:

Morris L. Cohen *How to Find the Law* (8th ed, St Paul, Minn: West, 1983)
J. M. Jacobstein and Roy Mersky *Fundamentals of Legal Research* (2nd ed, Mineola, NY: Foundation Press, 1981)
Miles O. Price *Effective Legal Research* (4th ed. Boston, Mass: Little Brown, 1979)

However, for the non-American lawyer there is now a slimmer and more practical guide published in this country:

> Robert Logan *United States Legal Research* (Hebden Bridge: Legal Information Resources, 1990)(Guides to legal research; no. 2)

7.55 The complexity of United States legal literature is a consequence of the federal legal system: the researcher has to cope not only with the mass of federal law but also the law of each individual state. While the law may often be similar from state to state because their courts follow similar common law principles (disregarding the anomalous position in the mixed jurisdiction of Louisiana) and their legislatures may adopt model laws such as the Uniform Commercial Code, variations, sometimes quite radical ones, do occur.

7.56 For the English lawyer there is also the problem of access to the material. Many academic libraries take basic materials and there are major collections in Oxford, Cambridge, and in London at the Institute of Advanced Legal Studies and the Middle Temple Library. The *Union List of United States Legal Literature in Oxford, Cambridge and London* (2nd ed, IALS, 1967) is very out of date but is of residual use in locating material. But no English library has a collection in printed form that could match the resources that would be available to an American lawyer. For this reason the importance of Lexis should be strongly emphasised. Lexis was in origin an American system and the vast bulk of federal and state legislation and case law (and many law reviews) is available in full text, and accessible in just the same way as the English materials. If regular use is made of the American database, it is well worth getting hold of the American version of the user manual. Details of the American libraries on Lexis are not given in the standard library contents list issued by Butterworths (Telepublishing), but a separate list can be obtained from them and they are also listed in Sarah J. Nichols *Law Databases* (London: Aslib, 1991); because there are so many libraries and files, using these printed lists is preferable to trying to battle with the on-screen versions. In the United States Lexis has an equally popular competitor, Westlaw, but though available here it is much less widely used.

7.57 Although it does not normally present great difficulties, the English researcher should bear in mind differences in spelling and usage in both legal and ordinary American English. The spelling point is particularly pertinent to Lexis searching, where, for example, to search for the word OFFENCE instead of OFFENSE would derail a search strategy. *Black's Law Dictionary* (6th ed, St Paul, Minn: West, 1990) and Bryan A. Garner *A Dictionary of Modern Legal Usage* (New York: Oxford University Press, 1987) are helpful here.

Textbooks and journals

7.58 The main American tools for finding books and journal articles were described in chapter 2 because the coverage of many includes English material, but an additional tool which is useful is Edward J. Bander *Searching the Law* (New York: Transnational, 1987). This follows a subject arrangement and under each subject are listed the leading texts, journal, treatises and bibliographies. A companion work covering the law of all the individual states is Francis Doyle *Searching the Law: the States* (New York: Transnational, 1989).

Legislation

7.59   Acts of Congress are officially issued in loose form and bound volumes as *Statutes at Large* in the same way as Queen's Printer copies of Public General Acts, but for most purposes the preferable source is the *United States Code* which is a compilation by topic, each topic being called a 'title', of the main legislation in force. It comes in three versions, the official version published by the government printer, and two versions published by rival commercial publishers, *United States Code Annotated* (West) and *United States Code Service* (Lawyers' Co-operative). The latter two, because of their extensive annotations, are to be preferred. The bound volumes have pocket part supplements and are reissued from time to time. Subordinate legislation is published daily in the *Federal Register*, and is consolidated in the *Code of Federal Regulations*.

7.60   State legislation follows a similar pattern with sessional laws and consolidations in the form of codes. The codes may cover the whole body of law or a part, such as a criminal code. Alongside the official versions, there are often commercially-produced annotated versions. The codes of some states are more important than others because they have acted as models which other states have followed; for example the Delaware Corporations Code. The National Conference of Commissioners on Uniform State Laws also produce model laws which may be widely adopted, such as the Uniform Commercial Code.

Law reports

7.61   Like the United States Code, the reports of the Supreme Court are available in an official series and two rival annotated commercially-published series. The official *United States Supreme Court Reports*, cited simply as US, go all the way back to 1790. The early volumes, like other early American reports which followed the English pattern, were known by the names of their reporters and may be still so cited. But when in 1875 simple sequential volume numbering was introduced, those volumes were retrospectively numbered as part of the main series in addition.

The *Lawyers' Edition*, cited L Ed, covers the entire series and is published by Lawyers' Co-operative. The *Supreme Court Reporter* (S Ct), published by West as part of its *National Reporter System*, starts in 1882. These two each have their own volume numbering system, but on both the equivalent volume number for the official series also appears.

7.62   Until 1880 there were numerous nominate reports covering the other federal courts. These were collected together in a reprint, *Federal Cases*. Since 1880 there has been the *Federal Reporter*, again part of the *National Reporter System*. Decisions of the district courts, the lowest level of federal court, were hived off in 1932 to another series, the *Federal Supplement*.

7.63   Reports of state courts were originally published as nominates, and in many states there continues to be an official state series, but virtually all English libraries that collect American reports will have them in the form of the *National Reporter System*. This is published in seven series covering geographic groups of states, the *Atlantic Reporter*, the *North Western Reporter* and so on. State decisions are also published in the *American Law Reports*. This series is not intended to be comprehensive like the *National Reporter System*, but provides in-depth annotations and commentary on selected cases. Before 1969 it also covered federal cases, but these are now separately covered by *American Law Reports Federal*.

7.64 There are a number of reports covering specialist tribunals or particular subjects, but because the coverage of the general series is much less selective than in England (*all* decisions of the final appellate court, and a very large number at intermediate appellate level, in each state are included in the *National Reporter System*), less reliance on them is needed.

7.65 American citation practice follows the English pattern except for date: the use of volume numbering rather than year as the preferred means of identification is universal so the square bracket/round bracket convention on dates does not arise, and the date is given at the end of the citation not at the beginning. In the case of voluminous series the Americans have a predilection for starting new series of volume numbering every so often; the abbreviation used for second series, third series, etc, which may momentarily perplex the English eye, is 2d, 3d, etc. It is the proper practice to cite first the reference in the relevant state reports and then the reference to the *National Reporter System*, which makes for long citations: the English lawyer should concentrate on the second citation. If only a state report citation is given, it can be translated into a *National Reporter* citation using the *National Reporter Blue Book* (in the unlikely event of needing to translate a *National Reporter* citation into a state report citation use *Shepard's Citations*, mentioned below, para 7.67). Thus a typical American citation may look like:

Hill v Bowen 8 Ill 2d 527, 134 NE 2d 769 (1956)

This 1956 decision is reported in volume 8 of the second series of *Illinois Reports* at page 527 and in volume 134 of the second series of the *North Eastern Reporter* (in the *National Reporter* system) at page 769.

Abbreviations for American series of reports are fairly fully covered by *Raistrick*, but an American equivalent is Doris M. Bieber *Dictionary of Legal Abbreviations* (3rd ed, Buffalo, NY: Hein, 1988).

7.66 The sheer volume of American case law means that Lexis (or Westlaw) is unquestionably the best finding tool. But there are printed sources. The *American Digest*, consolidated up to 1896 and thereafter in decennial, and more recently five-yearly chunks, is the main way to find cases by name or subject. Between consolidations it is kept up to date by the *General Digest* issued monthly and cumulated into bound volumes issued three times a year. *Corpus Juris Secundum* and *American Jurisprudence 2d*, published by West and Lawyers' Co-operative respectively, are more in the nature of encyclopedias, but their copious citation of authorities means that they are used largely as an entry into case law.

7.67 *Shepard's Citations* provides an elaborate means of identifying subsequent citations of a particular case. In American parlance, to 'Shepardize' means to note up. It performs the same function as *Current Law Case Citators* but its appearance is different because it operates entirely on the reference for the case not its name. Taking the example above, you would look up '134 NE 2d 769' to see if *Hill v Bowen* had been subsequently cited. A further system of notation indicates whether the case was followed, distinguished, or otherwise treated.

Commonwealth in general

7.68 Before looking at some of the major Commonwealth jurisdictions, it is worth mentioning some general comparative sources. A handy introduction is Sir William Dale *The Modern Commonwealth* (Butterworths, 1983), which apart from describing the legal development and the constitutional position of the Commonwealth as a whole has sections on each member country giving brief details of their legal system, constitution, courts and so on. Recent political and constitutional developments and other factual information on particular countries can be found in the *Commonwealth Yearbook* (HMSO). Although legal literature on the Commonwealth in general is not published at the same rate as it used to be when it had a higher profile, comparative works on particular subjects continue to appear from time to time. K.W. Patchett *Recognition of Commercial Judgments and Awards in the Commonwealth* (Butterworths, 1984) and J.D. McClean *Recognition of Family Judgments in the Commonwealth* (Butterworths, 1983) are just two examples covering areas where, because of treaty provisions and other factors, there are similar regimes throughout the Commonwealth.

7.69 *International Legal Books in Print*, mentioned in chapter 2, despite its shortcomings, is a tool for finding textbooks from Commonwealth countries. There used to be published an *Index to Commonwealth Legal Periodicals*, but unfortunately it has stopped, so national legal periodical indexes where they exist, or *Index to Legal Periodicals* will have to be used.

7.70 *The Law Reports of the Commonwealth* (not to be confused with the well-known Australian series *Commonwealth Law Reports*) provides wider access to the major decisions of Commonwealth courts. It started in 1980 and there are three volumes a year covering commercial law, criminal law, and constitutional and administrative law respectively. This series does include a few Privy Council cases. The *Appeal Cases* of course report many Privy Council cases, but some appear only in the law reports of the country concerned. As was mentioned in chapter 4, full sets of Privy Council judgments and related appeal documents are deposited in a number of libraries (see QR4.18).

The *Commonwealth Legal Bulletin* prepared by the Commonwealth Secretariat provides valuable information on legal developments throughout the Commonwealth and includes notes of cases and summaries of legislation.

7.71 As was mentioned in the introduction to this chapter, the main Commonwealth materials of use to English lawyers are law reports. Tracing these has been greatly facilitated by the publication of the *Bibliography of Commonwealth Law Reports* edited by Wallace Breem and Sally Phillips (Mansell, 1991). It is arranged by jurisdiction with, in federal jurisdictions, the federal material coming first followed by individual states. General series are listed alphabetically within each group and reports covering particular subjects are listed under broad subject headings. There are title and subject indexes to the whole work. The coverage, incidentally, is broad and includes both present and former members of the Commonwealth (so, for example, South Africa and the Republic of Ireland are covered); England and Wales, Scotland, Northern Ireland, the Channel Islands and the Isle of Man are also fully covered. A useful feature is that as well as bibliographical details of the printed version, availability of the reports on on-line systems is indicated.

7.72   Useful as the bibliography is, it does not extend to providing locations for the material listed, and gaining access to Commonwealth legal materials in general can sometimes be problematic for the English lawyer. Still of some assistance, though now very old, is the *Union List of Commonwealth and South African Law* (2nd ed, IALS, 1963) which covers legislation, law reports and digests of cases. Many academic law libraries will hold material, particularly law reports. There are major collections at Oxford and Cambridge, and, in London, at Inner Temple, Lincoln's Inn, the School of Oriental and African Studies, and the Institute of Advanced Legal Studies. The latter's already strong collection has been recently enhanced by the transfer of the Foreign and Commonwealth Office Legal Library, which, through official channels, had been able to build up an especially comprehensive collection of Commonwealth legislation. For those without ready access to the printed versions, Lexis includes a small range of law reports from Australia, New Zealand and Canada. These can be searched separately or simultaneously (together with all the English, Scottish and Irish material on Lexis) in the COMCAS library.

Australia

7.73   The standard guide to Australian legal research is Enid Campbell *Legal Research: Materials and Methods* (3rd ed, Sydney: Law Book Co, 1988).

Textbooks and journals

7.74   The three main Australian legal publishers, Law Book Company, Butterworths Australia, and CCH Australia, have long lists of current books and looseleaf services covering federal and state law and, in common with legal publishing elsewhere, often produce competing works on the same subject. A full listing of their works and much else besides can be found in Colin Fong and Graham Ellis *Finding the Law: a Guide to Australian Secondary Sources of Information* (Sydney: Legal Information Press, 1990). However, the provision of secondary material in English law libraries is of necessity fairly selective. That problem will be greatly eased by the recent launch by Butterworths Australia of an indigenous *Halsbury's Laws of Australia*. Hitherto there had only been an *Australian Commentary on Halsbury's Laws of England*. Unlike its English counterpart it will be entirely looseleaf, but otherwise will be a similar authoritative statement of the whole law, both federal and state, arranged by broad topics. It is to be hoped that its expense does not prevent it becoming widely available in English law libraries that aim to cover Australia.

7.75   The leading periodical is the *Australian Law Journal* published monthly. Other specialist titles, and university law reviews exist. The *Journal of Contract Law*, though published in Australia, has relevance throughout the common law world and is of a very high standard. Monash University Library produce an on-line service, *Australian Legal Literature Index* (ALLI), though it is not likely to be available here.

Legislation

7.76   Primary federal legislation is passed as *Acts of the Parliament of the Common- wealth of Australia*. A consolidation in bound volume form up to 1973 was published. Thereafter as well as the individual Acts as passed which will be bound up into annual volumes, there are also reprints in pamphlet form of individual Acts as amended. The same arrangement applies to subsidiary legislation which is passed as statutory rules:

there is a consolidation to 1956, annual volumes and reprint pamphlets of particular statutory rules as amended. Although there is not a direct equivalent of *Halsbury's Statutes* or *Halsbury's Statutory Instruments*, a work that performs many of the same functions is *Federal Legislation Annotations*, issued every three years with interim cumulative supplements. It lists in one alphabetical sequence by title all the Acts in the 1973 consolidation, subsequent reprints of Acts, and Acts passed since 1973 that have not been reprinted; at the end of the entry for each Act any regulations made under it are listed. The annotations include amendments and repeals, dates of coming into force ('operation dates' in Australia), and case law. Except crudely by title, the *Federal Legislation Annotations* does not offer a subject approach. That function is performed by the *Subject Index to the Acts and Regulations of the Commonwealth of Australia* published annually.

7.77 The states all have their own primary and secondary legislation in the form of consolidations of varying degrees of currency with subsequent annual volumes. Some also reprint individual Acts in amended form. In some cases, for example the Corporation Acts, the substance of the legislation follows the equivalent federal legislation, in order, as in the United States, to achieve uniformity across the states.

7.78 Recent legislative developments in both the Commonwealth and the states are given in two rival publications, *Australian Legal Monthly Digest* (Law Book Co) and *Australian Current Law* (Butterworths), both of which resemble our own *Current Law* (though the current parts of the second one are in looseleaf format).

Law reports

7.79 The Australian court system is one of some complexity. The supreme federal court is called, somewhat confusingly for the English lawyer, the High Court of Australia. It also hears appeals from state supreme courts. Beneath the High Court in the federal system is the Federal Court, but state courts also have federal jurisdiction in certain areas. There are also the federal Family Court and specialist tribunals.

7.80 The authorised reports of the High Court are the *Commonwealth Law Reports* (CLR)(ie the Commonwealth of Australia). Advance reports of High Court cases are published as the *Australian Law Journal Reports*, issued with the journal but paginated and bound separately. Since 1984 the authorised reports of the Federal Court have been the *Federal Court Reports* (FCR). Before that date decisions of the Federal Court were included in *Federal Law Reports* (FLR) . The *Federal Law Reports* no longer cover the Federal Court itself, but report cases decided by state courts exercising federal jurisdiction, courts of the two territories, the Family Court of Australia, and federal tribunals.

7.81 Roughly equivalent to the *All England Law Reports*, are the *Australian Law Reports* (ALR) which report cases from all the courts covered by the series mentioned above. As with the *All Englands* vis-à-vis other series, there may be duplication, but there may also be differences in coverage and timeliness. In the case of reports from the courts of the two territories (Australian Capital Territory and Northern Territory) ALR are in fact the authorised series, rather than FLR. Somewhat confusingly to the uninitiated, the territory reports, which have their own separately paginated sections at the end of each volume, are not cited as ALR, but as ACTR and NTR respectively. Moreover, the volume numbering of NTR (though not ACTR) differs from the volume numbering of ALR. Thus (1989) 90 ALR includes 90 ACTR and 64 NTR.

7.82   Each of the states has its own series of authorised reports. In New South Wales there was from 1960 to 1970 also a collateral series published commercially by Butterworths which sometimes causes confusion. The Butterworths series was called *New South Wales Reports* (NSWR); the official series was called *New South Wales State Reports* (NSWSR) until 1970 and *New South Wales Law Reports* (NSWLR) thereafter.

As in England there are also numerous specialist subject reports. Care is sometimes needed to differentiate series on the same subject from rival publishers, as with the *Australian Company Law Reports* (ACLR — Butterworths) and the *Australian Company Law Cases* (ACLC — CCH).

7.83   Although our own *Digest* includes many Australian cases, the indigenous aid for finding cases by subject is the *Australian Digest*, published by Law Book Company. The second edition in bound volume form is complete. A third edition in looseleaf format has started publication. The *Australian Legal Monthly Digest* covers recent cases and there is a noter-up table that cross-refers these to the main *Australian Digest*. For finding cases judicially considered the main tool is *Australian Case Citator*, also published by Law Book Company. It covers 1825 to 1959 in two bound volumes, and then there are four separate sequences covering 1960 to 1990 (though there are plans to consolidate these). A looseleaf volume cumulating quarterly covers the recent cases. As well as cases judicially considered it also covers discussion of particular cases in journal articles. As mentioned above in connection with legislation, there is also *Australian Current Law*, which digests cases and in the current binder has a table of cases judicially considered. It is cumulated in annual bound volumes. A particularly useful aid for the English lawyer, because it gives immediate guidance on whether Australian cases are likely to be relevant, is the *Australian and New Zealand Citator to UK Reports*, which gives references to Australian cases that have considered UK cases. The main volume which covers 1558-1972 is confined to cases reported in *The Law Reports*, *Weekly Law Reports*, and *All England Law Reports* and the only pre-1865 cases included will be those in the *All England* reprint volumes. The annual cumulative supplement covering 1973 to date is wider in scope and includes cases from other English series and indeed some Canadian, American and other overseas reports. Both volumes, however, are based only on cases that appear in the headnotes as having been actively considered — cases not mentioned in the headnotes and cases in the headnotes that are merely cited or referred to are not included.

7.84   Lexis coverage of Australian cases is limited to headnotes of cases in *Australian Law Reports* from 1973 (including *Australian Capital Territory Reports*, and from 1979 when they started *Northern Territory Reports*) — they are in the CASES file in the AUST library.

Canada

7.85   Like Australia there are both federal and provincial materials to cope with; an added complication is that the legal system of Quebec is a mixed one, following civil law adapted from French law in some private law matters but following common law in other matters. The position in Quebec has also resulted in an official policy of bilingualism throughout the country. Detailed manuals for Canadian legal research are:

Douglass T. MacEllven *Legal Research Handbook* (2nd ed, Toronto: Butterworths, 1986)

M.A. Banks *Using a Law Library* (4th ed, Toronto: Carswell, 1985)

Textbooks and journals

7.86 There is a large legal literature in Canada. A wide range of textbooks is published by the leading law publishers, Butterworths, Carswell, Canada Law Book, and, in Quebec, Walter Lafleur; likewise there is a full complement of legal periodicals in the form of university law reviews, professional publications and specialist subject journals. Fortunately, there is a comprehensive tool for finding both textbooks and articles: the *Index to Canadian Legal Literature*, which is issued as part of the *Canadian Abridgement* published by Carswell. A three volume consolidation was published covering materials to the end of 1984. This is supplemented by annual bound volumes and loose parts published eight times a year as *Canadian Legal Literature*, part of the *Canadian Current Law* service. An alternative publication (though not covering textbooks) is *Index to Canadian Legal Periodical Literature*. The main Canadian journals are also covered by the American products *Index to Legal Periodicals* and *Current Law Index*.

Legislation

7.87 A looseleaf consolidation of federal primary legislation, *Revised Statutes of Canada* was published in 1985 and most of the provinces also publish looseleaf consolidations of statutes. Acts as they are passed are issued in the *Canada Gazette* and there are official annual bound volumes. Subordinate legislation is also published in the *Canada Gazette*, but the last consolidation, the *Consolidated Regulations of Canada*, was back in 1978. There are commercially published annotated collections of statutory materials; the Canadian Criminal Code is produced in a number of rival formats, and individual codes from Quebec are published on the continental model.

7.88 The *Canada Statute Citator*, published by Canada Law Book, covers federal (but not provincial) statutes and includes amendments and dates in force as well as cases in which statutes have been judicially considered. As part of their *Canadian Current Law* service, Carswell publish in loose parts *Legislation* which are consolidated as the *Legislation Annual*. This covers both federal and provincial legislation and is in three sections: progess of bills, statutes amended, repealed or proclaimed in force (arranged by jurisdiction and alphabetically by title) and regulations (arranged by jurisdiction and title of enabling statute).

Law reports

7.89 Publication of law reports in Canada is prolific, and there is considerable duplication of coverage. The commercially published *Dominion Law Reports* is the main general series covering both federal and provincial courts. There are official series for the Supreme Court and Federal court, series for each of the provinces, regional series covering cases from groups of provinces, and an increasing number of subject-based reports.

7.90 Although there is quite a range of digests and finding aids, many devoted to particular provinces, the most comprehensive and most widely available in this country is the *Canadian Abridgment*, a vast multi-volume work. As well its own complex updating mechanisms in the form of replacement volumes, permanent supplements, and looseleaf supplements, it is supplemented by the loose parts of *Jurisprudence* and *Canadian Citations* which form part of the *Canadian Current Law Service*. The first of these provides summaries of recent cases from all the federal and provincial courts. Quite a large proportion of the cases summarised are unreported or not yet reported, but the publishers, Carswell, offer a photocopy delivery service for these. *Canadian Citations* covers both cases and legislation judicially considered. If you do not have access to the *Canadian Abridgement*, remember that selected Canadian cases appear in *The Digest*.

7.91   As with Australia, Lexis coverage is very limited: at present cases from Ontario Court of Appeals from 1986 and cases from the the Ontario Court of Justice (General Division from September 1990 and Divisional Court from March 1991) — they are in the ONTCA and ONTCJ files respectively in the COMCAS library. There are two main on-line databases produced in Canada, CAN/LAW derived from the reports published by Canada Law Book, and QUICKLAW which covers a wide variety of reports either in full text or in headnote form. The latter service now has a London node, but whether any UK law library makes use of it is not known.

New Zealand

7.92   New Zealand, being a smaller jurisdiction and being a unitary rather than federal state, has a less complex legal literature than Australia. Butterworths are the main legal publisher, though now CCH, the multinational legal publisher, has a toe-hold, and there are a number of periodicals, the *New Zealand Law Journal* being the leading general series.

7.93   Legislation is now published in a similar fashion to Australia: rather than attempting a global consolidation (the last of which was in 1957) particular Acts are reprinted from time to time, though these are produced in numbered bound volumes containing several Acts rather than as individual pamphlets as in Australia. There is an annual *Table of New Zealand Acts and Ordinances and Statutory Regulations in Force*.

7.94   The main series of law reports is the *New Zealand Law Reports*, but there are also now a number of specialist subject reports. The *Abridgement of New Zealand Case Law* is the main retrospective finding tool for cases. For recent cases there are two publications *Recent Law* and *Butterworths Current Law*, which also cover legislative developments. The *New Zealand Law Reports* from 1970 are on Lexis (the CASES file in the NZ library).

Other Commonwealth countries

This section is even more cursory than the foregoing, and can only give a few hints and tips as to possible sources.

Africa

7.95   Legal materials from Anglophone Africa are notoriously hard to get, though for some countries such as Nigeria they are quite prolific. The *Journal of African Law*, published by the School of Oriental and African Studies (SOAS) in the

University of London, is a general source of secondary materials. (The library at SOAS is one of the main sources of African legal materials in this country.) There is also one current general series of law reports published by Law Reports International in Oxford: *African Law Reports: Commercial Series*. South Africa has a well-developed and organised legal literature. Although its legal system is mainly based on Roman-Dutch law, it has imported many common law principles, so its law reports are sometimes cited in an English context, though less frequently than those from the countries already covered.

India and Pakistan

7.96   India has a vast, if somewhat disorganised, legal publishing output. The single most useful source is the *All India Reporter*, which covers both cases and legislation from the central and separate state courts and governments. Old Indian cases are quite often encountered in old English cases because of the volume of Indian appeals dealt with by the Privy Council, and indeed *The Law Reports* used to have a special separate series *Indian Appeals*. *All Pakistan Legal Decisions*, cited as PLD, is the source most likely to be encountered from Pakistan.

Malaysia, Singapore and Brunei

7.97   Malaysia, Singapore and Brunei follow English common law in many matters. The long-established *Malayan Law Journal* has been the main vehicle for case reports (as well as articles) from these jurisdictions, but started recently are the *Supreme Court Reports* which cover the decisions of the Supreme Court of Malaysia, the Courts of Appeal of Singapore and Brunei, and of the Privy Council (though in 1989 appeals to the Privy Council from Malaysia were abolished, and those from Singapore severely curtailed). These reports have a companion volume, *Supreme Court Journal*, containing articles. Finding aids for Malaysian and Singapore case law are well developed. *Mallal's Digest of Malaysian and Singapore Case Law* began publication in its fourth consolidated edition in 1990. Although primarily a digest of cases, it does list the main relevant legislation at the start of each topic. Since 1987 there has also been a comprehensive monthly publication which in contents and appearance is very similar to English *Current Law*, covering both recent cases and legislative developments: it was originally called *Butterworths Law Digest*, but was relaunched in 1991 as *Mallal's Monthly Digest*. There is a recent looseleaf consolidation of Singapore legislation.

Hong Kong

7.98   Hong Kong both as a UK dependency and as a commercial centre has traditionally been an area of interest to English lawyers. English barristers are still sometimes appointed as judges of the High Court, and English barristers may still be instructed to appear there. The temporary admission of English barristers to the Hong Kong bar for a particular case used to be commonplace, but due to local contention the policy is now much more restrictive and is confined to cases of unusual difficulty and complexity where there is no local counsel available. There is in fact quite a body of recent case law simply on the question of whether English counsel may be admitted. The relevant legislation is the Legal Practitioners Ordinance. Legislation in general may found in the looseleaf consolidation the *Laws of Hong Kong*, the current edition of which is in the course of replacement by an entirely new version which, in preparation for 1997, will for the first time give the text of the statutes in both English and Chinese. The main law reports are the *Hong Kong Law Reports*. There are now a number of locally published legal textbooks and the *Hong Kong Law Journal* has been published since 1971. Since 1985 Hong Kong has had its own version of *Current Law*, covering legislation and cases (many unreported); in fact it was originally called *Hong Kong Current Law* but since 1988 has been entitled *Hong Kong Law Digest*. It is published 11 times a year, and is cumulated as the *Hong Kong Law Yearbook*.

Caribbean

7.99 Finding out what legislation is in force for the various Caribbean islands has been revolutionised by the regular and timely publication of consolidated indexes for each one by the West Indian Legislation Indexing Project based at the Faculty of Law in the University of the West Indies on Barbados. The problem is that the index is sometimes more up to date than the holdings, in UK law libraries at any rate, of the actual texts. Legislation is often published as supplements to government gazettes and consolidations of varying degrees of currency exist for most jurisdictions. There is a one general series of law reports, the *West Indian Reports*, and relatively current individual series for the Bahamas, Cayman Islands, and Jamaica. The recently launched *Caribbean Law Review* carries notes of unreported cases as well as articles.

Pacific

7.100 Although not all are Commonwealth or common law jurisdictions the various Pacific islands are mentioned here. Except in the context of tax havens, they are not very frequently encountered by the English lawyer. There is now, though, a book published in Australia (where the area is naturally of greater significance): Jacqueline D. Elliott *Pacific Law Bibliography* (2nd ed, Hobart, Tasmania: Pacific Law Press, 1990).

European countries

7.101 For the English lawyer the law across the Channel may pose greater difficulties than the law, discussed above, across the Atlantic or across the globe. Few undergraduates study Roman law nowadays, which traditionally would have given some insight into civil law systems, and few English lawyers have a knowledge of European languages of the standard necessary to read legal texts. Nonetheless, the law of European countries is assuming ever greater importance.

Books and periodicals

7.102 One immediate difference from common law systems is the importance attached in civil law systems to authoritative commentary on the law published in textbooks and scholarly journals. Such writings, *doctrine* in French, are regarded as a source of law comparable to the decisions of the courts. There is a variety of legal bibliographies produced in most European countries (for an overview see Thomas Reynolds 'Secondary sources for research in European law' *International Journal of Legal Information*, vol 20, no 1, 1992, pp 41-53), but for the English lawyer the best places to start are sources already mentioned: *Index to Foreign Legal Periodicals*, *Bibliography of Comparative and Foreign Law*, and *Bibliographic Guide to Law*.

Catalogues, published or on-line, of libraries that collect European law is another obvious practical step.

Legislation

7.103   A distinctive feature of civil law systems is that much of their legislation is codified. Virtually all European countries will have a civil code, a criminal code, a code of civil procedure, a code of criminal procedure and a commercial code. Many other more specialised areas may have codes — France has over 50 separate codes. Usually they are available from commercial publishers in annotated form. These may be small pocket-sized books, like the well-known French series *Petits codes Dalloz*, or vast impenetrable tomes like those of Staudinger's *Kommentar zum Bürgerlichen Gesetzbuch*. Some of the more important codes have been translated into English as individual publications, for example the French civil code, the new Dutch civil code, the Swiss code of obligations, and several criminal codes in the *American Foreign Criminal Codes* series, but these one-off publications rapidly become out of date. Bear in mind the translations that may be available in general comparative looseleaf works.

7.104   New legislation is usually issued in official government gazettes — the *Official Journal of the European Communities* has made this format more familiar — such as the *Journal officiel* in France and the *Bundesgesetzblatt* in Germany. Consolidations of legislation, apart from codes, on the common law model, are rare, but exist for example in Switzerland.

An important source for the text of current legislation in English is *Commercial Laws of Europe* published monthly by Sweet & Maxwell. Access to the legislation (and court decisions) of European countries has been radically improved by the launch of *European Current Law* in 1992; it should be appreciated that this is not confined to coverage of member states of the European Communities. Like *Current Law*, to which it is a companion, it is a digesting service and does not provide the full text . It had a precursor in the form of the *European Law Digest* which goes back to 1973, but this was notoriously difficult to use, not least because the monthly parts were not consolidated in the annual bound volumes.

French legislation is available on Lexis. It includes the full text of the *Journal officiel* since 1955, all the codes, and many administrative regulations from various dates. They are in the LOIREG library. The text of course is entirely in French.

7.105   In most European countries the principle identifying feature of legislation other than codes is the date it was passed rather than as in England the title. There may also be given a reference number or citation to an official gazette; in German-speaking countries acronyms are widely used in place of titles.

Law reports

7.106   Although it is often said that civil law systems do not accord the decisions of the courts the same importance as do common law systems, in practice law reports are as indispensable to the continental lawyer as they are to the English lawyer even though they may not be used in quite the same way. The French term for this source of law, and there are cognate terms in most other European legal languages, is *jurisprudence*, not to be confused with its English usage meaning the philosophy of law.

Most reports of cases are commercially published rather than being official. There may be series covering particular courts, but the publication of cases in legal journals is widespread. Apart from the *Common Market Law Reports* which reports cases relevant to European Communities law from national courts as well as from the European Court of Justice itself, there are two sources for the text in English of decisions of European courts. One is *European Commercial Cases* which started publication in 1978 and is now issued by Sweet & Maxwell. Its coverage is quite wide and includes areas such as intellectual property, broadcasting, product liability, as well as more narrowly commercial fields like agency, and restrictive practices. The other is *International Litigation Procedure*. Although its coverage is wider than Europe, it is particularly strong on cases relating to the Brussels Convention of Civil Jurisdiction and Judgments. Its title suggests that it is merely a conventional journal, but while it contains some news items and summaries of legislation, it is principally a case reporting service. Summaries in English of European cases are also available, as mentioned above, in *European Current Law*.

The above sources, for the benefit of the English reader, report and cite European cases by the names of parties, but this is not the normal practice in Europe, where generally the official citation is simply by name of court and date.

7.107 Lexis includes the full text of several series of French reports as from various dates since 1959. They are arranged in two libraries, PRIVE covering private law cases and PUBLIC covering public law cases.

8. Directories and subjects adjacent to law

Introduction

8.1 The preceding chapters have been concerned with finding legal information. This brief final chapter offers some help with finding factual information that is not legal as such but which lawyers may need in connection with their work or which is incidental to a legal research problem, and with finding law-related information from other disciplines.

In this area more than most, some of the precepts discussed in chapter 1 should be borne in mind. If you are dealing with a non-legal matter do not assume, because you do not know of one or one is not on the shelves of your own library, that there is no reference work that will provide the answer. Asking people may well be quicker that looking at books. Going to an information professional may well be more efficient than trying to find the answer yourself.

Legal directories

8.2 There was a golden age which lasted for 200 years until 1976 when for most practical purposes there was but one legal directory, *The Law List*; now there is a profusion. There is a vast and wasteful duplication of information, yet no one source is entirely self-sufficient.

Solicitors

8.3 The official directory is now that produced by the Law Society, *Directory of Solicitors and Barristers*. The publishers Waterlows used to have the official franchise, but continue to publish what is now called *Waterlow's Solicitors' and Barristers' Directory*. Both list solicitors geographically by firm and alphabetically by name of solicitor; the latter has a list alphabetically by firm in its companion *Diary* volume. Date of admission of individuals and types of work carried out by firms are indicated. *The Lawyer's Diary* published by George Rose, and *Butterworths Law Directory* are alternatives giving much the same information, but it is probably fair to say that *Waterlow's* is better established; it remains to be seen whether the profession's preference gravitates to the Law Society's product. All are annual.

8.4   Alongside these purely factual sources are now two sources which offer more evaluative information: *The Legal 500* by John Pritchard (Legalease) and *Chambers and Partners' Directory: a User's Guide to the Top 1000 Law Firms and All Barristers' Chambers.* These aim to offer guidance on the specialisms and reputations of particular firms as well as giving factual information not found in conventional directories, such as number of staff, recruitment of trainee solicitors and history of the firm. Both of course are selective: qualification for entry is based mainly on size of firm, but the former includes editorial comment on smaller firms where appropriate and the latter includes smaller firms with notable expertise. In both the shorter entries are free, the longer entries are made on payment. Use as you would a *Good Food Guide.*

If you are interested in the current profile of particular firms or particular individuals, *The Lawyer* and *Legal Business* magazines often carry features. *Who's Who in the Law* gives biographical information on solicitors and other lawyers, but, in its first edition at any rate, provides somewhat uneven coverage.

8.5   If a solicitor cannot be found for some reason in a printed directory or if added information is required, such as details of when practising certificates were held or if there is a finding or order in respect of disciplinary proceedings, then it is best to contact directly the Law Society's Records Department (in Redditch not at Chancery Lane), who for a charge can provide information.

Barristers

8.6   There has been an enormous boom in the production of directories of barristers, partly due to relaxations on advertising by barristers and partly due to the advent of direct professional access. Until recently even information on the type of work undertaken could be construed as advertising; and accountants, architects and other professionals can now brief a barrister without going via a solicitor, but do not necessarily have the traditional contacts that solicitors have.

8.7   All the sources mentioned above on solicitors cover barristers as well, but the official directory is now that produced by the Bar Council itself, *The Bar Directory.* The main listing is by chambers arranged geographically and within location alphabetically by name or address of chambers. All chambers have a basic entry giving members with their date of call, but chambers may opt for an expanded entry which gives details of the type of work undertaken and expertise of particular members. At the front there is an index of chambers by type of work undertaken. At the back there are three lists of individual barristers: barristers in private practice, barristers in employment and non-practising barristers; these include Inn and academic qualifications as well as date of call and address. It is now the only directory to include non-practising barristers.

8.8   Of the alternative sources for barristers in practice the handiest (and cheapest) for basic information is *Hazell's Guide*, arranged by chambers with an index by name, though it does not give any details of type of work undertaken. A commercial rival to the official *Bar Directory*, intended particularly to provide information on areas of practice is *Havers' Companion to the Bar*, which is described — by itself — as 'the indispensable reference book for anyone instructing a barrister'.

8.9   There are a growing number of specialist bar associations (lists will be found in the *Bar Directory* and *Hazell's*) and some have produced their own directories, usually again with the aim of publicising areas of work undertaken. Examples are *The Modern Chancery Bar* (Chancery Bar Association), *COMBAR: the Commercial Bar Associaton Directory*, and *The Local Government, Planning and Environmental Bar Association Handbook*.

8.10   Of the sources already mentioned for solicitors, the Law Society *Directory* only gives an alphabetical listing of barristers; *Waterlow's* lists by chambers as well but only includes barristers in practice; *Butterworths Law Directory* and *The Law Diary* also include barristers in employment (but not non-practising). *Chambers and Partners Directory* includes all chambers but all barristers in a chambers are not necessarily listed. *The Legal 500* includes only selected chambers. However, both works give comment on reputation and specialisms.

8.11   If a barrister cannot be found for some reason in a printed directory further enquiries should be addressed to the Records Office at the General Council of the Bar, or to the Inns of Court.

Courts and judges

8.12   *Waterlow's* includes information on judges and courts at the front of its *Diary* volume, which is a companion to the *Directory* volume. *Butterworths Law Directory* has lists of circuit judges, recorders and district judges alphabetically and by circuit. However, *Hazell's Guide* is perhaps the most compact source of this information.

8.13   The fullest information on courts is to be found in *Shaw's Directory of Courts in the United Kingdom*, which as its title indicates covers Scotland and Northern Ireland as well as England and Wales. The Lord Chancellor's Department regularly prepare new editions of *The London County Courts Directory* (HMSO). This lists all streets in the London postal districts and indicates which county court district each falls in. To be thoroughly recommended, especially to the newly-qualified practitioner, is Andrew Goodman's *Court Guide* published annually by Blackstone. This gives all sorts of really practical information such as nearest tube stations, parking facilities, canteen facilities and so on. The same author also prepared the *Royal Courts of Justice Guide*, which again provided practitioners practical help in finding their way around the Kafkaesque labyrinths of the RCJ; it is to be hoped that a new edition will be prepared as at the time of writing all the rooms throughout the RCJ have just been renumbered. *The Lawyer's Remembrancer* includes lists of judges and courts together with a range of other useful information.

Legal services

8.14   *Waterlow's* includes a full section on legal services from accident investigation to shorthand writers, and there was published a little while ago *Butterworths Legal Services Directory* which may be reissued. The Yellow Pages has a heading 'Legal Services'.

Scottish and Irish lawyers

8.15   There are now two directories for Scottish lawyers. The *Scottish Law Directory* is long established. In Scotland it is commonly called the 'White Book', hence the title of its recently started rival, *The Blue Book: the Directory of the Law Society of Scotland*. The Faculty of Advocates also have recently produced their own directory which, like their English counterparts, is particularly aimed at giving an idea of the type of work undertaken by the Scottish bar. The Incorporated Law Society of Ireland publish an annual *Law Directory*; it also includes a list of Northern Ireland solicitors.

Overseas lawyers

8.16 There are three, rival, one-volume worldwide directories of law firms: *Butterworths International Law Directory*, the *International Law List*, and *Kime's International Law Directory*. All three are arranged by country. *Kime's* usefully includes brief notes (though of varying detail) on the legal system and legal profession of each country and also has an alphabetical index of all firms listed. *Butterworths* is the only one to include an alphabetical list of all individual lawyers mentioned.

8.17 However, often of more use than any of the above is the international section to the vast American directory, *Martindale-Hubbell Law Directory*. Currently it is only available as part of the whole work (which is also published on CD-ROM and is loaded on Lexis). In the 'Canadian and International Lawyers' volume there is first, on blue pages, a list of firms by country and major city with brief details. The particularly useful feature is that, as well as local firms, foreign firms practising in those cities are also listed. For example, in the Paris entry, after French firms, there are listed American firms in Paris, Brazilian firms in Paris and so on. The blue pages refer to the main entries where full professional biographies are given; this information is much more detailed than in the one-volume directories listed above. Not a directory as such but an evaluative guide to the large law firms worldwide is the *International Financial Law Review 1000: a Guide to the World's International Business Law Firms*. One of its more controversial features is a comparison of fees charged by lawyers in different countries.

8.18 All the above sources are necessarily selective, but many countries produce their own national law directories, though these are not necessarily widely available. Enquiries through the local bar association or other professional body, which may be found in *Kime's*, will usually be necessary. One directory that is fairly widely available is *Martindale-Hubbell* for American lawyers. It is arranged by state and cities within states and within cities by firm. On blue pages at the front of each volume is a listing by individual lawyer, though this is again arranged by state and city. A smaller alternative to *Martindale-Hubbell*, though necessarily with less information, is *The American Bar* published in two volumes by Forster-Long. This has the advantage of having a single alphabetical listing of attorneys in addition to the main sequence by state, city and firm.

8.19 If none of the above sources are available there are international sections in both *Butterworths Law Directory* and in *Waterlow's*. The former lists English firms with overseas offices and foreign firms with offices in England and Wales, though you need to read through the entries to distinguish the two categories. *Waterlow's* is slightly wider and includes some foreign firms that do not necessarily have offices here; it also distinguishes the categories more clearly. *The Legal 500* includes foreign firms in London.

8.20   The editor of *The Legal 500*, John Pritchard, has also now produced *Law Firms in Europe*, which is a similar mixture of factual information and opinion. The main sequence by country (which incidentally is not confined to EC member states) gives a run-down on the leading firms generally and those recommended for particular areas; it is in parallel text in English and French. If you have £500 to spare you could also buy a recent special report from Euromoney Publications, *Lawyers on Lawyers in Europe*, which aims to give ratings on which firms are regarded as the best in particular countries and for particular areas; it also indicates in which areas there is the most legal business. In the European context, though it is not a directory of lawyers, the *Cross-border Practice Compendium* prepared by the Conseil de barreaux de la Communauté Européene (published in this country by Sweet & Maxwell) should be mentioned. It gives details of professional regulation in each member state and on practice in the EC in general, together with addresses of the relevant professional bodies.

Solicitors' clients

8.21   Both solicitors for marketing purposes and prospective clients in choosing a solicitor are often interested to know which solicitors firm acts for a particular company or which companies are clients of a particular solicitors firm. There are at least three sources that provide this information via both permutations: *Crawford's Directory of City Connections*, the *Arthur Andersen Corporate Register* and the *Hambro Company Guide*. The latter two are published by Hemmington Scott, twice a year and four times a year respectively.

Law teachers

8.22   Both the Society of Public Teachers of Law and the Association of Law Teachers regularly issue directories to their members.

Law libraries

8.23   The main source is the *Directory of British and Irish Law Libraries* published from time to time by the British and Irish Association of Law Librarians. The main sequence is by constitutent countries of the British Isles (though the Isle of Wight is strangely listed on its own, separately from England) and alphabetically by town or city. Details of size of legal collection, opening hours, services and a contact name are given. There are separate indexes by name of organisation, type of organisation, contact name, and of special collections. A basic list of law libraries and other useful addresses is given at the end of the Quick Reference Guide (QR9).

Bodies holding records and registers

8.24   A remarkably useful work, though easily overlooked on the reference shelves because of its relative slimness, is Trevor Aldridge's *Directory of Registers and Records* (Longman). This contains a wealth of information on official records that may be needed in legal practice. As well as mainstream items such as birth certificates, wills, county court judgments and local land charges, it includes information on such diverse matters as the Bedford Level Deeds Registry, chancel repair liability, war-time debtors, closed burial grounds, registered residential homes, lotteries, and Jersey companies.

Past lawyers

8.25   Handy sources of information on well-known legal figures from the past are the *Biographical Dictionary of the Common Law* (Butterworths) edited by A.W.B. Simpson and the *Oxford Companion to the Law* by David M. Walker. There is in fact quite a body of material in this field; if research is needed, a full bibliography is given in Guy Holborn 'Sources of biographical information on past lawyers' (1992) 23 *The Law Librarian* 75-90, 119-145.

Subjects adjacent to law

8.26   Both in legal practice and for academic research it is sometimes necessary for the lawyer to stray into other fields. Solicitors in practice may need company and financial information for example; academics may need to carry out research in other social sciences or in philosophy or history. This section can only give the barest of outlines and it is not feasible to offer the same degree of evaluation as provided in earlier chapters; further advice should be sought if required from specialist publications and experts in the field. But it is hoped that it may give some idea of the possible resources available outside the law library.

Sources mainly for practitioners

Press coverage

8.27   Information on a particular topic, company or individual may be needed from the newspapers and non-legal periodicals and journals. There are manual sources, such as the *Index to the Times*, and the publication of the major daily newspapers on CD-ROM has been a boon. But because neither of those can be all that current and because of the vast number of sources that potentially might contain information, on-line sources are particularly valuable. One source that lawyers in particular may feel at home with is Nexis, a sister database to Lexis (though operated here by Lexis's American parent, Mead, not Butterworths Telepublishing). Like Lexis it is a full text database containing a very wide range of news and periodical sources. The sheer size of the database means that search strategies have to be carefully devised. Another widely used source is Reuter's Textline. This is available through a number of on-line hosts, including now FT's Profile. Originally it provided only summaries but it is now full text for most sources. English summaries are provided for some foreign language sources.

As well as providing a gateway to Textline, FT's Profile is the other major on-line source, covering all the main newpapers, and like Textline many sources of business, financial and market information. Searches can be confined to particular titles or to file groups such as UKNEWS covering the papers or UKBIZ covering *The Economist*, *Investor's Chronicle* and other similar business titles. A particularly useful file is the Hermes file of government press releases issued by the Central Office of

Information. The full text of back releases can be searched or the day's releases scanned for current awareness.

8.28   An alternative to using on-line sources is to use a fee-based research service. The BBC operate a Data Enquiry Service which will provide copies from their vast collection of press cuttings. There are different subscription rates and hourly charges depending on level of use. The Press Association News Library offer a similar service.

8.29   Many law libraries have Prestel, BT's viewdata system, mainly in order to access the legal database Lawtel. But there is a lot of current general information including news items on Prestel itself which should be borne in mind. Note that some information is charged for, usually on a per page viewed basis, though it is fairly modest compared to on-line databases.

Company, financial and business information

8.30   For detailed and up-to-date information on-line sources again often provide the best solution. Quite a number of databases are available via FT Profile. A selection of the most useful includes McCarthy Company and Industry, Press News and Comment, which has worldwide coverage; Global Scan, which covers credit reports and balance reports of companies from a number of countries; Infocheck, which has files on over 200,000 English companies; ICC, which provides full text company annual reports and accounts; Jordans Company Reports; and an on-line version of Extel cards, which again give information on annual accounts, new share issues, mergers and so on. As well as on-line sources, there are also the various services offered by Companies House itself in Cardiff. The activities of Companies House are publicised in its newsletter, *The Register*.

8.31   For the basic enquiry there are a number of printed directories, usually annual. Examples are the *International Stock Exchange Official Yearbook*, which lists companies and public corporations and *Kompass UK* (there are sister publications for other areas) which is in four parts, product and services, company information, financial information, and parents and subsidiaries. An alternative for the last kind of information is *Who Owns Whom*. The *Directory of Directors* is in two volumes, the first one listing directors by name and giving the companies they are directors of and the second listing companies, with brief details of the company including their directors. Information on directors and company officers will also be found in the *Arthur Andersen Corporate Register* already mentioned. Its sister publication *Hambro Company Guide* on the other hand gives more financial information on companies. Both, as was mentioned, list solicitors that act for particular companies; they also list other professionals such as accountants, auditors, stockbrokers in a similar way, as does *Crawford's Directory of City Connections*. The *Banker's Almanac* lists in volumes 1 and 2 banks worldwide by name with details of branches; volume 3 is a geographical index. Biographical information may be found in such publications as *Who's Who in the City* and *Who's Who in Industry*, as well as *Who's Who* itself. Statistical information is often also required; the monthly *Financial Statistics* (HMSO) prepared by the government Central Statistical Office is a basic source.

8.32   Because of the wealth of sources in this field, which may require considerable experience to use effectively and may not all be readily available, fee-based research services are an alternative well worth considering. These are proliferating. In London for example there is the Business Information Focus run by the City Business Library, Information for Business run by Westminster Central Reference Library, LBS Information run by the London Business School and the Business Information Service run by the British Library from their Science Reference and Information Service branch at Southampton Buildings. Similar services are operated by public and university libraries throughout the country. These together with the London services have formed a Business Information Network, managed by the British Library, which aims through cooperation to improve the quality of referrals and provide access to a wider range of sources.

Insurance and pensions

8.33 Related to financial information above is information on insurance and pensions. Two new publications *Insurance Journals Index* and *Pension Journals Index*, which come from the same stable as *Legal Journals Index*, have improved access to articles in this field; they are also available on the Legal Information Resources electronic database. There are also printed directories in this field such as the *Insurance Directory and Yearbook*.

Professional directories

8.34 Most professions produce published directories of their members. Annual directories are widely available in reference libraries for, among others, accountants, actuaries, architects, bankers, clergymen, dentists, doctors, opticians, company secretaries, stockbrokers and surveyors. If these are not available or do not provide an answer, contact the relevant professional body (lists will be found in for example *Whitaker's Almanac* and the *Directory of British Associations* (CBD) — both of which are extremely useful reference tools for other purposes too).

Shipping

8.35 Law firms dealing with shipping will need access to a variety of sources. Lloyd's produce a range of shipping related directories, including *Lloyd's Register of Shipping* itself. Lloyd's Maritime also offer an on-line database, Seadata, which includes ship particulars, ship movements, ship owners, managing agents, parent companies, casualties and demolition. There are 112,000 ships in the general database which includes 30,000 in the casualty database. The movement file dates back to 1985 and applies to 32,000 ships engaged on international seagoing trade (ie excluding ferries, tugs, pilot vessels, etc). The *Guide to Port Entry* gives detailed charts and other information on ports worldwide.

Intellectual property and patent documentation

8.36 Intellectual property is another area where non-legal materials may be required. For advice on sources of information here the British Library Science Reference and Information Service (based at the old Patent Office Library) is the best place to go. Among other things they are the primary repository for patents both English and foreign and operate the British Library Patents Information Service. On the same lines as the Business Information Network, there is also a Patents Information Network which is made up of 13 patent documentation centres located around the country.

Standards

8.37 Technical information may also be required on standards, usually in the context of a product liability or other negligence claim. The British Standards Institute based at Milton Keynes may answer enquiries using their on-line database Standardline (which is also loaded on CD-ROM).

Forensic science and medicine

8.38 Many law libraries will hold basic material aimed particularly at lawyers such as Bernard Knight *Lawyer's Guide to Forensic Medicine* (Heinemann) or J. K. Mason *Forensic Medicine for Lawyers* (Butterworths) and possibly some journals such as *Medicine, Science and the Law*. If more detail is needed it will usually be necessary to employ expert forensic assistance. If nonetheless research in this area is desired it will usually be necessary to use the facilities of a large scientific or medical library as few law libraries have more detailed technical works. In London the most readily accessible is the British Library Science Reference and Information Service (SRIS) — the Kean Street branch rather than the Southampton Buildings branch. They hold a range of monographs and specialist journals in this area. Journal articles could be traced through *Forensic Science Abstracts* which forms part of the *Excerpta Medica* abstracting service and is available of CD-ROM, or through the general medical database Medline which is also available on CD-ROM. The Home Office Forensic Science Service also prepare a database of forensic science literature, FORS, which is available via the on-line host DataStar — the SRIS at Southampton Buildings can undertake searches for a charge.

Parliamentary and government information

8.39 Parliamentary and government information has been touched on already elsewhere. But as well as the *House of Commons Weekly Information Bulletin*, the Public Information Office at the House of Commons, the *Civil Service Yearbook*, and government press releases in the Hermes file on FT Profile, which have been mentioned, there are a few other sources. *Public Bodies*, prepared by the Office of the Minister for the Civil Service (part of the Cabinet Office) and published annually by HMSO, gives a range of factual information on quangos and other related bodies. *Dod's Parliamentary Companion* is the main annual directory of MPs and peers, which as well as giving biographical details (and a photograph) lists any special interests. A slimmer directory, but issued more frequently, is *Vacher's*. For those who need to keep well informed of parliamentary and government activities there are commercial services, such as Parliamentary Monitoring Services, and quite a number of firms of Parliamentary consultants who lobby on behalf of companies or particular interest groups — they are listed in *Dod*. The main printed directory in the field of local government is the *Municipal Yearbook*, published in two volumes. In the EC field there are numerous directories. Both *Vacher's* and *Dod* produce European companions on the lines of their British ones; the latter gives full biographical details (and photographs) of member state government ministers responsible for EC matters, senior Commission staff, Court of Justice personnel, as well as all members of the European Parliament. The *Directory of European Institutions* (Butterworths/ Heymanns) and the Commission's own regularly produced directory are among the tools that may lead you through the Brussels bureaucracy.

Sources mainly for academic research

8.40 As well as the materials suggested below, some of the tools mentioned in chapter 2 should also be borne in mind, particularly *Index to Periodical Articles Related to Law*, general bibliographical tools, and the various indexes to theses. The sources dealt with below are mainly bibliographies of periodical literature, usually published in serial form; if other reference materials are needed it is well worth consulting *Walford's Guide to Reference Material*, an extensive work in three large volumes.

Social sciences

8.41 One of the leading bibliographical tools dealing with the social sciences in general is the *London Bibliography of the Social Sciences* produced annually by the British Library of Political and Economic Science (BLPES) at the London School of Economics. LSE of course have a large law faculty, whose research in interdisciplinary fields is particularly strong, and this is reflected in the library collections on which the bibliography is based. BLPES also prepare the *International Bibliography of the Social Sciences* which is published in four series, which are mentioned under their subjects below. The *Social Sciences Index* is an American index to the periodical literature and comes out the same stable as *Index to Legal Periodicals*, H.W. Wilson, so its format will be familiar to lawyers. The concept of the *Social Sciences Citation Index* will also be familiar to lawyers, since citators have been used by them long before scientists and others thought of them. This work lists articles that cite particular previous articles. Rather like using a leading case to follow up latter cases, this in an effective way into the literature as well as seeing whether a particular article has been endorsed or criticised. It is arranged in three parts: the citation index itself, a source index of the articles scanned, and a 'permuterm' index which indexes the articles by key words from their titles.

ANTHROPOLOGY

8.42 Since the pioneering work of Maine early this century anthropology has been of interest to lawyers, and law has always been of particular interest to anthropologists; legal anthropology is now quite a developed discipline with its own specialist literature and journals, such as *Law and Anthropology*. The two main guides to the literature are the serial publications *International Bibliography of Social and Cultural Anthropology* (part of the *International Bibliography of the Social Sciences*) and *Anthropological Literature* produced by the Tozzer Library at Harvard.

CRIMINOLOGY AND PENOLOGY

8.43 The *Criminology, Penology and Police Science Abstracts* has under various titles been published since 1960. Two other titles, which are American based, are *Criminal Justice Abstracts* and *Criminal Justice Periodical Index*. The Radzinowicz Institute of Criminology at Cambridge holds one of the leading libraries in this country and their catalogue was published by G.K. Hall, though it is now rather old.

ECONOMICS

8.44 The study of the relations between economics and law has a long history — Adam Smith gave lectures on jurisprudence — and the modern school of the economic analysis of law has generated much controversy and a concomitant literature. Well-established periodicals such as the *Journal of Law and Economics* will be indexed in the legal periodical indexes, but there is quite a body of law-related literature elsewhere. The *Journal of Economic Literature* published by the American Economic Association carries articles, reviews, surveys of the literature and a classified list of articles: section K contains the material on law and economics. Also published by the Association but in bound volume form, and so a little behind the *Journal*, is the *Index to Economic Articles in Journals and Collective Volumes*. The classification used is different and economics and law come under the number 916. The *International Bibliography of Economics* is another of the parts of the *International Bibliography of the Social Sciences*. *Contents of Recent Economics Journals* prepared by the DTI Library Service and published by HMSO is the main current-awareness tool.

EDUCATION

8.45 The current changes being witnessed both in academic and vocational legal education may make general educational literature of practical as well as purely academic interest to the law teacher. The law *of* education is also a subject that has come to the fore with the sweeping changes in the statutory framework of both higher and lower education, and has spawned a new journal, *Education and the Law*. That and the articles on legal education that appear in the *Law Teacher* and other legal journals will be caught by the legal journals indexes, but the main source for articles from elsewhere is the *British Education Index*. The main relevant headings in its subject thesaurus are 'Law in education', 'Law of education' and 'Law related education'.

POLITICS

8.46 The two main indexing services in this field are the *International Political Science Abstracts* and the *International Bibliography of Political Science* (part of the *International Bibliography of the Social Sciences*). Though now getting a little old, the chapter by Gavin Drewry, 'Judiciary and government', in *Information Sources in Politics and Political Science* (eds D. Englefield and G. Drewry, Butterworths, 1984) helpfully draws out some of the connections between law and politics.

SOCIOLOGY

8.47 The fourth part of the *International Bibliography of the Social Sciences* is the *International Bibliography of Sociology*. The *Sociological Abstracts* is the major American-produced tool. These may supplement articles in journals covered by the legal journal indexes, such as *International Journal of the Sociology of the Law*, *Journal of Law and Society*, *Law and Society Review* and *Social and Legal Studies*.

WAR STUDIES

8.48 The serial bibliography, *War and Society Newsletter* (published in Munich for the Militärgeschichtliches Forschungs Institut Freiburg), is mentioned because it does have a specific section on 'International law and military law', as well as covering a wide range of historical and other writings that might be interest to a researcher in this field.

Humanities

8.49   The *British Humanities Index* is the main general indigenous source covering the main periodicals, which might be of interest to those researching for example legal history or philosophy of law.

HISTORY

8.50   Legal history can hardly be described as a subject 'adjacent' to law — after all, it used to be a compulsory part of every undergraduate law student's syllabus — but it has not seemed appropriate to fit it in elsewhere in this book, and even here can only be very briefly covered. Undoubtedly the leading textbook is now J.H. Baker *An Introduction to English Legal History* (Butterworths), and that will give entry to the main literature. Also very useful to anyone starting out in this area is W.D. Hines *English Legal History: a Bibliography and Guide to the Literature* (Earland, 1990). Hines is also the compiler of the very useful 'Annual bibliography of British and Irish legal history' published in the *Cambrian Law Review*, which covers articles in general historical journals as well those in the specialist journals of which there are now at least four: *Journal of Legal History, American Journal of Legal History, Law and History Review*, and *Criminal Justice History*.

8.51   For the student of legal history wanting to look at general historical writings the following would be a start: the series of monographs produced in the series *Bibliography of British History* by Oxford University Press, the *Annual Bibliography of British and Irish History* and *Writings on British History* (though the latter is published somewhat in arrears).

PHILOSOPHY

8.52   The question whether the philosophy of law is a branch of philosophy or a branch of law is itself susceptible to deep philosophical analysis. But the practical answer is that there is a considerable body of material of relevance to the student or researcher of jurisprudence in general and specialised philosophy books and journals, as well as in the academic law journals. And there are also some journals, most notably perhaps *Philosophy and Public Affairs*, that specifically aim to bridge the gap between the two. The main English language tool is *The Philosopher's Index*. The principal headings likely to yield most material are: Jurisprudence, Justice, Law, Legal ..., Property, Punishment and Rights. Besides that and the main legal journal indexes, there is also *Current Legal Theory: International Journal for the Theory of Law and its Documentation*, which mainly covers material in European languages.

B.   Quick Reference Guide

Contents

QR9 Selected libraries and other useful addresses   330

This guide only covers generally available sources. REMEMBER ANY IN-HOUSE DATABASES. Many firms and libraries maintain their own indexes, manual or computerised, to journal articles, statutes, SIs, law reports or other materials.

QR1 Logical connectors and commands for on-line and CD-ROM databases

QR1.1 [1.36-1.45]

On-line or CD-ROM Database	AND	OR	NOT	Proximity x=words n=characters	Trunc-ation
Lexis	AND	OR	AND NOT	W/x	!
Justis (Celex, SI, SM, WLR)	AND, &	OR, ¦	NOT, !	WITHIN n OF/BEFORE	*
SCAD	AND, &	OR,/	NOT,\	—	*
Current Law	AND	OR	NOT	*x	*
UKOP	AND	OR	ANDNOT	—	$
Index to HC Papers (Chadwyk Healey)	AND	OR	ANDNOT	W x	*
Index to Legal Periodicals	AND	OR	NOT	—	:
Times and Sunday Times	AND	OR	—	—	*
FT Profile	+	,	—	//paragraph /sentence	*
Reuters Textline	AND, +	OR,,	NOT,—	/xW/ in order /xN/ in any order	*

QR2 Textbooks and other secondary sources

QR2.1 *Halsbury's Laws* [2.6-2.10]

Getting into it

— Consolidated index (vols 55 and 56)
— Indexes to individual volumes
— Consolidated table of cases (vol 54)
— Tables of cases in individual volumes
— Consolidated tables of statutes, SIs and European Communities material (vol 53)
— Tables of statutes and SIs in individual volumes
— Tables and index in annual cumulative supplement

Updating it

— Volumes of main work
— Annual cumulative supplement (two bound volumes)
— Noter-up (looseleaf 'Current Service — Noter-up' volume)

QR2.2 Books on a subject? [2.11-2.18]

— Library catalogues
— Raistrick *Laywers' Law Books*
— *Hammicks Law Book Catalogue* (annual bookshop catalogue)
— *Legal Books in Print* + *Law Books Published* (Glanville)
— *International Law Books in Print* (Bowker Saur)
— *British Books in Print* (annual hard copy, monthly microfiche or CD-ROM *Bookbank*)
— *Current Law*: in the body of main entries in the monthly digests; separately at the back in the yearbooks

QR2.3 Old books [2.17]

— Sweet & Maxwell's *Legal Bibliography of the British Commonwealth*
Vol 1: English law to 1800
Vol 2: English law 1801-1954
— J.N. Adams *Bibliography of Eighteenth Century Legal Literature*
— J.N. Adams *Bibliography of Nineteenth Century Legal Literature*

QR2.4 Where to get a book [2.18, 2.35]

— List of libraries, and information on library directories, at QR9
— Inter-library loan
— University library catalogues on-line via JANET network
— Law Notes Lending Library (Chancery Lane)

QR2.5 Articles on a subject? [2.19-2.34]

— *Legal Journals Index*: subject index
— *Index to Legal Periodicals* (American but main English titles)
— *Current Law Index* (American but main English titles)
— *Current Law*: in body of the main entries in the monthly digests; separately at the back in yearbooks
— *European Legal Journals Index* 1993-
— *Index to Foreign Legal Periodicals*
— *Legal Bibliography Index*
— *Index to Periodical Articles Related to Law*
— Lexis (*Estates Gazette* 1991-, *Law Society's Gazette* 1986-, *New Law Journal* 1986-, *Journal of the Law Society of Scotland* 1990- only)

QR2.6 Articles on a case? [2.24]

— *Legal Journals Index*: case index
— *Index to Legal Periodicals*
— *Current Law Index*
— *Current Law Case Citator*: 1947-1976 volume only
— T.M.C. Asser Institute *Guide to EC Court Decisions*: for articles, mainly in continental legal journals, on ECJ cases

QR2.7 Articles on legislation? [2.25]

— *Legal Journals Index*: legislation index (until 1990 one alphabetical sequence by title; 1991- five separate sequences according to jurisdiction)
— *Index to Legal Periodicals*
— *Current Law Index*

QR2.8 Where to get an article [2.35]

— Local union lists of serials, eg University of London, Inns of Court
— Inter-library loan
— Legal Information Resources Ltd document delivery service (see front of a recent issue of *Legal Journals Index*)
— Institute of Advanced Legal Studies distance services (subscribers only)
— *Union List of Legal Periodicals* (but last ed 1978)

QR3 Legislation

Public General Acts

QR3.1 Alternative sources for the text of Public General Acts [3.8-3.19]

— *Halsbury's Statutes of England*

   *   **Best source for most purposes**

      — arranged by subject, annotated, kept up to date

      — only statutes still in force

      — not official

      — excludes wholly Scottish Acts

— Queen's printer copy (HMSO)

   *   **For very recent Acts, citing in court, Acts no longer in force; otherwise only use if certain Act or section has not been amended or repealed**

      — arranged by date

      — official text, as originally passed

      — first text to appear

— *Statutes in Force* (HMSO)

   *   **For Scottish Acts, citing in court, photocopying; otherwise a less useful alternative if Halsbury's not available**

      — arranged by subject, kept up to date (but with delays sometimes), not annotated

      — only statutes still in force

      — official

      — includes Scottish Acts

— *Current Law Statutes Annotated* 1947-

   *   **Useful for: recent Acts, Acts no longer in force, commentary and finding green papers, white papers, debates etc preceding Acts, Scottish Acts; otherwise only use if certain Act or section has not been amended or repealed**

— arranged by date, annotated, text not amended

— includes Scottish Acts from 1991 (previously in separate Scottish edition)

— *Butterworths Annotated Legislation Service* 1935-

   * **An alternative for fairly recent Acts and Acts no longer in force**

      — arranged by date (but not strict chapter number order), annotated, text not updated

      — excludes Scottish Acts

— Lexis

   * **Useful for: heavily amended Acts, access to text when printed versions not available (eg home or office), finding statutes when printed indexes and tables inadequate**

      — full text of statutes in force as amended, with some annotations

      — not official

      — remember that each section of an Act is retrieved as a separate item

      — excludes Scottish Acts

— Looseleaf subject encyclopedias

   * **Useful for: most everday purposes, expert commentary, finding statutes by subject**

      — various arrangements, often annotated, kept up to date

— Handbooks and subject collections

   * **Useful for: personal purchase, carrying around, most everyday purposes, finding quickly statutes in mainstream subject areas**

      — various arrangements, often annotated, kept up to date only by new editions

QR3.2 Old Acts [3.20] (see also QR3.24)

— *Statutes of the Realm*

      — up to 1714

      — official

— Ruffhead's *Statutes at Large* (ed Runnington)

      — up to 1785

      — not official

— Other editions of *Statutes at Large* (see Sweet & Maxwell *Guide to Law Reports and Statutes* 4th ed 1962, pp 11-16)

— *Acts and Ordinances of the Interregnum 1642-1660* (ed C.H. Firth, HMSO, 1911)

QR3.3 Finding Acts by title — year and chapter number unknown [3.28-3.32]

— *Halsbury's Statutes*: alphabetical list in Tables and Index volume (softbound)

* **The main source**
  — gives volume and page number in main work
  — NB volume numbers prefixed with 'S' refer to looseleaf 'Current Statutes Service' volume
— *Statutes in Force*: alphabetical list in first binder
  * **Equally good; also for Scottish Acts**
    — gives chapter number as well as reference in main work
— Lexis
  * **Possible but expensive; could be useful where words in title only partially known**
    — Search example:
      TITLE(SAFETY W/8 SPORT) would retrieve all the sections of the Fire Safety and Safety of Places of Sport Act 1987 as well as of the Safety of Sports Grounds Act 1975
— Lawtel
  * **Especially for statutes not in the above because very recent**
— House of Commons weekly information bulletin: table of Public Bills in latest issue
  * **An alternative for very recent statutes**
— **Statutes in none of the above because no longer in force:**
  — Alphabetical list in Tables and Index volumes of 1st-3rd editions of *Halsbury's Statutes*
  — Table of short and popular titles in the Addenda and index volume (vol 16) of *Chitty's Statutes* 6th ed, 1913
  — Otherwise some form of subject search probably best

QR3.4 Finding Acts by chapter number and year — title unknown

— Annual volumes on the shelf of
  — Public General Acts (HMSO, Queen's Printer copies), or
  — *Current Law Statutes Annotated*: from 1947
  * **If this is the preferred version of text**
— *Halsbury's Statutes*: chronological table of statutes in Tables and Index volume (softbound)
  * **If this is the preferred version of text**
— *Statutes in Force*: chronological list (after alphabetical list in first binder)
  * **If this is the preferred version of text**
— *Chronological Table of the Statues* (HMSO, two black bound volumes)
  * **An alternative to find what title is if actual text not needed**
    — covers all statutes from 1235 to about two years ago
— *Current Law Statute Citator*
  * **An alternative to find what title is if actual text not needed**
    — all statutes from 1947; only pre-1947 statutes affected since 1947

— two bound volumes 1947-71, 1972-1988
— softback supplement 1989-
— latest monthly part of *Current Law*

QR3.5 Finding Acts in force by subject [3.33-3.36]

— *Halsbury's Statutes*: Tables of Statutes and General Index volume (softbound)
* **Best starting point (other than Lexis)**
    — NB two sequences:
        — Volume index: to the main bound volumes
        — Service index: to the looseleaf 'Current Statutes Service' volumes
— Looseleaf encyclopaedias, subject handbooks, textbooks, *Halsbury's Laws*
* **Shortcut for mainstream topics**
— Lexis: ENGEN library, STAT file (or STATIS file to combine with SIs)
* **At its best when searching for specific technical terms or concrete entities**
— *Index to the Statutes* (HMSO, two black volumes)
* **Usually only needed in preference to Halsbury's Statutes for Scottish Acts because at least two years out of date**
    — covers statutes in *Statutes in Force*
— *Current Law*: monthly digests
* **For very recent statutes not yet in Halsbury's or other printed sources**
    — use cumulative index in latest part or browse through main body of entries in each part
— *Current Law*: recent yearbooks (printed or CD-ROM)
* **An alternative if you know there has been a recent statute on a particular subject. Not worth the effort for older statutes**
    — in printed version use index at back (cumulative for 1987-89) or browse through body of entries in each yearbook

QR3.6 Finding Acts no longer in force by subject [3.37]

— Look at a relevant statute in force and see what it repeals
— *Halsbury's Statutes*: indexes to 1st-3rd editions
— Old editions of standard textbooks
— *Statutes at Large*: index (vol 10)
    — to 1786
— *Statutes of the Realm*: index
    — to 1715

QR3.7 Finding amendments and repeals [3.39-3.44]

— *Halsbury's Statutes*
* **Best starting point (but should be supplemented by latest Current Law and/or Lawtel). Does not include Scottish Acts**

— **Main work**: text as at date of issue of the volume. Look at notes to each section for details of amendments and repeals incorporated.

— **Cumulative supplement** (annual bound volume): under same volume and page number of main work. If actual text of any amendment not given in full, a reference to the looseleaf 'Current Statutes Service' volumes (or another volume of the main work) will be given. NB Includes annotations to statutes in looseleaf 'Current Statutes Service' volumes (statutes awaiting incorporation in a reissue of a bound volume). These appear at the end of each topic title within the sequence for a particular volume number and have '(S)' after the volume number.

— **Noter-up** (thin looseleaf volume): under same volume and page number as main work or 'Current Statute Service' volumes. NB Not always as up to date as the statute citator in the latest monthly part of *Current Law*, which should be checked next.

— *Current Law* statute citators

* **An alternative approach, but only references to year and chapter numbers of amending Acts given — not title or text of amendments. Sometimes more up to date than latest Halsbury's noter-up. Includes Scottish statutes**

— find statute by year and chapter number

— Statute Citator 1947-1971 (bound volume)

— Statute Citator in Legislation Citator 1972-78 (bound volume)

— Statute Citator in Legislation Citator 1989- previous year (softbound)

— Statute Citator in latest monthly digest for current calendar year (and, depending on time of year, in December monthly digest of previous year)

— Lawtel

* **The most up-to-date source for statutes from 1984**

— references not text

— find statute by title in the Legislation index

— Lexis STAT file in ENGGEN library

* **Most useful for heavily amended text**

Search examples:

TITLE(Income w/5 1988) and SECTION(434) will retrieve section 434 of the Income and Corporation Taxes Act 1988 as amended

TITLE(Vehicles Excise w/5 1971) and SECTION(Sch 4) will retrieve Schedule 4 of the Vehicles (Excise) Act 1971

— *Statutes in Force*

* **An alternative to Halsbury's Statutes, but usually less up to date. Includes Scottish statutes**

— Main work: text as at date of reissue of individual pamphlets

— Cumulative supplements: filed in binders at start of work

— *Chronological Table to the Statutes* (HMSO, two black vols)

* **Best source for finding when and how old Acts not included in any of the above were repealed. Otherwise, being at least two years out of date, of limited use. Includes Scottish Acts**

QR3.8 Finding commencement dates [3.50-3.58]

— Lawtel
* **Best source: updated daily, and covers all statutes since 1984**
  — find statute by title in legislation index
— *Is it in Force?*
* **Best printed source to start with, but issued only annually so may need to be supplemented (for preference by Lawtel or latest monthly part of Current Law). Covers statutes (including Scottish ones) passed since 1 January 1967**
  — Grey softbound volume, often shelved with *Halsbury's Statutes*
  — Arranged by year and alphabetically by title within year
  — Repeals noted (but without authority for repeal); commencement dates not given for repealed Acts or sections
— *Current Law*: Dates of Commencement Table in latest monthly part
* **Usually the most up-to-date printed source (other than HMSO Daily List), but only covers commencement orders issued in the current calendar year**
  — Arranged alphabetically by title

— *Halsbury's Statutes*: main work, cumulative supplement and noter-up
* **No particular advantage over a combination of above two sources where the information is more readily accessible. Source of commencement dates for pre-1967 statutes still in force**
  — Look at the annotations to particular sections or the section containing the commencement provisions
— *Halsbury's Statutes*: 'Is it in force?' division in looseleaf Noter-up Service volume.
* **An alternative to Current Law monthly parts for updating annual bound Is it in Force?, but not usually quite as up to date**
  — Two sequences: commencements to statutes listed in the main *Is it in Force?* and commencements to statutes passed since the last edition of *Is it in Force?*
— *Halsbury's Laws*: Commencement of Statues division in looseleaf Noter-up Current Service volume
* **An alternative to the above and to Current Law monthly parts, but again not usually quite as up to date**
  — Covers commencements since the last annual cumulative supplement to *Halsbury's Laws*
  — Arranged alphabetically by title
— HMSO *Daily List*
* **For finding commencement orders issued since the last monthly part of Current Law, if Lawtel not available**
  — Details of commencement orders are given at the start of the section listing SIs that appears at the end of each *Daily List*. If not stated, refer to the SI itself to find which provisions of the Act have been brought into force.

— Justis SI on-line database

  * **An alternative, but being updated monthly, not as current as Lawtel, and unlikely to be much more current than Current Law**

— Justis SI CD-ROM

  * **No particular advantage over printed sources. Could be useful for full text of commencement orders if no hard copy available**

    — Updated every six months

    — Search example:

      Title[Companies and commencement]

      will retrieve Companies Act commencement orders

    — If several commencement orders retrieved, look at latest first: effect of previous orders usually given in a note at the end

— *Current Law* statute citators

  * **An alternative to Is it in Force? and other printed sources listed above, but less straightforward to use for this purpose. A source for commencement dates of Acts passed from 1947 that have since been repealed. Includes Scottish Acts**

    — Bound volumes 1947-1971, 1972-88; softbound volume 1989-

    — For recent Acts commencement orders listed at start of entry; for older Acts check also for orders made under the particular section containing the commencement provisions

    — Only the SI number is given; refer to the SI itself for details of date and extent

    — If several commencement orders found, look at the latest first: effect of previous orders usually given in a note

— Lexis

  * **Probably an expensive approach unless other sources not available**

    — If only one or two sections relevant, find the text of sections themselves in the STAT file: the commencement date is given at the head of each

    — If a whole Act or large part of one relevant, find the relevant commencement orders in the SI file

— Telephone an official in relevant government department (identifiable from *Civil Service Yearbook*)

  * **For information on possible timetable for implementation when no commencement order yet issued**

Statutory Instruments

QR3.9 Alternative sources for the text of SIs [3.68-3.72]

— HMSO individually printed SIs

  — arranged by year and number

  — official text, as originally made

  — first text to appear

- includes all SIs of general application and *some* of local application; but some SIs of local application not published at all (see below)
- may subsequently be bound, or may be replaced by official bound volumes
- the only source for SIs not included in any of the sources below
— HMSO official bound volumes
  - go back to 1890
  - from 1961 arranged by year and number
  - before 1961 arranged by year and subject-matter (with tables to numbers)
  - official text, as originally made
  - do not include *any* local SIs nor short-lived SIs spent or revoked within the year
  - include some non-SI subsidiary legislation (unnumbered at the back of the last volume for the year)
— *Statutory Rules and Orders and Statutory Instruments Revised*
  - official text, as amended, of all instruments (other than local ones) in force as at 31 December 1948
  - arranged by subject-matter (with tables by number)
— *Halsbury's Statutory Instruments*
  - covers all SIs (other than local and wholly Scottish ones) in force
  - only selected SIs in full text, others summarised
  - full text of summarised SIs available to subscribers from the publishers on demand
  - arranged by subject
  - fully annotated, indexed and updated
— Looseleaf encyclopedias and subject handbooks
  - sometimes annotated
— *Supreme Court Practice, County Court Practice, Stone's Justices' Manual*
  - for SIs containing court rules
— Justis CD-ROM
  - full text of published SIs from 1987 (catalogue data only from 1980)
  - catalogue data for unpublished SIs from 1987
  - currently updated every six months
  - excludes some graphics
— Justis on-line database
  - as for CD but updated monthly
— Lexis: SI file in ENGGEN library
  - full text of all SIs in force (other than local ones), but check date of last update on file screen
  - excludes SIs containing double taxation agreements, which are separately searchable in the DTAX file
  - remember that every rule or regulation within each SI is retrieved as a separate item

— Unpublished local SIs
 — available from:

> Statutory Publications Office
> America House
> 6-8 Spring Gardens
> London SW1A 2BP
> *   **From 1922 (except 1942, 1950, 1951 and up to SI 940 of 1952)**

> Head of Search Department
> Public Record Office
> Chancery Lane
> London WC2A 1LR
> *   **As above up to 1960**

> British Library
> Official Publications and Socials Sciences Service
> Great Russell Street
> London WC1B 3DG
> *   **As above up to 1980**

— otherwise try your luck with relevant local authority

QR3.10 Finding SIs by title — year and/or number unknown [3.73-3.74]

— *Halsbury's Statutory Instruments*: index volume (softbound)
 *   **The only alphabetical list of all except the most recent SIs in force**
   — gives SI number and topic in main work (but not page number)
— *Halsbury's Laws*: consolidated table of SIs (in vol 53)
 *   **Likely to cover most SIs in force; next best printed source to the above**
— *Current Law*: alphabetical table of SIs in latest monthly part
 *   **For SIs too recent to be in the above two tables**
   — cumulative for the current calendar year
   — refer to December issue of monthly parts or the yearbook for the previous calendar year
— Justis CD-ROM
 *   **Particularly useful if precise title not known (but only goes back to 1980)**
   — search main database (from 1987) first
   — repeat search if necessary in catalogue database (F6) (from 1980)
   — search example:
     title[sheep scab]
   will retrieve Sheep Scab Orders
— Justis on-line

     *   **As above and more up to date, but probably an expensive approach, unless printed version not available**

— UKOP on CD-ROM (1980-)

     *   **An alternative to Justis CD for this type of search though will not give text**

     — limit the search to SIs using the 'categories' facility

— Lexis: SI file in ENGGEN library

     *   **More comprehensive than Justis CD and online, but an expensive approach.**

     — Search example:

          TITLE(Pension! w/10 Friendly Societies) will retrieve every regulation in the Occupational Pension Schemes (Friendly Societies) Regulations 1976 (SI 1976/598)

— Looseleaf encyclopedias: alphabetical tables of SIs

     — included in some but not all looseleafs (usual in Butterworths publications but not in Sweet & Maxwell's)

QR3.11 Finding SIs by year and number — title unknown

— Annual volumes on the shelf

     — from 1961 official HMSO volumes arranged by number within each year

     — before 1961 look at numerical table at front of first volume for the year

     — NB if official HMSO volumes taken, local and temporary SIs may have been bound by the library separately

— *Halsbury's Statutory Instruments*: chronological list of instruments in binder 1 of service

— *Table of Government Orders* (HMSO, pale blue bound volume)

     — arranged by year and number

     — omits unpublished local SIs

     — for SIs that were in force in 1948 references to the volume number and page of *SR & O and SIs Revised* are given

— *List of Statutory Instruments* (HMSO, monthly and annual): numerical list

     — gives the subject heading in the main list where details will be found

     — includes unpublished local SIs

— *Statutory Rules and Orders and Statutory Instruments Revised*: numerical table in tables volume (vol 25)

     — covers SR & Os (equivalent of SIs before 1946) and SIs in force in 1948, and SIs for 1949-1951

— *Current Law* yearbooks (1947-): numerical table of SIs

     — gives paragraph number in yearbook where full details of the SI will be found

— *Current Law* yearbooks on CD-ROM 1986-

     — search example:

          1989 *3 1841

will retrieve SI 1989 No 1841. (NB do not use a proximity search of less than three words)
— Justis CD-ROM and online
   — search example:
      Number[1990 No.953]
      will retrieve SI No 1990/953
      NB essential to enter full stop after 'No.'
— Lexis: SI file in ENGGEN library
   — search example:
      TITLE(1989 w/3 1246) will retrieve SI No 1246 of 1989
— Looseleaf encyclopedias: chronological tables of SIs
   — included in some but not all looseleafs (usual in Sweet & Maxwell publications but not in Butterworths')

QR3.12 Finding SIs by subject [3.75-3.78]

— *Halsbury's Statutory Instruments*
   * **Best starting point (other than Lexis)**
      — consolidated index in annual softbound index volume
      — index to monthly surveys in looseleaf service volume
      — cross-check monthly surveys by looking for the volume number and topic found in the main work in the *key* to the monthly surveys
— Looseleaf encyclopedias
   * **Shortcut for mainstream topics**
— Lexis: SI file in ENGGEN library
   * **At its best when searching for specific technical terms or concrete entities**
— Justis CD-ROM and on-line
   * **Effective for period covered**
      — full text searching from 1987
      — title information only from 1980
— UKOP (United Kingdom Official Publications) CD-ROM
   * **Titles only, not full text, so more limited than Justis**
      — limit the search to SIs using the 'categories' facility
— Lawtel
   * **Especially for very recent SIs, but depends on one's rapport with its subject approach**
      — from 1980
      — included in the main subject index
— *Index to Government Orders* (HMSO, two pale blue volumes + annual supplement)
   * **For Scottish SIs and for tracing powers to make orders other than by SI (neither are in Halsbury's). Otherwise a much less up-to-date**

alternative to Halsbury's SIs, though some may prefer its subject arrangement

— *Current Law*: monthly digests

    * **For very recent SIs not yet in other printed sources**

       — cumulative index to latest monthly part or browse through body of main entries in each monthly part

— *Current Law*: recent yearbooks (printed or CD-ROM)

    * **An alternative for recent SIs. Not worth the effort for older SIs**

       — in printed version use index at back (cumulative 1987-89) or browse through main body of entries in each yearbook

— *List of Statutory Instruments* (HMSO, monthly and annual): list by subject heading

    * **Only source for unpublished local SIs. A shortcut if you know subject and year but not number. But for recent SIs not as up to date as Current Law; for older SIs other sources generally preferable**

QR3.13 Finding SIs by enabling Act [3.79.-3.84]

— Lawtel

    * **Most up-to-date and convenient source for SIs made since 1980. Includes Scottish SIs**

       — find by title of enabling Act in SIs index from legislation menu

       — excludes commencement orders (which are covered in the statutes index)

— *Halsbury's Statutes*

    * **The best printed source, but may need to be updated for the most recent SIs (for preference by Lawtel or statute citator in latest monthly Current Law)**

       — look in the notes to particular enabling section of the Act in the main work

       — check annual cumulative supplement (bound volume) under same volume number and page

       — check looseleaf noter-up under same volume number and page

       — if particular enabling section is not known, all SIs made under an Act are listed at the front of the volume of the main work containing the Act

— Lexis: SI file in ENGGEN library

    * **Fast and effective, if cost no object. Unlike Lawtel will include all SIs**

       — Search example:

          AUTHORITY(Merchant Shipping w/6 1983) will retrieve all SIs made under the Merchant Shipping Act 1983

— *Current Law*: statute citator in latest monthly part

    * **Usually more up to date than the looseleaf noter-up to Halsbury's Statutes**

       — find Act by year and chapter number

— SI number, but not title, of orders, regulations, etc given against each section of the Act
— HMSO *Daily Lists*: list of SIs
* **A tedious plod, but the only safe way to check for very recent SIs made since the last statute citator in the Current Law monthly parts if Lawtel not available.**
  — read through the entries for every SI listed: the enabling power is given after the title
— Justis CD-ROM and on-line
* **Useful shortcut for SIs made since 1980**
  — search main database (from 1987) first
  — repeat search if necessary in catalogue database (F6) (from 1980)
  — search examples:
      7 within 80 of Animal Health Act 1981 will retrieve SIs made under all subsections of section 7 of the Act
      '7(1)' within 80 of Animal Health Act 1981 will retrieve SIs made under only subsection 1 of section 7 of the Act
  NB Allow a generous number of characters in the proximity operator to allow for SIs made under enabling powers in several sections of the Act
— *Current Law*: yearbooks on CD-ROM
* **Useful shortcut for SIs, except the most recent, made since 1986**
  — Search example
      Land Compensation Act 1961 * 10 s.32*
  will retrieve three regulations made under s 32(1) of the Act. NB use truncation symbol * after section number to catch all subsection numbers
— *Current Law*: statute citator 1947-71, statute citator in legislation citators 1972-1988, 1989-
* **A possible alternative to Halsbury's Statutes, but more long-winded. A way of finding, if they were ever needed, revoked SIs by enabling provision, or SIs that were made under an enabling provision now repealed**
  — find Act by year and chapter number
  — work backwards from the most recent citator; if several SIs given look at the most recent first before proceeding further: it may have revoked the earlier ones listed
  — for 1972-1982 and 1989- citators the number given (there are no titles) is of the SI itself; for the 1947-71 citator the number given is the paragraph number in the *Current Law* yearbook where the SI is digested
— *Index to Government Orders* (HMSO, two pale blue volumes)
* **Best source for Scottish SIs and orders not made as SIs. Otherwise a much less up-to-date alternative to Halsbury's Statutes. A way of checking by subject-matter what enabling powers exist where they have not been exercised**

— look at the table of statutes on the green pages at the front of volume 1, which refers to the relevant subject heading in the main work

— under each subject heading the text of the enabling power is set out and below, under the heading 'Exercise', the SIs are listed, or, if none, 'Power not yet exercised'

QR3.14 Finding amendments and revocations [3.89-3.93]

— *Current Law*: table of SIs affected **1947**-1988 in legislation citator **1972**-1988 and table of SIs affected in legislation citator 1989-

* **The simplest method covering up to the pre-current year**

— note this table in the 1972-1988 legislation citator in fact goes back to 1947

— covers SIs of whatever date affected since 1947

— arranged purely numerically; the SIs on the shelf will need to be consulted to find the text and title

— if more than one amending SI listed, look at the most recent first

— the effects of Scottish SIs issued in 1986 were omitted in error from the 1972-88 volume, but are included in the 1989- volume

— Lawtel

* **The most up-to-date source, covering SIs from 1980, but the enabling provision for the SI needs to be known first**

— select SIs from the legislation menu and search by title of enabling Act

— *Current Law*: monthly parts

* **The best manual source for updating the citator or Halsbury's Statutory Instruments, though the search has to be conducted by indirect means**

— note that there is no table of SIs affected as in the citator

— proceed by either a subject search or a title search

— by subject, look either in the cumulative index in the latest monthly part or browse through the body of main entries in each monthly digest: in the digests for new SIs amendments and revocations of earlier SIs are usually given

— by title, look in the alphabetical table of SIs in the latest monthly part under the same title as the SI you are checking: a later SI with the same title points to a revoking or amending SI

— to be on the safe side use both approaches

— *Halsbury's Statutory Instruments*

* **Slightly more complicated than using the citators, but gives titles and sometimes text of relevant SIs not just their numbers. Also more up to date, though a check in Current Law monthly parts and/or Lawtel still necessary.**

— check volume in main work; will include amendments and revocations up to date of reissue

— check annual cumulative supplement in the looseleaf service volume under the same volume number and topic

— check the key to the monthly surveys in the looseleaf service volume under the same volume number and topic

— HMSO *Daily List*: list of SIs

* **A very tedious plod, but the only safe way to check for very recent amendments or revocations made since the last Current Law monthly parts if Lawtel not available**

    — read through the entries for each SI listed (likely ones can usually be spotted by their titles): the numbers of SIs amended or revoked are given in the body of the entry under 'effect'.

— Justis CD-ROM

* **For the period covered an alternative, though probably of most use as a source of the text of SIs, if printed version not available, having checked citator**

    — search main database (from 1987) first

    — repeat search if necessary in catalogue database (F6) (from 1980)

    — search examples:

        1986/862 and (revok* or amend*)

    will retrieve SIs that revoke or amend SI No 1986/862

    NB In the printed version the number of the SI amended or revoked is usually given in footnotes; on the CD version the text of the footnotes is given right at the end of the SI

        Sheep Scab Order 1986 and (revok* or amend*)

    will retrieve the same information, but prefer a numeric search unless confident of precise title

        1938 No. 204 and (revok* or amend*)

    will retrieve SIs that amend or revoke Statutory Rule or Order 1938 No. 204. Use this format for numeric searches on pre-1946 orders which are SR & Os rather than SIs

— Justis on-line

* **Updated once a month**

— Lexis: SI file in ENGGEN library

* **Especially for heavily amended text. Quickest route if cost no object, but check date of last update.**

— *Table of Government Orders* (HMSO, pale blue bound volume + noter-up pamphlet)

* **Only source for tracing history of old SIs amended or revoked before 1947. About two years out of date, so of limited use for recent SIs.**

    — arranged numerically

    — SIs in force in bold

    — SIs revoked, spent or expired in italic

    — am. = amended; **r.** = revoked

    — for SIs in force at 1948 only post-1948 amendments indicated: for earlier amendments reference is given to *SR & Os & SIs Revised*

    — includes pre-1890 government orders

    — omits local unpublished SIs

— Looseleaf encyclopedias

* Often a convenient shortcut, but check date of last update in filing record

— text may be printed as amended or text of amending SIs given separately

QR3.15 Finding commencement dates of SIs [3.99]

— Text of SIs themselves (HMSO, *Halsbury's SIs,* Justis, or Lexis versions)

— commencement date almost always given at head

— *List of Statutory Instruments* (HMSO, monthly and annual)

— find SI in subject listing, commencement date given in entry details

— Lawtel

* For SIs from 1980, but need first to know enabling Act. Very up to date if text of SI itself not available

— find SI by title of enabling Act in SIs index from legislation index

— *London Gazette*

* Very rare: needed only for SIs whose commencement is dependent on the ratification of an international treaty by another state. Safer and easier to ring Foreign and Commonwealth Office Nationality and Treaty Department (see Civil Service Yearbook)

— look in quarterly indexes under 'Foreign and Commonwealth Office' and then in each issue in the State Intelligence section at the front again under 'Foreign and Commonwealth Office'

EC legislation

QR3.16 Types of legislation and numbering [3.100-3.106]

EEC, Euratom

Directives	Need implementation	Year/Number
ECSC		
Recommendations (Individual)	Need implementation	Year/Number
Recommendations (General)	Need implementation	Number/Year
EEC, Euratom		
Regulations	Direct effect	Number/Year
ECSC		
Decisions (General)	Direct effect	Number/Year
EEC, Euratom		
Decisions	Need implementation	Year/Number
ECSC		
Decisions (Individual)	Need implementation	Year/Number

EEC, Euratom

Recommendations   Not binding   Year/Number

EEC, Euratom, ECSC

Opinions   Not binding   Year/Number

QR3.17 Alternative sources for the text of EC legislation [3.108-3.114]

— *Official Journal of the European Communities*: L series
  * **Main source provided that you first have a full OJ reference. Only source for very recent legislation. Only source, if Celex not available, for material not reprinted in the commercial publications (eg legislation no longer in force)**
    — official text
    — published daily
    — cited as OJ
    — in English since 1973 (also published in all official languages)
    — Special editions 1972 and 1974 provide English translation of legislation in force at the time of UK accession
— *Encyclopedia of European Community Law*: C volumes (Sweet & Maxwell, 10 black looseleaf binders)
  * **Convenient for most everyday purposes**
    — full text of much (though by no means all) of the legislation in force
    — arranged by broad subject and chronologically within subjects
    — some annotations
— *Butterworths European Law Service*: legislation and commentary boxes
  * **Early days: may prove superior to the above, provided the pamphlets do not get lost**
    — started publication 1992
    — full text with commentary arranged in 31 titles
    — multi-coloured boxed pamphlets
— Celex on-line: sectors 3 and 4
  * **Extremely difficult to use. Prefer the versions offered by Justis or Lexis. Currency poor. However, usage is free to some designated libraries**
    — official database of the EC
    — full text in unamended form
    — in English from July 1979, otherwise in French
— Celex via Justis CD-ROM and on-line
  * **Probably the most convenient source of all, but reliant on data supplied by Celex so beware of currency problems**
    — CD updated every six months
    — search CD first then update on-line to minimise search costs
— Celex via Lexis: ECLAW file in INTLAW library

* **An alternative to Justis**

— *Completing the Internal Market of the European Community: 1992 Legislation* (Graham & Trotman, blue looseleaf binders)

* **Convenient alternative for the material covered**

— Subject compendiums (Butterworths European Information Services)

* **Handy paperback collections for mainstream areas**

— eg intellectual property

— Looseleaf subject encyclopedias

* **Sometimes a shortcut**

— eg *Butterworths Competition Law Service*

Encyclopaedia of Banking Law

QR3.18 Finding EC legislation by number [3.115]

— *Official Journal*: methodological index (annual and monthly)

* **As the number includes the year, straightforward to find the right annual index.**

— in two sequences: (1) number/year material and (2) year/number material (see QR3.16 above)

— from 1992 Directives listed first in the year/number sequence

— *Official Journal*: L series: recent issues

* **For very recent legislation since the last monthly index**

— browse through the contents list at the front of each issue

— *European Communities Legislation: Current Status* (Butterworths, two bound volumes + supplement)

* **Equally, or more, convenient. With telephone service, the most up-to-date source.**

— bound volumes reissued annually

— quarterly supplements

— telephone enquiry service

— covers all legislation in the special editions 1972 and 1974 and everything in OJ since (so excludes legislation repealed before 1972)

— arranged by year and within each year in two sequences: (1) number/year material; (2) year/number material (see QR3.16 above)

— gives full OJ references and title or subject-matter of main acts.

— *Encyclopedia of European Community Law*: Table of Community Secondary Legislation (at front of binder CI)

* **If OJ not available**

— two sets of tables: main table, and, for recent legislation since the last consolidation of the main table, a supplementary table

— each table arranged in three sequences: (1) Regulations; (2) ECSC Decisions and Recommendations; (3) EEC/Euratom Decisions and Directives

— gives just references to paragraph number in the encyclopedia where text (and OJ reference) is to be found (the first part of the number is the division number not the binder number)

— *Halsbury's Laws* volume 53: tables of European Communities materials

* **Possible shortcut**

— legislative material arranged in two sequences: (1) year/number material; (2) number/year material

— a third sequence of other materials, eg notices, resolutions, and non-ECSC recommendations

— gives full OJ references as well as paragraph numbers of where referred to in main work

— Celex on Justis CD-ROM and on-line

* **Quick and convenient**

— a search on the number alone is simplest, but will retrieve all occurrences not just the document itself — if several hits the earliest will be the document itself

— search example:

87/243

will retrieve Directive 87/243 and one Directive that amends it

— if preferred, using the manual, construct a Celex document number from the number you have and search specifically in the document number field

— search example:

DOCNUM[370L0524]

will retrieve Directive 70/524/EEC (a search on just 70/524 would give more than 60 hits)

— Celex via Lexis: ECLAW file in INTLAW library

* **Alternative on-line source**

— the same searches as above would be:

TITLE(Directive w/4 87/243)

DOC-NUMBER(370L0524)

— *Directory of Community Legislation in Force*: chronological index in volume 2

* **Only if you are familiar with Celex version of Regulation and Directive numbers**

— separate sequences for different categories of legislation within each year arranged in Celex format

— gives page number in volume 1, where full details given

— T.M.C. Asser Institute *Guide to EEC Legislation*

* **Covers EEC only; updated only every three years**

— separate numerical tables for Regulations, Directives and Decisions

— excludes legislation repealed before 1967 and minor legislation no longer in force; otherwise includes repealed legislation

QR3.19 Finding EC legislation by title — number unknown [3.116]

— Celex on Justis CD-ROM and on-line
  * **This, or Lexis, the best method**
    — beware of the Eurospeak in official titles, eg the Second Banking Directive is the Second Council Directive on the coordination of laws ... on credit institutions
    — search example (Justis):
      TITLE[second and credit institution*]
      will retrieve the above Directive 89/646
— Celex via Lexis: ECLAW file in INTLAW library
  — search example
    TITLE(second and credit institution)
— SCAD on CD-ROM
  * **An alternative for most legislation since 1983**
    — omits the minor legislation listed in light type in the OJ L series
    — bibliographic details only not full text
— *Legal Journals Index*: legislation index
  * **Occasionally a shortcut for recent or important legislation that is likely to have been commented on in the journals. Most effective on the electronic version**
    — in printed version, find the legislation index at the back of each part or volume
    — from 1992 separate sub-sequence of EC legislation
    — browse through under the following heads
      Commission Directive ...
      Commission Regulation ...
      Council Directive ...
      Commission Regulation ...
      First ..., Second ... etc
— Otherwise search by subject-matter

QR3.20 Finding EC legislation by subject: all legislation [3.117]

— Celex on Justis CD-ROM and on-line, or on Lexis
  * **Probably the best source**
    — search on free text: there is a system of subject headings but best ignored
— SCAD on CD-ROM
  * **Convenient for most legislation since 1983**
    — omits legislation listed in light type in OJ L series
    — various subject descriptors available, but search also on key words from the title
    — bibliographical details only, not full text

— *Encylopedia of European Community Law*: C volumes: indexes at back of binder X

    * **A convenient manual source for most legislation in force**

      — two sequences of index: main index and supplementary index (for recent material)

      — references are division numbers not binder numbers

— *European Communities Legislation: Current Status*: subject index in softback supplement

    * **Equally good manual source**

      — gives Directive or Regulation number in main volumes

      — numbers printed in italic refer to legislation no longer in force

      — numbers printed in bold (which may or not also be in italic) refer to originating Acts; numbers in ordinary type to amending Acts

— *Butterworths Guide to the European Communities*

    * **Very useful for a quick overview of main legislation in a particular area**

— David Vaughan *Law of the European Communities*

    * **Useful, especially for finding all legislation in a fairly broad area**

      — lists relevant legislation after commentary in each division

— *European Current Law*

    * **Useful for recent developments**

_ *Halsbury's Laws*: volumes 51 and 52

    * **Can be a shortcut**

      — as always check also the annual cumulative supplement and looseleaf noter-up under the same volume and paragraph number as the main work

— *Butterworths European Law Service*

    * **Should be very useful**

      — boxes arranged by topic

— *Directory of Community Legislation in Force* (twice yearly, two volumes)

    * **Official printed index derived from Celex. Difficult to use. Celex references possibly of use for an on-line update**

      — volume 1, the analytical register, arranges the legislation under 17 broad topics headings

      — volume 2 contains an alphabetical index to the analytical register

— Looseleaf subject encyclopedias

    * **Shortcut for mainstream materials**

— T.M.C. Asser Institute *Guide to EEC Legislation*

    * **Covers EEC only; updated only every three years; but a possible alternative**

      — main work 1983 + non-cumulative supplements

      — main entries arranged by treaty provision subdivided by topic

      — or use alphabetical subject index

— excludes legislation repealed before 1967 and minor legislation no longer in force, but covers other repealed legislation

— *Official Journal*: alphabetical index in monthly and annual indexes

* **For very recent legislation, or if all else fails**

QR3.21 Finding EC legislation by subject: Single Market (1992) legislation [3.118]

— Spearhead on-line via Profile or Justis (and other gateways)

* **Most up to date and useful source**

— produced by the Department of Trade and Industry

— summaries (not full text) of EC legislation adopted or proposed with details of implementation

— contact names in government departments responsible (the most useful feature) for further information

— see also CD version below

— Justis Single Market CD-ROM

* **Very useful if on-line versions not available or to do a preliminary search before going on-line**

— contains three databases:

— Spearhead

— Info 92 (Deloitte & Touche)

— European Update (European Commission)

— *Completing the Internal Market of the European Community: 1992 Legislation* (Graham & Trotman, blue looseleaf binders)

* **Convenient source for the text**

— Baker & McKenzie *Single European Market Reporter* (1 volume looseleaf)

* **Very useful**

— summaries (not text) of adopted and proposed legislation

— reports on progress and likely progress

— general commentary

— implementation in member states

— Euroscope (formerly EC 1992) on-line via Profile

* **Now wider than 1992**

— produced by Coopers & Lybrand in Brussels

— summaries (not text) of proposals and implementation

QR3.22 Finding amendments and repeals of EC legislation [3.119]

— *European Communities Legislation: Current Status* (Butterworths, two bound volumes + supplement)

* **The most convenient and, with telephone service, the most up-to-date source.**

— bound volumes reissued annually

— quarterly supplements

— telephone enquiry service

— covers all legislation in the special editions 1972 and 1974 and everything in OJ since (so excludes legislation repealed before 1972)

— arranged by year and within each year in two sequences: (1) number/ year material; (2) year/number material (see QR 3.16 above)

— where *part* of act affected the following abbreviations are used:

ad = added
am = amended
d = deleted (or repealed)
r = replaced (or substituted)

— where *whole* act no longer in force number printed in italic and the following abbreviations are used:

consld = consolidated
rpld = repealed
spent = spent
ssd = superseded

— Celex via Justis CD-ROM and on-line

* **An alternative, but not necessarily as up to date as the above**

— where an instrument is amended this is supposedly noted on the records for both the amended instrument (in the MODIFIED field) and the amending instrument (in the MODIFIES field) but in practice this does not always seem to occur, so prefer a free text search on the number of the instrument

— search example:

89/299

will retrieve Directive 89/299/EEC and any Directives mentioning it

— if a specific field search is required, because of too many hits, prefer the MODIFIES field to the MODIFIED field. It may also be necessary, using the manual, to construct a Celex document number.

— search example:

MODIFIES[389L0299]

will retrieve any instruments that have amended Directive 89/299/EEC

— Celex via Lexis: ECLAW file in INTLAW library

— search on '89/299' as above

— to confine search to enacted legislation (though because of time lag proposed legislation may be relevant) modify:

AND CITE(OJ L)

— The Celex 'Modifies' field is not a separate segment on Lexis, but comes within the cross-reference segment. To search for this:

CROSS-REF(389L0299 w/4 amend! or repeal!)

— *Encyclopaedia of European Community Law*: C volumes

* Not usually as up to date as the above, but can help

—amended legislation either reprinted as amended or amendments noted in annotations

— *Directory of Community Legislation in Force*

* A reasonably up-to-date alternative if you can find the entry for the legislation you are looking for

— reissued twice a year

— main entries arranged by broad topic in volume 1 (analytical register) list amending acts

— either find main entry by subject via the alphabetical index in volume 2 to the analytical register

— or find main entry by number in chronological index to volume 2; but these are Celex numbers, so you need to know how to translate from ordinary Regulation or Directive number

QR3.23 Finding UK implementation of EC legislation [3.120]

— *Butterworths EC Legislation Implementor*

* Very convenient and, with telephone enquiry service, very up to date, but only covers Directives

— twice yearly

— arranged by Directive number (with title, OJ reference and target date)

— omits repealed or spent Directives

— if only specific articles implemented these are only indicated if they are mentioned in the explanatory note to the implementing SI

— SIs on Justis CD-ROM and on-line

* A very good approach for implementation since 1987. Will capture all SIs relating to, not just implementing, EC legislation, but remember the possibility of implementation by Act for major directives

— full details of relevant EC legislation given in explanatory note at end of each SI

— only possible on main database, not catalogue database

— search example:

Directive within 50 of 84/169

will retrieve SIs on Farm Diversification Schemes made in accordance with EC Directive EEC/84/169

— Lexis: STATIS file in ENGGEN library

* Has the advantage over SIs on Justis, of complete coverage, and catching any Acts

— use the combined SI and STAT file STATIS

— search example:

Directive w/10 84/169

— Celex on Justis CD-ROM and on-line or via Lexis

    * **Supposed to cover national implementation, but very incomplete, but a possible starting point, especially for implementation by other member states**

        — information given in the PROV fields on the record for the document itself and also in separate National Implementation section (sector 7)

        — search for document as described above

        — if using sector 7, using the manual, construct a Celex document number, remembering to use the prefix 7 rather than 3

            — search example:

                DOCNUM[770L0524]

            will retrieve national legislation implementing Directive 70/524

— Single Market sources: see QR3.21 above

    * **Have the advantage of covering projected as well as actual implementation**

— *Legal Journals Index*: legislation index

    * **Possible shortcut, especially for recent material, as implementation often prompts articles**

        — on use see QR3.19 above

— *Current Law*: table of Statutory Instruments Enforcing European Legislation in latest monthly digest

    * **Of very limited use because merely lists in SI number order**

        — page number of table listed on contents page under 'European legislation'

        — cumulates in each issue

        — read through all the entries and try to spot the relevant EC legislation

Local and Personal Acts

QR3.24 Classification and numbering of Acts [3.121-3.124]

1948-

Public General	*Local*	*Personal*
c 1, 2, 3, etc	c i, ii, iii etc	c *1, 2, 3*, etc

1798-1947

Public General	*Local*	*Private*
Style of numbering varies		Not all officially printed before 1922. Only from 1870 same as modern Personal

1539-1797

Public	*Private*
Includes many Acts of local application printed only in official sessional volumes and *Statutes of the Realm* (to 1714), not in *Statutes at Large*	None printed before 1705; only privately printed thereafter

QR3.25 Alternative sources for the text of Local and Personal Acts [3.125-3.126]

— *Local and Personal Acts* (HMSO, Queen's Printer copies)
* **Virtually the only source**
   — arranged chronologically in unamended form
— *Current Law Statutes Annotated*
* **From 1991 only**
   — arranged chronologically in unamended form
— *Halsbury's Statutes*
* **Most of those relating to London**
— Lexis: STAT file in ENGGEN library
* **Most of those relating to London and the Lloyds Acts**
— *Statutes in Force*
* **Only about six of general interest**
— *Encyclopedia of Insurance Law*
* **Lloyds Acts only**

QR3.26 Finding Local and Personal Acts by title — year and chapter number unknown [3.127]

— *Alphabetical Index to the Local and Personal Acts 1850—1988* (Unpublished typescript, House of Lords Private Bill Office, 1991, 9 vols)
   — copies available at, eg, Law Society, Inns of Court, Supreme Court, Law Commission
   — includes cross-references from keywords as well as listing by first word of title
— Otherwise no alphabetical lists purely by title available (except in each annual volume): search by subject-matter instead

QR3.27 Finding Local and Personal Act by year and chapter number — title unknown

— Volumes on the shelf
— Tables in annual sessional volumes of *Public General Acts* and *Statutes at Large*
— *Chronological Table of Local Legislation* (see QR3.29 below)
— *Chronological Table of the Statutes* (see QR3.29 below)

— George Bramwell *Analytical Table of the Private Statutes 1727-1834* (see QR3.28 below)

QR3.28 Finding Local and Personal Acts by subject [3.128-3.129]

— *Index to Local and Personal Acts* (HMSO)

  * **The main published source for the period 1801-1966**

    — main index 1801-1947

    — *Supplementary Index* 1948-1966

    — arranged by broad categories and alphabetically by place or body within categories

— *Alphabetical Index to the Local and Personal Acts 1850-1988* (unpublished, see QR3.26)

  * **The most convenient source for the period, if available**

— Indexes to annual volumes

  * **The only source after 1988; an alternative to the above two if you have a rough idea of date**

— W.E. Tate *A Domesday of English Enclosure Acts and Awards* (University of Reading Library, 1978)

  * **The best source for enclosure Acts**

    — arranged by county with place name index

— George Bramwell *Analytical Table of the Private Statutes 1727-1834* (2 vols, 1813-1835)

  * **Only source before 1798**

    — main sequence in each volume arranged by regnal year and alphabetically by subject within regnal year

    — subject index at back of each volume arranged by topic and chronologically within topic

— Thomas Vardon *Index to the Local and Personal and Private Acts 1798-1839* (1840)

  * Except for 1798-1800 superseded by HMSO *Index*, but could be used as a cross-check

QR3.29 Finding amendments to and repeals of Local and Personal Acts [3.130-3.134]

— *Chronological Table of Local Legislation* (Law Commission, mimeographed typescript)

  * **Main source for amendments and repeals made 1925-1947; only source for 1948-1973. Includes effects of Public General Acts, Local and Personal Acts, and published SIs (but not unpublished local SIs)**

    — arranged by year and chapter number

    — includes all Local and Personal Acts 1925-1973 with details of amendments and repeals if any

    — includes those Local and Personal Acts passed 1798-1924 that have been amended or repealed between 1925 and 1973

— *Chronological Table of the Statutes* (HMSO, two black volumes): table of local and personal Acts

   * **Only source for 1974 to within the last two years. Notes effects as above**

     — find table at back of volume 2

     — arranged by year and chapter number

     — includes all Local and Personal Acts from 1974 with details of amendments and repeals if any

     — includes all those Local and Personal Acts passed before 1974 that have been amended or repealed since 1984

— Latest annual bound set of HMSO Public General Acts: table of legislation affected

   * **Depending on when published may update the above by a further year**

     — in the tables volume

     — Local and Personal Acts affected by other Local and Personal Acts, by Public General Acts or by SI during passed during that year

     — listed chronologically and by chapter number within each year after Public General Acts affected

— *Index to Local and Personal Acts 1801-1947*

   * **Only source for amendments and repeals made before 1925**

     — find Act by subject

     — repeals noted, including repeal by statutory rules or orders: but *not exhaustive for the period before 1900*

     — amendments not noted as such, but look in later Acts listed under the same subject heading

— Recent Local and Personal Acts on the shelf

   * **Only way of checking for possible amendments or repeals made by other Local and Personal Acts since last edition of Chronological Table of the Statutes**

     — simply look out for Acts that might conceivably impinge

— Lexis: STATIS file in ENGGEN library

   * **Only way of checking for amendments or repeals made by Public General Acts or non-local SIs since last edition of Chronological Table of the Statutes (or annual bound set of Public General Acts if later)**

     — search example:

       Imperial Institute w/4 1925

     will retrieve over 40 Public General Acts or SIs, including some since the last *Chronological Table* that amend the Imperial Institute Act 1925 (c xvii)

— The horse's mouth

   * **If there is an extant corporate body affected by a local Act, enquire (especially if they have a legal department) whether they can tell you what is in force**

QR3.30 Subsidiary legislation not published as SIs: examples and availabilty [3.135-3.142]

— Immigration Rules
  — published as House of Commons papers (HMSO)
  — reprinted in *Butterworths Immigration Law Service*
— Solicitors' Practice, Accounts, etc Rules made by the Law Society under the Solicitors Act 1974
  — reprinted in *The Guide to the Professional Conduct of Solicitors, Cordery on Solicitors*
  — *Law Society's Gazette* for information on recent changes; or the Law Society itself
— Financial services: SRO rule books etc
  — available in electronic version C-Text
— Rules, etc made by the Securities and Investment Board under the Financial Services Act 1986
  — reprinted in looseleaf services, eg
    Encylopedia of Financial Services (Sweet & Maxwell)
    Financial Services: Law and Practice (Butterworths)
    Robin Ellison *Pensions Law and Practice* (Longman)
    Linklaters & Paines *Unit Trusts* (Longman)
— Orders in Council (that are not SIs), Royal Proclamations, Instructions and Warrants
  — some in back of official HMSO bound volumes of SIs
  — in *London Gazette*
  — Civil Service Order in Council reprinted in *Harvey on Industrial Relations and Employment Law*
  — amendments and revocations noted in *Table of Government Orders* (HMSO, pale blue bound volume); appear after numerical sequence of SIs for each year
— Special Procedure Orders
  — published individually by HMSO
— Miscellaneous materials
  — try the government department concerned
— Bye-laws
  — ask the local authority or body concerned
— Traffic Management and Traffic Regulation Orders
  — in London ask the borough concerned
  — outside London ask the county council
  — advance notification (though not the text) may appear in the *London Gazette*: in quarterly indexes under 'Road Traffic Regulation Act 1984'

QR3.31 Quasi-legislation: codes of practice, government circulars, regulatory materials: possible sources [3.143-3.147]

— Looseleaf subject encyclopedias, specialist textbooks, journals
  * **The following is a very selective listing intended only to give an idea of the possibilities: this kind of material is easily overlooked**

  ACAS codes of practice:
  Sweet & Maxwell's Encyclopedia of Employment Law

  Rules of various arbitration schemes:
  Ronald Bernstein *Handbook of Arbitration Practice*

  Department of Health medicines and poisons circulars:
  Butterworths Law of Food and Drugs

  Department of the Environment circulars:
  Encyclopedia of Compulsory Purchase
  Encyclopedia of Environmental Health
  Encyclopedia of Planning Law
  Journal of Planning and Environment law

  Finance Houses Association code of practice:
  Encyclopedia of Consumer Credit

  Home Office circulars:
  Justice of the Peace

  Stock Exchange Admission of Securities to Listing:
  Weinberg & Blank on Take-overs and Mergers

  Trade association codes of practice:
  C.J. Miller *Product Liability & Safety Encyclopaedia*

  C-Text electronic database for SRO rule books etc, if available

— Otherwise try the body or government department concerned

Legislative history and proposals for legislation

QR3.32 Typical life-cycle of a new statute [3.149-3.154]

— Green paper
  For consultation
— White paper
  Firm government policy
— House of Commons (HC) 1st Reading
  Purely formal: Bill ordered to be printed
— HC 2nd Reading
  Debate on principle of the Bill
— HC Committee Stage
  Usually taken in a standing committee: clause by clause detailed consideration
— HC Report Stage
— HC 3rd Reading

— House of Lords (HL) 1st Reading
  Purely formal: Bill ordered to be printed
— HL 2nd Reading
— HL Committee Stage
  Usually taken on the floor of the House: a 'Committee of the whole House'
— HL Report Stage
— HL 3rd Reading
— HC consideration of HL amendments
— Royal Assent
— Commencement Order to bring Act into force

QR3.33 Finding pre-Bill proposals and reports [3.155-3.156]

— *Current Law Statutes Annotated*
  — details usually given in general note at start of Act, otherwise look at notes to particular part or section of the Act
— *Hansard*: 2nd Reading debate
  — almost always referred to by Minister introducing Bill
— Textbooks and commentary
— *Law Under Review* (Law Commission)
  — especially for recent proposals and reports not yet enacted, and for proposals not yet finalised
  — covers law reform projects in all government departments as well as Law Commission itself
— *Current Law*: yearbooks and monthly digests
  — Law Commission and other published reports summarised under the heading 'Law Reform'
— *House of Commons Weekly Information Bulletin*
  — lists recent green and white papers
  — cumulated in the *Sessional Information Digest*
— Catalogues of government publications
  — see QR6

QR3.34 Tracing progress of Bills [3.159]

— *House of Commons Weekly Information Bulletin*
  * **Best source**
    — separate tables of Public Bill and Private Bills
    — information of following week's business in the House will indicate whether a Bill has got any further since the issue was published (or telephone House of Commons Public Information Office)
— Lawtel
  * **Very up to date, but excludes Committee and Report Stages, and does not give Bill number**

— select either the public Bills or the private Bills option from the legislation menu

— summaries provided of selected Bills

— Weekly legal journals

  * **Convenient shortcut**

— Progress of Bills tables in *Current Law* monthly parts and *Halsbury's Laws Monthly Review*

  * **The latter more use than the former, but both of limited use in terms of currency and information given**

QR3.35 Finding debates on Bills in *Hansard* [3.162-3.166]

— *House of Commons Weekly Information Bulletin* and other sources listed above

  * **Especially for recent Bills**

  — will give date but not column number

— *Current Law Statutes Annotated*

  * **Very convenient for Bills enacted since 1950**

  — full details of debates given at end of general note at start of Act

— Sessional indexes to Commons and Lords *Hansard*

  — either separately bound or bound in back of last volume of session

  — Bills by title interfiled with all other material

  — an asterisked column number indicates a purely formal stage with no debate

  — will not usually include the Committee stage in the Commons: refer to separate Standing Committee debates

  — Commons and Lords in one series before 1909

— *Hansard* on CD-ROM

  * **Available from session 1988/89 but currently only covers Commons (not Lords or Standing Committees)**

— Polis

  * **For the experienced user only**

  — legislative debates available from November 1982

QR3.36 Legislative background to SIs [3.167-3.169]

— Commons and Lords *Hansard*

  * **For affirmative resolution instruments and some negative resolution instruments only**

  — sessional indexes or CD-ROM as above

  — the enabling section in the relevant Act will indicate whether the SI was made by either of these procedures

— Standing Committee *Hansard*

  * **For Commons debates not on the floor of the House**

— motion to refer consideration to a Standing Committee indexed in main Commons *Hansard*

— for debates on particular SIs look through list of Standing Committee debates in front of HMSO annual and monthly catalogues under title of SI or under 'Draft'

— Joint Committee on Statutory Instruments and Select Committee on Statutory Instruments: minutes of proceedings

* **Difficult to find consideration of particular SIs and of limited use if found**

— Joint Committee published as both HL and HC papers; Select Committee as HC papers only

— use catalogues of Parliamentary papers and government publications to trace (see QR3.36)

Proposals for EC legislation

QR3.37 *Relevant documents [3.170 and figure 3.29]*

— COM Documents

— text of proposal with explanatory memorandum

— *Official Journal* C series

— text of proposal without explanatory memorandum

— text of European Parliament Opinions

— Economic and Social Committee Opinions

— European Parliament reports: Series A

— *Official journal*: Annex

— debates of European Parliament in plenary session

— Economic and Social Committee reports

QR3.38 *Finding aids [3.171]*

— SCAD database on CD-ROM

— Celex on CD-ROM or on-line

— *Official Journal* C series on CD-ROM

— Single Market CD-ROM

— see also other single market tools at QR3.21

— Polis

— Printed indexes to *Official Journal* C series

— Specialist advice

eg Law Society Library Relay Centre, European Documentation Centre librarians, Information Offices of the European Commission and European Parliament (if you can get through), government departments (use Spearhead, DTI hotline, *Civil Service Yearbook*), House of Commons Public Information Office (see QR 9.9)

QR3.39 *Scrutiny at Westminster [3.172-3.174]*

— House of Commons Select Committee on European Legislation

— reports on European Documents published as HC papers
— Debates on European Documents on the floor of the House of Commons
    — Commons *Hansard*
— Debates on European Documents in the European Standing Committee
    — Standing Committee *Hansard*
— House of Lords Select Committee on the European Communities
    — reports published as HL papers
— Debates on the reports of the Select Committee on the floor of the House of Lords
    — Lords *Hansard*

QR4 Case law

Law reports

QR4.1 Deciphering abbreviations [4.31-4.33]

— Donald Raistrick *Index to Legal Citations and Abbreviations* (1981, — 2nd ed forthcoming)
  * **Best source**
    — remember filing order
    — includes references to reprints of nominate reports in *English Reports* and *Revised Reports*
— *Current Law*: monthly parts and yearbooks: table of abbreviations
  * **For new series since last edition of Raistrick**
— *The Digest*: table of abbreviations in front of volume 1(1)
  * **Covers nominates and all the main series, if Raistrick not to hand**
— *Halsbury's Laws*: list of reports in front of volume 1(1) and in cumulative supplement
  * **As above**

QR4.2 Finding English cases by name (of plaintiff or first party) — citation unknown [4.62-4.66]

— *Current Law*: case citators
  * **Best starting point unless case very recent indeed or old**
    — will include both cases reported and cases cited during the coverage period
    — bound volumes 1947-1976, 1977-78
    — softbound supplement 1989- to pre-current year
    — cumulative table of cases in latest monthly digest for whole of current calendar year (and December issue for previous year if necessary): references are to monthly issue and paragraph number.

NB at this stage only the first report to appear and All ER, WLR, and *Law Reports* references picked up; any other alternative citations only appear later in citator.

— *The English Reports*: table of cases

  * **Simplest source if case likely to be pre-1865**

    — gives full nominate report references as well as ER references

— *The Digest*

  * **Look here next if in neither of the above; the most comprehensive source for old cases; a cross-check on modern cases up to about a year ago; may help if not an English case**

    — consolidated table of cases to find right volume number

    — table of cases at front of volume of main work will give paragraph number (in old volumes asterisked numbers indicate small print Commonwealth cases): citation at foot of entry at that paragraph

    — check table of cases in annual cumulative supplement for more recent cases

— Lawtel

  * **Most up-to-date source for very recent cases in newspapers and main law reports**

    — updated daily

    — select the Decisions option from the main menu

    — back to 1980

— *Daily Law Reports Index*

  * **For recent cases in the all the newspapers; for slightly older cases that are proving hard to find because not ever fully reported**

    — look in cumulative parties index at front of the binder of weekly parts and each quarterly and annual part

    — back to 1988

    — case index at back of quarterly and annual volumes will indicate whether subsequently reported in the main series

    — also electronic verison

— *Legal Journals Index*: case index

  * **A double-check for recent cases not in Current Law or Daily Law Reports Index**

    — at back of monthly parts and in second part of quarterly and annual cumulations

    — also electronic version

— *Halsbury's Laws*: consolidated table of cases, and tables in cumulative supplement and looseleaf noter-up

  * **A double-check for cases not found in Current Law or The Digest**

— Lexis

  * **Of most use where details of name imperfect, where there is a possibility that the case is unreported, or where printed sources unavailable; otherwise an expensive approach**

— if confident that the case is post-1945 search on the NAME segment; if not, search on whole record in case it has been cited but is not otherwise on the database

— search example:

NAME(United Scientific w/8 Burnley)

will retrieve *United Scientific Holdings Ltd v Burnley*

— if you have a case with a common name and are confident of its approximate date combine with a date search

— search example:

NAME(Brown) **and DATE AFT 1988**

— remember other libraries apart from ENGGEN if a possibility that case is not English, eg EURCOM for ECJ cases

— *Law Reports Index*: table of cases reported and table of cases judicially considered

* **A shortcut for mainstream cases, if it is all that is to hand**

— Tables of cases in textbooks

* **Often the quickest way if subject-matter known**

— Tables of cases in indexes to particular series

* **Sometimes a shortcut if likely series known**

— Finding aids for cases from other jurisdictions (see QR7)

* **Bear in mind the possibility, if difficulty is encountered, that the case may not be English at all**

QR4.3 Finding English cases by name of defendant — plaintiff or first party and citation unknown

— Lexis (cases reported or cited 1945-)

— *All England Law Reports*: consolidated table of cases (1936-)

— *Daily Law Reports Index*: parties index (1988-)

— *Legal Journals Index*: case index (1986-)

— *Current Law* yearbooks on CD-ROM (1986-)

— *Weekly Law Reports* on CD-ROM (1984-)

— *Index to the Times Law Reports* (Professional Books, 1982-1988): index of cases

— *Times Law Reports* (W & T Clark, 1990-): table of cases reported

QR4.4 Finding EC cases by name [4.67]

— *Butterworths EC Case Citator and Service*: alphabetical list

* **Probably the most convenient source for ECJ cases**

— twice yearly (cumulated) with fortnightly updates (pink A4)

— by applicant only, but separate 'Nickname' table if another part of the name better known

— *Gazetteer of European Law* (1953-1983) vol 2 and *Case Search Monthly* (1988-): alphabetical index

  * **Alternative source for EC cases (though gap in coverage); includes cases from member states as well as ECJ**

  — listed by both applicant and defendant

  — the index gives a reference number which refers either to the main sequence of ECJ cases or one of the national sequences where full details will be found

  — refer to the instructions for use at the front of volume 2 of *Gazetteer* on entry elements in cases names

— T.M.C. Asser Institute *Guide to EC Court Decisions*: index of parties

  * **Another alternative but only updated every three years**

  — main work 1982 + non-cumulative supplements

  — listed by both applicant and defendant

— Celex on Justis CD-ROM or on-line: ECJ cases

  * **An alternative for ECJ cases, especially where only imperfect details of name known**

  — search on name as free text to be sure of getting it or if too many hits confine search to title field

  — search example:

    title[factortame]

    will retrieve various stages of the Factortame litigation

— Lexis: CASES file in EURCOM library

  * **If Justis not available and only imperfect details known**

    search example:

    NAME(Factortame)

— *European Current Law*: cumulative table of cases in latest monthly part

  * **Europe-wide not just EC**

  — from 1992 only

QR4.5 Finding European Court of Justice cases by number [4.67]

— *Butterworths EC Case Citator and Service*: numeric list

  * **The most straightforward approach**

— *Gazetteer of European Law* (1953-1983) vol 1 and *Case Search Monthly* (1988-)

  * **An alternative (though gap in coverage)**

  — master list of cases is by ECJ number; full details of all reports given

— T.M.C. Asser Institute *Guide to EC Decisions*

  * **Comprehensive but not updated as frequently as the above**

  — main sequence is by number

  — also includes index by date of judgment

— Celex on Justis CD-ROM and on-line

* **If you are going to look at text on this**
  — can search on just number but possibility of false drops
  — omit C- or T- prefixes
    — search example:
      case within 20 of 264/89
      will retrieve ECJ case C-264/89 and any cases citing it
  — if preferred, using the manual, construct a Celex document number
    — search example:
      DOCNUM[689J0246]
      will retrieve only ECJ case C-246/89
— Lexis: CASES file in EUROCOM library
  * **Especially if you need to look at the text on-line because not otherwise available**
    — search example:
      name(213/89)
      will retrieve Case 213/89
— *Halsbury's Laws*: consolidated table of cases and table in cumulative supplement
  * **Not comprehensive, but a useful shortcut, or if above not available**
    — chronological table of ECJ decisions at back of consolidated table of cases (vol 54)
    — chronological table of ECJ decisions after alphabetical table of cases at front of cumulative supplement
— Mimeographed advance ECJ judgments themselves
  * **Especially for very recent cases not in the above; but only possible if shelved in library in case number order!**

QR4.6 Finding English cases by subject [4.72-4.80]

— *Halsbury's Laws* and textbooks
  * **Although not case-finding aids as such, often the best way to start a subject-based research problem**
    — in *Halsbury's* use consolidated index and/or browse contents pages of each topic
    — check cumulative supplement and looseleaf noter-up under same volume number and paragraph number as main work
— Lexis: CASES file in ENGGEN library
  * **Likely to produce the most comprehensive results for cases since 1945 (and will lead to earlier cases cited since then); at its best when searching for specific technical terms or concrete entities; only way of finding unreported cases by subject**
    — formulate the search strategy broadly to start with and then narrow using the modify facility
    — think of synonyms and make full use of truncation and proximity facilities

— search example to find cases on measure of damages where a surveyor negligently values a house that subsequently needs substantial repairs:

surveyor **or** valuer **w/10** negligen**!** TRANSMIT
M [for modify] TRANSMIT
and damages TRANSMIT
M TRANSMIT
and value **or** price TRANSMIT
M TRANSMIT
w/15 cost **or** repair**!** TRAMSMIT

— *Current Law*: monthly digests and recent yearbooks (printed and on CD-ROM)

* **Usually the best manual starting place on the grounds that recent cases will cite relevant earlier cases; monthly digests most up-to-date all-round source; CD-ROM useful for searching for fact situations as well as legal concepts.**

— cumulative index to latest monthly part or browse through body of entries under main topic in each part

— CD-ROM, if available, for yearbooks 1986-

— otherwise, indexes (cumulative in 1989 and 1986 yearbooks) or body of entries

— *Halsbury's Laws*: monthly reviews and annual abridgements

* **An alternative to Current Law, but less comprehensive and less heavily used**

— *The Digest*

* **For in-depth research, especially where older cases likely to be relevant; also for selected Commonwealth authorities**

— consolidated index or browse through table of contents for each topic

— check annual cumulative supplement under same volume number as main work

— Lawtel

* **Most useful for very recent cases in the papers; otherwise a possible starting point for mainstream cases since 1980**

— in main subject index

— *Daily Law Reports Index*

* **Most useful for very recent cases (especially if you remember seeing one in the paper and cannot remember its name); back volumes worth checking for minor cases not fully reported if other sources do not yield anything.**

— key word index in binder of weekly parts, quarterly and annual parts

— also electronic version

— *Legal Journals Index*

* **A double-check for recent cases reported only in journals**

— subject index in monthly, quarterly and annual parts

— also electronic version

— *Law Reports Index*
  * **A shortcut for mainstream cases, if it is all that is to hand**

QR4.7 Finding cases on quantum of damages for personal injuries [4.83]

— Kemp & Kemp *Quantum of Damages in Personal Injury and Fatal Accident Claims* (3 volumes looseleaf)
  * **The basic bible**
— Goldrein and de Haas *Butterworths Personal Injury Litigation Service* (3 volumes looseleaf)
  * **Wider than just quantum but includes in binder 2 quantum summaries and quantum judgments**
— *Current Law*: table of damages for personal injuries or death
  * **Especially for very recent awards not in above**
    — cumulative table in latest monthly part and in each yearbook summarises the awards; the cases themselves digested in the main entries under Damages
— *Halsbury's Laws*: monthly reviews and annual abridgments
  * **Quantum cases a particular strength**
    — cumulative table to quantum cases in current monthly reviews filed in the 'Personal Injury' divider in looseleaf noter-up volume to *Halsbury's Laws* (not in the monthly review binder); also separate table in annual abridgment
    — cases themselves digested in the main entries under Damages
— Lawtel
    — injuries option from the decisions menu

QR4.8 Finding cases in which a particular word or phrase has been construed [2.47-2.50]

— *Stroud's Judicial Dictionary*
    — main work and cumulative supplement
    — superseded 4th edition still of use for old and Commonwealth cases
— *Words and Phrases Legal Defined*
    — main work and cumulative supplement
— *Current Law*: table of words and phrases in yearbooks and monthly parts
  * **Especially for recent cases not yet in the supplements to the above**
    — cumulative for the year in the monthly parts
— *Halsbury's Laws*: table of words and phrases in noter-up and annual abridgments
  * **An alternative to, or cross-check on, Current Law**
    — table in looseleaf noter-up volume of current service refers to monthly reviews filed in the other current service volume
— *Law Reports Index*
  * **An alternative for mainstream cases**

— under 'Words and Phrases' in the subject-matter index
— Lexis: CASES file in ENGGEN library
  * **Can be very effective as long as word not too common in ordinary usage**
    — search example:
      emergency w/10 meaning or defin! or constru!
      will retrieve cases on the construction of 'emergency', but also a number of false drops

QR4.9 Finding EC cases by subject [4.84]

— Justis CD-ROM and on-line
  * **Usually an effective approach**
    — *Common Market Law Reports* as well as ECJ available on on-line version
    — remember to use truncation symbol (*), wildcard character (?), and proximity searching (which is measured in characters not words) as appropriate
    — search example:
      (equal* or discrimin*) within 100 of (wom?n or sex*)
      will retrieve cases on sex discrimination or the equal treatment of men and women
— Lexis: CASES file in EURCOM library
  * **Equally effective approach**
    — includes *Common Market Law Reports* and *European Commercial Cases* as well as *European Court Reports*
    — search example:
      equal! or discrim! w/20 wom*n or sex!
      would be Lexis syntax for the same search as above. If it retrieved too many hits modify, eg, to cover equal treatment of redundancy:
      and redundan!
— *Gazetteer of European Law* (1953-1983) volume 2 and *Case Search Monthly* (1988-): subject index
  * **Probably the best manual approach (though gap in coverage)**
    — includes decisions of national courts
— T.M.C. Asser Institute *Guide to EC Court Decisions*: alphabetical subject index
  * **Comprehensive but not updated as frequently as the above**
— *Butterworths EC Case Citator and Service*: key phrase/sector index
  * **Only selected cases that have 'substantially contributed to EC law' included in this part of the work**
— David Vaughan *Law of the European Communities*
  * **Useful shortcut**
    — list of relevant cases after commentary in each division

— *Digest of Case Law Relating to the European Communities* (looseleaf)

   * **Official publication of the EC; coverage not yet complete and not very up to date**

     — planned to be in four sections:

       A ECJ decisions (except staff cases and cases on the Brussels Convention)

       B Decisions of national courts

       C Staff cases

       D ECJ and national court decisions on the Brussels Convention

— *European Current Law* (1992-)

   * **Covers all of Europe not just member states and not just EC law, but useful for recent decisions of national courts**

— *European Court of Justice Reporter* (1981-)

   * **Primarily a current awareness rather than a retrospective research tool**

     — a monthly digest by topic of all decisions of the ECJ

— The sources listed above for English cases

   * **For decisions of English courts relevant to EC law, though some ECJ cases covered by, for example, Current Law and The Digest**

QR4.10 Finding cases in which a particular English case has been cited [4.85-4.91]

— Lexis: CASES file in ENGGEN library

   * **Lexis at its best: more cases will almost invariably be retrieved than by any other means**

     — search example:

       Candler **w/5** Crane

       will retrieve all cases in which *Candler v Christmas Co* has been cited

     — if you have a case with a common name add date or key word from the subject-matter

— *Current Law*: case citators

   * **The main manual source for cases cited since 1947**

     — two bound volumes 1947-1976, 1977-88 and softbound supplement 1989- : references in the right hand column are to yearbook paragraph numbers where the citing case will be found

     — cumulative table of cases in latest monthly part (and if necessary December issue of previous year): cases in lower case are those that have been cited during the year and references are to monthly part and paragraph number

— *The Digest*

   * **The main source for cases cited before 1947; and a cross-check for cases thereafter**

     — find the digest entry for the case in the main work via the consolidated table of cases and the table of cases in the volume

— at the foot of the entry in small print the ANNOTATION section shows later cases in which it was cited

— check the annual cumulative supplement under the same volume number and paragraph number as the main work

— Lawtel

 * **Especially for very recent cases**

  — find the case from the decisions option, any later cases on the database that cite it are given at the foot

— *Index to the Times Law Reports* (Professional Books 1982-1988) and *Times Law Reports* (W & T Clarke, 1990-): tables of cases judicially considered

 * **May net material not in Current Law citators**

— *Weekly Law Reports* on CD-ROM (1984-)

 * **May net material not in Current Law Citators**

— *Daily Law Reports Index*: electronic version only (1988-)

 * **No case citator in printed version, but electronic version would pick any cases specifically mentioned in the summaries: might catch the odd case not in the above**

— *Law Reports Digest* (1865-1950): tables of cases judicially considered

 * **A cross-check on The Digest for older cases**

— *Law Reports Index* (1951-): table of cases judicially considered

 * **A shortcut for mainstream cases, but not as comprehensive as Current Law**

— *All England Law Reports*: table of cases reported and considered in consolidated tables

 * **Better than nothing, but limited coverage**

  — coverage of cases considered confined to those that were themselves originally reported in All ER or appeared in the All ER Reprint

— *Australian and New Zealand Citator to UK reports* (1 bound volume + annual cumulative supplement)

 * **For in-depth research or where above sources yield few or no English citations**

  — the main volume is confined to Australian and New Zealand cases that cite those cases that were originally reported *The Law Reports*, the *Weekly Law Reports* and the *All England Law Reports* to 1972, or in the *All England Law Reports Reprint* series; the supplement, 1973 to date, covers a wider range of UK reports

QR4.11 Finding cases in which a particular EC case has been cited [4.92]

— Lexis: CASES file in EURCOM library

 * **Probably the most effective approach**

  — includes *Common Market Law Reports* and *European Commercial Cases* as well as *European Court Reports*, so will pick some decisions of national courts as well as ECJ cases

— search on name or number

— search examples:

Harz w/5 Tradax

79/83

will both retrieve cases in which Case 79/83 *Harz v Deutsche Tradax GmbH* has been cited

— Justis CD-ROM and on-line

* **An equally good alternative**

— *Common Market Law Reports* on on-line version only

— *Gazetteer of European Law* (1953-1983) volume 2 case search table and *Case Search Monthly* (1988-) case tracker table

* **The best manual approach (though there is a gap in coverage)**

— arranged by ECJ case number

— only gives number of citing case: refer to main numerical sequences for details of the case

— includes decisions of national courts that cite ECJ cases

— importance of citation graded: cases in bold indicate substantial consideration, cases in italic indicate a mere mention; other cases are in normal type

— The sources above for English cases

* **For decisions of the English courts that have cited EC cases**

QR4.12 Finding cases on Public General Acts [4.93-4.96]

— Lexis

* **Lexis at its best: more cases will almost invariably be retrieved than by any other means**

— search on name of Act and if necessary section number; avoid searching on 'section', 's' or subsection numbers

— search example:

Employment **w/4** 1990 **w/15** 7

will retrieve cases citing s 7 of the Employment Act 1990

— *Halsbury's Statutes*

* **Together with Current Law statute citators the best manual source**

— find the statute in the main work from the alphabetical or chronological tables in the annual softback index

— check notes to particular section for any case references

— check annual cumulative supplement under same volume and page number as main work

— check looseleaf noter-up volume under same volume and page number as main work

— *Current Law*: statute citator

* **Usually slightly more up to date than Halsbury's Statutes, which, however, should be checked as well**

- statute citator 1947-1971, statute citator in legislation citators 1972-1988 and 1989- , and statute citator in latest monthly part (and if necessary December issue of previous year)
- arranged chronologically by year and chapter number
- any case references given under each section number
- Lawtel
  * **Useful for very recent cases and mainstream cases from 1980**
    - select statute citator option from main menu or legislation menu
    - find Act alphabetically by title
- *Daily Law Reports Index* (1988-): legislation index
  * **Useful for very recent cases; might catch some cases not in other sources**
    - in binder of weekly parts and at back of each quarterly and annual part
    - arranged alphabetically by title of Act
- *Index to the Times Law Reports* (Professional Books 1982-1988): statutes, regulations and rules referred to
  * **May net material not in other sources**
- *Times Law Reports* (W & T Clarke, 1990-): legislation index
  * **A cross-check on the Daily Law Reports Index**
    - arranged by year and chapter number of Act
    - look in latest monthly part and annual volumes
- *Law Reports Digest* (1865-1950): tables of statutes judicially considered
  * **For cases on statutes no longer in force and for pre-1947 cases**
    - arranged by regnal year and chapter number of Act
- *Law Reports Index* (1951-): table of statutes judicially considered
  * **A shortcut for mainstream cases**
    - arranged by year and chapter number
- *All England Law Reports*: table of statutes considered in consolidated tables
  * **A shortcut for mainstream cases**
    - arranged alphabetically by title

QR4.13 Finding cases on SIs [4.96-4.97]

- Lexis: CASES file in ENGGEN library
  * **Lexis at its best: more cases will almost invariably be retrieved than by any other means**
    - search on name of the SI and if necessary regulation or rule number
    - search example:

      Companies w/4 Unfair Prejudice w/6 1986

      will retrieve cases on the Companies (Unfair Prejudice Applications) Rules 1986
- *Law Reports Index* (1951-): table of Statutory Instruments etc judicially considered

* **The most useful feature of this tool**
— Rules of the Supreme Court listed first followed by other SIs by title
— *Halsbury's Statutory Instruments*
* **Some cases may be found in introduction to topic and annotations**
— *Law Reports Digest* (1891-1950): table of statutory rules and orders of court judicially considered
* **For older cases; no table in 1865-1890 volume**
— arranged alphabetically by title
— *All England Law Reports*: tables G-M in consolidated tables volume
* **Might possibly catch some cases not in Law Reports Index, but remember how the material is divided into different tables**
— six different tables:
G Rules of the Supreme Court
H County Court Rules
I Matrimonial Causes Rules
J Bankruptcy and Insolvency Rules
K Other rules
L Regulations
N Orders
— each table arranged alphabetically by title
— *Daily Law Reports Index* (1988-): legislation index
* **For very recent cases; will also catch some cases not in Law Reports Index**
— arranged by title interfiled with Acts and other legislation
— in binder of weekly parts and at back of each quarterly and annual part
— also electronic version
— *Index to the Times Law Reports* (Professional Books 1982-1988): statutes, regulations and rules referred to
* May net material not in other sources
— arranged by title interfiled with Acts and other legislation
— *Times Law Reports* (W & T Clarke, 1990-): legislation index
* **A cross-check on the Daily Law Reports Index**
— separate table after Acts, arranged by year and SI number; Rules of the Supreme Court separately listed
— look in latest monthly part and annual volumes
— *Weekly Law Reports* on CD-ROM (1984-)
* **May catch some cases not in other sources**

QR4.14 Finding cases on EC legislation [4.98]

— Lexis
* **The most comprehensive approach**
— CASES file in EURCOM library for cases from *Common Market Law Reports*, *European Court Reports*, and *European Commercial Cases*, which will be mostly (but not entirely) non-English cases

- — CASES file in ENGGEN library for English cases
  - — search example:

    Regulation w/4 3821/85

    will retrieve cases on EC Regulation 3821/85
- — Justis CD-ROM and on-line
  - * **An alternative electronic approach**
- — *Butterworths EC Case Citator and Service*
  - * **Probably the best manual starting point, but should be cross-checked against Case Search Monthly**
    - — separate tables by treaty provision, Regulation, Directive, and Decision
- — *Case Search Monthly* (1988-): law tracker
  - * **A good alternative to the above for period covered; will also catch some member state decisions**
- — T.M.C. Asser Institute *Guide to EC Court Decisions*: table of legal provisions
  - * **Comprehensive but not updated as frequently as above**
- — *European Current Law* (1992-)
  - * **A cross-check for recent material**
    - — Table 'Treaty provisions referred to' in fact includes Regulations, Directives and Decisions
- — *Law Reports Index* (1971-): European Community enactments judicially considered
  - * **Mainstream cases only**
    - — mostly English cases or English referrals to ECJ, but a few non-English ECJ cases reported in English series (mostly from ICR)
- — *Daily Law Reports Index*: legislation index
  - * **Only those cases reported in the English newspapers, but may help for important recent cases**
    - — by title (Commission Directive..., Council Regulation ... etc) interfiled with other legislation
    - — also electronic version

QR4.15 Finding cases on Local and Personal Acts [4.99]

- — Lexis: CASES file in ENGGEN library
  - * **By far the best way for cases since 1945**
    - — search as for Public General Acts
- — *Law Reports Index* (1951-): table of statutes judicially considered
  - * **The main manual alternative**
    - — by year and chapter number interfiled with Public General Acts
- — *Law Reports Digest* (1911-1950): Local and Personal Acts judicially considered
  - * **Only source before 1945; only available from the 1911 volume**
    - — separate table after Public General Acts and before Dominion statutes, arranged by year and chapter number

— *All England Law Reports*: statutes considered table B in consolidated tables volume

* **Might catch cases not in Law Reports Index**
  — separate table after Public General Acts, arranged alphabetically by title

— *Daily Law Reports Index*: legislation index

* **Especially for very recent cases**
  — look in legislation index in binder of weekly parts and at back of each quarterly and annual volume
  — by title interfiled with other legislation
  — also electronic version

— *Times Law Reports* (W & T Clarke, 1990-): legislation table

* **A cross-check on the Daily Law Reports Index for recent cases**
  — at back of annual volume, and cumulative in monthly parts
  — separate table after Public General Acts, arranged by year and chapter number

QR4.16 Unreported cases: where to find transcripts [4.20-4.25]

Much of the information below is based on that kindly supplied by the Supreme Court Library, Royal Courts of Justice, who issue a leaflet giving up-to-date information on the availability of transcripts and who may be able to offer further advice and information.

Unless otherwise stated, there is a charge (which may be quite substantial) for providing copies of transcripts. When ordering transcripts from shorthand writers it is usually essential to know the name of the case, the date, and the court (and, in the case of the High Court, whether sitting at the Royal Courts of Justice in London or at another court centre). The names and addresses given below for copies of High Court transcripts are only for cases heard in London; apply locally for sittings elsewhere.

QR4.17 House of Lords

Copies from

Judgments
Judicial Office
House of Lords
London SW1A 0PW
Tel: 071-219 3111

Available singly or on subscription

Appellate Committee proceedings (applications for leave to appeal)

Gurneys
St Stevens House
Victoria Embankment
London SW7
Tel: 071-930 4849

Reference copies	Some libraries may subscribe to current judgments. Sets of the 'printed case' (ie appellant's and respondent's advance written submissions) and appeal documents (eg transcript of court below), together with the judgments, are currently deposited annually at the following libraries, who also have extensive back runs:
	Advocates' Library, Edinburgh
	House of Lords Library
	Library of Congress, Washington
	Lincoln's Inn Library, London (from late seventeenth century)
	Distribution used to be wider and other libraries may have back volumes. The Supreme Court Library, Queen's Building, Royal Courts of Justice hold 1884-1967 (and judgments only 1976-).
Lexis	All 1980-

QR4.18 Privy Council

Copies from	Judicial Committee of the Privy Council Whitehall London SW1A 2AT Tel: 071-270 0485
	No charge
Reference copies	As for House of Lords, but annual distribution of appeal documents is as follows:
	British Library, Official Publications and Social Sciences Service
	Inner Temple Library
	Institute of Advanced Legal Studies Library (University of London)
	Lincoln's Inn Library
	Middle Temple Library
	University of Malaysia, Singapore
Lexis	All 1980-

QR4.19 Court of Appeal (Civil Division)

Copies from	Association of Official Shorthand Writers 2 New Square Lincoln's Inn London WC2A 3RU Tel: 071-405 9884
	It takes a minimum of two days to produce a transcript. Tapes only kept for six years but the

Association can arrange for authorised copying of reference copies back to 1951.

Reference copies   Supreme Court Library, Queen's Building, Royal Courts of Justice, 1951- . Photocopying not permitted.

Indexed by name of first party and date.

Published on microfiche by HMSO, 1951-1980 only.

Lexis   All 1980-

QR4.20 Court of Appeal (Criminal Division)

NB Some unreported cases may be traced through the *Criminal Appeal Office Index* published as a supplement to *Archbold* or available on-line from 1982 via Justis.

Copies from   Criminal Appeal Office
                         Room C 301
                         Royal Courts of Justice
                         London WC2A 2LL
                         Tel: 071-936 7344

Reference copies   Supreme Court Library, Queen's Building, Royal Courts of Justice, April 1989- (excluding appeals dealing only with sentence).

Arranged by date; indexed by name of first defendant.

Lexis   Only those reported in *The Times*, *Financial Times*, and *Independent* and those reported or summarised in various journals (including *Criminal Law Review*) 1980-.

QR4.21 Chancery Division

Copies from   Mechanical Recording Department
                         Room WB11
                         Royal Courts of Justice
                         London WC2A 2LL
                         Tel: 071-936 6154
                         Fax: 071-936 6662

Tapes erased after six years.

Reference copies   *Patent Court cases only 1970-*

British Library
Science Reference and Information Service
25 Southampton Buildings
Chancery Lane
London WC2A 1AW
Tel: 071-323 7919

May not be photocopied for six years.

Lexis

All Revenue list cases 1980-

All Patent Court cases 1980-

Otherwise only those reported in *The Times*, *Financial Times*, and *Independent* and those reported or summarised in various journals (see current Library Contents list) 1980- .

QR4.22 Family Division

Copies from

Mechanical Recording Department
Room WB11
Royal Courts of Justice
London WC2A 2LL
Tel: 071-936 6154
Fax: 071-936 6662

Tapes erased after six years

Reference copies

None

Lexis

Only those reported in *The Times*, *Financial Times*, and *Independent* and those reported or summarised in various journals (see current Library Contents list) 1980- .

QR4.23 Queen's Bench Divisional Court

Copies from

Marten Walsh Cherer
Midway House
27-29 Cursitor Street
London EC4A 1LT
Tel: 071-405 5010

Reference copies

Crown Office
Room C315
Royal Courts of Justice
London WC2A 2LL

Lexis

All 1983-

QR4.24 Queen's Bench Division Official Referee's Business

Copies from

Barnett, Lenton & Co
61 Carey Street
London WC2A 2JG
Tel: 071-405 2345

Reference copies

Handed-down judgments only: Supreme Court Library, Queen's Building, Royal Courts of Justice, November 1991- .

Arranged by date; indexed by name of first party.

Lexis	Only those reported in *The Times*, *Financial Times*, and *Independent* and those reported or summarised in various journals (see current Library Contents list) 1980- .

QR4.25 Queen's Bench Division

Copies from	Mechanical Recording Department Room WB11 Royal Courts of Justice London WC2A 2LL Tel: 071-936 6154 Fax: 071-936 6662 Tapes erased after six years.
Reference copies	None
Lexis	All Admiralty Court cases 1980- Selected Commercial Court cases 1980- Otherwise only those reported in *The Times*, *Financial Times*, and *Independent* and those reported or summarised in various journals (see current Library Contents list) 1980- .

QR4.26 Central Criminal Court

Copies from	Newgate Reporters Central Criminal Court Old Bailey London EC4M 7EH Tel: 071-248 9571
Reference copies	No modern ones but proceedings were published in *Old Bailey Sessions' Papers* 1730-1912. Also numerous printed editions of individual famous trials; many of these now collected in Chadwyck-Healey's microfiche publication *British Trials 1660-1900*.
Lexis	None

QR4.27 Other Crown Courts

Copies from	Contact chief clerk of the court for name of local shorthand writers.

QR4.28 County courts

Copies from	Proceedings of trials at county court trial centres and nominated child care centres tape recorded only from October 1991. Contact the court. Otherwise no formal record.

QR4.29 Magistrates courts

No formal record of proceedings

QR4.30 Employment Appeal Tribunal

Copies from	Employment Appeal Tribunal 4 St James's Square London SW1Y 4JU Tel: 071-270 3872
Reference copies	Supreme Court Library Queen's Building Royal Courts of Justice London WC2A 2LL Tel: 071-242 6587 Received by the Library six to eight weeks after judgment. 1979- Also available, by appointment, at the EAT Library
Lexis	All revised cases 1980-

QR4.31 Immigration Appeal Tribunal

Copies from	Immigration Appeal Tribunal Thanet House 231 Strand London WC2R 1DA Tel: 071-353 8060
Reference copies	Supreme Court Library Queen's Building Royal Courts of Justice London WC2A 2LL Tel: 071-242 6587 Received by the Library six to eight weeks after judgment.

QR4.32 Copyright Tribunal

Copies from	Copyright Tribunal Room 4/6 Hazlitt House 45 Southampton Buildings London WC2A 1AR Tel: 071-438 4776
Reference copies	At the above between the hours of 10 am and 4 pm

QR4.33 Lands Tribunal

Lexis	All 1980-

QR4.34 Special Commissioners of Income Tax

Reference copies Transcripts are made but are available only to the Commissioners and the parties. After 10 years deposited at:

Public Records Office
The Repository
Bourne Avenue
Hayes
Middlesex
Tel: 081-573 3831

QR4.35 VAT Tribunal

Copies from Combined Tax Tribunals Centre
15-19 Bedford Avenue
London WC1B 3AS
Tel: 071-631 4242 Ext 148

Available individually or on subscription

Reference copies Some libraries may subscribe

Lexis Selected cases 1980-

QR4.36 Searching for transcripts on Lexis [4.21]

To search for transcripts only

— Search example:

mareva **and** cite(transcript)

will retrieve only unreported cases on mareva injunctions

To search for cases other than transcripts

— Search example:

mareva **and not** cite(transcript)

will retrieve only reported cases on mareva injunctions

European Convention on Human Rights case law

QR4.37 Categories of decision [4.113-4.114]

— European Commission of Human Rights
— decisions on admissibility
— reports on the merits
— reports on friendly settlements
— European Court of Human Rights
— judgments
— Committee of Ministers of the Council of Europe

— resolutions under Article 32: decisions where case not referred to the Court

— resolutions under Article 54: execution of judgments of the Court

QR4.38 Alternative sources for the full text of cases [4.116]

— *European Human Rights Reports* (1980-)

* **Main commercially published series for Court judgments and Commission reports and selected other documentation**

— also available on Lexis in CASES file in EURCOM library

— *Publications of the European Court of Human Rights: Series A: Judgments and Decisions*

* **The official reports but publication in arrears**

— also *Series B: Pleadings, Oral Arguments and Documents*

— European Court of Human Rights mimeographed judgments (A4 format)

* **Advance publication of individual judgments**

— European Commission of Human Rights *Decisions and Reports*

* **The official source for reports on the merits, and selected other reports**

— European Commission of Human Rights mimeographed reports

* **Advance publication of individual reports on the merits**

— Committee of Ministers resolutions

* **Issued as individual sheets first in typescript then in printed form**

— Cited by DH number

— Printout of Commission admissibility decisions from Strasbourg database and on-line access

* **Only available at national Council of Europe human rights depositories**

— in UK at the British Institute of International and Comparative law (address at QR9.3)

— *Yearbook of the European Convention on Human Rights*

* **Full text of only a selection of Commission admissibility decisions, Commission friendly settlement reports and Committee of Ministers resolutions; very much in arrears**

QR4.39 Sources of summaries of case law [4.117]

— Press releases of the Commission, Court, and Committee of Ministers

* **The most up-to-date source if available, though means browsing through**

— *Human Rights Case Digest*

* **More organised but slightly less up-to-date source for the same material as above**

— Council of Europe *Information Sheets*

* **An alternative, though, not quite as up to date as above**
— *Yearbook of the European Convention on Human Rights*
* **Summaries of Court judgments and Commission reports on the merits for the year; but not up to date**
— *Digest of Strasbourg Case-Law Relating to the European Convention on Human Rights*
* **Comprehensive but not very up to date**
— Council of Europe *Stock-taking on the European Convention on Human Rights*
— Current Law yearbooks and monthly digests
* **See below**
— *The Digest*
* **See below**

QR4.40 Finding European human rights case law [4.118-4.119]

— *Current Law* yearbooks and monthly digests
* **For recent cases reported in EHRR and newspaper law reports**
— from 1986 with increasing coverage
— in main subject listing under 'Human Rights' and by name
— *Daily Law Reports Index*
* **For recent cases reported in the newspapers**
— under 'European Convention on Human Rights' in keyword index and in legislation index, and by case name
— *The Digest*
* **A selection of the more recent cases from about 1982**
— will be in volume 26 in the title Human Rights when reissued; currently only in continuation volumes G and H and cumulative supplement under the title Human Rights with volume 26 material
— *Digest of Strasbourg Case-Law Relating to the European Convention on Human Rights*
* **Comprehensive but not very up to date**
— volumes 1-5 by Convention article, volume 6 tables and indexes, looseleaf supplementary volumes
— Lexis: CASES file in EURCOM library
* **Includes full text of EHHR**
— European Commission of Human Rights *Decisions and Reports*: cumulative indexes to vols 1-20 and 21-40, indexes to individual volumes thereafter
— Council of Europe *Stock-taking on the European Convention on Human Rights*
* **Main cases described by article number**
— one mimeographed volume plus periodic supplements

— *Human Rights Case Digest*

   * **Especially for recent cases**

      — name and Article index in each issue and last issue of each year

— *European Human Rights Reports*: indexes to each volume

   — indexes by name and number, by subject and by Convention Article

   — also includes table of cases judicially considered

— *Yearbook of the European Convention on Human Rights*

   — alphabetical index includes subjects and names of parties

— Council of Europe *Information Sheets*

   — includes summaries of judgments and lists of Commission reports adopted

— European Court of Human Rights *Survey of Activities*

   — annual

   — includes complete numerical list of A series and details of cases

— European Commission of Human Rights *Survey of Activities*

   — annual

   — includes list of reports adopted

— British Institute of International and Comparative Law library

   * **Council of Europe human rights documentation depository; access to on-line Strasbourg database**

QR5 Treaties

QR5.1 Alternative sources for the text of a treaty [5.7-5.14]

— *United Kingdom Treaty Series* (1892-)
  * **Main source for treaties ratified by the UK**
    — issued by HMSO as command papers, but also bear own series number
    — may be shelved as a series, by command paper number, or in sessional volumes of Parliamentary papers

— *United Nations Treaty Series*
  * **Main source for all treaties from 1946, but publication about eight years in arrears**
    — should include all treaties entered into by members of the United Nations

— *International Legal Materials*
  * **Especially for important recent multilateral treaties which UK has not signed**
    — issued in periodical form by the American Society of International Law
    — selected treaties and other materials
    — cumulative indexes from time to time
    — available on Lexis from 1980 (ILMTY file in INTLAW library)

— *League of Nations Treaty Series* (1920-1946)
  * **Main source for all treaties before 1946**

— *Consolidated Treaty Series* ed. Clive Parry (1648-1919)
  * **Main source for all treaties before 1920**

— *British and Foreign State Papers* (1812-1968)
  * **An alternative to UK Treaty Series for many treaties after 1892; contains some pre-1892 treaties not in the command papers**

— Command papers in sessional volumes of Parliamentary papers (1800-1892)

* An alternative for UK treaties before 1892; some not also reprinted in the above

— National treaty series

* For non-UK treaties not yet in United Nations Treaty Series and not in International Legal Materials

— Foreign and Commonwealth Office *Miscellaneous Series* (and country series)

* An alternative source for selected treaties not yet ratified by the UK

— issued by HMSO as command papers, and usually shelved by command paper number or in sessional volumes of Parliamentary papers rather than by Miscellaneous (or country) number

— Looseleaf subject compilations of international legal materials, appendices to textbooks, etc

* Often a convenient shortcut

— Public General Acts and SIs

* For some treaties incorporated into UK domestic law, provided you know the title of the relevant legislation

— text of treaty sometimes printed as a schedule, but sometimes only referred to

— see QR3.1 and QR3.9 for alternative sources of the text of Acts and SIs

— Lexis

* A possible last resort if no printed sources available

— STATIS file in ENGGEN library would retrieve treaties incorporated by Act or SI (except Double Taxation Agreements) and would give text if given in a schedule

— DTAX file in UKTAX library contains all current Double Taxation Agreements

— *International Legal Materials* (1980-): ILMTY file in INTLAW library

— see also other contents of INTLAW library (mostly American material)

— Old compilations of treaties

* An alternative if available and Consolidated Treaty Series is not

— eg *Hertslet's Commercial Treaties* (1820-1925, 31 volumes) G.F. de Martens *Recueil de traités* (1791-1943)

— See also on old treaty series Clive Parry 'Where to look for your treaties'(1980) 8 *International Journal of Law Libraries* 8-18

Alternative sources for the text of EC treaties

QR5.2 *Treaties establishing the EC, accession treaties etc [5.15]*

— *Treaties Establishing the European Communities [etc]* (Office for Official Publications of the European Communities, two purple volumes)

*   **Offical edition reissued from time to time**

— *Encyclopedia of European Community Law* (Sweet & Maxwell, looseleaf): B volumes

— *Halsbury's Statutes* volume 50 (+ volume 50 section in Current Statutes service volume)

— Smit and Herzog *The Law of the European Economic Community* (New York: Matthew Bender, looseleaf)

— *Common Market Reporter* (CCH, looseleaf)

— Various compilations of EC materials for students

QR5.3   *Treaties entered into by the EC [5.16]*

— *Collection of the Agreements Concluded by the European Communities*

   (Office for Official Publications of the European Communities, several purple volumes)

— Foreign and Commonwealth Office *European Treaty Series*

   *   **Especially for recent treaties not yet in the above**

      — issued by HMSO as command papers and shelved by series number, or command paper number or in sessional volumes of Parliamentary papers

— *Official Journal of the EC*: L series

   *   **For very recent treaties**

QR5.4 Finding treaties by date or subject [5.17-5.22]

— Clive Parry and Charity Hopkins *An Index of British Treaties 1101-1988* (HMSO, 4 vols)

   *   **The main source up to 1988 for treaties ratified by the UK**

      — volumes 1-3 cover 1101-1968

      — volume covers 1969-1988 and updates vols 1-3

      — main sequence with full details arranged by date

      — three subject indexes:

         — multilateral treaties by subject

         — bilateral treaties by country subdivided by subject

         — bilateral treaties by subject subdivided by country

— M.J. Bowman and D.J. Harris *Multilateral Treaties: Index and Current Status* (bound volume and annual cumulative supplement)

   *   **The best source for multilateral treaties (though does not cover every single multilateral treaty there is)**

      — main sequence with full details arranged by date

      — bound volume goes up to June 1983

      — cumulative supplement in two parts:

      Part A: Additional treaties (ie some pre-1983 treaties omitted from bound volume and post-1983 treaties)

      Part B: Noter-up to treaties in bound volume

— table of other multilateral treaties after main sequence in bound volume lists treaties referred to but not detailed in full

— Peter H. Rohn *World Treaty Index*

  * **For treaties 1900-1980 not found in the above; includes many treaties not in UN or League of Nations treaty series**

  — main sequence chronological by date of signature

  — party index covers both bilateral and multilateral

  — key word index

— Indexes to government publications (see QR6)

  * **An alternative for treaties published by HMSO as command papers in the United Kingdom Treaty Series and the FCO 'European Communities' and 'Miscellaneous' series. Especially for recent treaties**

  — search by subject and/or party

— Indexes to the *United Kingdom Treaty Series*

  * **Possible shortcut for recent treaties**

  — recent indexes issued annually

  — by subject

— *International Legal Materials*

  * **For recent treaties not in UK Treaty Series or Bowman and Harris**

  — look through recent parts

  — cumulative indexes

  — also on Lexis

— *United Nations Treaty Series*: cumulative indexes

  * **A long haul, but a source for treaties from 1945 not in Parry or Bowman and Harris, if Rohn not available**

  — cumulative indexes covering 50 volumes each

  — in two sequences, chronological and alphabetical

— *League of Nations Treaty Series*: cumulative indexes

  * **A source for treaties 1919-1945 not in Parry or Bowman and Harris, if Rohn not available**

  — indexes covering 20-40 volumes: look in each unless approximate date known

  — each index in three sequences:

    — chronological index of all treaties

    — chronological index of general international agreements (ie multilateral treaties) only

    — alphabetical index under both country and subject for bilateral treaties and under subject only for mulitilateral treaties; within each heading arranged chronologically

— *Consolidated Treaty Series*: indexes

  * **Main source for treaties before 1919 not in Parry or Bowman and Harris; but only possible to search by date and party**

  — three indexes:

— general chronological list
  — excludes colonial, postal and telegraphic agreements
  — arranged by date with full details of treaty
— special chronological list
  — as above for colonial, postal and telegraphic agreements
— party index
  — by country (with former territories grouped with their modern equivalents)
  — within country arranged chronological
  — title of treaty not given; only name of other party, date, and volume reference
— Looseleaf subject compilations of international materials, appendices to textbooks etc
  * **Often a shortcut**

QR5.5 Checking parties and status of treaties [5.23-5.28]

— M.J. Bowman and D.J. Harris *Multilateral Treaties: Index and Current Status*
  * **The best starting place**
    — find treaty in main work and then check cumulative supplement
— *Index of British Treaties*
  * **Only up to date to 1988, but may help**
    — find treaty in main chronological sequence and then check volume 4 for any additional information
— *Supplementary List of Ratifications, Accessions, Withdrawals, etc*
  * **For recent information, but tedious to use**
    — issued four times a year as part of the *UK Treaty Series* (command papers published by HMSO)
    — arranged by subject-matter
    — plough through each list
— United Nations *Multilateral Treaties Deposited with the Secretary-General: Status as at ...*
  * **Not very up to date, but may help for a non-British treaty not in *Bowman and Harris***
— Treaty Records section of the Foreign and Commonwealth Office
  * **To make sure no very recent changes, having checked printed sources**
    — telephone them (number in *Civil Service Yearbook* under Nationality, Treaty and Claims Department of FCO)
— Rohn *World Treaty Index*
  * **Only up to date to 1980, but may help with retrospective information**
    — full details of parties, entry into force etc in main chronological sequence

QR6 Other official publications

Sources for finding official publications

See also sources mentioned at QR3.33-3.39 on finding Bills, pre-legislative reports and law reform proposals

QR6.1 Sources covering both HMSO and non-HMSO publications [6.14-6.25]

— UKOP CD-ROM

    * **The best source by far for publications from 1980 to within the last three months or so. Virtually the only source to cover both HMSO and non-HMSO publications.**

    — updated quarterly

    — searchable by any element, eg title, author, chairman, subjects

    — also includes publications of international organisations sold by HMSO

— Stephen Richard *British Government Publications: an Index to Chairmen and Authors 1800-1982* (4 volumes)

    * **Indispensable as chairman the commonest identifying feature of government reports, though not now very up to date**

— Polis

    * **For the experienced user**

Coverage is as follows:

Parliamentary Questions	
House of Commons	October 1980
House of Lords	November 1981
Non-legislative debates and Early Day Motions	November 1981
Legislative debates	November 1982
House of Commons papers and Bills	May 1979
House of Lords papers and Bills	November 1981
Command papers	May 1979
Public General Acts	May 1979

Local and Personal Acts	November 1982
Statutory Instruments laid before the House	November 1982
Ministerial deposits in the Library	June 1983
Selected UK official publications	January 1982
EC legislative proposals	January 1983
Other selected EC documents	January 1984
Selected international offficial documents	January 1986
Pamphlets in the Libraries	January 1983
Books in the House of Commons Library	January 1985

Sources covering HMSO publications only

QR6.2 *All categories of HMSO publications [6.14-6-18]*

— *HMSO in Print* on microfiche

   * **Often the best starting point if UKOP not available, though limited for subject searching**

   — quarterly

   — entries by title, author, chairman, department, series title and Parliamentary paper number

— HMSO monthly and annual catalogues

   * **The main manual source if an approximate date is known**

   — arranged in the following sequences

      — HL papers by session and number

      — HL Bills by session and number

      — HL Hansard

      — HC papers by session and number

      — HC Hansard

      — HC Bills by session and number

      — Command papers by number

      — All publications (except Bills, Acts and Hansard) alphabetically by department, body or committee

      — Alphabetical index to all of the above by keyword, chairman, or personal author

   — note that the annual catalogues are based on the calendar year so contain material from, and listed under, different Parliamentary sessions

   — some Parliamentary committees are numbered 1st, 2nd etc and are listed before the letter A in the main alphabetical list

   — some Parliamentary committees are listed in the main alphabetical sequence under 'Select...' if that is their official title, eg Select Committee on Science and Technology, others directly under their name if that is their official title, eg Home Affairs Committee

   — do not include SIs

   — before 1966 annual catalogues grouped in five yearly volumes with continuous pagination and consolidated index

-- HMSO *Daily List*

* **For publications since the last monthly catalogue**
  — no cumulation or index, so no alternative but to read through every one
  — also available in the HMSO section of Prestel
— HMSO database on-line

* **Especially for complex or recalcitrant searches; for HMSO publications goes back further and is more up to date than UKOP**
  — from 1976
  — updated monthly
  — available via Blaise or Dialog
— *Committee Reports Published by HMSO Indexed by Chairman*

* **No particular advantage over annual and monthly catalogues which now also index all chairmen**
  — quarterly with annual cumulation

QR6.3 *Parliamentary papers [6.19, 6.24]*

— *Index to House of Commons Parliamentary Papers* on CD-ROM

* **An alternative if UKOP on CD-ROM is not available**
  — from 1991/92 session
  — updated twice a year
  — based on Polis rather than HMSO data
— *Parliamentary Papers: General Alphabetical Index* 1900-1949; 1950-1958/59; 1959/60-1968/69

* **More convenient than looking through HMSO catalogues**
— Peter Cockton *Subject Catalogue of the House of Commons Parliamentary Papers 1801-1900* (Chadwyck-Healey, 5 volumes)

* **Has revolutionised finding nineteenth century papers**
  — arranged by broad topics subdivided by narrower topics and within each sub-topic by bills, reports of commissioners and accounts and papers
  — detailed subject index to main sequence in volume 5
  — gives full references to both printed version and Chadwyck-Healey microfiche edition
— *Parliamentary Papers: General Alphabetical Index* 1801-1852; 1852-1899

* **A poorer alternative if the above is not available**
— Sessional indexes to bound sets of Parliamentary papers

* **If papers kept in this form and date of relevant session known; will also translate an HC number or command number into volume and page reference in bound set**
— *General Index to the House of Lords Papers* 1859-1870; 1871-1884/85

* **Only source for the period other than individual sessional indexes**
  — originally issued with the official papers

— facsimile reprint (Dobbs Ferry, New York: Oceana, 1976)

QR6.4 *Parliamentary debates and questions[6.20, 6.25-6.26]*

— *Hansard* on CD-ROM (1988/89-)

* **Excellent, though only one session can be searched at a time**

— only Commons *Hansard* (not Lords or Standing Committee debates)

— one disk per session with intermediate cumulating disks issued after Christmas and Easter recesses

— Polis

— see QR6.1 above

— Telephone the House of Commons Public Information Office

* **Often the simplest solution, especially for recent material**

— will, within reason, use Polis to answer enquiries

— House of Commons *Hansard*: fortnightly indexes, indexes to bound volumes and sessional indexes

* **A long business unless you have a good idea of date to start with**

— printed sessional indexes currently issued very much in arrears

— House of Lords *Hansard*: weekly indexes, indexes to bound volumes and sessional indexes

QR6.5 Common examples of Parliamentary papers and their categories [6.9]

Annual reports and accounts of public bodies and quangos — HC papers, HMSO, the body itself, or not published at all: see the annual *Public Bodies* (HMSO)

Charity Commissioners reports — HC papers

Criminal Injuries Compensation Board reports — command papers

Criminal Law Revision Committee reports — command papers

Criminal statistics — command papers

Crown Prosecution Service annual reports — HC papers

Green papers — command papers (or HMSO or department concerned)

Immigration Rules — HC papers

Judicial statistics — command papers

Law Commission reports — HC papers or command papers

Legal Services Ombudsman annual reports — HC papers

Monopolies and Mergers Commission reports — command papers

Ombudsman (Parliamentary Commissioner for Administration) reports — HC papers

Royal Commissions — command papers

Select Committee reports — HC or HL reports

Treaties — command papers

White papers — command papers

QR6.6 Command paper series and abbreviations [6.10]

1833-1869	1 – 4222
1870-1899	C 1 – C 9550
1900-1918	Cd 1 – Cd 9239
1919-1956	Cmd 1 – Cmd 9889
1957-1986	Cmnd 1 – Cmnd 9927
1986 to date	Cm 1 –

QR7 Law outside England and Wales

QR7.1 General comparative sources [7.6-7.14]

— *Oxford Companion to Law*
* **For quick enquiries on foreign legal systems**
— Rene David *Major Legal Systems in the World Today*
* **Academic introduction to comparative law**
— *Modern Legal Systems Cyclopedia* (looseleaf)
* **Detailed descriptions of legal systems, but bias towards needs of American lawyers**
— *Martindale-Hubbell*: Canadian and international law digest volume
* **Very useful brief summaries of the laws of over 60 countries**
— *International Encyclopaedia of Laws* (looseleaf)
* **In course of publication, but promises to be detailed account of laws worldwide**
— *International Encyclopedia of Comparative law*
* **Mainly for academic research; not yet complete; not updated**
— Collections of 'laws of the world' on various subjects
* **Do not overlook; often a shortcut; some may provide full text translations of legislation**
— *Bibliography of Foreign and Comparative Law Books and Articles in English*
— *Index to Foreign Legal Periodicals*
* **Articles mostly not in English**
— *Foreign Law: Current Sources of Codes and Basic Legislation in Jurisdictions of the World* (3 volume looseleaf)
* **Invaluable guide to legislation (and also other sources of foreign law)**

311

Other jurisdictions in the British Isles

QR7.2 Scotland [7.15-7.26]

— *The Laws of Scotland: Stair Memorial Encyclopaedia*
   * **A first port of call, though not yet complete**

QR7.3 Sources for text of Acts applying to Scotland only [7.21]

— Public General Acts (Queen's Printer copies and HMSO bound volumes)
— *Statutes in Force*
— *Current Law Statutes Annotated* 1991-
— *Scottish Current Law Statutes* 1949-1990
— *Parliament House Book* (looseleaf)
   — selection of legislative materials for the practitioner

QR7.4 Finding-aids that cover Scottish Acts [7.21]

— *Current Law*: monthly parts and yearbooks 1991-
— *Scottish Current Law*: yearbooks 1948-1990
— *Current Law*: statute citators
— *Index to the Statutes* (HMSO)
— *Chronological Table of the Statutes*
— *Is it in Force?*

QR7.5 Finding-aids that cover Scottish cases[7.23-7.26]

— *Current Law*: monthly parts, yearbooks and case citators 1991-
— *Scottish Current Law*: monthly parts, yearbooks and case citators 1948-1990
— *Green's Weekly Digest* 1986-
— *The Digest* (selected Scottish cases in the small print cases)
— Lexis, full text of:
   Reported cases

Session Cases	January 1950-
Scots Law Times	January 1950-
Scottish Criminal Case Reports	January 1981-
Scottish Civil Law Reports	February 1986-

   Unreported cases

Scottish House of Lords decisions	July 1986-
All Inner House decisions	January 1982-
All Outer House decisions	January 1985-

QR7.6 Northern Ireland [7.27-7.33]

— Paul O'Higgins *Bibliography of Periodical Literature Relating to Irish Law* (1966, supplements 1973, 1983)

— *Irish Legal Journals Index* 1993-

QR7.7 Legislation [7.28-7.31]

— *The Statutes Revised, Northern Ireland*
  — all legislation affecting Northern Ireland in force at 31 March 1981 except United Kingdom statutes passed at Westminster since 1920 that extend to or apply only to Northern Ireland
  — separate A4 annual cumulative supplement
— Public General Acts, *Statutes in Force* or *Current Law Statutes*
  — for United Kingdom statutes not in the above
— *Halsbury's Statutes*
  — includes details of extension of UK statutes to Northern Ireland but does not include text of all UK statutes applying only to Northern Ireland
— *Northern Ireland Statutes*
  — from 1972 made as SIs at Westminster, but with separate numbering as well as SI number
— *Northern Ireland Statutory Rules and Orders*

QR7.8 Law reports [7.32]

— *Northern Ireland Law Reports*
  — also on Lexis 1945-
— *Northern Ireland Law Reports Judgments Bulletin*
  — also on Lexis 1984-
— *Index to Northern Ireland Cases 1921 to 1970* (plus 1975 supplement)

QR7.9 Finding-aids for legislation and law reports [7.33]

— *Current Law*
— *Bulletin of Northern Ireland Law*
— *Index to the Statutes* and *Chronological Table of the Statutes, Northern Ireland* (HMSO, Belfast)

QR7.10 Isle of Man [7.34-7.38]

— John Glasson *Trusts, Tax and Estate Planning Through the Isle of Man* (Key Haven, 1989)
— Comparative works and journal articles on tax havens
— Bibliography of Manx legal literature in W. Twining and J. Uglow *Law Publishing and Legal Information: Small Jurisdictions of the British Isles* (1981)
— Types of legislation:
  — (1) Acts of Tynwald (which require Royal Assent)
  — (2) United Kingdom statutes extended to the Isle of Man by Orders in Council (which are UK SIs)

— (3) Manx Government circulars (which are subordinate legislation made under 1 or 2)

— *Subject Guide to the Acts of Tynwald including Alphabetical and Chronological Lists of the Acts* (annual)

— *Subject Guide to, and Chronological Table of, Acts of Parliament Extending or Relating to the Isle of Man* (2nd ed, 1992)

— *Subject Guide and Chronological Table to Subordinate Legislation* (1981)

— Central Reference Library, Government Buildings, Douglas, Isle of Man

— for information on and copies of legislation

— *Manx Law Reports* 1972-

— *A Book of Precedents: a List of Constitutional and Privy Council Judgments Affecting the Isle of Man from 1523 to 1986*

— *Manx Law Bulletin* 1983-

QR7.11 Channel Islands [7.39-7.42]

— A.G. Chloros *Bibliographical Guide to the Law of the United Kingdom, the Channel Islands and the Isle of Man* (2nd ed, 1973)

— *Tolley's Taxation in the Channel Islands and the Isle of Man* (annual)

— Comparative works and journal articles on tax havens

— Types of legislation:

— (1) United Kingdom statutes extended to particular islands by Orders in Council (which are UK SIs)

— (2) Primary legislation passed by the legislatures on each island and then required to be sanctioned by Her Majesty by Orders in Council (which are *not* UK SIs)

— (3) Legislation passed by the legislatures on each island under general powers granted by Orders in Council (Jersey) or under common law powers to legislate (Guernsey)

— (4) Subsidiary legislation made on each island under powers delegated by 1, 2 or 3 above

QR7.12 *Jersey [7.43-7.46]*

— Paul Matthews and Terry Sowden *The Jersey Law of Trusts* (2nd ed, Key Haven ,1990)

— F. de L. Bois *A Constitutional History of Jersey* (1972)

— Series of legislation:

— *Laws* (formerly *Recueil des lois*) ie category 2 above

— *Regulations and Orders*, containing

— regulations of three years duration (category 3 above)

— regulations (or rules) of the States of indefinite duration (4 above)

— acts (for eg commencements and treaties)

— orders made by Committees of the States

— *General Index of Legislation*

— *Jersey Law Reports* 1985-
— *Jersey Judgments* 1950-1984
— *Jersey Law Reports Index 1977-1986*
  — covers both the above for the period concerned
— *Table des décisions* 1884-1963; 1964-1978
  — no recognised law reports or judgments in the English manner before 1950
  — 1884-1963 volumes a digest in French of the decisions filed at the Royal Court
  — 1964-1978 volume a digest mostly in English of cases not reported in *Jersey Judgments*

QR7.13 *Guernsey [7.47-7.49]*

— D.E. Thompson *Guernsey Company and Trust Law Handbook* (Guernsey Financial Services Commission, 1992)
  — reprints relevant legislation
— Sir John Loveridge *The Constitution and Law of Guernsey* (1975)
— Series of legislation:
  — *Laws* (also called *Orders in Council*, formerly *Recueil d'ordres en conseil*) ie category 2 above
  — *Ordinances* (formerly *Ordonnances*), containing both legislation made by the States under Laws and under common law powers
  — *Orders of the Royal Court*, containing rules of the Court and defence regulations
  — *Statutory Instruments* (*not* UK SIs) made by Committees (ie Ministries) of the States under Laws
— Alderney and Sark each have their own *Orders in Council* and *Ordinances*
— *Guernsey Law Journal* (1985-)
  — digest of legislation and cases (including Alderney and Sark) and occasional articles

Other common law jurisdictions

QR7.14 Republic of Ireland [7.50-7.53]

— Textbooks published by Butterworths Ireland, Roundhall Press, and in Sweet & Maxwell's *Irish Law Texts* series
— *Gazette of the Incorporated Law Society, Irish Law Times, Irish Jurist*
— *Acts of the Oireachtas*
  — index 1922-1982
— *Irish Current Law Statutes Annotated* 1984-
— *Statutory Instruments*
  — index 1922-1979
— *Irish Reports, Irish Law Reports Monthly*

— All written judgments of superior courts distributed 1976-

   — indexed in *Index to Irish Superior Court Written Judgments 1976-1982* and in 'pink lists' supplement to *Gazette of the Incorporated Law Society*

— *Irish Digest* to 1983

— *The Digest* (selected Irish cases among small print cases)

United States

QR7.15 *Textbooks and journals [7.54-7.58]*

— *Legal Books in Print* and *Law Books Published* (Glanville)

— *Law Books and Serials in Print* (Bowker)

— Edward J. Bander *Searching the Law*

— Francis Doyle *Searching the Law: the States*

— *Index to Legal Periodicals* (also on CD-ROM)

— *Current Law Index* (also on CD-ROM)

   — aims to be a more user-friendly version of the above and with fuller coverage

QR7.16 *Federal legislation [7.59]*

— *United States Code*

   * **The official unannotated version, but commercially published annotated versions usually to be preferred:**

      — *United States Code Annotated* (West)

      — *United States Code Service* (Lawyers Co-operative)

— *Statutes at Large*

   — equivalent of Queen's Printer copies of Public General Acts

— *Federal Register*

   — published daily containing the equivalent of SIs

— *Code of Federal Regulations*

   — consolidation of above

QR7.17 *Law reports [7.61-7.67]*

— *United States Supreme Court Reports* (US)

   * **The official edition, but commercially published annotated versions often to be preferred:**

      — *Lawyers' Edition* (L Ed) (Lawyers' Co-operative)

      — *Supreme Court Reporter* (S Ct) (West) from 1882 only

— *Federal Reporter* 1880-

   — part of West's *National Reporter System*

— *Federal Supplement* 1932-

   — part of West's *National Reporter System*

   — District Court reports, hived off from the above

— *Federal Cases*
  — reprint of pre-1880 federal nominate reports
— *National Reporter*
  — comprehensive collection of state reports arranged by region (with additional separate reporters for California and New York)
  — likely to be the only (printed) source of state reports available
— *National Reporter Blue Book*
  — converts a state report citation to a *National Reporter* citation
— *American Law Reports*
  — selected cases only but commentary and annotations
  — from 1969 state cases only
— *American Law Reports Federal*
  — as above for federal cases from 1969
— Lexis
  * **For text of all American law reports if printed copies not available; by far the best way to research American cases**
— Printed finding aids:
  — *American Digest* and *General Digest* (West)
  — *Corpus Juris Secundum*
  — *American Jurisprudence*
  — *Shepard's Citations*

QR7.18 Commonwealth in general [7.68-7.72]

— *International Legal Books in Print*
— *Commonwealth Legal Bulletin*
— Wallace Breem and Sally Phillips *Bibliography of Commonwealth Law Reports* (1991)
— Institute of Advanced Legal Studies *Union List of Commonwealth and South African Law* (2nd ed, 1963)
— *Law Reports of the Commonwealth* 1980-

QR7.19 Australia [7.73-7.84]

— Colin Fong and Graham Ellis *Finding the Law: a Guide to Australian Secondary Sources of Information* (1990)
— *Halsbury's Laws of Australia* 1991-
— *Acts of the Parliament of Australia*
  — consolidation to 1973
  — individual Acts as passed
  — reprints of individual Acts as amended
— *Statutory Rules*
  — consolidation to 1956

— individual Rules as passed
— reprints of individual Rules as amended
— *Federal Legislation Annotations* (three yearly with supplements)
    — alphabetically by Act
    — includes all Acts in the 1973 consolidation and passed since 1973
    — annotations:
        — whether reprinted
        — amendments and repeals
        — operation dates
        — regulations made under Acts
        — case law
— *Subject Index to the Acts and Regulations of the Commonwealth of Australia* (annual)
— *Australian Legal Monthly Digest* (Law Book Co)
— *Australian Digest*
— *Australian Case Citator* 1825-
— *Australian Current Law* (Butterworths)
— *Australian and New Zealand Citator to UK Reports*
    — see QR4.10
— *The Digest* (selected Australian cases in the small print cases)
— Lexis: CASES file in AUST library
    — only headnotes of *Australian Law Reports* 1973-

QR7.20 Canada [7.85-7.91]

— *Index to Canadian Legal Literature*
    — part of the *Canadian Abridgment*
    — books and articles
    — supplemented by *Canadian Legal Literature* issued as part of the *Canadian Current Law* service
— *Index to Canadian Legal Periodical Literature*
— *Revised Statutes of Canada* (looseleaf, 1985-)
— *Canada Gazette*
    — statutes and regulations as passed
— *Consolidated Regulations of Canada* (1978)
— *Canada Statute Citator*
    — federal statutes only
    — amendments, repeals, dates in force, and cases
— *Canadian Current Law: Legislation*
    — federal and provincial statutes
    — three sections:
        — progress of Bills

— amendments, repeals, and entry into force
— regulations by enabling Act
— parts consolidated as the *Legislation Annual*
— *Canadian Abridgment*
    — vast digest of case law
— *Canadian Current Law: Jurisprudence*
    — digest of federal and provincial cases by subject
    — includes many unreported cases
— *Canadian Current Law: Canadian Citations*
    — cases judicially considered
    — legislation judicially considered
— Lexis: ONTCA and ONTCJ files in COMCAS library
    — only Ontario Court of Appeals cases 1986- and Ontario Court of Justice cases 1990-

QR7.21 New Zealand [7.92-7.94]

— *New Zealand Law Journal*
— *Statutes of New Zealand*
    — consolidation 1957
    — Statutes as passed
    — Statutes as amended reissued in numbered bound volumes, *Reprinted Statutes of New Zealand*
— *Table of New Zealand Acts and Ordinances and Statutory Regulations in force* (annual)
— *Abridgment of New Zealand Case Law*
— *Recent Law*
— *Butterworths Current Law*
— Lexis: CASES file in NZ library
    — *New Zealand Law Reports* 1970-

Other Commonwealth countries

QR7.22 *Africa [7.95]*

— *Journal of African Law*
— *African Law Reports: Commercial Series*

QR7.23 *India and Pakistan[7.96]*

— *All India Reporter* (AIR)
    — includes legislation as well as cases
    — covers both central and state materials
— *All Pakistan Legal Decisions* (PLD)

QR7.24 *Malaysia, Singapore and Brunei [7.97]*

— *Malayan Law Journal*
  — main series of law reports as well as articles
— *Supreme Court Reports* 1988-
— *Supreme Court Journal* 1988-
— *Mallal's Digest of Malaysian and Singapore Case Law* (4th ed, 1990-)
  — also lists main relevant legislation for each topic
— *Mallal's Monthly Digest* 1987-
  — until 1990 entitled *Butterworths Law Digest*
  — covers both cases and legislation: similar to the English *Current Law*

QR7.25 *Hong Kong [7.98]*

— *Hong Kong Law Journal*
— *Laws of Hong Kong*
  — looseleaf consolidation, in course of replacement by new English/ Chinese bilingual edition
— *Hong Kong Law Reports*
— *Hong Kong Law Digest* 1985-
  — until 1987 entitled *Hong Kong Current Law*
  — similar to the English *Current Law*
  — monthly parts cumulated as the *Hong Kong Law Yearbook*

QR7.26 *Caribbean [7.99]*

— *Caribbean Law Review* 1992-
— Annual cumulative indexes to primary and secondary legislation in force in each of the Islands prepared by the West Indian Legislation Indexing Project based at the Faculty of Law, University of West Indies, Barbados (distributed by US publisher William Gaunt)
— *West Indian Reports* 1959-
— *Law Reports of the Bahamas* 1965-
— *Cayman Islands Law Reports* 1980-
— *Jamaica Law Reports*
  — current series being published retrospectively with coverage from 1933, but still very incomplete

QR7.27 *Pacific [7.100]*

— Jacqueline D. Elliott *Pacific Law Bibliography* (1990)

QR7.28 European countries [7.101-7.107]

— Individually published translations of particular codes
  — only very selectively available
— *Commercial Laws of Europe*

— monthly, translations of texts of legislation
— *European Commercial Cases*
  — monthly, translations of text of cases
— *International Litigation Procedure*
  — includes translations of cases from European countries; strong on Brussels Convention cases
— *European Current Law* 1992-
  — similar to the English companion
  — covers all European countries, not just EC member states
  — precursor: *European Law Digest* 1973-1991
— Lexis
  — French legislation from 1955 in the LOIREG library
  — Various French law reports from 1959 in PRIVE and PUBLIC libraries
  — both of the above are in French!

QR8 Directories and subjects adjacent to law

Legal directories

QR8.1 Solicitors [8.3-8.5]

— Law Society *Directory of Solicitors and Barristers*
  * **The official directory of solicitors**
— *Waterlow's Solicitors' and Barristers Directory*
  * **Probably the most used directory**
— *Butterworths Law Directory*
  * **An alternative**
— *The Lawyer's Diary*
  * **An alternative**
— *The Legal 500*
  * **Evaluative guide to the leading firms**
— *Chambers and Partners' Directory: a User's Guide to the Top 1000 Law Firms and All Barristers Chambers*
  * **Evaluative guide to the leading firms**
— Law Society's Records Department at Redditch
  — for details of eg practising certificates held, disciplinary findings, etc
  — searches charged for
  — address at QR9.8

QR8.2 Barristers [8.6-8.11]

— General Council of the Bar *The Bar Directory*
  * **The official directory**
    — includes, selectively, details of work undertaken, expertise etc
    — only directory to include non-practising barristers
    — by chambers and alphabetically

— *Hazell's Guide*
  * **The handiest tool for basic information (but no details of type of work undertaken)**
    — by chambers and alphabetically
— *Havers' Companion to the Bar*
  * **Designed especially to provide information on areas of work undertaken, though not included for every barrister**
    — by chambers and alphabetically
— All the directories listed above for solicitors
  — not all both by chambers and alphabetically
  — *The Legal 500* includes only selected chambers
  — *Chambers and Partners' Directory* lists all chambers but not all barristers; evaluates only selected chambers
— Specialist bar association directories, eg
  — *The Modern Chancery Bar*
  — *COMBAR: the Commercial Bar Association Directory*
  — *The Local Government, Planning and Environmental Bar Association Handbook*
— Records Office of the General Council of the Bar (address at QR 9.8)

QR8.3 Courts and judges [8.12-8.13]

— *Waterlow's Solicitors' and Barristers Diary*
— *Hazell's Guide*
— *Butterworths Law Directory*
— *Shaw's Directory of Courts in the United Kingdom*
  * **The most detailed guide**
— *The London County Courts Directory*
  — a listing by street indicating which County Court district each falls in
— Andrew Goodman *Court Guide*
  * **A practical guide to facilities, etc for the court user**
— *The Lawyer's Remembrancer*

QR8.4 Legal services [8.14]

— *Waterlow's Solicitors' and Barristers' Directory*
  — at the back
— *Yellow Pages*

QR8.5 Scottish and Irish lawyers [8.15]

— *Scottish Law Directory*
— *The Blue Book: the Directory of the Law Society of Scotland*

— Faculty of Advocates *Directory*
    — includes details of type of work undertaken
— *The Law Directory* (Incorporated Law Society of Ireland)

QR8.6 Overseas lawyers [8.16-8.20]

— *Martindale-Hubbell Law Directory* : Canadian and international lawyers volumes
    * **The most detailed source other than indigenous directories**
        — in the blue pages at the front it lists separately under each city in each country (a) firms of local lawyers and (b) firms of foreign lawyers practising there
        — full professional biographies of members of the firms are given in the main section arranged by country and city
— *Kime's International Law Directory*
    * **Probably the most useful alternative**
        — separates local lawyers and foreign lawyers under each country
        — includes brief notes on professional regulation etc for each country
— *Butterworths International Law Directory*
    * **An alternative; only source with alphabetical list of individual lawyers**
— *International Law List*
    * **An alternative**
— *Waterlow's Solicitors' and Barristers Directory*: international section
    — A selection of English firms with overseas offices and foreign firms with offices in England and Wales; a few other overseas firms
— *Butterworths Law Directory*: international section
    — A selection of English firms with overseas offices and foreign firms with offices in London, but categories not clearly distinguished
— *The Legal 500*
    — includes foreign firms in London
— *International Financial Law Review 1000: a Guide to the World's International Business Law Firms*
    * **An evaluative guide**
— *Law Firms in Europe*
    * **From the same stable as The Legal 500**
— *Cross-border Practice Compendium* (Sweet and Maxwell)
    * **For details of professional regulations for lawyers practising in EC member states**
— National directories of lawyers, eg *Martindale-Hubbell* for American lawyers, *Canadian Bar List*, etc

QR8.7 Solicitors' corporate clients and companies' solicitors [8.21]

— *Crawford's Directory of City Connections* (annual)
— *Arthur Andersen Corporate Register* (twice yearly)

— *Hambro Company Guide* (quarterly)

QR8.8 Law teachers [8.22]

— Society of Public Teachers of Law and Association of Law Teachers directories

QR8.9 Law libraries [8.23]

— *Directory of British and Irish Law Libraries*
— See also list of useful addresses at QR9

QR8.10 Bodies holding records and registers [8.24]

— Trevor Aldridge *Directory of Registers and Records*

QR8.11 Past lawyers [8.25]

— A.W.B. Simpson *Biographical Dictionary of the Common Law*
— *Oxford Companion to the Law*
— Guy Holborn 'Sources of biographical information on past lawyers' (1992) 23 *The Law Librarian* 75-90, 119-145

Subjects adjacent to law

Sources mainly for practitioners

QR8.12 *Press coverage [8.27-8.29]*

— Indexes to newspapers and newspapers on CD-ROM
— Nexis (on-line)
— FT Profile (on-line)
— Reuter's Textline (availabe via FT Profile and other on-line hosts)
— BBC Data Enquiry Service
  — fee-based service
— Press Association Newpaper Library
  — fee-based service
— Prestel
  — for very recent news

QR8.13 *Company, financial and business information [8.30-8.32]*

— FT Profile
— Companies House
— *International Stock Exchange Yearbook*
— *Kompass UK*

— *Who Owns Whom*
— *Directory of Directors*
— *Arthur Andersen Corporate Register*
— *Hambro Company Guide*
— *Crawford's Directory of City Connections*
— *Banker's Almanac*
— *Who's Who in the City* and *Who's Who in Industry*
— *Financial Statistics* (monthly, HMSO)
— Fee-based research services (addresses at QR9.6):
  — Business Information Focus (City Business Library)
  — Information for Business (Westminster Central Reference Library)
  — LBS Information (London Business School)
  — Business Information Service (British Library Science Reference and Information Service)
  — Public and university libraries in the Business Information Network (contact the above for details)

QR8.14 *Insurance and pensions [8.33]*

— *Insurance Journals Index* 1992-
  — also available electronically
— *Pensions Journals Index* 1992-
  — also available electronically
— *Insurance Directory and Yearbook*

QR8.15 *Professional directories [8.34]*

— For lists of professional bodies see *Whitaker's Almanac* or *Directory of British Associations*

QR8.16 *Shipping [8.35]*

— Various Lloyds directories, including *Lloyd's Register of Shipping*
— Seadata (on-line)
  — ship details, movements, and casualties
— *Guide to Port Entry*
  — charts, etc of ports worldwide

QR8.17 *Patents and intellectual property [8.36]*

— British Library Science Reference and Information Service and libraries in the Patent Information Network (address at QR9.5)

QR8.18 *Standards [8.37]*

— British Standards Institute at Milton Keynes
— Standardline (on-line)
— Standards Infodisk CD-ROM

QR8.19 *Forensic science and medicine [8.38]*

— British Library Science Reference and Information Service (Kean Street branch) — address at QR9.5
— *Forensic Science Abstracts*
    — part of *Excerpta Medica*
    — also on CD-ROM
— Medline
    — also on CD-ROM
— FORS (Home Office forensic science on-line database available via DataStar)

QR8.20 *Parliamentary and government information [8.39]*

— *House of Commons Weekly Information Bulletin*
    — includes eg full lists of government etc
— House of Commons Public Information Office (telephone and address at QR9.7)
— *Civil Service Yearbook* (also on CD-ROM)
— Government press releases in Hermes file on FT Profile (or hard copy from Central Office of Information)
— *Public Bodies* (annual, HMSO)
— *Dod's Parliamentary Companion* (annual)
— *Vacher's Parliamentary Companion* (quarterly)
— *Municipal Yearbook*
— *Dod's European Companion*
— *Vacher's European Companion*
— *Directory of European Institutions*

Sources mainly for academic research

QR8.21 *Social sciences [8.41]*

— *London Bibliography of the Social Sciences* (annual)
— *International Bibliography of the Social Sciences* (IBSS)
    — four different series listed separately below
— *Social Sciences Index*
— *Social Sciences Citation Index*

QR8.22 ANTHROPOLOGY [8.42]

— *International Bibliography of Social and Cultural Anthropology* (part of IBSS)
— *Anthropological Literature*

QR8.23 CRIMINOLOGY AND PENOLOGY [8.43]

— *Criminology, Penology and Police Science Abstracts*

— Criminal Justice Abstracts
— *Criminal Justice Periodical Index*

QR8.24 ECONOMICS [8.44]

— *Journal of Economic Literature*
   — law and economics: section K
— *Index to Economic Articles in Journals and Collective Volumes*
   — law and economics: section 916
— *International Bibliography of Economics* (part of IBSS)
— *Contents of Recent Economics Journals*

QR8.25 EDUCATION [8.45]

— *British Education Index*

QR8.26 POLITICS [8.46]

— D. Englefield and G. Drewry *Information Sources in Politics and Political Science*
— *International Political Science Abstracts*
— *International Bibliography of Political Science* (part of IBSS)

QR8.27 SOCIOLOGY [8.47]

— *International Bibliography of Sociology* (part of IBSS)
— *Sociological Abstracts*

QR8.28 WAR STUDIES [8.48]

— *War and Society Newsletter*
   — a bibliographical publication, includes section 'International law and military law'

QR8.29 HUMANITIES [8.49]

— *British Humanities Index*

QR8.30 HISTORY [8.50-8.51]

— J.H. Baker *Introduction to English Legal History*
— W.D. Hines *English Legal History: a Bibliography and Guide to the Literature*
— 'Annual bibliography of British and Irish legal history' in *Cambrian Law Review*
— *Bibliography of British History* (OUP)
— *Annual Bibliography of British and Irish History*
— *Writings on British History*

QR8.31 PHILOSOPHY [8.52]

— *The Philosopher's Index*
— *Current Legal Theory: International Journal for the Theory of Law and its Documentation*

QR9 Selected libraries and other useful addresses

QR9.1 Libraries

NB Admission and charging policies vary. It is essential to telephone before visiting in person.

See also

> *Directory of British and Irish Law Libraries* (British and Irish Association of Law Librarians)
>
> *Guide to Libraries and Information Units in Government Departments and Other Organisations* (British Library Science Reference and Information Service)
>
> *Aslib Directory of Information Sources* (Aslib)

Any specialities are noted

QR9.2 Professional libraries

Law Society Library
Law Society's Hall
113 Chancery Lane
London
WC2A 1PL
Tel: 071-320 5946

*   EC law

Gray's Inn Library
5 South Square
Gray's Inn
London
WC1R 5EU

Tel: 071-242 8592

*   Public international law, foreign law in English not covered by other Inns

Inner Temple Library
Temple
London
EC4Y 7DA
Tel: 071-797 8217
* Commonwealth, especially Canada, Caribbean, Hong Kong, India
Lincoln's Inn Library
Lincoln's Inn
London
WC2A 3TN
Tel: 071-242 4371
* Commonwealth, especially Australia, New Zealand, Malaysia, Singapore
Middle Temple Library
Middle Temple Lane
London
EC4Y 9BT
Tel: 071-353 4303
* EC law, United States
Supreme Court Library
Queen's Building
Royal Courts of Justice
The Strand
London
WC2A 2LL
Tel: 071-936 6587
* Transcripts of certain cases (see QR 4.16–4.31)
Bar Library
Royal Courts of Justice
The Strand
London
WC2A
Tel: 071-936 6420

QR9.3 Academic libraries

British Institute of International and Comparative Law
17 Russell Square
London
WC1B 5DR
Tel: 071-636 5802
* Council of Europe human rights documentation
Institute of Advanced Legal Studies
17 Russell Square
London
WC1B 5DR
Tel: 071-637 1731
* Major research library, especially Commonwealth, US, Western Europe, public international law

Kings College
Library
The Strand
London
WC2R 2LS
Tel: 071-873 2313

* Medical law; German law

London School of Economics
British Library of Political and Economic Science
10 Portugal Street
London
WC2A 2HD
Tel: 071-405 7686 Ext: 2421

* Especially European, US, UN and other official publications

Queen Mary and Westfield College
University of London
Mile End Road
London
E1 4NS
Tel: 071 975 5555 Ext: 3327

* Commercial law

School of Oriental and African Studies
University of London
Thornhaugh Street
London
WC1H 0XG
Tel: 071-687 2388 Ext: 2270

* Oriental and African law

University College London
Gower Street
London
WC1E 6BT
Tel: 071-387 7050 Ext: 2588

* Roman law, Soviet law

Bodleian Law Library
St Cross Building
Manor Road
Oxford
OX1 3UR
Tel: 0865-271463

* Major research library

Squire Law Library
Old Schools
Cambridge
CB2 1SD
Tel: 0223-333318

* Major research library

QR9.4 Government libraries

Board of Inland Revenue
New Wing
Somerset House
The Strand
London
WC2R 1LB
Tel: 071-438 6648

Departments of the Environment and Transport Legal Library
Room P3/072
2 Marsham Street
London
SW1P 3EB
Tel: 071-276 5750

Department of Trade and Industry Solicitors Library
10/18 Victoria Street
London
SW1H 0NN
Tel: 071-215 3054

Home Office
Queen Anne's Gate
London
SW1H 9AT
Tel: 071-273 3398

Lord Chancellor's Department
Trevelyan House, Room 13
30 Great Peter Street
London
SW1P 2BY
Tel: 071-210 8592

QR9.5 Public libraries

British Library

(a) Official Publications and Social Sciences Service
Great Russell Street
London
WC1B 3DG
Tel: 071-323 7536

(b) Science Reference and Information Service
25 Southampton Buildings
Chancery Lane
London
WC2A 1AW
Tel: 071-323 7474/7496

*   Business information; intellectual property law; patent documentation

Kean Street
London
WC2B 4AT
Tel: 071-323 7288

* Forensic science and medicine

City Business Library
1 Brewer's Hall Garden
London
EC2V 5BX
Tel: 071-638 8215

Holborn Reference Library
32-38 Theobalds Road
London
WC1X 8PA
Tel: 071-413 6343/6

* English law for general public

Westminster Central Reference Library
35 St Martins Street
London
WC2H 7HP
Tel: 071-798 2036/2034

* Official publications

QR9.6 Fee-based business information services

Companies House
English and Welsh enquiries:
Tel: 0222-380801 or
Postal Search Section
Companies House
Crown Way
Cardiff
CF4 3 UZ

Scottish enquiries:
Tel: 031-243 4061 or
Postal Search Section
Companies House
100-102 George Street
Edinburgh
EH2 3DJ

Business Information Focus
City Business Library (see above)

Business Information Service
British Library Science Reference and Information Service
Southampton Buildings (see above)

Information for Business
Westminster Central Reference Library (see above)
LBS Information
London Business School
Sussex Place
Regent's Park
London
NW1 4SA
Tel: 071-724 2300

QR9.7 Parliamentary information

House of Commons Public Information Office
House of Commons
London
SW1A OAA
Tel: 071-219 4272

House of Lords Information Office
House of Lords
London
SW1A OPW
Tel: 071-219 3107

QR9.8 Professional bodies

The General Council of the Bar
3 Bedford Row
London
WC1R 4DB
Tel: 071-242 0082

Records Office Tel: 071-242 0934

The Law Society
Law Society's Hall
113 Chancery Lane
London
WC2A 1PL
Tel: 071-242 1222

Ipsley Court
Berrington Close
Redditch
Worcestershire
B98 0TN

QR9.9 European Communities information

This list appears at the back of every bimonthly issue of *European Access* published
by Chadwyck-Healey and is reproduced from it with kind permission.

List of useful addresses

Sources of European Community Information in the United Kingdom and Ireland

Offices of the European Commission

Windsor House
9/15 Bedford Street
Belfast BT2 7EG
Tel: 0232-240708

4 Cathedral Road
Cardiff CF1 9SG
Tel: 0222-371631

7 Alva Street
Edinburgh EH2 4PH
Tel: 031-225-2058

8 Storey's Gate
London SW1P 3AT
Tel: 071-973-1992

39 Molesworth Street
Dublin 2
Tel: 010-353-1-712244

European Parliament: Information Offices

2 Queen Anne's Gate
London SW1H 9AA
Tel: 071-222-0411

43 Molesworth Street
Dublin 2
Tel: 010-353-1-719100

European Investment Bank

68 Pall Mall
London SW1Y 5ES
Tel: 071-839-3351

Euro Info Centres: *Information service aimed specificially at small and medium-sized businesses in matters relating to the EC and European markets.*

United Kingdom
Local Enterprise Development Unit
Ledu House
Upper Galwally
Belfast BT8 4TB
Tel: 0232-491031

Birmingham Chamber of
Industry and Commerce
75 Harborne Road
PO Box 360
Birmingham B15 3DH
Tel: 021-454-6171

Federation of Sussex
Industries and Chamber
of Commerce
Seven Dials
Brighton BN1 3JS
Tel: 0273-26282

Bristol Chamber of
Commerce and Industry
16 Clifton Park
Bristol BS8 3BY
Tel: 0272-737373

Wales Euro Info Centre
UWCC
The Guest Building
PO Box 430
Cardiff CF1 3XT
Tel: 0222-229525

Exeter Enterprises Limited
University of Exeter
Haley Wing
Reed Hall
Exeter EX4 4QR
Tel: 0392-214085

Scottish Development
Agency
21 Bothwell Street
Glasgow G2 6NR
Tel: 041-221-0999

Yorkshire and Humberside
Euro Information Network
Westgate House
Wellington Street
Leeds LS1 4LT
Tel: 0532-439222

Liverpool City Libraries
William Brown Street
Liverpool L3 8EW
Tel: 051-298-1928

London Chamber of
Commerce and Industry
69 Cannon Street
London EC4N 5AB
Tel: 071-248-4444

Manchester Chamber of
Commerce and Industry
56 Oxford Street
Manchester M60 7HJ
Tel: 061-236-3210

Norwich and Norfolk
Chamber of Commerce
and Industry
112 Barrack Street
Norwich NR3 1UB
Tel: 0603-625977

Thames-Chiltern Chamber
of Commerce and Industry
Commerce House
2-6 Bath Road
Slough SL1 3SB
Tel: 0753-77877

Highland Opportunity Ltd
Development Department
Highland Regional Council
Regional Buildings
Glenurquhart Road
Inverness IV3 5NX
Tel: 0463-234121

Euro Team
Business Advice Centre
30 New Walk
Leicester LE1 6TF
Tel: 0533-554464

Centre for European
Business Information
Small Firms Service
11 Belgrave Road
London SW1V 1RB
Tel: 071-828-6201

Kent County Council
Springfield
Maidstone ME14 2LL
Tel: 0622-696130

Northern Development
Company
Great North House
Sandyford Road
Newcastle NE1 8ND
Tel: 091-261-5131

The Nottinghamshire
Chamber of Commerce and
Industry
309 Haydn Road
Nottingham NG5 1DG
Tel: 0602-624624 Ext.123

The Southern Area
Central Library
Civic Centre
Southampton SO9 4XF
Tel: 0703-832866

Shropshire Chamber of
Commerce and Industry
Industry House
16 Halesfield
Telford TF7 4TA
Tel: 0952-588766

Ireland

Cork Chamber of
Commerce
67 South Mall
Cork
Tel: 010-353-21-509044

Irish Export Board
Merrion Hall
PO Box 203
Strand Road
Sandymount
Dublin 4
Tel: 010-353-1-695011

Galway Chamber of
Commerce and Industry
Hynes Building
St Augustine Street
Galway
Tel: 010-353-91-62624

Shannon Free Airport
Development Company
The Granary
Michael Street
Limerick
Tel: 010-353-61-40777

Sligo European Business
Information Centre
16 Quay Street
Sligo
Tel: 010-353-71-61274

Irish Export Board
c/o Industrial Estate
The Cork Road
Waterford
Tel: 010-353-51-78577

Rural Information Centres: *new EC initiative to provide
information service of relevance to rural areas. In pilot phase at
present but likely to expand soon.*

Centre for Regional and Rural
Development Studies
University College Galway
Galway
Tel: 010-353-91-24411 Ext.3042

Scottish Agriculture College
Cleeve Gardens
Oakbank Road
Perth, PH1 1HF
Tel: 0738-36611

European Documentation Centres: *Major collections of EC
documentation housed in university (U)/polytechnic (P) libraries.
In addition to serving the academic community most EDCs also
provide an information service to the public. There are EDCs at:*
Aberdeen (U); Wye College, Ashford (U); Bath (U); Queens,
Belfast (U); Birmingham (U/P); Bradford (U); Sussex,
Brighton (U); Bristol (U); Cambridge (U); Cardiff (U); Essex,
Colchester (U); Ulster, Coleraine (U); Lanchester, Coventry
(P); Warwick, Coventry (U); Dundee (U); Durham (U);
Edinburgh (U); Exeter (U); Glasgow (U); Surrey, Guildford
(U); Hull (U); Keele (U); Kent, Canterbury (U); Lancaster (U);
Leeds (U/P); Leicester (U); LSE, London (U); QMC, London
(U); Polytechnic of North London (P); Royal Institute of
International Affairs, London; Loughborough (U); Manches-
ter (U); Newcastle (P); East Anglia, Norwich (U); Notting-
ham (U); Bodleian, Oxford (U); Portsmouth (P); Reading (U);
Salford (U); Sheffield (P); Southampton (U); Wolverhampton
(P); Cork (U); Dublin (UCD/Trinity); Galway (U); Limerick
(National Institute)

European Reference Centres: *Small collections of basic EC
documentation in academic institutions. There are ERCs at:*
Aberystwyth (U); Chalfont St Giles (Buckingham College);
Chelmsford (Essex Institute); Cleveland (P); Exmouth (Rolle
College); Edinburgh (National Library of Scotland); Halifax
(Percival Whitley College); Hatfield (P); Inverness (High-
lands Regional Council, Library Service); Ipswich (Suffolk
County Library); London (Ealing HE College); Northampton
(Nene College); Preston (P and Public Library); Reading
(Bulmershe College); Sheffield (U); Stirling (U); Swansea (U);
Wrexham (NE Wales Institute)

For further details and addresses of EDCs and ERCs contact
Ian Thomson, Chairman of the European Information
Association, University of Wales, College of Cardiff, PO Box
430, Cardiff CF1 3XT. Tel: 0222-874262

EC Depository Libraries: *Comprehensive collections of EC
documentation intended to serve the general public.*

Commercial & Social
Sciences Library
Central Library
William Brown Street
Liverpool L3 8EW
Tel: 051-225-5434

Central Reference Library
City of Westminster Library
St Martins Street
London WC2 7HP
Tel: 071-798-2034

British Library
Boston Spa
Wetherby LS23 7BQ
Tel: 0937-546044

National Library of Ireland
Kildare Street
Dublin 2
Tel: 010-353-1-765521

Oireachtas Library
Leinster House
Kildare Street
Dublin 2
Tel: 010-353-1-789911 Ext.264

Other sources

Confederation of British
Industry
Centre Point
103 New Oxford Street
London WC1A 1DU
Tel: 071-379-7400
CBI Initiative 1992
Tel: 071-836-1992

Consumers in the European
Community Group
24 Tufton Street
London SW1P 3RB
Tel: 071-222-2662

Dept of Trade and Industry
Ashdown House
123 Victoria Street
London SW1E 6RB
Tel: 071-215-5000
1992 Hotline: 081-200-1992

Local Government International Bureau
35 Great Smith Street
London SW1P 3BJ
Tel: 071-222-1636

Obtaining European Community documentation

The majority of EC documentation is published by the Office for Official Publications of the European Communities (OOPEC), 2 rue Mercier, L-2985, Luxembourg. Tel: 010-352-49-92-81. Telex: PUBOF LU 1324 b.

To obtain material published by OOPEC, to find out subscription and standing order details and obtain free sales catalogues contact the appropriate sales agents:

HMSO Books (PC 16)
HMSO Publications Centre
51 Nine Elms Lane
London SW8 5DR
Tel: 071-873-8372

Government Publications Sales Office Sun Alliance House Molesworth Street Dublin 2 Tel: 010-353-1-710309	Postal address: Government Stationery Office EEC Section 6th Floor Bishop Street Dublin 8 Tel: 010-353-1-781666

Some free items issued by EC institutions, the documentation from the Information Offices in the Member States, EC publications issued by commercial publishers and certain other categories of material are not available from OOPEC or their sales agents. The addresses of the Information Offices are given above. Other addresses for this type of material include:

Council of Ministers Information & Documentation Rue de la Loi 170 B-1048 Brussels Belgium Tel: 010-32-2-234-61-11	Court of Justice Internal Service L-2920 Luxembourg Tel: 010-352-4-3031
DG ... Commission of the EC Rue de la Loi 200 B-1049 Brussels Belgium Tel: 010-32-2-235-11-11	Economic & Social Committee Press, Information & Publications Division Rue Ravenstein 2 B-1000 Brussels Belgium Tel: 010-32-2-519-90-11
European Centre for the Development of Vocational Training Bundesallee 22 D-1000 Berlin Tel: 010-49-30-884120	European Foundation for the Improvement of Living & Working Conditions Loughlinstown House Shankill Co. Dublin Tel: 010-353-1-826888
European Investment Bank Information/Public Relations Division L-2950 Luxembourg Tel: 010-352-4379-3142	European Parliament General Secretariat L-2920 Luxembourg Tel: 010-352-4-3001

Other European organisations

HMSO are agents for the documentation of OECD and the Council of Europe. Contact the address in the previous column. If you need to contact the organisations direct the following addresses can be used:

Council of Europe Information Department F-67006 Strasbourg France	OECD 2 rue André Pascal F-75775 Paris Cedex France

The documentation of EFTA and WEU can only be obtained from:

EFTA Information Service 9-11 rue de Varembé CH-1211 Geneva 20 Switzerland	WEU Information and External Relations Services 43 avenue du Président Wilson F-75775 Paris Cedex 16 France

Index